CHASING AMERICA

Dennis Watlington

THOMAS DUNNE BOOKS ⚑ ST. MARTIN'S PRESS
NEW YORK

CHASING AMERICA

Notes from
a Rock 'n' Soul
Integrationist

THOMAS DUNNE BOOKS.
An imprint of St. Martin's Press.

www.stmartins.com

Book design by Irene Vallye

Vinyl record photograph on title page by Stephen de las Heras

Acknowledgments art by Wesley Gott

Library of Congress Cataloging-in-Publication Data

Watlington, Dennis, 1952–
    Chasing America : notes of a rock 'n' soul integrationist / Dennis Wallington.—
1st ed.
        p. cm.
    ISBN 0-312-27189-1
    EAN 978-0-312-27189-3
    1. Watlington, Dennis, 1952– 2. Screenwriters—United States—Biography.
3. Television writers—United States—Biography. 4. African American screenwriters—
Biography. 5. Racism—United States. I. Title.

PS3623.A8695Z477 2006
812'.6—dc22
[B]
                                                                    2005051901

First Edition: February 2006

10 9 8 7 6 5 4 3 2 1

To my wife Anne

You were always the endgame inspiration. And if this dream comes, I'll see myself as you knew me.

To Richard Nicholson

No one has had a lengthier influence on my adult life. Somewhere in the woods of the great Northwest state of Washington resides the wisest spiritual consigliere a street kid could have encountered. Richard Nicholson is a bigger-than-life combo of gumbo that hovers near the six-foot-five-inch, two-hundred-eighty-five-pound dimension. Imbedded in his impressive girth is the gentlest demeanor that much power and mass can emit. My meat-and-potato guru, who moves smartly in oversized rainwear, communes with the steady rainfalls of freedom. His insistence that the universe prefers human love as its drug of choice steered me away from contributing to the negative impact that power, greed, and fear has on so many of our planet's inhabitants. The high ceiling of positive, interactive souls is where Nick managed to fix my glare. It's the big man's shellac that coats California's heartbeat, and I'm honored to thank Nick for his wise mentorship and selfless supply of invaluable inspiration.

ACKNOWLEDGMENTS

No one chases our great country without assistance. To my three children—Avery, Keelan, and Arielle: You special beings have shown more resilience enduring the tumultuous ups and downs that were perpetrated upon you by parents who staked your security's claim upon the wet napkin that is Blackwriting opportunities. To Arielle, my Amazonian heartthrob: As this is written you are engaged in your freshman year at the Millbrook School. When you took on the transformative task of joining a new community, sans parents, you showed me that you are far more capable at the game of life then any of us had the right to expect from a thirteen-year-old child. You have the most powerful spirit and will I've ever encountered in someone so young. The day you scored an A+ in prep school algebra, you ascended to a class all your own. To Keelan, who taught himself to become a jazz pianist before taking on the classics during his collegiate excursion: You are the most multitalented individual I have ever known. My gifted son—if it's Oxford you want, then the Watlington family will do whatever we can to support your dream. To Avery, the sturdy one, whom I left as a child: Your sacrifice cemented my biggest regret. I'm glad that we found the rudiments of a new beginning because the courage it took to develop into such a fine man without a father is awesome. It is my good fortune that your perseverance has allowed for another shot at the father/son thing.

To my wife/editor, Anne: It's up to the editor and his or her ego to contend with the unfair distribution of recognition and fortune that exists between a writer and his wordsmith, but the writer knows the value of a capable steward. You have influenced, salvaged, manipulated, plundered, enlightened, burdened, cheerled, and wept over our quarter century of work. You've stood at the gate and administered the security that ushered 90 percent of every word, from soap operas to the legit theater, I've ever written. The last draft of *Chasing America* is the best we could possibly achieve seated in front of your glass fortress. Since the days when we were kids and everyone thought we were nuts to write and produce our own play, you've filtered my why-not-ism so that the best of my bolts made it to the page. This completion of our difficult gut check only happened because we always played our best game when it mattered most. This is our Super Bowl. Win or lose, we've made it to the big game.

This book took just short of five years to complete. In its final year, at a time when Pedro Martinez and his Beantown crew finally moved the "curse" off the plate that ended eighty-plus years suffering, from Radatz through the Rooster, the well-earned elation in my rural environment of Berkshire County, Massachusetts, and its Connecticut neighbor, contributed a significant slice of *Chasing America*'s development. I was the unusually tinted oddity suffering from an odd occupation. The retail store workers up and down Route 7's strip offered unstinting support. As personal relationships, disappointments, and joys grayed with the twenty seasons that have passed, this aggregate of women and men played into the spirit of my climb through my first full prosaic effort. To my rural teammates, this book's future carries your stamp.

A third of the book was written somewhere between the hours of 4:30 A.M. and 7:00 A.M. in the parking lot of the Shop & Stop supermarket in Canaan, Connecticut. My appreciation goes to the entire staff, paying special attention to Pam Hill, Jeff, Christine, Aaron, and Anthony Sullivan, the hardest working man in America. Anthony's focus on responsible behavior provided mental tonic every time I needed to replenish my initiative. His effusive good will surpassed anyone's during the book's odyssey. I send special regards to the early morning blue-collar cashier beauties that received me and shared wonderful musings before the patron' arrival.

United States Post Office, Southfield Branch: To Linda Barzie, my valuable courier who rode all the ups and downs over the twenty seasons the book took to cook. Her warmth provided a special contribution to the lengthy slog. To Stanley M. Segalla in Canaan, the old booze merchant who doubled as my "Old Man in the Sea." providing a dose of early century New York and all of its rich immigrant-laden wisdom. To Ken's Barbershop in Great Barrington, my regards to Ken Tenbroeck. It is impossible to underestimate the value of a White Barber in a rural area who cuts Black hair well. For the better part of a decade I have sat in Ken's chair and watched in amazement as he de-intimidated my appearance, keeping me presentable during the numerous New York meetings that helped bring these pages to fruition. To his fellow worker, Nancy Donovan, although she hasn't quite garnered her ability to sheer the naps, her work on my ungainly beard and her melodious companionship nourished my fondness for the rural Caucasian. To Salisbury Bank and Trust Company in Canaan, you've drafted your folks well. I couldn't have handled my meager bank statements as easily without Megan Pezzee's smile. To Jerry Callinan and Fran English, two cats who somehow managed to give money a good name. Jerry, one of my favorite "big men," looks solid enough to have been assigned the task of protecting the blind side of the great, young New England Patriots' quarterback, Tom Brady. Both men play like aces. Thanks guys.

I don't drink, but I welcomed the opportunity to buy for others at the Cordial Shop so that I could groove with Claudia Dionne, a courageous young woman whose reserve pulled victory from the jaws of personal defeat. Claudia's mother, Beatrice Bunce, and her calming presence explain why her daughter has stood so tall under pressure. I have absconded morsels of her courage with each firewater purchase. Thank you, ladies, for your part. Dos Amigos, rest in peace. Before this wonderful little Mexican restaurant in Great Barrington burned to the ground, it set an eternal flame beneath this project.

I am particularly grateful to Manhattan's Beacon Hotel on Seventy-fourth Street and Broadway, where the pulse of the Upper West Side resides in your living room. Over the last ten years whenever in New York City, I made a beeline for the pigment palace where the staff looked like my brothers, sisters, cousins, uncles, and friends. The diversity is also Caucasianally expressed by a wide array of people with particular attention paid to Mary Rix, a loving mound of competence and imagination with a healthy dose of Brooklyn washing it all down. My thanks to Daryl Stokes, Eryk Gorski, Anna Matos, Jim Tracy, Mini Dindial Sing, Isa Almonte, Wilbia Garcia, Marcy Gofay, Alan Leuto, and the housework crew. I've written half of the book under the Beacon's roof, with a host of people teasing, questioning, and rooting me on to completion. I could not have found a better hothouse for *Chasing America*'s growth. It's lush variety of international tourists emits a global mist enriching every elevator ride.

A special inspirational note to Walter Rosenblum, my favorite twentieth-century photographer. This gentle film avatar's D-day photographic heroism was only exceeded by his camera's humane lenses that exposed the hidden light behind the facial expressions of children consigned to the lower tiers of Western largess. He taught me the rudiments of the uncompromising focus that humanist, artistic expression requires. In the year 2000, a twenty-year-old bolt of pixieish power was unleashed upon me. Jules Shell entered my life during a San Francisco-area film shoot, and her untainted creative energy jump-started my jaded professional ethics, knocking ten years of procedural plaque off of my operational gums. Her first experience in a Black Holy Roller church produced one of my favorite memories. I've discerned that every young feisty Midwestern college grad should experience a Black church for one afternoon during their initial post-graduate summer.

To Stanley Buchthal: With the urging of Barbara Kopple, you laid your instincts on the line by optioning this book for a film before it was half complete. I'm sure if you know that at the time of the deal, given a debilitating rough patch of life I'd been mired in, you had a better chance of casting Katherine Hepburn in your next project than seeing the book's completion. But my desire to run with the big dogs like you helped pull me through. I'm sure when the book reaches the screen, it will be your special brand of broad based do-it fluid powering the engine. To Peter Geer, whose timely, sensitive generosity saved the entire effort before it was a third completed. Thank you. To Jim Sadwith, whose boundless friendship and support often brightened my darkest hours. To Reverend John Collins and his wife Sheila: I'm so proud of what you have done with your lives. The freedom school you established during the New York City strike in the early sixties turned me on to the rich American vein that is African American history. Seated in that unforgettable, multiple week window, I absorbed the likes of Phyllis Wheatley, the great poetess whose work charmed George Washington, and George Washington Carver, the great American contributor whose work with the peanut made Skippy rich. Long before the official call, you guys got me going on the Black pride initiative. Thank you for your laminated insights. To Ellen Stapleton for providing a human laboratory through which the material was filtered at a critical point in the book's development. In addition to being a beloved sister-in-law, her proud middle class sensibilities added a unique ear to the process. To Nina Rosenblum and the Tisch School of the Arts, thank you for making me a filmmaker. To David Debin, the most soulful of my bigger brothers, despite our current frozen frame positioning, I loved every time I was lucky enough to be in your presence. To John Terenzio, who was my most heartfelt friend from lower mid-year at the Hotchkiss school into our high thirties, and godfather to my cherished Arielle: I'm sorry our impasse muted my ardor in giving the depth of our friendship its full due, but, in truth, there is no one I spent more time with who was brighter, funnier, or more passionate about living than you. It was my bad not delivering the anecdotes. Sorry, J. T. To Lydia Butler: In addition to your having worked on *Tar and Feather*, the very first thing I ever wrote, you subsequently emerged as the untrumpeted generator that made the *Bullpen* run. Your lifelong friendship has been a "treasure" trove. Thank you, baby.

To Michael W. Fuller, (6/28/1963–6/21/2004), Associate Director of Admissions at Millbrook School: Never in the Watlington family's good fortune had someone come, enriched, and passed away so quickly. Your persistent, thorough recruitment of Arielle has left an indelible mark that will color the fortunes of her sociological inclusion for generations. When we met, we were complete strangers, and your perception of our family's odd pulse was a pure blast of oxygen. During my frequent stops at the tree on campus that commemorates your presence, I park beside your memory and refuel my perspective by remembering your unsolicited selection as the shooting-star ex-jock turned prep-school administrator that brought the important propellant that defines the dignity that supports the foundation that is the wonder of New England's fine preparatory hamlets. Your guts will be riding with me for the rest of my stay on the count, so R.I.P., brother man. To Bob, Sandy, and Brad Haiko: Bob, Sandy, and I arrived together on the Hotchkiss campus in the fall of 1969. Because of Bob's youth and Sandy's gorgeous youth, they were amongst the closest faculty members that a couple of grizzled ex-pavement criminals, like Noel and I, could relate to. Our lives and friendship have only grown over the last thirty years. Bob's photographic art has matured wonderfully over his three decades of heading the photography department at the 'Kiss, and whenever I have needed a good eye and thoughts that accompany such vision, Bob was always the guy. To Brad, who I've known since he was little more than a mushroom, I dig the way you've grown up so far help, and like your dad, you're one of those special "guys."

To Charles Barkley, for bringing a full court of solid young contemporary Black do-it fluid to the public square. Jim Brown, who conveyed principled Amer-I-Can values: You have been a role model my entire cognizant life. After Gretzkying football's record books, you made me dare to think I could be an actor, and you've kept Dr. King's racial self-empowerment issues alive without the ignorance of racist opportunism being a factor allowing for the door to remain open to our White national relatives. You've been blessed with the gift of only needing one block to make big plays. Keep on running. David Kelly is a grassroots influence and his unsurpassed ability to tell diversity rich American stories on prime time television is rivaled only by Rod Serling's mid-century reach. In addition to his sterling block of work, he has my graditude for placing more Black people on the bench than anyone in U.S. history.

To Sean Desmond, my editor, the indespensible catalyst who contained this book when I was spilling all over the place. His skill, patience, and encouragement, not to mention his competitive marathon-length stamina, guided a projected two-and-a-half year project to its five-year completion. Without Sean's sensitive leadership, the book's title would have never proceeded beyond its first word, as I would still be engaged in the chase.

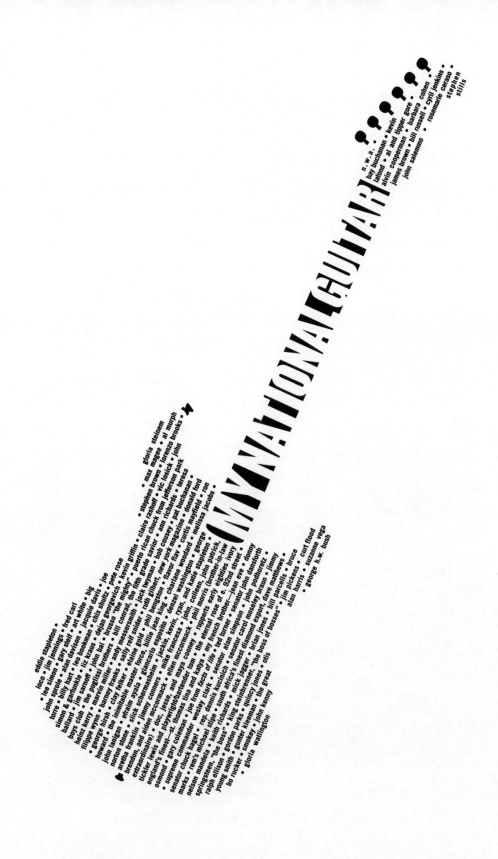

AUTHOR'S NOTE

The following names are not the real names of
the people described in this book:

Bruce Barrett
Clark Billings
Willie Leach
Guner Stalin
Joni
Ben Janks

CHASING AMERICA

PROLOGUE

The biggest adventure you can ever take is to live the life of your dreams.

—**Oprah Winfrey** (Oprah Winfrey has not endorsed this book, but I endorse her.)

Great Barrington, Massachusetts

The morning marks the end of my beginning. As I sit on a bench in an old gym, my lungs are sore from exertion and my knees throbbing from abuse. I've limped to the painful conclusion that my active participation in team sports is over. I've been playing basketball for forty years. I love the sport. It's one of the few level playing fields in America: One set of rules fits all. The instant thrill of grabbing a big rebound in a tight game is one of the things I have lived for.

The twenty-year-olds have finally broken me down. I hung in there for a long time, but after my forty-fifth birthday, my sky hook melted into a ground hook. The young boys lost respect and turned my dominance off like a faucet. This court doesn't lie, and it disposed of me as dispassionately as it received me all those years ago. What the hell am I going to do with this middle-aged body wrapped around an athlete's heart?

I learned how to play ball in the ghetto back in the sixties. The game transcended basketball, becoming manhood ball. Every time you stepped on the court, you put your good reputation at risk. I'd never lost a game in my life because I never cheated a teammate with less than my best effort. It's the only way I knew how to play. My ghetto toughness on the court is my last strong tie with my street past.

On the way home, as I mourn the extraction of my athletic molars, I'm burning up colonial turf from Pittsfield, Massachusetts, to the Connecticut border on Route 7, the Berkshire Strip. I wanted my family to live in a state where Teddy Kennedy had a seat at the poker table. Massachusetts is also Crispus Attucks territory. He was a Black man reputed to have been the first patriot to die for America in the Revolutionary War. It makes sense to me that a Black man would be the first person to go blood for our great miracle.

I stop for a cup of coffee in a little diner in Sheffield. I'm inhaling my caffeine in an atmosphere where tired White workers come and go, often with their work splattered on their clothing. The waitress is sexy and inviting in a blue-collar, single-mother sort of way. It's an odd place to be contemplating my recent conclusion that I am distinctively proud of my slave ancestry and the depth of my Americanism. I am from a line of South Carolina stock that goes back almost three hundred years. Their courage, strength, perseverance, and creativity are all qualities that define America's great human resources. In my darker moments I choose to think of my people as swindled forebears who sacrificed the most, the longest. Depends on whether I wake up on the half-empty side of the bed as opposed to the half-full.

When I arrive home I notice that my two cats, a skunk, and a one-eyed wild turkey are eating from the same bowl of cat food. Talk about diversity. I creep by, careful not to disturb the skunk, my symbol for American racial turmoil—black, white, and filled with foul gas. I make my way to the shower, peeling off knee braces and layers of bandages. I've chosen Miles Davis's last live concert to score the final meeting of my basketball muscles and hot water. The shower feels good, the Advil has kicked in, and the pain in my joints is subsiding. Bob Dylan's "Blonde On Blonde" has joined my retirement party. Succumbing to my inability to leave well enough alone, I'm oddly annoyed by a nagging memory from the previous night. Dinner with my pal, Ari, was unsettling.

I met Ari, a man in his late twenties, at a health club in Great Barrington. African dark with a shaved head and Schwarzenegger's body, he stood out like a bruised thumb. Our initial attraction was that we were pigment brothers. When Ari told me that he owned a Mexican restaurant, Dos Amigos, I got a kick out of this unusual young brother, a business owner in a White town. It takes special doses of self-esteem and communication skills to pull that one off.

Ari was born to a teenaged mother in Seattle and was put up for adoption at birth. After two years in foster care, he was adopted by a Jewish couple and has been a proud Jew ever since. We began to check each other out while riding the stationary bike. Ari revealed that he was engaged to be married.

"She's a White woman," he muttered under his breath.

He studied me, searching for the smirk that often emerges on the faces of many Black people when the topic of interracial marriage is mentioned, a nasty little friction that engenders suspicion and confusion in the tribe. I was a curiosity to him: Black and imposing enough to fit comfortably in Willie Horton's inner circle, and yet, I was grinding away beside him in an all-White club. I strung him out a bit, effecting my street-nigger frown. Ari looked forward and pedaled faster, wishing he'd never opened his mouth.

"Hey, man, my woman's White, too," I replied.

"Oh yeah, you're joking?"

Ari's surprise was justified. Interracial marriages are microscopically rare. "I've been with my woman twenty years. Seen fire and rain in that deal," I tossed.

Ari studied me and smiled. "What's it like being married to a White woman for that long?"

"She's not a White woman, she's my wife," I wheezed breathlessly.

My answer wasn't great, but it was the best I could do on my eighth mile. We made plans to have dinner out with our women.

"So what's a big Black Jewish guy doing owning a Mexican restaurant in the Berkshires?"

My wife's question was the appropriate icebreaker, as she and I greeted Ari and his fiancée, Heidi, in a sushi restaurant. Anne's provocative inquiry delighted Ari. He sensed that the task of feeling each other out would be easy.

There was a fifteen-year gulf between the couples. Anne and I weren't quite old enough to be their parents, and they weren't quite young enough to be our children. What do interracial couples talk about? Generally, on these rare occasions when more than one of us comes upon each other, we declare ourselves righteous taboo-busters. The subliminal message is: We're different and we're proud. But that was a painful bore, like belonging to a cult. The worst thing about being a part of an unpopular minority group is that you're stuck with each other, whether you like it or not.

Heidi was an American who had grown up in Germany. She'd never read America's racial-orientation manual. Untainted and fresh, all she knew was that she was in love with the man of her dreams.

"Is integration better or worse than when you two got together?" Ari asked.

"Better," we lied reflexively and moved past that question quickly.

Anne and I often disagree over this issue. She's a bigger believer than I am. I wasn't going to tell Ari that I felt integration was about as firm as a punctured waterbed. Those who practice integration are on the outside looking in. Anne and I dodged the heavy stuff, being careful to avoid triggering a *Who's Afraid of*

Virginia Woolf? scenario. We filled the air with funny anecdotes about our world of cross-marriage.

I didn't have the stomach to tell them that the easy part of a Black-White marriage is the love you share. Real love will trump pigment every time. It's the sense of alienation that you experience from both races that undermines that love. This stigma gnaws on many a good union until it breaks down. You have to be a little crazy to be able to ignore it. Anne and I are a couple of gypsy writers who have had the flexibility to build our lives outside of the mainstream. We were bogus role models, but we put on a good show.

Did I mislead him? I don't know. I'd invested my life in the notion that by the twenty-first century we would have moved beyond the race-ignorance and fear that continue to plague us. Holding on tightly to my vision of America has left a number of perceptible scars. Color-free peace in America is a large order. I'm too far down the trail to change, but should I be an advocate?

My thoughts about race are outdated, somewhat illusory. In these times of racial confusion, I am left to ask: What shape does my America take? I've clung to the distant images of my youth. King's integration initiatives are my blueprint. I've bobbed and weaved, seeking to elude the resegregated version of America that followed the great one's vision.

John Fogerty is shouting from my speakers: "Some folks are born made to wave the flag. Ooh, they're red, white and blue." Have Black integrationists invested too much in a withering Caucasian culture? When the great Jackie Roosevelt Robinson dashed to an early grave on the base paths of our national ignorance, was he running in the wrong direction? The number of colored people on the planet continues to swell, and at some point their discordant voices will harmonize. In America, are future members of a worldwide majority working to preserve the outsized appetites of an eventual minority? Or is our often-maligned, all-encompassing diversity the embryo that will grow into the leader of a new multicultural planet? Did I stumble into something progressive by falling in love with an Irish-Catholic cop's daughter from a red-assed, multiethnic Northeastern suburb?

My wife's father and I once traced our paths backward to the 1965 Harlem riots and discovered that we were within three city blocks of each other, he a captain peddling law and order, while I searched for a back alley carrying a television set. Fifteen years later I showed up at his dinner table fearing that my Sidney Poitier impression would fall short of its mark. How was I going to tranquilize the life of an ex-ghetto heroin addict, Black as Beulah and divorced with a young son? When he would inquire about my livelihood, how was I going to utter the words "out-of-work actor"?

On the day that I was to make my official request to be accepted as Anne's man, we arrived at the family home in Merrick, Long Island, and it took every ounce of courage I possessed to get out of the car. In my criminal days, the cardinal rule was never do anything to piss off a cop. I was afraid that making love to a White cop's daughter out of wedlock challenged that rule. It was the closest I'd ever come to what the death-row boys must feel like on their way to the gas chamber. My wits deserted me for a moment, and I said something absurd: "Go in the house and turn off all the lights. Maybe I won't look so dark." Anne laughed and gave me a look that said *It's time to take your medicine.*

The house was a modest suburban dwelling, which increased my fear, given the fact that most of the White folks I rolled with were rich. At the door a robust, white-haired Irishman greeted us, offering me a strong hand to shake. I looked into his eyes and read neither fear nor anger. He was civil cool. I believe I was rescued by the Irish Catholic moral tenets that were imbedded in the old guy. It was as though the Pope had saved me from getting my ass shot off. The cautiously pleasant evening's proceedings marked my induction into the White faith, where I would subsequently acquire a visa that allowed me to view meat-and-potatoes White Americans up close. Sitting at the dinner table in this fantastical enclave, inconceivable challenges awaited us all. After a lifelong period of checkered admiration for the prototype, for better or worse, I was now a Cleaver, and recollections of the old Beav' in action would have to see me through.

My life is that of a willing rogue with a spirited appetite for walking the tightrope between the races. I live in two Americas: the White one we sell versus the one that includes us all. The latter is the America I am constantly chasing. As long as I am willing to pay the exorbitant Black tax, a tariff placed upon my admission to the mainstream, I can hold my own in the struggle to juggle both worlds. Often the tax gets so high that many Black folks say "The hell with it." But it's impossible to embrace the entire American miracle with one arm—it takes both.

Dover Plains

My daughter, Arielle, and I are on a train to New York City, where I am to put her on the Jitney, a bus line that runs between Manhattan and the Hamptons on Long Island. Arielle is going to see her grandmother for their annual visit. It's her first train ride, and the wonder in her eyes is inspirational. When you marry upstream against the racial tide, one of the unique perks is often the special children that are spawned. Arielle is self-assured, affable, athletic, and creative, carrying a can't-miss tag in today's society. Her golden face is the embodiment of an African-Irish blood mix that echoes the magic that is America. Oceans and centuries divide her ancestors, and yet common earth-diggers who tended the tobacco and potato fields have formed a genetic agreement, setting up shop in Arielle's little body—a patented U.S. bottle of diversity. Its vintage is the best yet produced in our country's slow movement toward its creed. When I was my daughter's age, the absurdity of racial disconnection was wildly different.

BLACK
LIFE

People must prove to the people a
better day is coming.

—**Curtis Mayfield,**
"Choice of Colors"

ONE

Harlem, U.S.A.

Leola Watlington was born in the small town of Georgetown, South Carolina, in the early 1920s. She was a strong, spiritual child, whose religious convictions shielded her from Jim Crow's licking stick. So deep was her belief in those old-time Negro rituals that upon her arrival as a nineteen-year-old on Harlem's doorstep she was virtually immune to the status quo. With God as her compass, she would take on any foe, from the neighborhood school system to the freaked-out, desperate heroin addict, with equal force. She and the Lord made their own rules.

Leola was also blessed in an odd way by the fact that she was the spitting image of Aunt Jemima, midcentury America's ideal Black matron. After Hattie Mc-Daniel won her Oscar in 1939 for *Gone With the Wind*, my mother and others like her were ensured a secure place in the homes of White America. White people liked my mother. She was a big woman, five-foot-eight and 220 pounds of atomic might that demanded respect. She worked hard, insisting on giving her employers more than their money's worth. Leola was the queen of the domestics and wore her crown with distinction in 1956.

As a four-year-old, I viewed my mother as a higher form of life. Though obviously female, she transcended gender as a dominant man-woman. The things she could lift astounded. Watching her move a couch with my father stripped me of any notion of male supremacy very young. In fact, in the Black community my perception wasn't unusual—women ruled. As a child, I was scared to death of her. She would easily carry me under one arm as though I were a purse. Leola was an ardent spare-the-rod, spoil-the-child activist in that concept's heyday. I earned some severe beatings by today's standards, but I'm not claiming abuse: It was just tough-ass survival-influenced child rearing. She subscribed to the Almighty's divine instruction, and I began falling short of that mark from the outset.

Domestic workers, like my mother, who worked for White families in the fifties were the least vulnerable to the myth of White superiority. In the privacy of their homes, people shed their armor, and the domestics were often awash in White frailties. My mother saw her employers as painfully human and often spoke of them as flawed people. This had nothing to do with color; it was based on religious perfectionism. Her employers fell in love with this asexual mass of physical and spiritual dynamism. She was a great cook, with Joe Louis's left hook.

Leola's post-slavery hunger made her an advancement freak. She learned by working for White people that there was a big world just beyond her fingertips, and she was determined that we would nab our share. She felt White folks had been "over blessed" with resources that pointed the way to Hades, but she respected White ingenuity and its magical connection to formal education. To her, the answers to the great divide between the races were embedded in the pages of a textbook. Leola theorized that the key to White success was their desire to learn more than they needed to know.

The belief among Black people was that you had to be twice as good to get half the chance a White person was afforded. My mother felt that twice the education would do the trick. "Be better than the White man" was her cry from the moment I was born in Harlem Hospital. "Know what they know," was Leola's mantra.

I was two years old when my mother began to drill the alphabet into me. She would punch, slap, and, on occasion, whip me if I gave a wrong answer. I was blessed with an extraordinary memory, so by three years old I could spell my name and count to fifty. I didn't know what any of it really meant, but I never missed a cue. "Black people have to sound 'telligent," she ruled.

The Step 'n' Fetchit docility assigned to Negroes enraged my mother. The fake smiles and eyeball-rolling on the faces of Black performers, which pleased White folks, were painfully phony to Black folks. We knew that people like Louis Armstrong and Hattie McDaniel were quite different offstage. We were a secret society of actors toiling as shit-colored children on their best behavior. A successful workday was doing your job while drawing as little attention to yourself as possible, and then making a beeline back to Harlem.

The domestics were different; they fancied themselves quasi-insiders. My mother took full advantage of this position by bringing me to her place of work and seeking to ingratiate me with her extended family. This was my introduction to show business. I entertained my mother's employers by doing an Elvis impersonation. She even bought me a tiny pair of blue suede shoes. They went wild. The part of my act that drew gasps from my audience was when I spelled words like *peach* and *apple*. I would close with a flourish by spelling my difficult last name.

I'd sneak a guarded look at my mom. Her smile told me that there had been no screw-ups, at which point I would approach the people and shake each hand. I did countless variations on that routine—on buses, subways, for Delancey Street shopkeepers, who were the toughest audience, all under the watchful gaze of my mother. I felt obligated to please her, so I began to develop the act, adding new and more difficult words, like *orange* and *ocean*. Somehow I'd glommed on to Paul Anka's song "Diana," and that worked its way into the act. My mother rewarded my efforts by making me her favorite.

This was not my preferred designation, for it carried a heavy burden. Her insistence that I sound smart before I really knew anything was taxing. People above sin are tough to please. If I messed up, the threat of her going upside my oversized head loomed large. I was terrified of her wrath. While many Black children my age were told "You're not good enough," driving their self-esteem into the ground, I was burdened by something quite different. Being better than white folks was demanding work.

"Did you see the look on them people's faces when you spelled that word?" I smiled and nodded in the affirmative, but the truth was that I had been too busy looking at her. White people didn't impress me nearly as much as she did. By my fourth year, my mother's game plan was gaining momentum. I sounded smart and had amassed reams of useless information.

One day she contracted a minor illness that required medical attention. Her employers would not let her go to a run-of-the-mill ghetto hospital, which was more veterinarian than human; they insisted she get the best of care. This is how my mother and I wound up at Mount Sinai—a bright, clean, polished cathedral, heaven-like in comparison to the colored facilities. As my mother was being attended to, I sat in the waiting room and was approached by a nice White lady who would change my life.

In the early fifties to a Black four-year-old, White people glowed like God. Everything on television was White. Hopalong Cassidy wore a big white hat, and Elvis, my hero, managed to be Black with white skin. Christ was White, and my mother worshipped him with a nearly insufferable zeal, so it all made sense to me.

I began whistling "Hound Dog," hoping the White goddess would respond. "That's good," she said. We talked a little Elvis. She then asked, "What's your name?" I heard music as I focused upon her angelic face. She looked just like the blond schoolteacher in one of the *Our Gang* comedies.

"Dennis Watlington," I said.

"What a nice name," were the words that came tumbling out of her aura.

"I can spell it," I replied, and she challenged me to do so. The shit was on. I exhausted my whole act, and it blew her away. I was a real spectacle, an affable talking chimp.

When my mother came back, the White lady soaked her with praise on her parenting, and Leola inflated like a parade balloon. I'd scored a big crossover hit. The mighty and the petite were smiling upon me, one physically imposing, the other, a demure, filter-lit blond—both gushing. Wow!

Suddenly I was whisked away to a room where several White men in long white coats formed a semicircle around a hospital bed I was seated upon. I must have been wearing shorts because I remember the cold metal my legs hit as I swung them nervously. The men asked me what seemed like an endless stream of questions, and they became increasingly impressed by my answers. Later I saw them talking to my mother. I was comforted by her body language: She stood tall in the company of White people, which distinguished her from the average Colored person. It looked like something big was up. On the bus ride home my mother was strangely silent. She was no longer smiling.

"What's the matter?" I asked.

She wouldn't answer, preoccupied in thought. After a moment she blurted out, "They want you to go to a school for smart White children downtown."

Confused by her demeanor, I said, "That's good, right?"

She didn't answer, preferring to look out the window. Suddenly I began to deflate. This magical afternoon was left wanting because of my mother's peculiar behavior. Years later she told me that the doctors who made the recommendation were psychiatrists, and she feared that I might be crazy.

Mount Sinai Hospital had a scholarship fund for the disadvantaged and I was certainly eligible. To my parents the offer was baffling, a rare opportunity at a time when such gifts were unfathomable.

The hospital sent me to a private pre-kindergarten for well-off White children. It was my first experience with White peers, and I quickly discovered that they did things differently. I recall protesting a ridiculous nap rule. My nursery mates were nice enough, and the education part was fun, but this nap thing was unacceptable. It all came to a head when during naptime I couldn't sleep, so I got up and began to walk around. The teacher ordered me to go back to my cot, and I began to run. The teacher chased me around the room, and I accidentally ran into the snack table. As the graham crackers and juice went flying, so did I, right out of the program.

The spirit of Jackie Robinson was a big thing at that time. If Jackie had performed as poorly as I did, it would have set baseball back twenty years—or so it seemed from my mother's reaction. Boy, did I get my ass kicked for that one. I'd blown the act, went out into the big time, and fucked it up. It was like my mother was an agent who had gotten me my big break, and I showed up for rehearsal drunk and was fired.

My mother and I had worked toward this opportunity for four of my five years, a considerable investment. Humbled and pained, I decided to lay low as I prepared to enter kindergarten.

In September 1957, we left our crowded West Harlem apartment when my brother Calvin was born. My father, an army veteran, had a little pull, and we landed a bigger place in East Harlem, the other side of the moon.

The Jefferson Housing Project was brand new when the Watlington family arrived. Here my parents would raise five children: Robert, Jr., Gloria, myself, Calvin, and closing the loop with our baby sister, Harriet. While West Harlem was predominantly Black, East Harlem was everything. In 1957 the Puerto Rican migration was in full motion, and new housing projects were built to help accommodate the influx. The neighborhood surrounding the projects was on life support. The postwar upgrade in American life had turned the historic birthplace of Burt Lancaster and Eugene Lang into a sieve. Italians, Irish, and Jews were on their way to the suburbs. Those who were better off had moved to the Levittowns that were being built. The tougher, poorer slices of the ethnic loaf left behind were there to greet us with a two-by-four.

It was a hard-boiled neighborhood. Welfare had not kicked in yet, so it was dog-eat-dog, no excuses. If you didn't work or hustle on the streets, you starved. We were all working-class poor people who were forced to interact, although the White ethnics that hadn't assimilated feigned a bogus superiority.

The Italians had the upper hand: pure guinea mob-savagery scared the hell out of everyone. They controlled the bottom line. Every Italian guy sought to infer that he was connected. The Irish Paddy boys were standoffish and the quickest to leave, but in the street wars they carried the message that you could never beat a Paddy boy, you had to kill him. The Jewish culture of shopkeepers and businessmen was a strong presence. The Puerto Ricans were the new kids on the block with a debilitating language deficit. Black folks quietly cultivated a rage while trapped in a pool of hungry immigrants.

My mother transcended all barriers. The Italians loved her cooking. Soul food's lure brought the pasta boys home with my brother after school. The Italian mothers reciprocated, and the word *mangia* found its way into everyone's vocabulary. Puerto Ricans loved Jesus, so Leola loved Puerto Ricans. Somehow her broken Spanish and Italian kept up with their broken English. This diverse pool of influences was available to me, because everyone respected or feared my mother. Her presence overwhelmed the neighborhood. Leola could be violent when she had to be, but only on the side of the Lord, much like America.

In my first year in East Harlem, my mother led me to Public School 102, where I was enrolled in kindergarten. She was still pissed off about my unfortunate turn in the White world and viewed public school as my just dessert. I felt terrible about my predicament.

When I arrived, I discovered that most of my classmates didn't speak English. What was I going to do with all of these English words I could spell that flew over the heads of my classmates? I hated it; kindergarten was a bitch. It was only a half a day, from 8:00 to 12:00, but seemed like forever. The kids hadn't been through my mother's stringent boot camp, so they seemed retarded. "What do you mean you can't spell *balloon*? Idiots!"

My teachers were nice enough: two White women, one short and fat, the other, tall and thin. Their easy demeanor and warm-smiling faces were comforting, but my early interaction with White people had taught me to listen for the sound of the other shoe when it landed. They comported themselves much like American nuns sent to an underprivileged country to do missionary work. Although the neighborhood was predominantly White, the class was 98 percent Black and Puerto Rican.

The students were between five and seven years old, either from the island and speaking no English, or from the South and speaking bad English. There was no Head Start program, no multilingual social experiments to fall back on. In fact, the opportunity to live in this country or the ability to vote in a general election was the big prize. We were the children of a group of people who were jockeying for position on a life raft. Over the next twenty years this neighborhood would become pure pigment. Little did I know that many of my classmates would become the parents of the future prison population explosion.

The reverse culture shock I experienced after my flirtation with the White school was so profound that I became an elitist, with my wide nose pointed upward. I had inside information on what the real America was like. I'd tumbled out of the major leagues into a pick-up game.

One very important thing happened during my kindergarten year. I had my first fist fight. Some guy pushed me out of line. I pushed him back. I'd never had a physical confrontation before and was surprised when he kicked me in the stomach and punched me in the jaw. I was dazed but unhurt. I charged into him and clumsily kicked his ass.

If you couldn't fight in a tough neighborhood, you were a social cripple. You might be able to slink through physically, but your spirit was dead on arrival. In 1957 the ghetto was still engaged in bare-knuckled mayhem. A few switchblades and zip guns (which were essentially souped-up slingshots) were around, but you proved yourself by how good you were with your hands.

After I had pummeled my adversary, we were pulled apart. I discovered something that would serve me well for the rest of my ghetto life. Blows from someone my own size was light action. I'd been in with the heavyweight champion of the universe, my mother. After having my ass whipped by the mother lode, everything else was mashed potatoes. Between the ages of five and seventeen, I may have had about three hundred or so fights. Many were inconsequential; others were well-advertised main events, like schoolyard battles in front of half the student population. Regardless of the opponent, my confidence was always bolstered by the knowledge that no one ever hit harder than my mother. That first fight taught me that I had to be violent when pushed, a prescription I was never very comfortable with, but this grim reality would govern my young life.

This primitive school environment offered little challenge, so I acted out with a vengeance. My teachers liked me, but that only fueled my bad behavior. The well-deserved ass-whippings I received at home didn't seem to make a difference. I was headed for trouble.

By the second grade, I was the best reading-writing-and-spelling machine in my class. I got off on it. Having the right answers come to me so often with such ease was a beautiful high. In order to maintain my attention and a semblance of good behavior, I was given my own group of five underachievers to teach. That was a great feeling. The group sat in a circle, and I had my fellow students read aloud for me. I loved the responsibility, but it didn't keep me from getting in trouble.

I'm not sure why, but I remember being in the closet in my classroom among a number of coats, so it must have been winter. I started a fire, and it quickly grew out of control. Someone smelled smoke, and, after a head count, my teacher knew who was missing. She ripped open the door, unveiling me in a coughing jag. Losing her temper, she yanked me out of harm's way, then grabbed a fire extinguisher and unleashed a white foamy fluid throughout the closet. Whipped cream has spooked me ever since.

I knew that I'd done it this time. My teacher escorted me by the ear to the principal's office. I was placed on immediate suspension and had to remain in the office until my mother arrived to pick me up. Uh-oh! I sat in a puddle of fear and confusion. When my mother arrived, she looked twice as big and considerably more menacing than usual. I was made to sit on a bench outside the principal's office and wince while listening as my mother gave a Holy Roller sermon that made the glass portion of the door vibrate. I could hear a booming litany of "my child this" and "my child that" that rattled my bladder.

The door to the principal's office finally opened, and my mother grabbed me by the collar. I thought she was going to kick my ass, but she dragged me down the hallway without saying a word. I didn't know what was up. We came to my classroom, and, in front of all of my classmates, she bent me over her knee. I began to struggle, but she overpowered me and pulled my pants down. With my ass prominently displayed, she began wailing the daylights out of me. The stinging pain paled in comparison to the raucous laughter of my classmates. I struggled and broke her grip in between blows, and, with my legs tangled in my underwear, I fell to the ground, exposed for everyone to see. My mother then dragged me from the classroom into the hallway and ordered me to pull up my underwear and trousers.

Several of my classmates ran to the door to hear the post-humiliation commentary, while I stood there and fought back the desire to cry. My mother screamed at my classmates, "Back inside!" They scattered, unwilling to tempt her wrath. I stood there, frozen in time, when my mother said, "I ain't finished with you yet. I love you, and I'll do whatever it takes to save you from your stupid, hard-headed self."

She slowly turned and began to walk down the hallway. I apologized from a distance. She stopped and turned to me, and, as I moved closer to her, I discovered her eyes were moistening. She said, "I'm sending you home." That appeared obvious, since I'd just been suspended for a week. "Maybe down home you can learn something I can't teach you up here." She picked up her pace, and I accelerated to keep up.

"What do you mean, 'down home'?" I asked.

She blurted out the words that would set my life on its ear.

"Down South."

TWO

It was early morning in 1958 when I awoke on the road to nowhere. My uncle Junior drove southward into a blinding sunrise. My mother had made good on her decision to send me "down home" to my grandmother in Georgetown, South Carolina. As I sat upright in the backseat, my uncle pulled over to the side of the road on the outskirts of a sleepy, faceless Southern town. He told me that he wanted to grab a couple of hours of sleep.

What the hell am I supposed to do? I thought.

"Sit still," he commanded.

I complied for about ten minutes before starting to fiddle nervously with a yo-yo. I attempted to do a trick called Around the World. The yo-yo hit the window, and the sound jolted my uncle awake. Angry, he threw me out of the car and scatted me off into the nearby brush, which looked like a forest to me. It was cold, and I couldn't for the life of me figure out what the hell I was doing there.

The fire episode in school had led to my banishment. Initially, "down home" had sounded like a pretty good idea. It meant escaping the never-ending taunts of my friends and classmates who chimed, "I've seen your hiney, all black and shiny." That was then, but now, standing in the woods, planted in the early-morning sticky dew, gave me big cause for pause.

Shivering, I was scared to death. I

wanted to go back to the car, but I didn't want to antagonize my uncle, for that was a possible ass-whipping in the making. So I sat on a tree stump and tried to whistle. I went through my Elvis repertoire, but in those days no one could resist Elvis, and his music attracted a muskrat and other frightening, furry living things. As they came toward me, I freaked out. A lifelong Manhattanite, I was thinking *Where's the fucking concrete?* and ran like hell.

When I got to the car, I was frantic and banged on the window, preferring my uncle's wrath to the wilderness. When he saw how scared I was, he let me in and comforted me. I begged him to move on, and thankfully he granted my wish. The sound of the car's ignition was sweet music.

Eventually our brown car pulled up in front of an old house that scared me to death. It was huge and dysfunctional-looking, conjuring up ugly pictures I'd seen of sharecropper poverty. My grandmother and a brood of kids came running toward the car. I ducked beneath the seat. "Get up, boy," my uncle shouted at me. When I looked up, the car was surrounded with what seemed like thousands of little barefoot cousins bouncing with excitement. It was like being at the zoo.

My grandmother opened the door and invited me out. What a sight she was—five-foot-three or so and built like solid oak; she was a dead ringer for Harriet Tubman. With a bandanna wrapped around her head, she wore a thick, all-purpose, floor-length, quilt-like skirt. Mama Sis was the name the cousins were chirping at her. What a woman! I ran to her and hugged her tightly. She pressed my head into her dress, which was so full it felt like a mattress. I wouldn't let go, and she looked down at me and asked, "You shy?" I nodded in the affirmative, which was news to me.

Over the next eternity (in real time, a year and a half), I would grab a handful of this paradise every chance I got. I was introduced to my horde of cousins, which confused the hell out of me. Who were all these poor Colored kids? I later figured out that my grandmother had nine children, and most of them had sent one or more of their kids "down home." It was usually the grandchildren who didn't handle the northern way of life very well. This was the family's reform school.

Luckily, my grandmother was a loving warden. She was strict but kind, and religious down to her last petticoat. Her face didn't resemble my mother's very much, but they both exuded the same confidence that makes one the leader of the pack. And we were a pack! I continued to hold on to her like a cat dug into a rug while she hugged my uncle. He pulled me off of her.

"Let the boy stay here if he want," my grandmother chided.

But my uncle, tired and cranky, would hear none of that. He groused, "There's too many of them down here for him to be sticking to you like that."

It was then that I said my first words, "You mean all of them live here all the time?"

My grandmother said, "You'se all my children. You all started from me."

Ugh!

When we entered the house, it was shocking how poor they were. There were no lights or electricity—zero. There were kerosene lamps that were lit only after nightfall. The poor in the projects up North lived like kings compared to this insanity. This big, drafty two-story house was something out of *The Grapes of Wrath*. There was no running water. All heat was provided by wood-burning stoves. The kitchen was scary, charred, and battered from age. I became sick to my stomach from the smell of burning wood. In the family's sitting room there was an assortment of chairs and crates and a huge stove with a sooty pipe that extended all the way to the ceiling. This was where the brood gathered to do family business. It was at this point that I lost it. I was tipped over the edge by the sorrow that gripped me when I realized that this was the room where the TV should be. A quick calculation rendered the painful verdict: no electricity, no television.

This was Southern, Black, pre–Second World War poor. I flipped out and started to cry. My grandmother tried to calm me, but the reality went through me like a hot knife. I was inconsolable. My uncle picked me up and held me on one of his shoulders and began to carry me away, kicking and screaming. The brood followed as he climbed the stairwell. We came to the top of the stairs and entered an enormous loft that had a number of barely adequate partitions providing an open kind of privacy.

I was still squealing as my uncle put me down. Suddenly, I was stunned into silence. Seated behind one of the partitions was a ninety-four-year-old woman. She was the oldest living thing I'd ever seen. One of my cousins said, "That's Miss Sue." She was frighteningly thin and shriveled; her face seemed weblike. She motioned for me to come closer to her and slowly offered her hand. I reached out and touched it. I could feel the bones upon contact in this prunelike extremity. She croaked, "I'm Miss Sue, and if you take care of me, I'll take care of you."

I didn't want to know what that meant. My cousin said, "She mean the bucket." I looked down. Beside her bed was a tin bucket half-filled with urine. Apparently, all the cousins took turns emptying it and attending to Miss Sue's other needs. That wasn't the worst of it. The kicker was that we also took turns helping her use the bucket. There was absolutely no way I could have guessed that my mother was this angry with me. I had been sentenced to hard labor. I ran for the stairwell and hurried down. My uncle and several of my cousins took off after me.

I spent three nights crying myself to sleep, keeping everyone awake. I was exhausted and depressed in the daytime. My two oldest cousins, Kenny and Diane, ran the brood. At thirteen and fourteen years of age, they were ancient to me. Kenny had come over the first night and started smacking me around, trying to get me to shut up. Diane was kind and more patient. Kenny led the charge that I was a spoiled rich mama's boy from the North. It was my introduction to the concept of relativity. No matter how poor you think you are, you're rich to somebody. For my entire stay he would give me heat over that myth, even though I suffered every hardship he did, wearing the same rags.

I'd thought southern Coloreds liked and respected Coloreds from the North. I was wrong. The other cousins picked up on the notion that I was soft. I'd become the upper middle class White guy who goes to Rikers Island. These were tough kids. You could see the cynical wisdom flow from their indignant faces as they laughed amongst themselves at their inside ground-billy jokes, which were at my expense. I stayed close to my grandmother. I was wearing her dress out.

On my fourth night, I was wailing my homesick solo to the displeasure of my other cellmates, when my grandmother emerged carrying a lantern. This time she had her hit person's face on. Everyone was fed up; it was time for her to act to protect the majority.

"You come with me, boy," she said and ordered me to stand. When I asked her where we were going, she said, "To the chicken coop."

"What!"

She grabbed a blanket and ordered me to follow. We went downstairs and out into the backyard. It was lights-out black, not dark, black—you couldn't see your hand in front of your face. I followed the lamp off into the distance.

"Where are we going, Mama Sis?" I asked.

"If you can't live with us," she said, "I have the place for you. The chickens don't mind if you cry, 'cause they'll be passing on soon."

"What?!"

I sobered up quick. It was clear I'd overplayed my hand. In less than a week, I'd gone from enjoying *The Soupy Sales Show* on weekday afternoons to the chicken coop. After walking a quarter of a mile, we came to a huge tin-and-mesh-wire shack. You could hear what seemed like a million chickens clucking in whispers. My grandmother asked me to hold the lamp as she opened a padlock and pulled the door that dragged a noisy path through the moist dirt.

We stepped in, and she led me to a corner where there were several twenty-five-pound bags of feed.

"Am I going to sleep here?" I asked.

She didn't answer. She just positioned the bags of feed into a little bed. She motioned for me to lie down.

I raised my voice in anguish. "I'll be good, I'll be good, I'll never cry again, I promise!"

"If you don't appreciate what the Lord gives you, he'll give you less," she purred.

It took years for me to figure that one out. At the time, I was completely blown away. I stopped protesting, because the louder I spoke the more I stirred up the chickens. She ordered me to lie down, placed the blanket over me, walked away, and closed the door. The same scraping sound cementing the verdict.

This was the big test. I was about to rid myself of any phobia of incarceration. I felt an unexpected shot of calm and composure as I focused on the odd but relatively cool sound of chickens clucking. The next thing I remember was waking at dawn and being surprised by how many chickens there were—a hundred or more. The rooster let loose his blast, sounding distinctly more powerful than those I'd heard on television.

From that moment on, I was over any and all homesickness. I was a southerner.

Despite the living conditions that I never got used to, I was beginning to ease up and accept my sentence. Living with a mob of relatives makes for a hot bed of competition, and I discovered that I liked to compete and win. The prize was access to my grandmother, won by those who worked the hardest. This meant chores, chores, and more chores.

Mama Sis believed in hard work, just like my mother. They were both nuts about it. My grandmother was two generations removed from slavery. Slaves were drilled with the work ethic "Don't stop 'til you drop." My grandmother ran our household much like a plantation. When we weren't in school, we worked in the fields for the better part of the day. The heat in the fields was treacherous. My grandmother used to say, "The heat is there to let you know the work is serious." Amen!

We worked the land, which consisted of a big garden where we planted an assortment of vegetables. At harvest time my grandmother employed a process that enabled her to can and preserve food for our winter needs when the land rested. With the exception of a two-year-old cousin, everyone worked.

I could be picking peas one day and assisting Uncle Junior as he repaired the roof the next. I was expected to overcome my fear of heights on the spot, which I did looking down in horror. Phobias were considered silly because they made hard work more difficult.

Six days a week, my relatives were amazingly sane and stable. They accepted life's grim realities with dignity, under the watchful eye of the Lord or his able messenger, my grandmother. In short, we took what life gave us and made it better. During my boot-camp period, my cousins squeezed all of the delusions that I'd absorbed from northern television out of me. If I wanted to see my favorite cartoon characters, Heckle and Jeckle, I had to draw them.

The chicken chores were another swift jolt of advanced reality. I'd never killed anything bigger than a cockroach in my life. A skinned chicken looked so different from a live one that I'd never made the connection. The first time I saw a chicken get its head chopped off, I screamed. My uncle Junior looked at me in a way that made me feel foolish. I held my tongue as the headless creature banged from wall to wall like a pinball.

"This is how you eat, boy," my uncle said as he handed me a hatchet, grabbed another chicken by the neck, and held it over the chopping stump. "Hurry, boy, it's got a lot of fight in it." The poor thing was scrambling for its life. "Swallow hard and do it," he commanded. It was like the first time one jumps off of the high diving board at the swimming pool. Thwack! I did it!

We killed fifteen chickens that afternoon for consumption and sale. The headless victims were tossed in a sack, and my uncle said, "We buy 'em and raise 'em, so we can feed you. We can't afford store-bought food, so you do what you have to do. These ain't people, they'se food."

"I thought in church they said not to kill?"

"You got that wrong boy."

"How?"

"They mean thou shall not kill in church," he said, brushing me off. "Let's go pluck these things before night falls, and stop asking so many damn questions."

We had a huge tub of boiling water bubbling in the backyard. We dunked the chickens in the pot in short intervals so that the feathers would loosen, while being careful not to cook the meat. When the feathers loosened, we began to pluck them, a horrible job. It was like giving someone a shave, one hair at a time.

When we completed the job, it was dusk and my uncle took me to his special place. It was one of the plum trees on the far end of the property. We climbed to the center of the tree, which provided a breathtaking view of the sunset. He said that he'd never missed a chance to watch the sun go down from his perfect angle on the world. The mass murderer of poultry had a poet's soul.

I was beginning to admire my uncle Junior. I wasn't afraid of him anymore. As long as I respected his role as my grandmother's overseer, he was pretty cool. He was like Superman, with a quick, correct answer for just about everything. Whenever he couldn't answer, he simply replied, "Shut up and work."

He became my role model. If he could do it, then I could do some version of it. He frequently took me on his plum-tree excursions. As we watched the orange horizon, he talked about the Korean War and how much he had loved the armed services. He was disappointed that he hadn't gotten the chance to fight. He was tied up in the kitchen feeding the real soldiers. He wanted a chance to die for his country, so he could die an American. He figured, "You can't live it, but you can die it."

Southern Life dies when night falls in a house with no electricity. One of the benefits of hard work was that you generally fell asleep faster, but aside from that, it was just too damn dark. On occasion my oldest cousin, Diane, would read to us by kerosene lamp, but kerosene was costly and we didn't waste anything, so these sessions were few and far between.

My cousin Julius talked of how much he liked school, which was still several weeks away. He felt reading and writing indoors beat working in the fields. That sounded good to me. I never thought I would look forward to going to school, but I was learning how things once taken for granted became jewels when the game changed.

I was taking to my universe quite nicely. I missed my mother, but there were a number of things I didn't miss about her. So it was something of a wash. With no telephone, we communicated by mail. I received a letter every two or three weeks. I began to think of her less and less.

As the calluses outfitted my feet from living the barefoot life, a sense of self-preservation came over me, and I began to enjoy it. If this were all there was to life, I would have easily grown up to become a successful American. Early to bed, early to rise, nose to the grindstone, strong, and overbearingly religious. Weren't those the qualities for success? I wasn't aware that just beyond the limits of our property there was another reality, one for which all the wonderful attributes I was acquiring would be of little value.

My grandmother was going to visit a relative in a town fifty miles away. Since my arrival, I hadn't left the property, had never been to town or seen anyone except family and the church crowd. As a reward for all my sucking up to her, she decided to take me along. My deceased grandfather, Big Jim Bradley, had worked for the railroad, and my grandmother was afforded the opportunity to travel on the train at a large discount. She had a shrine to my grandfather in her bedroom cubicle. He was a big guy, with Paul Robeson's height and upper-body presence. She wouldn't answer many questions about him, except to state her mantra, "He was a good man and took care of his family."

It was a beautiful day for travel on this late-summer afternoon. My uncle dropped us off at the train station, and we headed for the waiting room. I had visions of gumball machines dancing in my head. I sped up, but my grandmother barked, "Slow down!" I stopped in front of the well-appointed facility and could see the gumball machines and a soda fountain beneath a huge overhead fan. The first White people I had seen since coming south were resting comfortably. My grandmother continued walking until we were past the joint. Suddenly, confusion set in. "Where we going, Mama Sis?"

"To the waiting room," she answered calmly.

"You passed it."

"We'se going to *our* waiting room."

Her reply made me smell a rat. We continued to walk until we came to a hot, dirty little shack with no ventilation and no concessions. It stank. At this point, as the flies began sizing us up, I became angry.

"Why are we in here, when the other place is better?" I wanted to know.

My grandmother flashed the face of a lioness about to administer tough love to one of her cubs. She whacked me across the lips and said, "This is for the Coloreds."

Stunned, I asked why. She told me how Coloreds had it harder. "Why?" I still wanted to know as my lip swelled from the blow. She took a piece of tissue from her purse and began to dab at my bruise.

"Down here, we live different. Takes more life to live if you Colored."

This was the first time I was ever hostile toward my grandmother. I'd taken my share of her whacks with a good attitude, but this felt different. I wanted to take her on. But the look in her face was scary. It was the look of an honest person who had just told a vicious lie. I didn't trust that look, so I choked back my indignation and kept my mouth shut.

On the train, we didn't talk to each other. I looked out the window as the countryside flew by. I snuck a look at her, and I thought she was embarrassed about the way she'd hit me. She never changed her facial expression. She wore a mask of proud sorrow. I reached for her dress and pulled closer. She extended her arm outward and pulled me to her quilt. Mama Sis never looked at me; she continued to look forward as though she was carved in wood. I was seeing the effects of Jim Crow up close. Racism was big enough to have cracked my grandmother, and I didn't think anything could do that.

The next day, when my uncle and I were back on that damn roof, I asked him why we couldn't sit in the same room with the White people. He told me he didn't want to talk about it.

"Why?"

"Because the last thing I want to think about on a roof is crackers. Now shut up and concentrate."

I started to pout. "When White people down here look at Colored, they see slaves," he said. "They think we cheated them out of something by getting free, so they have it set up where we can't get no mo' free. It wasn't like that in Korea. Men act different when they think they're going to die."

"It's not like that up North," I whined.

"Who you kiddin'," he laughed. "That's the reason I'm down here."

"You like it better down here than New York?" I challenged.

"Damn right. You can work your whole life up North and never own a thing. This is ours. If you stay out of the line of cracker fire, you can live a better life," he crowed. I smiled but thought he was crazy.

THREE

September rolled around, and we were about to start school. My Southern school experience was a fourteen-carat-gold bitch. The first red flag was that we weren't going to get new clothes for school, and none of my cousins expected any. I was again facing our sub-poverty. We had this mass laundryfest two days before school was to open. We washed the same rags we always wore. I later learned that my mother was sending five dollars a week for my care, but that money dissolved in our pot of needs. As I turned the ratty fabric in the boiling water, I was praying that the clothing would melt away.

That Sunday in church, a nine-hour affair, I spent much of my time praying that my nightmare would end. As the season changed, it seemed time to split. I was ready to get off for hard work and good behavior. I thought my mother would surprise me and let me come home. God knows, I'd paid enough for my crimes. On this day, before school started, I pleaded with God to send me north, and refused to believe that time was running out on my prayers. I talked to God honestly and felt I had a good case. Where was the mercy? It was not to come.

The following morning I found myself standing with the brood, dressed in rags, preparing to walk two and a half miles to the Colored school. As if entering a new school wasn't bad enough, you had to walk a marathon to get there. Unfortunately, the situation was even worse than I imagined.

The first thing I discovered was that everyone in my class was dressed better than I was. The shocking discovery that not all Black southern kids were poor hit hard. I was the poorest of them all. How could this be? Crisp jeans and nice shirts surrounded me. They teased me brutally because I was dressed like trash with a relatively sophisticated pattern of speech. They couldn't sync the two together, and this made me ripe for ridicule. It was like the strange feeling one gets when a dark-skinned African speaks with a Liverpudlian accent. I was a space alien. I had no supplies and carried my notebook in a paper bag. Thank God I'd perfected the art of sounding smart. That seemed to garner my teacher's respect, but with the students, I was an outcast.

Contrary to my northern experiences, where unsettled immigrants and displaced southern Blacks didn't have a clue, I found the kids in this class to be far more confident and self-assured. Their families had been rooted in these parts for centuries. In this pre–civil rights environment, a Negro class system was firmly in place. The lighter skinned you were, the more apt you were to be doing well. If your hair was straight or loosely curled, that was another ticket to the front ranks. The thinking was: The more of the master's blood you had in you, the better off you were. The darker your skin, the more hell you caught. If you were dark-skinned, you'd better be dressed well or your parents had to drive a Thunderbird. The last option for a darkie was that he'd better be a hell of a fighter and able to scare people. I had none of these assets going for me. I was dark-skinned, poor, and raggedy, with an unusually large head and a funny northern accent.

Lunch was tough because I couldn't afford the ten cents for the meal. A nest of Black women cooked the soul food. Each day another wholesome, scrumptious meal, with accompanying warm wonder biscuits, passed me by. As I gnawed on my scraps drawn straight from the earth, my classmates waved drumsticks dipped in gravy under my nose. What pain!

They took education seriously "down home." The teachers had permission to beat you with paddles and straps and they would take care of business on the spot. I would later discover that guards in correctional facilities used the same approach. It didn't work too well in lockup, but it was very effective in the classroom. You paid attention, completed your assignments, and spoke when you were spoken to. Once, I was caught stealing food in the cafeteria and was taken to the principal's office. He gave me one of his renowned thrashings. It didn't quite come up to my mother's best, but it was close. He probably had to ration his energy more carefully.

I learned more that school year than at any other time in my life. There were no excuses for misbehavior. Jim Crow vitriol didn't exist because the teachers and administrators were all Black. Black-on-Black cruelty was just as painful.

There was nowhere to hide. If you were considered poor amongst southern Black people, you were at the bottom of society. Black working-class people had little sympathy for the Black poor. The fact that I was hungry was my parents' fault; the holes in my clothing were just my tough luck. I learned more about racial and class harassment from middle-class Black folks than I did from Whites.

I often spent my long pain-in-the-ass walk home from school with my cousin Kenny ragging on me about being such a large-headed asshole. It was one of his favorite pastimes, so I would block him out until he shouted, "Here they come!" ripping me from my thoughts. It was his air raid signal. We would run and literally dive through the air behind a set of bushes, eluding a barrage of bottles and other lunch refuse. Every day on the way home, the White kids, who went to a different school and traveled by bus, would pass us and throw all the garbage left over in their lunch boxes in our direction. It was a sport, like skeet shooting. "Look at the niggers, get the niggers!" I'm convinced that this daily exercise contributed to my lifelong physical agility. We zigged and zagged, then hit the dirt. It became a challenge, which lessened the humiliation.

My teacher, Miss Beck, was a member of the most prominent Black family in Georgetown. They were professional Negros—doctors, lawyers, business people, the cream of light-skinned-Black southern royalty. Miss Beck liked me. She thought I'd done a good job dealing with all the bullshit I was enduring. She encouraged me not to lose my spirit, and I became her pet.

She once took me to her family home. It was beautiful, filled with all the modern comforts of the twentieth century. There was a big television in the sitting room. It had been months since I'd seen one, and I became filled with excitement, feeling I'd stepped into a fantasy world. The poor really take it on the chin when they are exposed to prosperity. The ache of feeling "less than" expands. I was reminded of my southern Christmas when we all sat around and tried to deal with being too poor to enjoy the holiday. I'd dropped the notion that Santa existed, so that I wouldn't think that he'd singled me out to hate. My grandmother would give the family the "God loves us" rap, but it didn't stand up when we were around people God had blessed. I refused to believe that God really loved me when he had given some other kid the bicycle.

As I stared at the blank television screen, I began to lust for a better life. I was cursing God when Miss Beck entered the room. I straightened and stared at the television, hoping that she would take my hint.

"Put that notion away, boy."

Her words hung in the air like a guillotine's blade.

Why?" I asked.

"Because TV isn't good for children," she scolded.

What kind of cockeyed bullshit thinking was that? "Please, just a few minutes," I said. Miss Beck stood on her word and steered me from the room.

I was there to help her staple the programs together for a school event. She led me to a little den. On the way there we passed through the kitchen, where I saw an assortment of store-bought food. I wanted to scream, "This is torture!" but I just moved very slowly, allowing my eyes to stock up at the expense of my empty stomach.

By the time we began our chore, I was thinking that she was cruel. I stapled away until I couldn't take how I was feeling anymore. I threw it across the desk. Miss Beck was startled by this outburst, and her kind demeanor changed into abject disapproval.

"That's no way to behave, young man," she scolded.

I apologized, but my disappointment had settled in. She handed me the stapler and motioned for me to get back to work. I stewed in an anger I didn't understand. As soon as the work was done, Miss Beck told me to prepare to leave. I cleaned up the errant scraps of paper and moped along as Miss Beck led me back through the kitchen of my discontent. I closed my eyes so that I would not gape at those labels. My foolish antics caused me to bang my leg into a table, and it hurt like hell. I screamed from a mixture of frustration and a pain that throbbed in my upper thigh.

When I started crying, Miss Beck shook off her annoyance and began to comfort me. She was childless and husbandless. I'd figured that she'd gotten her fill of kids on her job, but she put her arm around me and assured me that my leg would be fine. I was wallowing in self-pity (which was up to my shoulders at this point). Then she said a few of the magic words I yearned to hear. "You think you'd like some cookies and milk?"

My anguish could now spot the Cavalry. Out of a package? I wondered.

"Yes, I'd like that, Miss Beck," I responded, trying to sustain my anguish, not wanting to risk her rescinding the offer.

I had three chocolate cookies and a glass of cold milk. This was a real departure from my grandmother's sugar bread and water. Composed and ready to catch every crumb that fell, I could have eaten ten more of those cookies, but I decided to quit while I was ahead.

This trip to Miss Beck's palace had turned into one great tease. All the things I was missing in life were right there at my fingertips, and yet these tantalizing trappings of contemporary life were not to be mine. I gave Miss Beck a hug as I was leaving. After I'd taken a few steps up her walkway, I heard her say, "Cheer up. God loves you."

I didn't turn back. I just hung my head as I began my long walk back to the poor side of town.

That evening my blues intensified. After finishing my homework by candle-light, I had one last chore and it was a killer. I was on Miss Sue duty that week. The specifics of the job were to change her linen, clean up her cubicle, and then help her urinate into the bucket. Her ninety-plus-year-old thighs were the most frightening thing I'd ever seen up to that point in my life. I had to hold her steady over the bucket, which was tricky because you couldn't see the bucket beneath her. You prayed that her aim was true. She was taking longer than usual and became too heavy for me to hold. She slipped from my grasp, fell into the bucket, and yelled in that croaky way of hers. I had to turn her over on the bed and pull the bucket off of her ass. What a mess! The bucket had seared a ring print into her ancient backside. As I toweled off her buttocks as she mooned me, I thought I would die from embarrassment.

I sat her upright. She was in a daze. As I cleaned her up, I could hear my cousins giggling. We tried again and this time were successful. It's a terrible feel-ing to dump an old person in a bucket. She sensed how bad I felt and told me she had something for me. She rummaged through her bag and came out with two cookies that were older than she was. She placed them in my hand, and when I held them between my thumb and forefinger, they crumbled into pow-der. I smiled and thanked her, and she seemed pleased. I wasn't sure if this wasn't her way of paying me back for dropping her, but I just kept on smiling.

As I approached my ninth birthday, I began to flourish in my diminished in-nocence. I'd learned that people seem to have a much better time being cruel than nice, so I developed thick skin and tried to stay a moving target. Now, when the White kids on the school bus threw their garbage at me, I would stag-ger and do an exaggerated imitation of having been shot. This turned them on, and after a few times going through my act, they began to cheer me. I became their favorite victim. In my final month of school, I could smell the goal line. The end was near, and I celebrated the fact that I wouldn't have to walk this in-sufferable two and a half miles home for much longer.

With three days left in the school year, I was in a particularly good mood on my walk home, when I saw in the distance an imposing vehicle coming toward me. It grew bigger and bigger as it drew near. Before I knew it, the largest truck I had ever seen had slowed to a halt. The driver was White, which should have given me pause, but the sight of this monstrosity forced me to gape. The driver looked in my direction, and I quickly turned away in fear.

I moved on, picking up my pace and eventually breaking into a trot. The truck began to follow me. It picked up speed, and I began to sprint. My panic provoked a misstep, and I went sprawling. As I skidded on the pavement, I heard a grating redneck twang. "Aw, you all right?" The man got out of the cab and approached me, and I jumped to my feet. He was a good-looking blond guy who resembled Peter Graves in the TV series *Fury*. I was surprised by and distrustful of his broad smile. He knelt beside me and examined my skinned knee through my patched pant leg. "You have to watch where you're going," he said cheerfully.

"I was watching your truck," I muttered under my breath. He laughed heartily, and, despite his kindness, I held my breath, waiting for the other shoe to drop.

"You live close to here?" he asked matter-of-factly.

When I pointed out that I lived a couple of miles up the road, he offered to give me a ride, and my response to his generosity was, "Why?"

He had a puzzled look on his face when he said, "I don't know many people who would rather walk than ride."

I took the bait, and for an instant became a nine-year-old child who couldn't resist the opportunity to ride in the mother of all trucks. I followed the stranger. The engine roared as I fixated on the complicated dashboard.

"You coming from school?" he asked.

Before answering, my distrust began to well up. "You from the North?" I asked.

"No, I've been living here all my life," he answered while keeping his eyes firmly on the road.

"Then why you helping Coloreds?" I whispered.

There was a lengthy pause before he answered, and I began to expect the worst, like he might be crazy and want to rape or kill me. Finally, he broke his silence.

"You Coloreds are people too."

"What?" I wondered out loud.

He represented everything I'd been trained to fear, yet exhibited none of the behavior. He told me that he had been in the war—he didn't specify which one—and that he'd served with Coloreds.

"Colored boys are some courageous sons of a gun, and don't you ever forget that."

My head was all screwed up now.

"I like kids." He smiled as he continued to look forward.

Delightfully confused, I felt ten feet tall as we continued down the road. When we pulled up in front of my house, everyone came running to see this huge mystery that dominated half the block. When the driver's door opened and out climbed this Troy Donahue-esque stud, no one knew what to make of him. I followed him out of the same door. As he reached up to help me down, the shock on my cousins' faces was captivating. Their envy melted when the stranger said, "You kids want to take a look inside my truck?" They jumped at the opportunity and, in an instant, were crawling all over the inside of the cab. As the stranger looked on, he placed his arm around my shoulder. I could see off in the distance my uncle Junior, who would not approach us. He seemed to be threatened by the blond stranger.

After a few minutes, the comic-book superhero shook my hand, climbed back into his truck, and roared off. We all waved enthusiastically until his vehicle was but a dot in the distance.

Uncle Junior approached and asked, "Who was that?"

"I don't know," I answered honestly. "He was in the war, like you, and say he like Coloreds."

"Don't you ever do that again. Crackers pick little boys up and kill them or fuck them all the time."

Uncle Junior walked away, spoiling the thrill of my first taste of putting people before color.

I blurted out, "You're jealous!"

He stopped in his tracks and came back at me, and, in a fit of inexplicable anger, he kicked my ass. Despite the pain from his blows, I felt sorry for him. I knew the White knight gnawed on his inadequacies because Uncle Junior had earned the right to be my hero. I rolled up into a ball on the grass, and all I could think about was getting out of the damn South.

The South was pure racial confusion. It was overwhelming and disfiguring. The word *nigger* meant little to me because we used it all the time, yet it was the worst thing a White person could call you. I didn't get it. I thought of TV and returning to my White heroes—the Lone Ranger, Superman, Roy Rogers, and Soupy Sales. I refused to believe they would hurt me just because I was Negro.

I'd seen so much anger and cruelty in the Black world. Black schoolmates humiliated me by passing off urine as lemonade and trying to convince me to drink it. I had lost respect for Black adults because I'd seen them reduced to children whenever in the presence of White people. In my mind, the separation between Black adults and myself was minimal. They were executive children— talented and resourceful but with zero power in the eyes of the world.

Unfettered by all of the pertinent complexities that were over my head, I callously called life as I saw it. As my sentence in the South drew to an end, I longed for the softer tones of northern White condescension.

Finally, my mother called off the dogs and sent the price of a train ticket, signaling the end of my nightmare. The night before departure, I didn't pack; there wasn't one single thing that I wanted to take with me. I'd carried my rags outside the night before and torched them. My grandmother was annoyed when she approached my little bonfire. She tried to lay her anger off on my using matches, but I could see that the fire hurt her pride.

Mama Sis told me that God gave me less because I was stronger than most. "The meek shall inherit the earth," she preached.

"That's jive," I said, then braced for the physical onslaught.

She looked at me, and her eyes began to moisten. I'd never seen her so vulnerable. It was as though a moment of doubt had lodged itself between the bricks of her faith. I began to feel terrible for her. She read my sympathy and proudly professed, "The smoke is making my eyes water. Put that fire out." Mama Sis turned and walked away. I continued to burn the rags until they were ashes, then raked their remains into the wind.

On this blessed morning, as I helped my grandmother build a fire in the kitchen, she masterfully whipped the batter for a special pancake breakfast in my honor. My cousins began to drift into the kitchen to contribute to the effort. I was excited and wanted everything to move quickly. Sweat caused by the stove's heat appeared on my grandmother's brow. I looked up and caught several sweat droplets that fell from her chin. This wasn't the official goodbye between us, for she was taking me back to New York on the train, but it was the end of wood-burning stoves and a return to electricity.

During breakfast my uncle Junior issued what amounted to a toast. "To the boy with the big head, the big mouth, and the big heart." On that flattering note I exited my nightmare.

As we rode on the train, my grandmother wore her usual stoic expression, staring straight ahead, trying to lend dignity to the Colored section. I was bursting with excitement, even though the long ride was as harrowing as my walk to school. What lay ahead for me? Was the North going to be the oasis I'd built it up to be in my homesick fantasies?

It was 1960. I couldn't imagine that the new decade the train was speeding into would explode into a million pieces, and that when the debris settled the country wouldn't resemble my grandmother's world. My generation's courage and arrogance would replace her quiet, compliant dignity.

Crossing over into the North was an experience that was palpable. We had to change trains somewhere north of Washington, D.C. The new car we sat in was racially mixed. We went to the concession stand, and the White concessionaire referred to my grandmother as "ma'am." He was respectful, and his smile seemed genuine. When we returned to our seats, as I sucked on my drink, I noticed that my Mama Sis's face had softened, and a smile had emerged. The sixties were about to begin.

FOUR

In the fall of 1960, I spent a short time as my father's favorite kid. When Robert Watlington felt especially good about one of us, he would award his favorite "the seat." That special place was on the floor between his legs as he watched television. I hated watching television with my dad: CBS News was painful to me, but those dour, boring men were the rage with him. I had to survive golf and the Arnold Palmer revolution in order to hold on to my throne. My dad had caddied for most of the summers of his youth, and the game was in his blood. A Black golf enthusiast living in the ghetto had a tough go of it, unless he enjoyed putting with a broom. It was also "in the seat" that I learned about professional baseball and my father's intense hatred for the New York Yankees. To my father, the Yankees represented everything he hated in White men: They were exclusionary, powerful, smug racists who always won.

My father had once lived and died with the exploits of the old Negro Leagues, or "nigger ball" to him. His Black manhood had chafed when Jackie and Campy couldn't prove what he had believed his entire life: Black men were better athletes than White men. Joe Louis provided the first dose of Viagra for the impotent Black male's self-esteem. Everyone's psyche remained erect as the Brown Bomber annihilated the sons of European immigrants by the bushelful. But facts hurt, and at their best in 1953, Robinson, Campanella, Newk, and his other beloved Dodgers couldn't beat those fucking White boys. To a Black man who grew up before 1950, everything was about race, and the way the Yankees sneered at the desegregation of baseball while continuing to whip everyone's ass was a tough pill to swallow. Dad's theory was that when Branch Ricky had gone hunting for the man to integrate baseball, he had made a bad choice. To my father, social experiments weren't worth shit if you didn't win. His rap was powerful.

"I've seen at least sixty boys in nigger ball better than Robinson. Robinson wasn't no baseball player, he was a football player! If Ricky would have went just for talent, instead of all that social shit, he could have had about ten or eleven niggers that would have kicked the Yankees' ass. Who wouldn't want a veteran like Satchel in one of them big World Series games? Jackie's game was short, and he still made them Paddy boys look silly. Branch Ricky may have wanted to be Abraham Lincoln, but there ain't no place for that in baseball. He didn't have the guts to win, just tinker round the edges. White so-called heroes always half-step when it come to niggers, except Sinatra! A good guinea with a great heart is just a Colored man with oily skin."

It was wild watching him vent as he sparred with his self-hatred. When the Dodgers lost, he was merciless as he kicked the hell out of "charcoal Jackie and that fat spic, Campy, and Step 'n' Fetchit Newcombe, the heartless," which was a reference to Black pitcher Don Newcombe's lack of intestinal fortitude.

But on an October afternoon in 1960, as my father was lighting up Kool cigarettes one after another, the Pittsburgh Pirates came to bat in the bottom of the ninth inning in the seventh game of the World Series. The score was tied 9-9, and my father had all but resigned himself to the fact that the Yankees would win. He bemoaned that his "favorite spic in the world," Roberto Clemente, hadn't made the difference. I was dozing off as Bill Mazeroski stepped to the plate.

"Good, he's a Polack, so he might be dumb enough to handle the pressure."

That one confused me. I didn't really know what a Polack was. The faint crack of a bat meeting the ball set off an explosion that boggled the mind. As the player with the black hat rounded the bases, my father ran around the living room. Bill Mazeroski emancipated my father.

Robert Watlington was born in White Plains, New York, at the beginning of the century, mired in Jim Crow's tar. Family history suggests that his ancestors were part of the Underground Railroad, a group of slaves led by the great Harriet Tubman, who burrowed a path from the South to Canada and its moderately less hateful racial environment. There must have been some sexual activity with the Canadians, because the Watlingtons who came back across the border were light-skinned to the point of Caucasian in some cases. Robert had light brown skin, which made him the dark sheep in the family. His confusion was profound:

to be the darkest in a group of lightly tinged Negros was a hard pull for a young adolescent.

I'm not completely sure how it went down, but both my father's parents were dead by the time he was eleven years old. He was the youngest of three brothers, stuck in the relative wilderness that was White Plains, New York, at the time. Robert would later joke that "the plains didn't get much whiter than White Plains." One of the brothers, Taft, disappeared from the face of the family's historical record. My dad didn't say much about him, except that he believed that he was alive and that they would someday meet again. Robert's oldest brother, Leroy, was blind. After death's wicked sweep through the family and Taft's subsequent flight, the responsibility of caring for Leroy was placed on Robert's shoulders. Three days a week, he took his brother on the trolley to New York City. Robert and Leroy would travel to Upper Manhattan, which is now East Harlem, where Leroy attended The Lighthouse, a school for the blind. One could only imagine what it was like to pull into Grand Central Station in 1920 in turn-of-the-century transportation.

"Horseshit used to be a big problem," he'd often chortle. "And the waiting."

"What?" I asked.

"When you have a blind brother, you are forced to be patient."

Leroy became a successful radio engineer and lived a long and fulfilling life. But Robert's noble work exacted a cost. Holding down a job at twelve and attending to Leroy had shut down his education.

"Nobody finished school back in those days," he explained, "especially niggers, but if I could of, I'd be something more."

Despite his many responsibilities, Robert found the time to get hooked on sports. Like many others in the frigid Northeast, he skated on the frozen ponds. He became a good enough figure skater to compete in local tournaments. "They wouldn't let a nigger win something that White in those days, but I loved the challenge." His initial interest in golf was about money. "It was the best dollar, and all the caddies were Black in those days. Walking in the sun beat working in the sun." Subsequently, the golf bug seized him. Only golf fanatics can explain this particular malady, but his experiences on the course as a young man provided the best memories of his life. He bragged of his low scores as he watched those interminably long Arnold Palmer–Gary Player clashes. He could break down a golf swing with an MIT grad's facility.

When he was in his twenties, Robert and a friend opened a small gym for prizefighters in Manhattan. He was on his way, until a brick wall found him. "The Paddy boys moved in and wanted to turn us into janitors in our own place. Typical White boy, bully shit—we do all the work, they get all the money. We were ready to take them on, until the Depression washed it all away. Before you knew it, tough White guys were selling pencils on the street." Robert hustled between odd jobs and soft scams. Once he spoke of his hand in distributing a new syphilis-buster, penicillin. "Best profit I ever made on the streets." He taught himself to read and began to affect the persona of a hip Harlem elitist filled with dreams and ambitions.

He bounced and juggled well into his thirties, playing that sweet Harlem groove called jive. Frustrated and loving the scene in equal measures, he coasted until World War II. The war energized Robert. He saw this as his last chance to convince White America to change the way it felt about his skin, hoping against hope that his willingness to risk his life to protect her interests would better his individual lot. He was a good soldier and won an important citation of honor. The photo of him receiving this award from a commanding officer was the highlight of his visible life. I used to stare at that photo of the White man with the shiny bars and metals on his chest, shaking my father's hand. That picture cemented my respect for him and created a thousand bullshit scenarios in my fantasies about his courage.

After the war, it was the beginning of a national opportunityfest. Blacks and European immigrants fought for turf in a newly created middle ground dividing the rich from the impoverished. Education, housing, and jobs were plentiful. In Robert's heart he was first in line after all the bullshit he'd been through, but he was continuously passed over or turned away. He realized that the immigrants he had welcomed to his country had blown by his weathered, aging ambitions, trampling them in their understandable desire to escape the bitter taste of the Depression. For Robert, the Depression continued. A daily showering of crushed initiatives whacked his spirit. Finally, after a lengthy and disappointing search, his life's work found him. The tools of his business were sponges and rubber gloves, oddly similar to a surgeon's instruments, but sadly his tag would be that of a janitor. America's ship had come in, and old Robert was left holding a mop, seething internally when called "boy" by the children of immigrants.

"That army medal wasn't worth shit! I'd have done better if I'd died in action." As he wallowed in his stillborn condition amongst the many others in Jim Crow's womb, he happened to be having dinner one evening, when he laid eyes on a shy raw-boned, nineteen-year-old slave-bred South Carolinian Harriet Tubbinesque bolt of a woman called Leola. Somehow, the jaded northeastern hipster and the young tobacco-brewed religious zealot decided to make a go of it.

"They beat the Yankees," Robert screamed! "That fucking Polack buried his foot right in old Stengel's pin-striped ass!"

"What's a Polack," I asked?

He struck a near reverential pose and said, "They are great fucking people."

I was left to figure out if that was because they were dumb or because they were good baseball players.

FIVE

"Colored, Colored," **went** the alarm to friends in the building who didn't have television. It was a special alarm reserved for those up for a real novelty—someone Black on television. In today's TV you would have to program nudity during the family hour to generate the same excitement. The first shows that featured Blacks were the mammy shows, especially my beloved *Beulah*. Louise Beavers as Beulah was a work of art. Hattie McDaniel and the other blown-up Black beauties were my taste. I knew those women, and they were strong, hard-working, pride-filled, religion-packed contributors to the development of the American family. It was like having my mother on TV.

It was 1961. The typhoon rolling in from the South called civil rights was building momentum, and on the horizon many of the Black symbols of family, morality, and civility would be horse-and-buggied into oblivion. At the time, one of the most respected White men in America was TV host and columnist Ed Sullivan. He was an Irishman with a keen eye for talent and a lot of guts. When Louis Armstrong, Mahalia Jackson, and the master of performance electricity, young Sammy Davis, Jr., would appear on our tiny screen, a bizarre sense of inflated esteem would grip everyone in the room. Sullivan would call Louis over, sweating and grinning in appropriate inoffensive measures, and Ed would tell the country that this boy was all right, implying that America shouldn't think so poorly of us. We were just a harmless, talented lot.

Jammed in front of the small circular screen with faulty reception, we watched Mahalia Jackson sing a sublime Black American experience. As we rose and fell on every note, we placed our meager self-esteem in the hands of this rotund Black angel who was special enough to break the heavy chains of exclusion.

"That Ed Sullivan is all right," yelled one of the viewers.

"He gave a Colored a chance," opined another.

"There's some good White people out there," one woman declared.

"Them niggers probably had to dress in the bathroom!" sounded a voice of skeptical reasoning.

Everyone laughed, and we would slowly descend back into our insidious depression as Ed Sullivan introduced Robert Goulet.

Ed Sullivan gave me my first glimpse of the man who would lead my spirit beyond the walls of niggerdom: Sammy Davis, Jr. In my opinion, he was among the most fascinating Black men of the twentieth century and stood tall alongside other important civil rights leaders of my youth. Without education, Sammy had fought his way into White America's heart, banging his head against concrete racial barriers throughout the country. With a prodigious talent as his compass, Sammy leapt onto Las Vegas stages in the Jim Crow era and worked his ass off as a salesman for my freedom. He placed double effort into his every move on stage, assuring the public that he was willing to trade the very best of himself for a chance to be a whole American.

Sammy and Sinatra, another great civil rights activist, fought the battles for racial equality in the back alleys of America, where the cuts were deeper. They completed a long pass on the playing fields of racial discord when they integrated New York's Copacabana in the fifties. To me, my guys were making major contributions right up there with those of the courageous folks integrating lunch counters in the South. Sinatra was the first hip integrationist. He let Sammy hang out with him on the top of the show-business mountain. They were cool about it; they shared the same rhythms. A ghetto kid could relate to Frank and Sammy because they played on hot pavement.

By the early spring of 1963, the March on Washington was brewing. It was the culmination of a cultural push that had begun after the Second World War. The moral high groundism of Martin Luther King, Jr., was at its peak. His subsequent Nobel-worthy initiatives were unprecedented. The right to vote and integrated bathrooms were all the rage.

Around this time, I experienced a different kind of emancipation. My mother had cut the remaining strands of our umbilical chord, and the streets were mine to take. My age had reached double digits, which meant I had to navigate the neighborhood on my own. Her organic wisdom understood that the sooner you were forced to test yourself against the world, the better off you'd be. The pre-March hype swirled around me as I was learning the streets of Harlem. While my parents panted over our first sociological bump since Reconstruction, I smoked my first joint.

Alfred Mealy, the pied piper of East Harlem, was five years older than me, a lot of wisdom in Black time. At sixteen, he was in his ghetto prime—a superb, resourceful street hustler who dressed in silk suits and alligator shoes with no socks. He was light-skinned ("high yellow" was the term on the street), not quite White but well situated on the pigment chart. The best time in the life of a ghetto flash is between the ages of twelve and twenty, when youth, sex, drugs, and street adventure come together, climaxing in waves of raw pleasure. For many, the dream portion of their lives is over by their mid-twenties. In 1964, Alfred was in his prime, electric, everything I wanted to be.

"Women love this golden dick," he'd brag.

Alfred was the best storyteller I'd ever heard. His broad eloquence was right out of the DeWolf Hopper school of theatrical bombast. His brown-flavored tales would keep a young kid's attention on a summer night, until balloons filled with water would come raining down from the roof, signaling it was time to shut up. Alfred's stories of his many trysts with White women in Greenwich Village—his reward for plying them with marijuana—were akin to a wet dream. I asked Alfred if marijuana would get me some White pussy.

"No, you're too Black," he said sympathetically, as if I had an incurable disease. There was nervous laughter among my friends as everyone checked their pigment levels. I laughed off Alfred's joke and posed as the butt of my own humiliation. Alfred liked that and told me, "You got heart . . . for a spook."

Later that week I bumped into Alfred, and the aura of his cool drew me to him. He was headed for Jefferson Park.

"Where you going?" I asked.

"To get my head right."

"What?"

"To get my head right."

I didn't quite know what that meant. When we reached the back of the park, he pulled out a skinny, anemic-looking cigarette.

"What's that?"

"Reefer," he replied.

He lit the cigarette and took a much bigger drag from it than I'd ever seen anyone take. Then, amazingly, he wouldn't let the smoke out. As Alfred started to gag, he held on to the smoke as though he were riding a wild bronco. Finally, he let go. His eyes immediately glazed over, then moistened.

"Are you okay?" I asked.

"Yeah, man, this shit is a bitch. You want some?"

"No," I blurted out.

"Okay, ain't nobody ever going to beg you to smoke their shit."

"What's it like?"

"It's the best thing next to pussy," he exhorted through what seemed to be an additional layer of cool he'd suddenly acquired. "This is your chance to go somewhere you've never been before."

"Is it like a cigarette?" I chortled as I inched toward my fate.

"You ever smoked a cigarette?"

"A few times." Actually I had smoked regularly since I was nine.

"Well, you smoke reefer like a cigarette. You just don't let the smoke out, until your lungs can't hold it no more."

"Will it make me crazy?"

"Fuck you, man!"

He started to walk away. I gave chase.

"You what's wrong with niggers. All their adventure is caught up in their dicks." He then turned and, with the sweeping majesty of Othello, said, "Niggers have to find adventure in their minds."

He approached me with an odd seriousness I hadn't seen in him before. "You know the only way you are going to beat being a nigger?"

"How?"

"By breaking the chains on your mind." My street Rasputin gripped me. "Niggers are still slaves in their own mind. You want to stay a nigger?"

"No," I said tepidly.

"Then smoke this."

He handled the joint like an English king did a sword when someone was about to be knighted. I shook nervously as I held the joint in my hand. In a half-hour I would be in this new place called high.

I became a junior mate on Alfred's crystal ship. I earned money by hunting down bottles and cashing them in for pennies and nickels, helping to seed my new pot jones. As seen through the eyes of a stoned eleven-year-old, the ghetto was beautiful. The sounds and the pace made for a funky carnival. Even the gang fights and various other forms of terror seemed like great theater under the influence—environmental insanity at its finest. Alfred was right: The pot did break the chains. I felt special and now wanted to stand out.

The Jefferson Park Boys Club of America was a godsend to a poor kid who wanted something more. It was a way out, or, more importantly, a way in. Education had yet to become a viable option in most ghetto-children's minds, so the fact that the Boys Club offered major awards for hitting the books was unique. In the early sixties, the egghead line in the ghetto was a short one, so those of us who qualified were escorted onto a golden carpet. Despite the darkness of my complexion or the accuracy of my emerging jump shot, I had gained access to a remarkable opportunity. I was knocked for a loop after being accepted into the Boys Club scholarship program, and everyone treated me like an Alice who was about to step through the mirror into White wonderland. The only place I could find the real deal was in the back of the park with my guru.

"The fact that the world is run by White folks don't mean shit," Alfred preached. "The real players have a color of they own, so it's about can you play. I know yo' head sure big enough." He laughed, breaking my attentive trance. "Eighty percent of the world is illusionary bullshit. Find the twenty percent, and go for what you know. The rest ain't worth more than a bluff."

My best friend, Mikey Gay, and I were serious egghead wannabes, vying for attention and athletic superiority. I was the better athlete, while he edged me out narrowly with the books. When we discovered that we were both being considered for a scholarship ("What's a scholarship?") to White prep schools ("What's a prep school?"), our competitive juices boiled over. Successful Boys Club alumni were sending poor kids who showed promise to elite East Coast prep schools. If you were chosen for consideration, it set off a long process. For two summers you would go to a prep school for six to eight weeks and learn how to become a Black White kid. If you passed muster and kept your nose clean, you would attend one of the better high schools in the world.

The Boys Club had been helping the children of European immigrants hunt for mainstream opportunities for decades. Despite the problems the unscrubbed ethnic newcomers had encountered, their Whiteness had eased their path toward the big prize of that time period, assimilation. The first generation of Blacks and Latinos who competed for these scholarships ran into a host of additional obstacles. We had to contend with the Jackie Robinson syndrome: a slippery journey of being a first or an only. The spirit of the March on Washington had White folks in a giving mood, which often bordered on the ridiculous. We went from "Use the back door" to "Come in, take my house, take my money, take my daughter." Wow! Many of these gestures reeked with guilt, a sign of weakness. It was written in the mean streets' charter: Thou shall exploit any perceived weaknesses.

I talked to Alfred about these new developments. He complimented me for moving up in the world and said, "If shit ever gets tough, just say the name Martin Luther King as much as you can. Right now, that name is better than money with White folks. You can play in the White folks league because you one of the best reading niggers in the ghetto. Just remember that eighty percent of them is full of shit too. It's just that their stakes is higher and you got to be ready. Don't make a lot of sense you heading into the White world not knowing everything you can about White folks." He encouraged me to listen to White radio stations. "Stretch your shit," was his way of putting it.

I had left White music behind once I hit the streets, around the time Elvis was in the army. The Frankie Avalon–Fabian pap would have put my newly acquired ghetto card in jeopardy. But Alfred continued to prod, so I started listening to Murray "the K" Kaufman, Herb Oscar Anderson, and that bunch. I responded to the call of Lieber and Stoller at the trial end of Tin Pan Alley's influence. Overnight Dick Clark became the coolest White man in America. He was Ed Sullivan plus. He didn't just book the great soul singer Jackie Wilson; he seemed to like him. Watching Dick Clark plugged me in to the other America. What I saw was just lame and clumsy enough to douse any presumptions of White superiority.

My mother's crude method of strong-arming me into becoming an exceptional reader had made school a snap. White folks who cared judged us primitive souls on a very steep curve. Since my education numbers matched and in some cases surpassed those of my White peers, it made me almost a genius in the warped judgments of educational administrators in the ghetto. It was all coming together. A strange new confidence started to emerge.

One day, in the back of Jefferson Park, as Alfred and I were smoking a joint, he said, "White folks are the key."

"The key to what?" I asked.

"Everything. They have the guns, the money, and the confidence to dream. I'm not talking about these fake White folks that live around here. I talking about Eisenhower, Truman." He rattled off about twenty names I'd never heard before. "And then there's Ralph Bunche, the only nigger in the game."

"What about Martin Luther King?"

"That nigger's bluffing. You hear about this thing they talking up in Washington. Ain't no way that nigger gonna stand under J. Edgar Hoover's nose and fuck with him. Never happen!"

Alfred wasn't always right. That summer King would change the nation forever with his dream speech. As my family watched the news, my parents seemed confused, not knowing what to believe or whom to trust. Did this mean it was going to be easier to be a Negro? Or were we being set up for another debilitating disappointment? Was White America really listening to a Negro who wasn't singing or shucking and jiving? During the March, while King spoke his ballad for a new America, we all fidgeted as my father studied the TV screen. He started to puff on his Kool cigarettes. "I've been around a long time, and there ain't never been anything like this." He became excited. "And with TV, the whole world is going to know that niggers been getting the shit end of the stick." We cheered Sammy, Belafonte, Brando, but the biggest cheer in that intoxicating moment of Black hope was reserved for Charlton Heston. Once Moses made the scene, we knew that this was something different.

Nineteen sixty-three was a good year for my father. His freedom stock had risen, and the Dodgers swept the Yankees. The Yankees would not win another championship until the year before his death in 1978, by which point he had become a devout Reggie Jackson fan. After the final game of the 1977 series, he crowed, "I hope that after Reggie's three big ones, he finds a way to piss on George Weiss's grave" (referring to the Yankees' general manager in the fifties).

One fall day a phenomenon occurred that would shake the ground around us. As the afternoon school session was about to begin, my teacher, Miss Selego, a fair but severe disciplinarian, came into the classroom crying. She removed her glasses and looked shockingly vulnerable. The toughest White woman ever wept openly. My best friend, Gary Hamilton, began to laugh hysterically, and I joined his laughter. A voice came over the loudspeaker: "It has just been confirmed that President John Kennedy was shot and killed today in Dallas, Texas. We will have further instruction on how you should proceed."

Miss Selego had gathered herself and said, "A terrible thing has happened." She broke up again, and Gary and I both let out bigger laughs. Miss Selego lost it and started to scream at us. "What the hell are you laughing at? He's going to be replaced by that damn Texan, and you can kiss your civil rights goodbye."

The voice from the sky came back, alerting the classroom that school was closed and we should go home and say a prayer for the Kennedy family. As we filed out, I went to Miss Selego and apologized for laughing.

"You don't understand, Dennis. The last thing this country needs now is a president from the South," she uttered as if she were in mourning.

Boy, was she wrong! The Kennedys were one of the greatest collection of public servants in the twentieth century, and I admire them greatly, but JFK getting popped turned out to be the best thing to happen to Colored folks since Lincoln. Jack Kennedy would never have gotten the deals for Black people that LBJ did. A rough-hewn, experienced politician with a strong whiskey gut and knowledge of where all the bodies were buried was just what the doctor had ordered. LBJ hammered home the completion of our legislative freedom package.

When the Civil Rights Act of 1964 was signed, I witnessed through my pot-induced haze the sheer exhilaration of Black folks dancing to the intoxicating tune of emancipation, the sequel. At the time, few were sophisticated enough to understand what the legislation meant. The fact that the bill had the word "rights" in its title provided a Coltrane-like rush. "Who would have ever thought that a cracker would lead the way," my mother shouted to her God. President Johnson's speech on the bill forced my parents to grudgingly trust the overseer. By the end of the speech, Johnson had transformed himself into a family uncle who was passing for White. His nose and other features were scrutinized for Negroid affectations.

"Only a president with some Colored in him would sign a bill that helped niggers," said a friend.

Adam Clayton Powell, Harlem's heroic congressman, was feted as LBJ's capable sidekick. These architects of the new Reconstruction were sizzling. They had fattened the hog; ham was in and pigs' feet were out. With Martin Luther King spending his moral capital judiciously, the golden age of Nigras was upon us.

SIX

In 1964, around the time that the Boys Club selected me as one of the golden ones, I met George House, or Mr. George, as he was called. He was my first important adult mentor. Mr. George and his wife, Berta, lived in our building and were friends with my parents. He was a thirty-eight-year-old native Floridian who seized the opportunity to expose me to the ways of the proud "new Negro" that was emerging from the foam of the growing wave of civil rights. Mr. George was a bit past his prime to benefit from the new opportunities for Negroes, so when he discovered that I had been chosen for a scholarship, it fired up his vicarious circuits. He was in constant regret over his thin academic résumé, having been denied the opportunity for a top-flight education in the apartheid Florida of his youth, and drew a positive hard-on from his self-appointed mentoring stance, which I welcomed.

Mr. George encouraged me to be aggressive when dealing with important White folks. He figured that I could get away with more by being a novelty. "Legal larceny" was the term he would use when discussing "the ways of White folks."

"White man has mastered the art of stealing legally. The guinea boys and the Paddy boys are starting to learn how that game is played. Now, with you, it's our turn."

Mr. George's influence was particularly strong during a period when he took me with him on weekends to wash White folks' cars. It was on Long Island, the Whitest place I'd been since the feed store in Georgetown, South Carolina. Mr. George had connected with people out there and made a deal to wash and wax the cars belonging to a slew of pretentious, pipe-smoking, nouveau-White beneficiaries of postwar largesse.

In his pitch he purred, "Me and the young man will take you back to the showroom." As we buffed and shined the chrome, Mr. George drilled his wisdom into my skull. "The only way to compete with the White man is on school property. Niggers been shot trying to get good schoolin'. You have the chance of a lifetime, boy."

As dusk turned to nighttime we would ride the Long Island Railroad. Mr. George called it the White train, because very few Black people who weren't domestics ever rode on it. Most of the domestics were off on the weekends, and Mr. George and I were the only Blacks in a car filled with White folks who were returning to the city after a weekend of Long Island fun. My arms hung uselessly from scrubbing countless hubcaps and fenders.

"The only thing the White man has over a Black man is privileges, and they ain't White privileges, they'se American privileges," preached Mr. George as he continued his relentless drumbeat.

"Mr. George, why didn't you go after White privileges?" I asked.

"They wouldn't let me. When I got my diploma, it wasn't worth shit, so I couldn't move forward even a little bit." As he pondered his misfortune, the ugliest mask I would ever see him wear emerged. "I didn't know how to believe. When I was your age, things were hell in Florida. There wasn't no Colored dream. Reverend King done brought the twilight zone to niggers. Your scholarship is proof of that. A nigger had to be better than Beethoven to get an opportunity like yours."

By the time we reached Penn Station, Mr. George had me feeling as though I was Columbus getting ready to explore this new territory called Privilegedville. At that time, I would always seek out Alfred's street sauce to balance Mr. George's straight-arrow rap.

"White folks ain't nothing special. Except when shit goes down, they got the guns. But you don't have to fuck with that. You going into the arena of words and figures. A nigger can make words dance, and you got a gift for twirling them motherfuckers. That's why they want you. I ain't learning you all my shit for nothin'. Man, use it."

As Alfred toked, I realized that he always sounded better to me than anyone else. Was it the truth or was it the weed?

"You the new nigger," spouted the wise seventeen-year-old ghetto head that Alfred pumped from.

"You can stand with the White boys and hold your head up," rang Mr. George's words.

"It's your job to find out if all this civil rights stuff is bullshit or not," Alfred chided.

"Remember, boy, your people are behind you," instructed Mr. George. "If you wasn't ten times as good as them, they wouldn't have picked you."

Whoa . . . why me? I couldn't smoke enough reefer to get clear about that one. In fact, I stopped smoking reefer and began to blame it for my predicament. Why the fuck did I want to carry the banner for my people? That was insane to me. I needed all of my senses reporting back to me accurately in these confusing times, so the pot had to go.

At the end of the school year, I was sitting in the principal's office with my mother. The principal informed my mother that I'd been chosen for a program called Open Enrollment, a New York City Board of Education plan to allow poor kids to go to better White schools in the outer boroughs. The principal told us that I would be attending Riverdale Junior High School in the Bronx.

"Is the school all White," my mamma asked?

"It's predominantly Jewish," he answered.

"Good," my mother said, "I know them."

I was at the perfect age, at the perfect time, for a Black kid in northeastern America. If you could read above grade level, well-fixed White folks were trampling over each other to sponsor you. A reasonably well educated Black child made White folks, who were mainlining civil rights, orgasmic.

"What's a Peddie?" I asked when my mother told me that she had received a letter from the Boys Club Scholarship Program. They were assigning me to the Peddie School in Heightstown, New Jersey, for the summer. The reality of the letter unnerved my mother, who hated the loss of control that came with being in over one's head.

She became angry. "Shut up," she said for no reason.

"What did I do?"

"That shut up was for whatever you were going to say."

"Okay."

My mother's real problem was that she had to come up with a long list of clothing, towels, and other accessories we couldn't afford. She was such a proud lady that our poverty was off limits to her ego. When confronted with a tight situation like this, she would lash out and create pain elsewhere. Our options were to borrow or steal, and for my mother the latter was unacceptable. Mr. George pitched in and gave me a jacket and socks.

My father remained distant, cloaking his inadequacies with silence. He wasn't sure what to make of my opportunity. He didn't trust the White world. "If they turned Joe Louis into a monkey, no nigger is safe," he opined.

My mother did everything she could to meet these challenges. Fortunately, her new extended church family offered their help, particularly Reverend John Collins, a White Methodist minister. We weren't Methodists, but it was the only church in the neighborhood that wasn't Catholic, and Reverend Collins put forth a vigorous effort to reach out to the Protestant minority.

I grew to like Reverend Collins immensely after testing his patience repeatedly, searching for White weaknesses. His fortitude was comforting given some of the experiences we'd had with White males. White men who came up in the ghetto without an official reason were usually up to no good. The majority of them were freaks who were lusting for young Black and Puerto Rican boys. Once, while coming down the back stairwell in my project building, I heard a male begging and screaming. I ran to the action, where I discovered a pathetic White man who was pleading for his life.

"Get the fuck out of here!" shouted the brother of a good friend of mine. "He slurped my thang, and now he doesn't want to pay," he spewed angrily. "Get the fuck out of here," he shouted as I ran back up the stairs.

Five minutes later, when the commotion had subsided, I went back down and saw the poor bastard lying in his own blood. He was moaning. I ran and told my mother, and she called the cops. When they arrived, the White man told them he was the victim of a robbery attempt. The cops bought his story, even though the man never explained how he had wound up in the hallway.

Reverend Collins passed inspection. He was a bonafide Christian hero with good intentions. In the winter, before I was to begin attending the Peddie School, there was a public school teachers strike. Reverend Collins set up a makeshift school in the church. Initially, I wanted no part of it, but my mother forced me to go. I lucked out. Reverend Collins's school would be my first exposure to African American history. The revelation that Ralph Bunche didn't have a monopoly on this "credit to one's race" business was an invaluable discovery. I plunged into a pool of obscure Black heroes, like the artist Henry Owassa Tanner and thespian Ira Aldridge, as well as the great George Washington Carver, who invented peanut butter. I was left to ponder a thought for the rest of my life: If Carver did so much for the peanut, why did Skippy make all the money?

On the early summer day I was to leave for the Peddie School, my mother was in a panic. After all of the effort she had put in to get me ready for school, she'd forgotten to secure a way to get me there. We went to the church and discovered Reverend Collins was out of town saving someone else. My mother and I were in a dark mood as we sat on the church steps, and I watched her struggle with her ego, unable to admit that she was stumped. I was very careful not to make eye contact with her. Suddenly, the church's junior minister, Reverend Fernandez, approached us. Like a good man of the cloth, he was drawn to the bent posture of the thwarted. He made a sensitive inquiry, which released just enough humility in my mother to allow her to share our problem.

He put us immediately at ease and offered to drive us to the school. Reverend Fernandez drove an old model Oldsmobile from the fifties. Initially he couldn't get the car started. We held our breath until the car revved up. Once we were on our way, I asked a question about New Jersey because I couldn't remember ever being there.

"Shut up! The man was good enough to take us, he don't want to be bothered by you."

That put an end to my questions for the rest of the trip. When we arrived at the campus, it was like a scene out of *Lost Horizon*, Shangri-la within shouting distance. We were mesmerized by the ivy-covered walls and manicured lawns. Thoughts of movies I'd seen rushed through my mind. I tried to come up with a character or situation that compared with this mind-blowing vision we were gaping at. I was dumbfounded, with no images to hold on to. My mother too was overwhelmed by the idea that I was going to reside in this rich White training ground for seven weeks. It was the first time I'd ever seen her completely flabbergasted. She was speechless. Reverend Fernandez put his arm around her and offered words dipped in soothe.

"This is something different, huh, Mrs. Watlington?"

"It's all right," she replied.

Tough to the end, she fought a stream of liquid that was forcing its way down her cheek.

That summer there were ninety-one students at the Peddie School—ninety well off to enormously wealthy White kids, and me! These kids had privileges infinitum, and I was one of those underprivileged civil rights babies they'd sort of heard about. Many of the students had never seen a Black kid up close. The ages ranged from eleven to eighteen. I was the youngest kid in the school.

Who planned this thing? I found myself wondering after my mother and Reverend Fernandez hotfooted it out of the joint. The Reverend had to get back to the church, and my mother, who had overcome her emotions and returned to granite, dumped me like a stork does a bundle on the doorstep. Later I unpacked my ghetto dreck in the presence of my new roommate. Brent seemed to have everything: He was White, rich, and handsome, with a tan as deep as a Colored man's. He had a new typewriter and a to-die-for record player. It took forever for his parents to unpack his clothing, and I felt smaller and smaller with each wealth-soaked item that materialized. It dialed up the humiliation of my southern experience. Brent's parents walked over to my bed, where I was hoping that I had turned invisible. His father bent down and placed his hands on his knees. Our faces met twelve inches apart as he said, "How are you, young fella?"

"Fine," I said as my reflection bounced off of his blue pupils.

Brent's mother looked at me with the affection of a first-time Fresh Air Fund patron. "I brought you something," she said as she pulled out a fancy can of White folks' cookies. The brand name was unrecognizable to me. She gave me six cookies, which was odd but welcome, until I tasted one.

What is this!? I thought as I swallowed hard and smiled. "Thank you very much."

The cafeteria was a welcome shock. I'd never seen so much food in one place—and all the milk you could drink. In my family every morsel of food was carefully doled out, except the beans! If you went into the refrigerator without permission, you placed your well-being in serious jeopardy. I had never had more than one small cup of milk at a given meal in my life. One of the reasons for our hunger was my parents' great pride. They were incapable of taking something without having overworked for it. This duo preferred deprivation to welfare. They trusted nothing but hard work for an honest dollar, even if it meant having too little to eat. My father got paid once every two weeks. Our pattern was one okay week and one hungry week. In the bad week the harsh interrogations over stolen food from the refrigerator were constant.

My first meal at Peddie was an unrecognizable dish loaded with beef. These people were obviously trying to make me look bad by allowing me to feed myself to death. It was orgasmic. As I stockpiled my plate, I snuck a glance at the teacher in charge, thinking he might stop me, but no problem. Then, just as I was about to dive into my bounty, the teacher said, "Young man, you are not using your utensils properly."

I stopped in mid motion, my fork inches from my mouth. *What!* my mind screamed as the other students focused on me. After a pause, I blurted out, "Come on, man!"

The teacher's look was one with which I would grow very familiar—the constipated WASP expression of disapproval. "We comport ourselves a bit more congenially at this school."

What the fuck, I again thought, *is congenially?*

The teacher proceeded to give me my first lesson on how to use a knife and fork, White-folks style, and totally screwed up my rhythm, hammering my style with his rule book.

"Look, I'm hungry. Can't we learn how to eat after we eat?"

The table cracked up with laughter. The teacher glowered, and the students tried to suppress their amusement.

"We'll work on this later," he said with an ominous Dracularian tone.

I attacked the food with my knife and fork, matching the ferocity of the blades on the skates of the great Messier. My performance at the table brought me a lot of unwanted publicity. Geeky White cats went wild recounting my confrontation with the head of the table.

The southern kids were the oddest. Although they repeatedly called me "nigger," they were much more comfortable with Black folks. Their ideas about me may have been a bit antebellum, but unlike the others, they didn't treat me like a space alien.

I talked an office secretary into letting me make long-distance calls once a week. I called Alfred for some comfort and support, but he was stoned almost beyond recognition.

"What's the matter, man," he responded with slow, lethargic pauses, his breathing curiously audible. "I'm with some new shit that's going down." He became energized, offering a flash of vintage Alfred. "What the fuck I told you, man, about the eighty percent and the twenty percent. You taking my shit up in the halls of White folks and fucking it up."

I then checked in with Mr. George. "White folks have rules for everything, even though they'se relatively rule-breaking folks. Learn every White rule there is and then watch and learn how they break them."

"Find the Jews," my mother said. My mother knew that in many wealthy Jewish kids' lives there was a Beulah figure tucked away. This might enable them to relate to me.

The summary of my advisors was to bluff my ass off, learn the rules, and find some Jews. For the next several days, I studied the upperclassman for Semitic signs that might indicate they were safe to approach. I needed all the help I could get as I tried to adjust to a life that was run by bells and whistles. Luckily for me, my powerful slave genes emerged. I began to gain a reputation as an athletic talent among my peers, and soon I was playing with and against the upper grades. I could compete and even excel against varsity guys. Jocks were often the most likely to screw up during the school year, so the summer school was loaded with them.

Tom Triola, at fullback, and Bob Monahan, at halfback, were prime stud seniors on the football team. They were my first up-close White male crushes. The knowledge of my superior speed had made its way around the campus, and Triola invited me to play on his team on the main campus lawn in the after-dinner touch football game. It was Triola's team against Monahan's team.

I discovered the very first time I ever went up against rich White guys that they were significantly inferior on the ball field. Regardless of age, I was stronger and quicker than most White athletes who competed against me that summer. The ethnic White boys that I grew up with were hard core compared to their rich counterparts. In our neighborhood, these preppies would have been soft, slappable putty. They had been sheltered from the brass knuckles of reality and were easy to break down. I ran wild on upperclassmen and embarrassed them on a level playing field. The older guys on campus gave me a nickname: Spitfire. The Spitfire was a popular car among rich teenagers in the mid-sixties. This name led me to the discovery of a lifelong passion: Brian Wilson's music.

A big part of my life was inspired, influenced, and saddened by Wilson's genius. I boarded Wilson's Beach Boy train during the "Little Deuce Coupe," and "409" period. The fact that my nickname was one of those sleek vehicles that Wilson wrote about enabled me to identify with this goofy-looking group of White boys with candy-striped shirts. Wilson helped me deal with my fears about being a poor Black kid in this bafflingly different environment. "In My Room" was a song I could never have listened to at home without being branded "faggot," but it became my theme song.

Except for Sinatra and Elvis, White popular singers floated dead in ghetto waters. There was a full frontal assault on the early Beatles in the ghetto. Black folks were upset because a good deal of the Beatles early songs were covers of Black classics, done well. In 1964, because of the hair thing, I heard more brothers talk about "fucking" the Beatles than listening to their music. But I was a long way from the primal beat of my homeland. The music of my borrowed world was a fascinating mixture of the British invasion and the Beach Boys.

One of the Southern bigots was a James Brown fan, and he dug having me around to authenticate his musical choice. In those days it was easier to find a rib joint in Utah than a rich White boy who dug James Brown. My bigoted friends and I bonded over Brown's "Papa's Got a Brand New Bag." I taught them how to dance and untangled their humorous misrepresentation of hip Black language.

I was starting to do pretty well in school. In the first few weeks, it was more schoolwork than I could imagine. An A+ ghetto student was about a C− in a joint like Peddie. These classes were no-nonsense affairs. If you acted up, they would administrate you to death with all the penalties and demerits, but you got the message and you didn't screw around. In the school I had gone to in the South, they eliminated the bureaucracy and just whipped your ass. The results were the same: no disruptions and serious attention paid to education. I'd learned enough about my classmates to know what major fuckups they could be, but in class the teacher was lord and master. How could they turn it on and off like that? I posed the question to the great Alfred Mealy.

"White folks know the difference between digging and fucking."

"Oh?"

"Keep bluffing," he chided. "You can master that White game, but they can't ever be niggers. It's your driver's seat if you want it."

I thought about what Alfred said. I could tell from my James Brown sessions that White boys just didn't have that special indefinable Black "thing." I could outrun, outtalk, outdance any of them, and I was catching up in class. I didn't have any of the cool material things they had—no radio, record player, watch, tennis racket, or parents to drive up and visit each weekend. In fact, I didn't have one visitor the whole summer. Yet, I not only was surviving, I was cooler. Could being Black and cool be better than being rich and White?

"Did you get to know any of those Jewish boys?" my mother asked. This was her mantra.

"Ma, it's hard to pick out rich Jews from regular rich White folks."

"That's stupid," she said. "Next time you get in a good crowd, find the way to say the words *mazel tov*."

"What?"

"*Mazel tov*."

"What's that?"

"It's good. It means celebration, warm feelings." Her fondness for the Jewish family she had worked for was profound. "I don't care how gussied up they might get with their money and other things, but they respect pain."

The next day in math class, one of my classmates did something extraordinary on the blackboard, and the instructor led a cheer. I shouted out, "Mazel tov!" Out of the nine or so students, four looked at me curiously, while the others thought I was probably expressing some unidentifiable junglism. Suddenly, the ethnic division sharpened. "It means good feeling." Again, half thought I was crazy and the other half smiled.

I spent the next couple of weeks observing ethnic differences. I sized things up by color or shading. The WASPs and the Irish were White. Italians ranged from White to Sicilian Brown. Jews also had a consistent layer of pigment that really came out in the sun. The sun was an important defining element when parsing Caucasians. Italians and Jews generally cooked well, while the Irish and the WASPs tended to peel. Subdividing White folks into groups was an important tool for my survival. Divided, they seemed less imposing.

I concluded that an eleven-year-old from the ghetto was the equivalent of a fifteen-year-old rich kid. Some of the kids closer to my age cried over some of the silliest things. If my roommate Brent's parents didn't call, he would cry. When I first met him, I felt small and intimidated by his Ricky Nelson exterior.

He had it all, or so I thought. I was to discover that he was a babe in the woods. This was the first time he had ever been away from home. He had this great modern record player, the kind that you would fantasize about with your face pressed against the glass of a store window, but he listened to such lame shit. He had a lot of Disney stuff, and he was into something called Spin and Marty. Mouseketeers and the whole bit were driving me crazy. He wasn't Ricky Nelson; he was the Beaver. He only vaguely knew who Dick Clark was, much less anyone on the Black music scene.

I borrowed a Beach Boys album from one of my southern bigots and planned my attack. One day, as Cubby and Annette warbled on as Mouseketeers, it was enough to make my ass hurt.

"You'll never get no pussy with that music." His eyes widened as though I had said a dirty word, which I guess I had.

"Don't say that, you have a filthy mouth!"

"Pussy, pussy, pussy . . . and that shit will never get you any. You a man!" I shouted.

"I'm not a man, I'm a kid," he uttered.

"Well, you rooming with a man, so that kid stuff is out."

"I want to meet a good girl someday," he spoke with his chin resting on his chest.

"My Uncle Womp, from a place called Lenox Avenue, told me man don't want a good girl, he want a bad girl who does good things."

With Brent in a weakened state, I put on the Beach Boys Concert album, and with the rich beginning guitar rift of "Fun, Fun, Fun," his eyes popped open as though he had snorted a hit of cocaine. I could see that I had broken his cherry, and from that moment on we were cool cellmates.

During one of the after-dinner football games, I was kicking some ass on the field, when I heard this voice. "Hey, Spitfire!" Many would yell my name because it was cool, but this voice cut the air differently. After we scored and there was a break, I ran over toward the voice. "Hey, Spitfire," he again shouted.

"Hey man." I afforded him my standard opening. He smiled and revealed one of the friendliest faces I'd ever seen.

"My name is Jim Sarnoff."

"Hi, I'm really Dennis beneath all the Spitfire jive."

Jim was a junior, about five or so years older than I. He attended Peddie during the regular school year, so he must have been a lousy student. Despite the age difference, Jim and I became friends. We sat together on a bus during a school trip to see Sinatra in *Von Ryan's Express*. On the highway we passed the RCA compound in New Jersey. Someone yelled out, "Hey, Sarnoff, there's your grandfather's place." That sent my eyebrows soaring. I was to learn later that Jim's grandfather was General Sarnoff, one of the pioneers of twentieth-century communication as head honcho of RCA and NBC.

I'd stumbled upon a winning ticket in my Semitic lottery. In the summer of 1964, Jimmy was a great substitute for a big brother. Whenever I would stub my toe on my ignorance about the ways of White folks, Jimmy would break it down for me in ways I could understand, without a hint of condescension. He was a valuable agent who protected my sanity. We would remain close for decades.

I was cruising. Everyone loved old Spitfire. It was too good to be true. A frightened ghetto kid was able to compete. At a time when Black folks were being attacked by dogs and hoses, I had my White folks in check. As the term wound down, I was comfortable and my grades were climbing.

I competed with the master's kids at their own game and closed out the summer in good shape. I could not have done it without the advice of some of the best Black street minds on tap. With Alfred's, Mr. George's, and my mother's counsel, I was able to handle the heat. I was the chocolate bar that wouldn't melt.

On the last day, while saying my goodbyes, my favorite Southern bigot, matted down with emotion, said: "You're the only nigger I've ever really cared about." It was touching; he'd come a long way in eight weeks from his original assessment of me as "just another nigger." The use of the word *nigger* didn't bother me because the sentiment was heartfelt. He gave me his Beach Boys Concert album, and after we shook hands for the final time, he awkwardly sought to hug me. This was so traumatic for him that I let him off the hook by slapping five.

"Have a good life, you crazy little . . ."—he caught himself, not wanting to use one *nigger* too many, then resumed—"son of a bitch."

When I arrived back home, I was heralded by many in the neighborhood for my successful first step on the road to education, riches, and White folks. It was intoxicating. Everyone thought I was some sort of genius, which was bullshit, but my experience was so foreign to the average ghetto dweller that I became the poster boy for newly freed Negros looking for tangible signs of change. I was living proof that King's early returns were positive.

What a year it had been! I started out a frightened eleven-year-old and emerged by year's end as a bonafide neighborhood celebrity. Mr. George said, "I'm proud of you. You're on your way." My enthusiasm was tempered by the fact that they didn't know anything about White folks or their world. Having learned just how little the races knew about each other, it seemed certain that the integration bus was destined to blow out a lot of tires.

By November, on my twelfth birthday, I begged my mother to pay off on a deal we had made: If I did well at Peddie she would buy me two Sinatra albums. She didn't usually go as high as seven dollars on a birthday gift. "Anything to get those 'Bleached Boys' out of my house," she sighed. I was driving her to the edge of madness with "Fun, Fun, Fun."

On my birthday, after the house had settled down and my mom and dad were asleep, I put on my father's trench coat and fedora. The hat barely fit on my head because my noggin was already a size bigger than my dad's. I played my favorite Sinatra song, "In the Wee Small Hours of the Morning." I was scared shitless, and Sinatra's music understood pain and confusion. I knew that my life would only become more difficult. There was no joy on this birthday, just the relief of having made it over the first hurdle on the road to this thing called White success. The further I sank into my purported ascendancy, the more distressing it felt. As another Sinatra classic, "I Get Along Without You Very Well," played, I stared out the window with my dad's trench coat slung over my shoulder, Sinatra-style. I wanted to go back to the simplicity of being anonymous, but I was one of the chosen. There was no alternative but to bluff it out.

SEVEN

During my first year at Riverdale Junior High School in the Bronx, I discovered that the well-intentioned effort to integrate Colored children from the ghetto with their middle- and upper-middle-class White peers was doomed. The streets of the sixties were producing the most drug-influenced, emboldened Black people in our history. When an entire busload of Black kids from the Black West Side of Manhattan came into Riverdale, the school went into shock, realizing immediately that they had made a big mistake. We were the first generation of young Black people who weren't particularly interested in being credits to our race. When we arrived, the White folks were expecting a cachet of Sidney Poitiers and Arthur Ashes. Instead, street-savvy disciples of the renowned Harlem drug kingpin Nicky Barnes greeted them. Throw in a significant slice of this new religion thing called the Nation of Islam, and the good White people of Riverdale were in for a lesson in society's changing tide.

Although this was a public school, it looked more like a private institution. It was a large three-storied complex with several athletic fields, a basketball court, and several handball courts, all perfectly kept. The teachers carried themselves with a higher professorial bent than anything most ghetto-dwellers had ever seen before. For me, it was reminiscent of my experience at Peddie, another high-powered, focused institution for privileged White people. Some of the kids dressed in jackets and ties, others were less formal, but they were all bright-eyed, bushy-tailed upper-middle-class offspring of the first immigrant class to hit the jackpot.

At the first school party, there was a battle over whose music would dominate the proceedings. The Beatles were in a class by themselves, but so was James Brown. The English invasion, led by the Dave Clark Five, crashed into a brick wall called Rufus Thomas, the Stax Records artist. If not for the brilliance of Berry Gordy's Motown crossover, there might have been a riot. Everyone settled down over both Smokey Robinson and the Miracles and the Four Tops. The Black students watched the tangle-footed White teenagers stumble through the new dance steps that were second nature to them. We pronounced the Whites inferior in the only area that really mattered in junior high school—teenage cool. We didn't understand that clumsiness, an unpardonable sin in the ghetto, was an acceptable part of being White.

Among the racial turmoil that evening, I received an invitation to sing with a rock 'n' roll band. A couple of my White classmates, a guitarist and a bass player, had heard me sing when we were hanging out in the boys room. The bass player invited me to his house to listen to music. I played the Alfred role and turned them on to pot for the first time. They buzzed up quick, and we bonded over music. We listened to The Blues Project, led by Dylan's keyboardist, Al Kooper. One of the best things to happen to America occurred when talented, visionary White boys got their hands on the blues. They nourished the baby well, extending its life by decades. As we continued to play, and the smell of the marijuana grew sweeter, the groove was a fit.

I made the mistake of telling my best friend, David Pryer, about the band I was in and my secret love for rock 'n' roll. David was a Five Percenter, part of an offshoot of Elijah Mohammad's Nation of Islam, which was beginning to receive national attention thanks to Malcolm X's breathtaking, acidic eloquence. David ragged on me unmercifully about my refusal to join his sect. The Muslims were for separatism, Black individual pride. They were profoundly religious and moved in lockstep. The seriousness of their struggle left little room for flexibility. They were the Black race's new conservative wing, and despite periods of murky leadership, the Nation of Islam had compiled an excellent record of turning indigent, self-destructive Black nomads into model citizens.

David had a thousand and one well-crafted, sensible reasons for hating White people, but I didn't want to hate anyone. One of us was for separatism and the other for rock 'n' roll. My budding philosophy about life was solidifying and at its core was the belief that separatism ain't American. Our fights got ugly at times. I was a traitor, an Uncle Tom, and so on and so forth. The Black colony got word of my apparent flirtation with the enemy and began to shun me. This was a delicate situation. The music I was interested in was on the White side, but the girls were on the Black side. Ultimately, the fishnet stockings won out, and I began to shy away from the band, before quitting altogether, a painful decision and a mistake.

I was born to throw a football, able to do it instantly and all at once. One fall day, I was tossing a football with my brother Robert and demonstrating how I had been taught to throw a tight spiral. While hurling the ball to my brother, we were approached by a burly tank of a man with an easy, confident smile. He moved with a nimble grace, despite his weight, which inflated his air of intimidation.

"Hey, Watly, who's that boy throwing the ball?"

My brother was known as Big Watly. He knew this man whose voice boomed even during normal conversation. The man quickly informed me that he was a basketball coach who had put together some legendary sandlot teams. He'd coached some of the better ballplayers in the ghetto at that time. I decided to give him a show.

I aired it out about forty yards, from one project building to another. I had grown several inches over the summer, and my slave genes were beginning to cut my body into definitive muscle.

"Hey, you," yelled the impressive figure.

"Who, me?" bluffing disinterest.

"Yeah, you, ya big-head motherfucker!"

No one had mentioned my oversized head all summer.

"Come here," he commanded.

I went to him, and my brother made a formal introduction.

"Dennis, this is Chuck Griffin," he said.

"How ya doin', son. I like the way you throw that ball." He began to massage my apprehension, sticking out his hand. "You do have a big head, but that's all right."

I was impressed but not amused. It was the first of many fire-and-ice applications Chuck would lay on my ass.

"I'm thinking of starting a football team," he boasted.

He talked about a new football league that had been started by someone at a poverty program called Haryou-Act. These poverty programs provided services to a starved community. Chuck was one of the ambitious Black men who had seized the moment.

Chuck Griffin had been born in Mississippi in the early twenties, which was no time to be a Black man. He came from a "fine" family, which meant that his father was a minister who was placed in the awkward position of leading his congregation through White man's hell. The Black ministers in Jim Crow America had the most difficulty soothing the bruised spirits of the darkest darkies because many of their lives had been stillborn, but Chuck Griffin was one person who couldn't stand the niggering down of his people.

When he was a teenager, he was working as a nigger on a construction project. An exposed live wire became the focus of everyone's attention. A foreman told Chuck to pick the wire up. At first Chuck thought that the man was joking and sought to laugh it off. When the foreman insisted that he handle the dangerous wire, Chuck refused. That was a major offense, a Black man refusing the madness. Chuck had said: "Enough!" This young boy, barely in his teens, was ready to die. The foreman was forced to back down. The other Blacks were directing their eyes and attentions elsewhere, fearing that the White man might think that they stood behind Chuck's mini-insurrection. One of the Black Toms chastised Chuck for his outrageous behavior, which made the foreman feel better.

That night, just as the Griffin family was about to turn in, they received the requisite visit from the responsible White male contingent. These upstanding pillars of the community, who happened to wear white hoods, wanted to discuss the matter. The leader calmly stated that the group was doing the Griffin family a favor by consulting with the elder Griffin before they would be forced to hang his son. They told Reverend Griffin that they had a lot of respect for him and understood what a good boy he was. They thought they owed him a warning: Put that young buck in check or lose him for eternity. Chuck's father was ready for them. He had already made plans for Chuck to stay with family members in Chicago. This pleased the group, and they complimented the Reverend on his profound understanding of how things worked in Mississippi. They considered the matter closed as long as they didn't have to see that little troublemaker anymore.

Chuck's father swallowed and offered a plethora of nigger "yes, sirs" and "thank-yous." Inwardly, he burned, as he had to beg for the life of his son as well as the safety of his family. He was well aware of how many Black families had been awakened by a ring of fire surrounding them. Chuck's father had given in to survival. Chuck was livid. He had been a warrior from birth, blessed with a Robesonian streak of individuality. That night his respect for his father was dampened and remained so for many years to come. He felt betrayed, not understanding that his father had chosen the only avenue that would preserve his life.

The entire family subsequently joined Chuck in Chicago, and they prospered. There were six children. One sister became an opera singer, a brother was a minister and accomplished jazz pianist, and another was a gifted artist whose specialty was beautiful wall-sized murals. They were all high school graduates with some college experience, except Chuck, who was the black sheep of the flock.

Chuck didn't have a special artistic designation, but he was imbued with charisma; he was a gifted speaker, and the women loved him. He joined the navy during the end of the Second World War at the age of seventeen. The navy toughened him, and his fortitude increased. He made clear to all involved on the ship that he wasn't accepting any cracker shit. "If you come after me, you better not miss, because I'm the kind of Negro who will do anything to fight nigger treatment. If you think I'm just talking, try me." He made it clear that he didn't join the navy to fight for White folks and be treated like shit. Chuck's presence and seriousness made its point, and the White boys didn't fuck with him. He once said about this incident, "I never felt more free than when I was ready to die."

After he left the navy, he came to New York, somewhat estranged from his family. He married into a great family from the Bronx and started to settle down. But fate had much bigger plans for this proud new Negro. When he sent me off running to gather my friends for this football idea, he was planting the seeds for the most colorful anti-poverty community center ever.

After my age hit double digits, not only did my mother force me to deal with the streets, but on one foggy morning she woke me up to say, "Get a job!"

"What?" I mumbled as I scratched for my equilibrium.

"Ain't no grown-ass nigger gon' to live on me!" she phrased definitively.

The moment we were old enough to lie about our age on the application for working papers, we were hurled into the workforce. I got a job as a delivery boy for the Drug Loft, a pharmacy on Second Avenue, and earned fifty-four dollars a week, plus tips. I was fucking loaded. On a good week I made more than my dad did. My mother was a straight egg about my bonanza. Her steadfast rule was that you kept what you made, but if you mismanaged your money, your ass was left bare to show. I had it all: positive notoriety, unheard of opportunities and fat pockets.

My job was also an education in sociology. I delivered prescription drugs in the wealthiest neighborhoods in Manhattan: I was courier to the elite. My route was from Ninety-sixth to Fifty-ninth Streets, between First and Fifth Avenues. I had a big, thick truck bike with a basket attached to its handlebars. Rich people's desperation for drugs was the same as that of the ghetto-dweller, except White folks legalized their habits. My boss told me that more than half of the drugs I delivered were for the head and not the body. They were getting high for many of the same reasons Cooty the Wino from around the block got high.

Overnight my landscape changed. Between my attendance at Riverdale Junior High School and working in midtown Manhattan, my existence went from almost total Black to two-thirds White. It was the damndest thing. One of the best things about my job was my coworker Skito. Skito was in his early twenties and from my neighborhood in East Harlem. I didn't know him before the gig, but his Puerto Rican culture in those days was always mine for the taking.

Skito immediately took me under his wing, despite being twice my age. He gave me respect when he discovered what a hard worker I was and how much of his work I was willing to do. My background also intrigued him. Blanco Tongue was the nickname he gave me. He had never met a Black kid from the neighborhood who spoke White so well. Skito's influence set off a series of events that would help me grow up in a hurry. The first was sex. Skito was married with two kids and was a woman magnet. I called him the Trash Magnet because the girls who came around were nothing to write home about. But he had a lot of them. I told him about my two sexual experiences on the back stairwell.

He laughed. "That ain't fucking, that's just rubbing." He vowed that he would make me a real player. "You old enough for your dick to get hard, right?"

"Uh, yeah, all the time," I responded meekly.

Then he delivered his state-of-the-penis address. "The only part of you that makes you a man is your dick. Nothing else matters. Women say they want a house, car, maybe children; don't believe it. If they want you, really want you, it's because of your dick." He paused to measure the impact his words were having. I was a wide-eyed pupil, so he poured it on. "Only your dick can bring out those sounds in a woman, and that's what they want."

I was confused. I couldn't imagine my mother making "those" sounds, but I wanted to impress my newest mentor so I nodded persuasively. One night during the Christmas holiday season, we had so many deliveries that we worked overtime. Skito and I rolled dice to see who would buy dinner. I won, so we went to a coffee shop on Seventy-eighth Street and Lexington. I had never been in a coffee shop before. My family had never risen above the street hot-dog vendor level, so this was heady stuff for me. It was beyond my imagination to assume I could enter a "class" White establishment like a coffee shop. Skito pulled my coat.

"They want money; we got money, that's it." He was buying, so I followed him in. He ordered three cheeseburgers.

"What's that?" I asked. He was surprised that I didn't know what a cheeseburger was. He took me over to the grill, and I witnessed one of the most beautiful exhibitions of culinary artistry imaginable. Three beef patties were sizzling.

"You like cheese?"

"Yeah!" My eyes were fixated on the meat when the cook put thick orange slices of American cheese on the burger. When they melted, covering the entire thing, I saw God.

Skito shook me back to reality. "Snap out of it. It's hamburger, not pussy." I couldn't wait to get back to the store and eat my fantasy. While racing up the avenue, Skito yelled, "Slow down, you got to be cool. I got a surprise for you." What could be better than my orange burger? "I got a girl coming, and I want to fuck her in the basement."

"So what," I said.

"You ever see two people fuck?"

"No."

"Well, you gonna."

Shortly, I would find myself perched behind several large boxes of Kleenex and mouthwash positioned in front of a crack, which gave me full view of Skito and a trashy, peroxide blond with horrible zits and a body that flooded your joint with blood. The juice from the burger ran down my chin as Skito pulled out all the stops, fucking the willing body every which way. The Puerto Rican was making it with the White girl, for the Black kid enjoying his first cheeseburger—pure American poetry.

Skito, the Body, and I smoked a joint as we walked east on 77th Street. The Body pleasantly promised to have sex with me the next time we met, which would never happen. But that thought enriched my masturbation file tremendously.

Skito put his arm around me and said, "Cocolo, you got it made."

"I would be nervous with a woman like that," I confided.

"Someday, that kind of pussy will be below you. You got good schools and you could still hang in the block. Nobody's got double shit like that, and you're only twelve. If ever there's going to be a Cocolo for president, it is you."

He laughed with paternal delight at his revelation. Maybe I did have it all or at least a hundred times more than most Black kids in the history of Black kids. Riding the bus uptown on First Avenue as the gaudy excitement of Christmas lights and decorations flashed around me, things certainly seemed like they were going my way.

EIGHT

An antiseptic mist shrouded the hospital corridor. I was in a wheelchair being hurried down the hall by a nervous orderly. The next thing I knew I was in a
room with a needle in my arm. A nurse extracted what seemed like every drop of
blood out of my body. Several doctors began to confer over my limp presence.
They discussed what to do for my twin terribles: heroin withdrawal and an advanced case of hepatitis. My liver was burning. They couldn't treat both, so they
chose the hepatitis. The withdrawal would be my problem. Once I was secured
in my isolated room, I experienced the most horrible night of my life. I have yet
to ever endure anything more frightening or more difficult than that first night of
cold turkey, hepatitis-style.

The pain and the chills were so violent that I spaced out and saw angel wings
swirling around me with blinding speed attacking my mid-section. I wanted
to die because death had to be easier. I tried to smoke a cigarette,
but it tasted like stale urine on the back stairs of a project
building. I prayed that if the wings ever left, I would
never stick another spike in my arm. I begged God,
whoever that was, to believe my sincerity. I begged
the sky to forgive my hundreds of robberies, or
"stings," of innocent people—anything for a
chance to see the morning in less pain. Finally, a nurse came in and gave me a pill. I
began to throw up, until there was nothing

but painful substance-less heaves. Mercifully, I passed out and was reborn the following morning.

It was the spring of 1969, and Martin Luther King's body had been cold for nearly a year. Nixon's new law-and-order initiatives clashed with Black skulls. The anti-war crowd followed the civil rights movement through the doors of civil disobedience. Black powerless radicals gasped as their oxygen frayed. Bobby Kennedy might have been able to clean up the mess, but he soon followed King's induction into the Dead Martyrs Hall of Fame.

These were the problems that whipped through the world as I lay in a Harlem Hospital bed. I'd been using heroin for three years. Imagine a powder that comes at you in mere granules, yet is powerful and seductive enough to make you piss on your grandmother's bible if that is what it takes to make it with the White lady. I'd rather have fought in a war than have been a heroin addict. A junkie's life is focused. No responsibilities, obligations, or accountability, except for swallowing the thought of dying any time you go into your arm.

As the pain subsided and my strength returned, I was forced to deal with a new term I'd not heard before—sobriety. With sobriety comes clarity and reflection. Sober reflections hurt, and I held on to that hospital bed for dear life. It was the safest place I'd been in a long time.

"Man . . . you should be shot in your face with a shit pistol," was the bowie knife Mr. George threw at me that tore through my heart. This was his reaction to the news that I'd been booted out of my prep school future. In the summer of 1965 I went away to the Darrow School/Williams College ABC program. A Better Chance (ABC) was another of the many well-intended, poorly conceived programs that hurled Black bodies aimlessly at the deep-rooted, complex problem of exclusion. The Darrow School summer session was the last mile in my migration toward the corridors of upper-class learning, a plantation for eggheads. If I did well at Darrow, I would begin the following fall at the George School in Bucks County, Pennsylvania.

I was disappointed with Darrow from the outset. After having worn the distinction of being the only Black student at the Peddie School, I was now one of a number of Colored wannabes. Where was the sport in that? Many of my classmates were from the South, and their mission was to dodge that noose. They were a veritable gaggle of baby John Lewises, with comparable, explosive internal wiring. These guys were smart as hell and labored over every educational detail.

I felt that if I was going to put in the effort to be at this special level, I wanted the distinction of outdoing White folks on their turf. Competing with a bunch of Black people for the attention of a few Whites was not my scene. The thrill was in being the main nigger, not just another nigger. Despite a poor effort, I was devastated when they gave me the boot. My excommunication from the church of learning was humiliating, leaving me angry and looking for trouble.

My mother went off; our second trip down this road. She had hardly gotten over the time I was thrown out of baby prep school. Here again I had blown another of those rare gems in Black life—the solid White opportunity. It was as if a bomb had gone off. Everyone turned their backs on me in disgust, except my father who never bought in to what he termed "White hocus pocus." My mother's disappointment played out in her attempts to make life miserable for me.

When I went back to Riverdale for my ninth year the embarrassment was overwhelming. Teachers were offended because they had given me a great deal of special attention in my preparation. I'd been dropped from such a high that I bounced three times. The first bounce was out of prep school, the second was the rapid dissipation of my prestige in the neighborhood, and, as a result of one and two, the third bounce was the beginning of the Black urban male's most devastatingly debilitating experience—heroin! I went down like a torched village.

A mass of humanity dressed in surgical gown and mask stood over my bed. It was Chuck Griffin. I hadn't seen or heard from him since he had dropped me off at the hospital three days earlier. Chuck removed his mask. I tried to joke with him about the possibility of catching something, but his frown didn't give an inch.

"I thought you was going to die the night I brought you in here. After we left the hospital I was already thinking of how we were going to use your dead ass as a symbol."

I again attempted a stab at humor. "Does that mean it was a bad thing I didn't die?" Again his locked features blew me off. "Why didn't you come see me?" I asked.

Angrily, he replied, " 'Cause I didn't want to!"

Chuck was desperate over his exhausting losing battle with kids like myself. He was trying to resurrect our community center, the East Harlem Federation Youth Association. A few tiny years earlier, when the center had been thriving on the good sense and goodwill of those with money who cared, he had proclaimed, and we had believed that we were "Number one on the planet Earth!" The center Chuck had established had twenty-five different progressive, creative options for young, street-tough kids to take part in. He brought falconry, chess, archery, a gospel choir, and a special brand of smash-mouth ghetto football to within the fingertips of potential felons. When the first wave of compassion-fatigue hit the ghetto shores, Chuck was forced to go around begging for small contributions to keep the lights on. Moneyed White folks had inexplicably cut his funding off at the knees.

His indefatigable pursuit of our dream had been endless, despite the fact that several of his main kids were spending all of their potential on smack right before his eyes. One day he gathered us all together and asked us to go to City Hall to see a small group of people and show them what heroin was doing to our lives. Everyone agreed to do it but then disappeared. Chuck and I were a bit tighter then the rest: I was his quarterback and point man, the kid who could melt liberal hearts utilizing pretty White words. He came and found me on the streets and hauled me downtown, where I bared my junkie soul in front of some old, overfed White people. But all I could think of was robbing them so that I could go to the cooker.

The last straw for Chuck happened at a football game on the day I was brought to the hospital. A couple of players and I shot up in the locker room just before kickoff. I had played on heroin before, but this was a different feeling. We received the ball first, and when I ran out to the field, I felt like I was moving in slow motion. I whispered to one of the other players who had shared my needle, "Hit me real hard in the head with your helmet because I'm too fucked up to call the play."

We rammed helmets, which I thought would shake me capable, but it only made things worse. The first play was a simple handoff, which I managed to execute. The second play, Chuck called for a pass from the sideline. I ignored his order; the last thing I wanted to do was to drop back to pass and get clobbered. I called another running play. It was stuffed for no gain. Chuck was jumping up and down like a madman. He again signaled for a pass. I had to pull the trigger. I dropped back to throw the ball and went into a dream. I had no idea where my receivers were, and the next thing I knew I was back in the locker room with a doctor and the team assistant.

Chuck came in at half time and asked the doctor about my well-being. The doctor replied, "Get this boy to a hospital immediately."

Chuck and I were both shocked.

"Did he break something?" Chuck asked.

"I wish it were that simple," the doctor said. "It's my guess that he either has yellow jaundice, or worse, hepatitis."

"Is that something serious?" Chuck questioned. "How do you get that?"

The doctor paused and asked, "Should we talk about this in private, Chuck?"

Chuck looked me over and replied, "Hell no, let that nigger know."

The doctor spoke, "If we don't get this boy to the hospital immediately, he could die."

Despite noticeable recovery over the previous few days, I was too weak to withstand Chuck's continued verbal pounding from which my hospital bed offered little protection.

"I couldn't stop thinking of how disappointed I was in you, you little big-headed junkie motherfucker," he screamed. "I couldn't figure out how I failed niggers as smart as you in a time when White folks' checkbooks is flying open. What the fuck was I supposed to sell folks, when my main nigger took himself out shooting that shit?" He became enraged, like he was going to hit me.

"I'm sick!" I yelled.

"Nigger, I want to kick you and your fucked-up liver out that window. I ain't knitting a motherfucking baby booty for you over this shit! I've instructed anyone who know you, except your mama, that they better not come anywhere near this motherfucking hospital. 'Cause I'm gonna play hard cards with yo' Black ass. I want your over-intelligent dumb ass to fry in your heroin oil for a while. Then we see what we got. It ain't easy to escape the gravitational pull of the ghetto."

Chuck left me in a puddle of shock.

It was almost three years to the day since I had watched Earl Taylor as he stood over a bottle cap filled with white powder. He had carefully injected a half-filled eyedropper of water into the bottle cap. Earl then removed several matches from a matchbook, struck them, and began to cook the substance. He had made a little device out of a bobby pin, which enabled him to hold the bottle cap over the flame, until the bottom of the cap became red-hot as the liquid sizzled. This recently tarnished golden boy gazed with fascination at Earl's deft handling of the most popular process to hit the ghetto since welfare applications. I was dying to try it but was afraid of needles. Earl drew the fluid into the eyedropper, which now sported a sleek hypodermic needle on its tip. He injected the fluid into the pit of his left arm, and, without the slightest hint of discomfort, he calmly rode the fluid. That was the coolest thing I had ever seen. In minutes he was into a world he controlled. As he began to nod off into a dreamlike comfort, his voice changed, it slowed down and became melodic in a blues-laced way. He began talking wonderful, sweet street shit.

"Little Watly, what you lookin' at? You act like you want some. You want some?" he offered.

"I don't want to die," I uttered inquisitively, testing the waters of temptation.

"You don't want to die?" He began to sink into a nod with his voice trailing off like a withering radio signal.

"What!" I shouted.

Earl shook out of his nod, not missing a beat in his thought process. "You don't want to die. Why?"

I didn't have an answer as he passed me a small cellophane envelope, which I almost dropped. That got his attention. Suddenly he became as alert as a cadet. He took the cellophane package from me, reached in his pocket for a nail file, opened the cellophane package, and scooped a portion of the powder on the file's tip. "Bring your head over here," he said.

I moved forward gingerly. Earl grabbed me by the back of the head and literally brought my nostril to the file.

"Sniff! You might get sick, so be ready to run to the bathroom to throw up."

He scooped another portion and placed it below the last virgin nostril I would ever have. I immediately became sick, ran to the bathroom, and tried to throw up but couldn't. Instead I developed a small nosebleed. I was starting to feel the effects of something odd and wonderful. I didn't know how to handle the feeling. When I emerged from the bathroom, Earl and several other seasoned dope fiends awaited my return. They inspected me for signs of pain or discomfort. When they discovered that I was getting off with only a mild nosebleed, they broke into comforting smiles and kudos. I felt as though I had been christened.

"I ain't never seen a nigger pop his drug cherry so easy," one of my teachers beamed.

I got the feeling I might be suited for this. Earl gave me a few more snorts and then cut me off.

"One thing you got to learn about this game is that you gets your own shit."

He turned stainless steel. It was my first lesson about the frigid temperatures of a junkie's heart. I became invisible. All the other junkies ignored me, concentrating on the depth of their high. I asked once more for another snort and was met with a collective, resounding "No!" I felt as though I had been raped, but I loved the feeling.

Heroin and welfare came in at about the same time—twin symbols of the Black urban meltdown in the last third of the twentieth century. I could respect the fact that the mob was into heroin for the profit. But what were the pols in Washington thinking when they passed a new slavery initiative? Welfare was a cheap, poorly constructed buyout of a confused people. Fresh from the stultifying humiliation of exclusion, too many Black folks opted for a deadly exchange, trading assimilation for cheese and oily peanut butter with the Department of Agriculture stamped on it. A proud race whose personal trademark was hard work went into the tank.

We'd always worked twice as hard for half as much, when suddenly we wanted to work half as hard for twice as much. The desired forty acres and a mule had descended into forty bags of dope and a Cadillac. At this time a new role model emerged in the ghetto—the dynamic drug dealer, a figure so powerful that it trumped the old-fashioned numbers runner's Cadillac with the Rolls Royce.

Dope dealers were a spectacle wherever they went. They were the neighborhood stars, and every sighting had the glamour of a funky film premier. I remember praying that my very attractive sister Gloria would catch the eye of a big pusher who would then cut me in. When the drug money arrived, many of the neighborhood's top athletes took advantage of their celebrity by seizing the moment. Basketball was an excellent way to market heroin to young people. The street basketball legends emerged as glitter salespersons flaking for the Italians. Just as Michael Jordan's relationship with Nike saturated the world with rubber footwear, the best of the neighborhood players helped to ignite the early sixties heroin boom.

My hero was the great Pee Wee Kirkland. I was once in attendance when Pee Wee showed up at the annual Wagner Easter Basketball Tournament. The tournament was one of the crown jewels of sports in East Harlem. Pee Wee arrived in a Rolls Royce, dressed from head to toe in white silk with a tasteful white beaver fedora tilted perfectly on his head. When Pee Wee ran on the court to warm up, the packed joint went wild. He completed magical layup after magical layup to the tune of "Jimmy Mack" by Martha and the Vandellas. He danced at the foul line in between his practice free throws. The screams got louder. Only Smokey Robinson at the Apollo scored higher on the shriek meter.

It also helped that he was one of the greatest athletes in the world at that time, who routinely scored 40 points or more against the best basketball talent in the country. Adding insult to devastation, his floor game piled up assists faster than his minions could sell off his deuce bags. Pee Wee led his team to a championship that day. He picked up his MVP trophy and boogied out the gym to the endless beat of Martha and the girls. It was impossible for a human to be any cooler.

He had made it to the top with an independence that was breathtaking. What a role model! To hell with education—that was for fools and White folks. Pee Wee had laid down the gauntlet, coloring our vision with his flamboyant agenda. I had no way of knowing that my hero was a puppet, a snake-oil salesman for the noveau White underbelly. Pee Wee would become one of a horde of battered ghetto stars who once shined brightly but subsequently spent the second half of their lives feeding penitentiaries and graveyards. Many were left to contemplate their roles as unwitting laborers who, along with our national legislative branch, constructed the new slave ships. These ships glazed in white powder would carry millions of Black men and women on our most ignoble journey.

The nurse awakened me with the news that she had to stick another object up my ass. I asked her if she could give me a little time to get myself together and offered her a cigarette. She accepted and took a break. As she puffed on a Kool cigarette, I became frustrated, asking myself, "What have I done? Why didn't I die? Junkies die, few hang around to suffer." The nurse ordered me into one of those embarrassing positions and did the deed. In my discomfort, I realized that a good way to screw yourself was to go after that high. Painful memories invaded my consciousness as the nurse hovered.

At the beginning of my heroin usage, it had been all nickles and dimes. One day I ran into my good friend Donald Ford. We'd known each other since kindergarten and, because of the project's proximity factor, were practically brothers.

"The only way you can be a junkie is to be a junkie," Donald said.

"I ain't no junkie," I protested.

"Anybody who uses this shit is a junkie or a junkie-to-be. You have to decide how bad you want the high. Like me, I'm the whole thing. Hang with me for a while. I'll show you how to do this thing."

Several hours later Donald and I were walking on 110th Street and Madison, when he suddenly stopped and struck a pose, much like a hunter's dog might do, and said, "A 'book!"

"A what?"

"A pocketbook."

He was focused on a middle-aged Black woman who was about to turn onto 110th going west toward Fifth Avenue. Donald accelerated, each stride pregnant with athleticism. He was always amongst the fastest in the neighborhood.

"Come on!" he yelled.

I followed, and within a flash we were both upon the poor woman. My discomfort was compounded by the fact that she wore glasses. We bull-rushed her. Donald snatched the 'book, and I clumsily ran into the woman, knocking her down. The insult had chafed the injury. We ran like the wind, with my heart pumping like crazy. I had crossed a line.

When we were in the clear we opened the pocketbook, and it was a bonanza—ninety-five dollars. We quickly went through her wallet and other possessions, discovering nothing more valuable than welfare and hospital cards and a handful of mints. We threw that stuff away and immediately headed for the West Side to cop some dope.

The most popular purchases on the streets were two-dollar envelopes or deuce bags. We bought twenty bags, which was by far the most I had ever been in possession of at one time. We found a suitable building and went up on the roof. I went for my file to begin snorting. I placed the file beside me as I began to open up one of the bags. Donald grabbed the file and threw it off the roof.

"What the fuck you doing?" I screamed.

"You ain't wasting good dope on that shit. If we tap the vein we'll get three times as high."

I'd been wrestling with the big question: to shoot or not to shoot for several weeks. "I'll try it," was my response.

Donald, seeming to relish the opportunity to indoctrinate me, cooked up some dope. I wanted to skin-pop, which involved making a surface puncture— the usual step people took between snorting and mainlining. But Donald took the shoestring out of his sneaker and began to tie my arm up. He hit a vein, and it hurt like hell. After striking blood he continued to draw my blood into the syringe only to shoot it back again. I was puzzled but soon discovered that this was called *booting*, a procedure that brings on the high faster. As I studied the precision of Donald's medical maneuver, I went into a state of shock, only to wake up several hours later from the feeling of raw ice encased around my genitals.

After my awakening, Donald and two strangers told me that I had overdosed and almost died. Only their smart, panic-free maneuvers had enabled them to awaken me by burning my crotch with ice. It was a ceremonious atmosphere, honoring my complete baptism into the bowels of the heroin culture.

While gaining my junkie legs, my best friend, Ben Janks, thought I was too soft. "If they weak enough to rob, it's their problem," Janks argued. The hardest part of being a junkie was having to stick up a lot of people, and the rule of thumb was to attack the weakest mark. An old nigger named Thumbtack taught me that the key to "taking someone off" was patience. "You got to keep your dick soft. If you jump at the first piece of pussy that come down the road, you'll soon be huntin' penicillin. A woman might shine but so do plastic." This requires some translation. The woman is the asexual victim, the clap is getting busted, and the penicillin is the lawyer.

Thumbtack was brilliant. He was twenty years my senior, but heroin addicts are ageless because they're all funneled toward the cooker. We were all the same age, but Thumbtack was first among equals. At the age of fourteen, I was at the bottom of the smack democracy. I was useful because at my age I had the flexibility and maneuverability to hang on a rope from a roof as many as two stories down. I would tape a portion of one of the windows with masking tape so I could muffle the sound when breaking it, then open the window from the inside, crawl in, and let Thumbtack and the others into the apartment. They would go through the apartment with breathtaking speed, cleaning out anything of value. Organization and cunning leadership were Tack's forte, so the execution was always first-rate.

We did about four of those heists and never came close to getting busted. There was a racial angle that aided our success. An unstated but well understood axiom amongst Black street criminals was that you only robbed your own people, which included Puerto Ricans. There were plenty of White people in our neighborhood, and yet we rarely opted to put the hit on them. We knew that the law treated you a lot differently if you went after White people. "They don't care much mo' about niggers than they do dogs, so yo' bust is much lighter," Thumbtack would say. His ruthless business mind was that of a calculating African mercenary who sold his people to the slave merchants in an eye blink. "If they dumb and helpless enough to add up to one good shot of heroin, then they servin' me well." Thumbtack was a junkie, and few understood bottom line wants and desires like a dope fiend.

I talked to him about my prep school washout with White folks, and he counseled, "White folks hate niggers, and as long as you understand that, then they be's fine with you. Just don't challenge their hatred." He would always laugh after saying that. I wasn't sure that I agreed with Thumbtack, but then again, he seemed to always be right.

Janks was a great friend who held the distinction of being the first one in class to expose himself to the girls in the sixth grade, opening a can of unconsummated sexual games for us all. He was from a broken family and lived with his father. Single-parent families were unusual in those times, and many of us envied the freedom Gary's father allowed him. His father was a good provider, so Gary was television-and-stereo rich, which was how I defined wealth in those days. In 1963, as Janks taught me to ride his new bicycle, he was living a ghetto kid's fantasy.

By early 1967, Janks and I had both fallen off a cliff. It had been years since we had seen each other before our paths crossed on a West Side smack hunt. We were both shocked and pleased that we'd reunited, even if it was over the cooker. We started to hang out and pull robberies together, and we always managed to answer the bell whenever our habits screamed. The hundreds of junkies were picking off the neighborhood innocents so fast that we were fighting each other over them. Janks started to get restless and wanted to make a bold move, break new ground. He wanted to go downtown and take off White people, a frightening thought.

"We should go American," Janks said. "White people steal every day, why shouldn't we take them off?"

We argued for weeks over this. It was not morality that fed my reluctance. It was the fact that I knew White folks weren't to be fucked with. The first responsibility of the police on the island of Manhattan was to protect White people. The reason for Janks's and my success in the ghetto was that the police response time was slower in Harlem, giving us criminals confidence that we could complete the task. I tried to explain this to Janks, and his response was odd. He was not anti-White, but his twisted brain somehow felt that he was discriminating against White people by excluding them. His convoluted understanding of the merits of diversity was pushing us to the edge of a cliff.

One cold, desperate night when our habits were howling, Janks broke the rule of patience and took on a guy with no apparent handicaps. My friend only barely managed to come out of that episode with his life. It turned out that Janks's mark was also on the prowl, and a nasty fistfight left his jaw swollen and his anger aglow. "We going after White folks!" he screamed. I gave in. I set some ground rules: there would be no weapons. Neither of us had a gun, but we used knives and pipes all of the time. They were essentially props that I had never had to use. My second ground rule was no burglaries. In White apartments the cops were much more likely to shoot, often to kill.

This left us one option, what we called a yoke. This was a fairly straightforward two-man technique: One person grabs the victim from behind, placing one's power arm around the neck and bringing the sting to the ground. If done right you don't hurt the victim; the suddenness of the action is intended to stun. Your partner then grabs the pocketbook, and you both burn hell running, putting precious distance between you and the disoriented victim. The yoke was used primarily for pocketbooks, so women were the targets. It was less a gender thing than the fact that it was their unfortunate custom to carry pocketbooks.

Janks and I were walking down Fifth Avenue, just above 110th Street. As the numbers descended I began developing an unusual case of jelly legs. Normally, once I was committed to a sting, I blocked out all fear. But this was different.

"Best way to die is to hurt Whitey. They will junk the few reasons that they have to let you live and disappear your Black ass." That was Alfred's take on the idea of robbing Whitey. At this point Alfred was strung out to the gills, but his discipline remained intact when the question was obvious suicide. "In order to rob someone you have to be able to blend away after the sting. How the fuck a nigger as Black and greasy as you gonna blend?"

It was a very good question as we passed Ninety-sixth Street and Fifth Avenue. The quick change was miraculous. We went from urban barbed wire to the elegance and grace of the most celebrated avenue in the world. Junkies in the doorways turned into doormen, whose hands massaged the door handles of limousines. "Are you sure you want to fuck with this?" I asked. Janks's response was not quite as bold as it had been twenty blocks earlier. "Jail ain't that bad, and death means it's over. So it's not really a big thing, huh?"

We walked on the Central Park side of the street, in the shadows, moving lightly and watching. We came upon a young blond nurse who no doubt worked at Flower and Fifth Avenue Hospitals—a beautiful angel of mercy. Janks and I both spotted her and gave each other a look that said that if she turned east on Ninetieth Street we would strike. The reason we chose Fifth Avenue was because after the sting you could scale the wall of Central Park and lose yourself in its vastness. Janks and I were dressed in dark clothing that meshed with our dark faces—two heroin-desperate, enflamed panthers. I watched the nurse, with three-fourths of me hoping she would turn into the quiet, less well lit block, one-fourth of me hoping she wouldn't turn at all. I was close to pissing in my pants. She turned.

Janks and I locked eyes, which was a signal to cross the avenue. The lights on the avenue were so bright that the opulence blared. We entered Ninetieth Street and quickly closed the distance. I signaled that it was time to strike. With a burst of acceleration, I collared the woman from behind in a stun move, careful to cover her mouth, hoping to mute her instinctual urge to scream. The moment I had her going backward, it exposed the arm that carried the pocketbook. Janks yanked it with a snapping motion, paralyzing her grip. It was a flawless maneuver.

Now the breathless part began. We knew we had three screams to work with. If we weren't over the park wall in three screams, the fourth scream could cost us our lives. We both had better-than-average speed, a professional prerequisite. Our victim was too disoriented to scream at all, but a couple of innocent bystanders began a chorus of "Stop, stop, police, police!" We hit the wall like marines. Janks tossed the pocketbook over the wall, and we scaled it within feet of each other. On the other side of the wall there was a row of shrubs that separated the wall from the park. Janks scooped up the 'book and dashed through the interference. I was right behind keeping a keen eye on him, careful not to separate or I'd never get an accurate accounting of the proceeds. As Janks emerged beyond the shrubs, I heard a muffled thud, much like the sound of someone hitting a beach ball with a baseball bat.

As fate would have it, a cop on horseback was on patrol and happened to be passing by in that fraction of a moment, when Janks emerged from the shrubs and ran blindly smack-dab into the horse's ass. He was knocked out cold and lay spread-eagled on the ground as the cop tried to calm his horse. I continued running into the park, where I stayed, laying low, until it became safe to sneak out. I went on the lam for two weeks in Brooklyn, sweating out the possibility that

Janks would rat. I expected as much. Ratting was almost a matter of course among us tough guys, but he didn't. That image of Janks on the ground being foamed over by the startled horse was the last one I would ever have of him.

As I crept around Central Park, burrowing through nightfall, I could think of only this episode's stinging moral that I would observe it to the letter for the rest of my criminal life: Don't fuck with White people!

NINE

My mother came in flaunting her nursing experience, acting as though she put on her surgical mask differently than anyone else. I hadn't seen her since I had arrived at the hospital. If I was looking for sympathetic warmth, she slipped me a harsh reality pill, whacked me on the back, and made me swallow without water. Leola was furious. She slammed the chicken she had brought me down on the table so hard that the pieces flew off the plate and into the air, somehow landing in their original positions. Leola railed on, jabbing my sore spot about the good White opportunities I had screwed up. She scoffed at the notion that my underprivileged background had anything to do with my current occupancy in the shit house.

"I write you off into God's hands," she said, "and if you die it's your own fault, because the Lord rolled up his sleeves and did some special work on you. If you choose to go out in those streets and slop around in all that White man's sin, all I can say is, if you was shivering in the gutter and I was carrying a blanket, I'd walk on by."

I respected my mother because her principles never wavered. Her tough love was a pain in the ass, but it was always solid. She would never give an inch, so it was up to me to give in if there was to be any movement. Her brick wall approach, along with Chuck's sledgehammer, were my only visitors, so I gave up on self-pity fast.

As I munched on her world-class fried

chicken, she gathered her things together and warned, "Young niggers die every day, every day, every day . . ." Her voice petered out as she left the room. My mother was right. Over the previous three years I had had at least a dozen death misses.

Two years earlier I had been locked up in a small police unit in the Johnson Housing Projects. This was where they brought perpetrators and interrogated them before determining if they required further processing. There was a delicious bit of irony attached to my arrest. I had been a flawless criminal for two years and was only getting better at it when I was apprehended, booked, and charged with assault and robbery with a deadly weapon. The kicker was that I hadn't done it. I'd gotten away with so many terrible things for so long that it was hard for me to get angry when the law of averages caught up to me. Besides, I was intrigued by the opportunity to earn my lockdown stripes.

I was given my one phone call, and I called my mother. She startled everyone but me when she said, "Put the nigger under the jail!" After a series of puzzled looks, a White cop took me off into a little room, my hands cuffed behind my back. He sat me in a chair and started to come on to me in a very friendly way.

"Save us all a lot of trouble by admitting you did it. It would be easier on everyone."

I said defiantly and, oddly enough, truthfully, "No, I didn't do it."

He became upset and said, "If you weren't a bad apple, why doesn't your own mother want you?" I didn't have an answer. He asked again if I had committed the crime.

Again I stated with abject conviction, "No, I didn't do it!"

The cop's face changed, turning into a red mask of anger. "That's what I hate about you little Black motherfuckers," he said. "You're a bunch of lying pieces of shit."

He then slapped me so hard that I went flying from the chair. Because I was cuffed I had no way of breaking my fall. I fell hard on my shoulder, my good cheek smacking the floor. The cop came after me, grabbed me, and gave me another shot in the face, which numbed my jaw. I felt certain that this was it; my life was to conclude in one of those street-hot scenarios that produce legends in my circle. Killed in the line of action by the police. Junkies repeatedly offered up a toast for any of us who met such a noble fate.

Lying prostrate on the floor awaiting the final blow, I looked upward, where there was a hulking Black male figure. He was so massive that he blocked out the hallway lights, darkening the room. From my floor-level view, I caught a glimpse of his badge. *Whack!* Another shot to the face.

A booming voice shook the room as it roared, "Leave that boy alone. Ain't supposed to be beating that boy that way. Leave that boy alone. You gonna kill that boy in here. What you crazy?"

The cop came to his senses. I'd been saved. I glanced at the doorway at my savior, a cop who was Black enough to see that I was a kid and not an animal.

Given my mother's response, I immediately became a fifteen-year-old ward of the state. That ass-whipping marked the beginning of a close association with the juvenile criminal justice system. I was considered guilty until proven innocent, and they shuttled me off to Spofford Youth House, a pubescent Rickers Island. I was to be held at the facility until further court proceedings.

Chuck visited me in lockup. "You'se a dumb motherfucker, and I don't have time to elaborate," he boomed at me. I protested my innocence, but it rang hollow because I was a bonafide threat to civil society. Chuck gave me the best piece of advice that anyone can give a first-timer about to take the big dive. "Fight the baddest motherfucker you can find, because win or lose, niggers who are scared of him will respect you."

I arrived at Spofford in the Bronx, one of the city's human ashtrays. My clothes and possessions were taken away, and I was processed on to a cell floor labeled D5, the toughest of them all. In prison the big eat the small. To forestall some of the savage, predatory behavior among inmates, they divided us up according to size and/or age. My height and weight qualified me for the toughest cellblock. It didn't scare me. One of the good things about being a junkie is that there are few lines of fear to contemplate.

I went into D5 and immediately saw a couple of guys I'd known from the streets. There was a strange, familial atmosphere, but I would soon learn that incarceration was no joke. My first morning I was among fifty or sixty burgeoning baby criminals being herded into the showers. The showers had a lengthy wall with twenty spouts protruding. No attempt was made to preserve privacy. After going through that nakedfest, we were shuffled back to our cells, where we got dressed in our facility togs, which consisted of jeans and a powder-blue T-shirt with our number stenciled across it in bright red ink.

Breakfast was at 7:15 A.M. When the bell rang, we were to respond immediately by quickly lining up military-style. I had been my own man for the previous few years, and with the exception of my mother and Chuck, I didn't respond to order, so when the bell rang I lollygagged, coolly shuffling to the lineup. I noticed that I was the only one who responded that way. It should have set off a light bulb that guys every bit as tough as me were hopping to command. With a tough guy's smirk on my face, I challenged the system.

The guards were called supers, and the super on duty was as big as Mean Joe Green and country-nigger tough. As he approached me, he grabbed a ring of keys and, before I could move whacked me in the jaw with the keys. I saw stars. He then lifted me up by the pants and collar and flung me ten feet into the line. Everyone laughed at the morning entertainment. I would discover that the supers' tolerance for bullshit would barely fill a thimble.

A terrible pain was shooting from ear to ear, and any attempt I made to bring my teeth together was pass-out painful. I told the super about my pain, and he said, "Fuck you! Maybe that will keep your mouth shut." This had to be a violation of some sort, but it was a period when kid criminals had no advocates, thus no rights. The cute days of Leo Gorcey and the Bowery Boys were a thing of the past. The new juvenile portrait was that of a Black and Puerto Rican kid who barely ranked above the discarded animals at the ASPCA.

A quasi-friend of mine, whom I had known on the street, dropped by and whispered in my ear, "The more you bitch, the less they hear."

From that moment on I marched to the beat of the super's drum. Once you got the lay of the land, it was like being in a very cool club. The guys in my cell block all had mid-sized to big-time offenses on their rap sheets. It was a good groove, but I knew that the test would come: I would have to earn my stripes.

The supreme leader of D5, Willy Leach, had everyone terrified on the block, except for a small circle of elite criminals. I had made eye contact with Leach a couple of times, and each time he had tried to intimidate me with his street glare. I ignored him, seeking to avoid confrontation, but he quickly rose to the top of my list of concerns. Leach approached me and asked me for a cigarette. I gave him a cigarette. He asked me for a light. I handed him a book of matches. He seemed to be a bit miffed over the fact that I didn't make an effort to light his cigarette.

That night at dinner we had pie for dessert. I discovered that pie was served once a month as a major treat and was a very valuable commodity. All sorts of deals were made over pie. It was a phenomenal sight, hundreds of guys working the floor brokering deals using pie as currency. Willie Leach approached me and asked for my pie. This was it, my make-or-break moment in this joint. Chuck's words echoed in my mind, "Fight the baddest nigger!"

I took my pie, put it on the floor, and jumped high in the air as though rebounding, before landing heel first in the pie, smashing it to bits. "Now eat it!" I said. The shit was on! Leach and I got into a slam-bam, hard-nosed clash. Several punches were traded in the face, which is how ghetto cats scored a fight. It lasted only a few minutes, but it had Hearns-Hagler written all over it. The supers separated us, and, as they dragged us out of the cafeteria, there was a huge buzz about me, the new guy who had a lot of heart. Chuck's advice had been right on the mark.

We were thrown into confinement for three days. I didn't know what Willie's next move would be. While in confinement, I tried to analyze his character, wondering if he was really tough, which meant we would go for the mutual respect, or would his bully's underbelly force him to stab me in the back. When we got back to the cell block, we looked at each other. Leach tried to bluff me by hardening his face with anger as though he wanted to continue the beef. I slapped on my street mask. We stared each other down for what seemed like a long time. My knees sent a few wobble warnings up my spine, but I hung tough. Suddenly, Leach smiled in a way that offered friendship, which loosened my hard glare and evoked a smile in response. We shook hands, brother-style, slapping each other five repeatedly. Willie Leach and I were great friends from that point on.

Willie Leach's history was serious street matter. He had come into the system when he was only eight years old, busted after killing his father in his sleep. For years Willie had endured horrendous whippings around the clock for imaginary offenses. Finally, when Leach couldn't take it anymore, he waited until his father had passed out from a big booze hit.

"I would have never done it if he was sleeping regularly," he told me, "but when he was under the weight of that Sneaky Pete, he'd pass out for dead."

Leach sliced his wine-soaked dad's gullet. Abused-child advocates hardly existed in those days. The abuses that Leach had put up with would get his father arrested in today's world, but in Leach's day it was every screwed child for himself. Leach was stamped a social monster to be caged in perpetuity. He was anything but a monster. Had he not been dead on arrival, I can think of a number of honorable paths he could have traveled upon. Leach was the product of harsh concrete and high-grade insanity. His whole life had been spent under the system's microscope. Leach consigned himself to being a lifer.

It was jungle free-form, dynamite-fisted mayhem. Many of the inmates were able to get heroin very easily. My favorite cell mate was Loco, a Puerto Rican kid. True to his name, he was crazy fearless. I once saw him swallow several bottle caps to win a bet. He had a great sense of humor and a big heart. His mother brought him heroin twice a week. She would take a stick of Wrigley's chewing gum, get rid of the gum, and fill the silver wrapper with as much heroin as she could, then slide the silver wrapper back into the outer packaging.

Loco, Kitty Boo, Washout, and Stinky were all members of the ruling guard. Leach ushered me into that circle shortly after our fight. The super who had disconnected my jaw was very tight with Leach and the ruling hierarchy. When he discovered that I had been invited into the circle, he gave me a favorable second look. It was mandated that we go to school for three hours every day. That was a joke. We would sit around and listen to Black radio, WWRL, Frankie Crocker and that bunch, and we would challenge each other in dance-offs, testing who could lay the sweetest licks on Berry Gordy's endless tide of Motown brilliance.

The super would allow several of us to skip school and mop the cell block down for extra cigarettes. He was the role model of choice for Leach's consortium. "You ain't nothin' but young boys to me because I can whip all of your asses," the super chided. "You dumb for being criminals and dumber for getting caught. You niggers ain't nothin' but a bucket of dried snot, and there ain't nothin' lower than that in the world." Dried snot was his favorite reference to our status in society. "You niggers gotta find a way to strengthen your legs, 'cause you got a long climb from where you at. Most snot-dipped niggers never make it." We loved the guy.

As they ran me through the system, I protested my innocence vigorously. In court I played up my White side, leaking signs of superior education and verbal facility. My mother had been forced to give up valuable time at work, so she was in no mood for my bullshit. The three options that the judge was considering were reform school, home under strict probation, or a novel idea for a Black kid—a halfway house. My mother wanted me home; the prosecutor wanted reform school. I wanted this halfway house thing.

My legal aid attorney let me speak on my own behalf to the judge, and I put on a show. I sang my tales of woe with the seductive charm of the great Jolson. It was all bullshit. I pulled out all the stops and was going to win this old bastard through the sheer intensity of performance. The high point of my rap was when I drew upon a passage from Hemingway's *Old Man and the Sea*. Back in my Peddie days, old White guys had gone nuts for this novel. I talked about the main character's reference to the great DiMaggio. It was Sammy time; the act was working. If the judge hadn't been wearing that robe, he would have applauded. Although he had not made a decision, he dropped halfway house hints all over the place. I didn't know what a halfway house was, but it wasn't reform school, like Warwick or Otisville, or my mother, who was building up a head of steam like a Mexican bull.

Shortly after completing my floor show, the volcano erupted. My mother blistered the judge with a verbal equivalent of a public caning, accusing him of having fallen for my jive. "I know my child. Best thing for that boy is for somebody to sit on his head!" she bullied. "Look at his record. This is the fifth time I had to take time off work to come down here. Taking food off my table over that little big-head fool. And who the what is Hemmingway? Either put the boy away or give him to me. Ain't no halfway nothin', and if you don't see that, you ain't fit for your job, sucker!"

The judge burned red in my mother's Carolina-hot woodshed. He flexed his muscles and smacked her with a contempt citation and had her removed from the court. She was locked in a little cell behind the judge's chambers until she calmed down. The look she gave me as they carted her away was so angry and fierce that I told the judge, "Please, Judge, don't send me home. I'd prefer life in prison, without parole."

I returned to Spofford that night and drew on Willie Leach's Ph.D. in the criminal justice system to get the dope on this halfway house business. We were in the bathroom stroking Loco through withdrawal sweats. Loco's mother had gone to Puerto Rico, cutting off his heroin supply, and the turkey was kicking his ass. As Loco, battling nausea, caressed the toilet bowl, Leach told me that a halfway house was supervision without bars. "They send you to school in the local neighborhood, hoping that you could make it in society. You the first nigger I ever heard of going to one of those things. That's for White boys. Was the judge Colored?" he asked.

"No, an old White man, but he was the soft kind."

I cautioned that the judge had not made his decision. Leach couldn't get over the fact that I was even being considered for a halfway house. He wondered out loud, "How could a Black, greasy nigger like you . . ." He was muted by his incredulity.

I had been reluctant to reveal my background, fearing that it would float a scent of weakness, alerting the sharks. I dropped my guard to help clear up his confusion and revealed my prep-school past and all of my many dealings with the good side of White folks. He was wide-eyed with amazement. It was the only sign of kidlike curiosity I would ever see on the face of this fifteen-year-old man/boy. You would have thought I was Dorothy telling him about my trip to Oz, particularly when I described the mounds of food available in the White world with no one looking over your shoulder.

I asked Leach, "If you were on the outside as a regular guy, what do you think you would be doing?"

"I don't know." He scowled.

"You ain't just a blank page," I prodded. "You have to have some sort of want."

"This is what I'm gonna be," he said. "There ain't no other world for me. I got to be proud of my criminal shit, 'cause this is it."

Loco began to battle the dry heaves. Leach massaged his back and his neck, easing Loco's hiccuplike gags. The hot sweats ensued, and Leach, with the cool of a doctor, delicately sponged him down with cold, wet toilet paper. After the crisis we picked up on our conversation.

"What you gonna do with your White people stuff if they let you out?" he asked.

"I don't know what I'm gonna do," I replied, "but I'm glad that my mother pushed me into book learning and how to talk White-folks talk."

"Why?" Leach pushed.

"Because that shit is magic. I may have beat Otisville and Warwick because of my White game. I don't know where it is going to take me, but like King's trying to say, a nigger who can read gets over a lot better than a nigger who can't."

We continued to talk about the virtues of literacy for a while. Then a cloud of doom descended around Leach. He sounded like a man who was approaching his checkout date, suggesting that he was past his prime at fifteen. The experience was reminiscent of the final scene between Doughboy and Tré in John Singleton's *Boyz n the Hood*. We see Doughboy's sensitive resignation to his inevitable demise in a world where violence is the favorite pastime and early death offers a sense of relief. Like Doughboy, Leach was social dead meat and he knew it. Our cold, gray, unfeeling animal shelter turned warm, and the pain stung as Leach sipped his hemlock. It was clear to me that my only chance of beating Leach's fate was to maneuver my way around the shipwreck.

TEN

Boredom mounted at the hospital as the weeks crawled along. I was surprised one afternoon when two men entered my room. It was one of those aura moments, live animation at its ripest. One of the men was a tall, handsome light-skinned Black man dressed in hip clothing. I didn't know who he was, but he looked like a someone. The other man could be summed up in one word—Belafonte. I mean *the* Harry Belafonte—White people's perennial choice for the best-looking Black man in America.

What the fuck was he doing here! Was I having a relapse and becoming delusional again? Maybe this was part two of the angel-wing attack. "Are you really Harry Belafonte?" I asked. He laughed. Once he began rapping, you could hear that West Indian melody in his voice. He said he had come to see me because he cared about me.

"Why?" I asked.

"Because you survived a traumatic experience," he said. "You don't give up on young survivors, because they can win in life."

That was the first time I'd been drug-free long enough to accept encouragement without my deflectors up. And the fact that it came from a superstar didn't hurt.

The man with Belafonte was his bass player, and both were committed to trying to reach out to young people in trouble.

"A lot of people are working hard for boys like you," asserted the calypso man.

Mr. Belafonte pulled out a business card and gave it to me. My self-esteem soared. I didn't know what the hell I was going to do with his card, but its raised lettering was so cool. He told me that if I could stay off the junk and get an education, I'd be amazed at what I could do. This was my first exciting non-heroin moment in years.

After Mr. Belafonte left, I felt like my bed was in a state of levitation. I fantasized about him adopting me. After a heady ride through my feel-good cloud, my bed and I nose-dived back to reality, sobered by my truths. These bolts of opportunity had come my way before. They would excite me, and I would embrace them with a junkie's energy moments before a sting, only to wither quickly because after one whiff of my master—the White lady of the streets—I had to sleep with her. Unlike most street niggers, I had been offered more good moments than I deserved. After my many screw-ups, I had little confidence in my ability to do anything right.

On that stormy day in 1968 the courts decided against my mother's wishes and sent me to a halfway house. At that point the complexion of my incarceration changed. I was on a bus with boys straight from family courts all over New York State. I was one of twenty or so kids between the ages of fourteen and sixteen who were being driven to the Ernie Davis Home for Boys in Syracuse, New York, the state's version of incarceration lite.

When we arrived at the home, classic sports history descended on us immediately. The home had been founded by the legendary Syracuse football coach Ben Schwartzwalder. Coach Schwartzwalder and Ernie Davis had had a special relationship that resulted in Davis's becoming the first Black Heisman Trophy winner, breaking the Jim Crow lock on the award. They won a national championship together, and their chemistry exemplified Dr. King's best aspirations. Tragically, Ernie contracted leukemia and died at age twenty-three after being drafted by the Cleveland Browns and momentarily paired with one of the most powerful and important Black men in the second half of the twentieth century, a former Syracuse alum himself, the great Jim Brown. Unlike Brown, whose glare could whup your ass, Ernie Davis was a beloved, more mainstream national treasure. If you can imagine General Colin Powell in shoulder pads, that was Ernie Davis. He commanded such respect and admiration that he owned Syracuse. Upon his death, the outpouring of love and compassion had led to positive developments. My new home was one of them, an oasis in the desert of juvenile incarceration.

The head of the home, Don Muchi Grasso, was a hefty Italian known as MG to the kids. You learned quickly that he was honest and fair with a good a sense of humor, but the word was out that you shouldn't take his kindness for weakness. In our first meeting in a quaint, homespun dining room, I said, "This ain't like no jail I ever saw."

He responded, mimicking my dialect, " 'Cause this ain't no jail. Our purpose is to show you why you don't need jail."

Skeptically, I offered, "Good luck,"

He laughed, grabbing a hold of his awning-sized belly, and said, "If there wasn't something good in you, you wouldn't be here." Suddenly, his joviality fled, leaving a pair of no-bullshit eyes for me to stare into. "If you got the goods. I assure you, we're going to find it."

MG instructed me to check the room-assignment list that was posted on the house bulletin board, where I discovered that I would be rooming with a B. Barrett.

"What the hell is a B. Barrett?"

I was soon to find out. As I approached the room I heard the Beatles song "I'm Down" blasting. I stepped into the room, and there stood an utterly goofy, extremely pale, somewhat buck-toothed guy with a pile of red hair.

"What's your story?" I asked.

"Oh, come on. Give me a break before we go into the story thing," he chortled.

"Correct me if I'm wrong," I said, "but we are criminals, ain't we?"

He laughed, plopped on the bed, and asked, "Do you like the Beatles?"

"The stuff on the radio, 'Yeah, yeah, yeah'?" I said. "Not particularly."

"The Beatles are everything." he stated definitively. "Repeat after me: the Beatles are everything." I laughed. "Come on, come on, come on, repeat after me: The Beatles are everything!"

I gave in and said, "The Beatles are everything."

We laughed, and Bruce said, "There, you've just been baptized."

After our little ritual I said to him "All right, repeat after me."

"What?"

"Smokey Robinson is the ultimate pretty nigger."

Puzzled, he said, "What?"

"Say it!" I commanded.

He shrugged his shoulders and said, "Okay, Smokey Robinson is the ultimate pretty nigger. What the hell is that about?"

"Smokey is my man. No one in music gets the bitches off like Smokey, which is my thing."

Bruce scratched that shroud of red hair and asked, "Do you drink beer?"

"Hell no!"

"I never met a beer I didn't want to fuck," he asserted.

"You're a strange guy," I said.

"You think so?" His energy seemed to leave him, bringing on a state of solemnity.

"What you doing here?" I asked.

"My dad put me here," he answered.

"Why?"

"Because he drives a Maserati."

"What's a Maserati?"

"It's a car for young guys that only old guys can afford."

"And . . ." I replied, trying not to seem ignorant.

"And I hate my father," he snapped.

"So far, this communication thing ain't working, man."

"He's an asshole. He shat on my mother, left the family, and got a really young girlfriend who I can't stand. So I started a lot of fires. I tried to burn down his business, and he really took offense to that. So he ran me through the courts, and all of this and that and that and that, and this is where they decided to put me. I'll tell you something—grownups are for shit!"

Blood rushed to his pale face, and his red hair turned to fire. After a moment he calmed down and asked, "What are you here for?"

"I was busted for assault and robbery with a deadly weapon."

Bruce looked at me wide-eyed and said, "That's neat," and I laughed. "You know I once met a Colored guy."

"Just one?" I teased.

"Yeah, just one, you know, and he was all right," he said. "He sang a lot, which was great. He worked on weekends at my dad's office building. He cleaned the joint. My mom and I used to have lunch with my dad on Saturdays. My dad was always two hours behind schedule, so we'd do a lot of waiting. I would watch the Colored guy work, mostly wondering, 'How do people become Colored?' I started to talk to him. He never said more than he had to, but his eyes were always shifting back and forth. He was a big guy, and I couldn't figure out why he was always so nervous around me. Are Colored guys normally nervous types?"

"Nah," I said. "It was probably because you were White."

Bruce went to the record player, put on a Jefferson Airplane record, and started to get into "White Rabbit." He closed his eyes and began caressing Grace Slick's lyric. It was the first time I had ever seen a White guy do rock 'n' roll as religion. After Grace blasted the last note, with Bruce accompanying her on air drums, he turned to me and said, "White guys are nothing to be nervous about. If I make you jumpy, just give me a whack and I'll calm down. Okay?"

Bruce and I rode on a wave of mid-sixties energy. As goofy as he looked, he was pretty amazing. He was the kind of guy who could go into a department store in Syracuse, and, by the time he came out, he would be in a completely different outfit from head to toe, all stolen.

He used to say, "It's easy to steal as long as the people are watching you."

"What?" I said, a word I used a lot with Bruce.

"Come on," he said, "who expects anyone to steal in front of them."

"White people expect me to steal in front of them."

"That's different. I bet you could get away with stealing in front of Colored people."

We made each other laugh, and our color difference melted. It was a very useful and telling experience for me because Bruce was not cool in any Black way. He looked like the worst of the geeks, and yet getting to know him erased that perception. He taught me that you can't judge White folks from the outside or you miss half the fun.

I loved the Ernie Davis Home. MG believed in a level playing field, and we were encouraged to become family. After a few months of positive vibes of communication wrapped in warm-hearted discipline, it became clear that if I was to be stuck in the penal system, White justice was the way to go.

A delightful old Black woman named Sadie was the cook. The quality of her food rivaled that of my mother's, but she had a voice that was so terrible it should have gotten her arrested. Every morning we were awakened by her ear-rupturing rendition of Richard Harris's "MacArthur Park." Those of us who were assigned to set up the breakfast table would stuff napkins in our ears as she strangled Jimmy Webb's lyrics.

I had scored surprisingly high on a placement test and wound up in an excellent public high school called Nottingham. The school was attended by predominately middle- and upper-class White kids, but many of them had surrendered to the call of the new counterculture, so they were intrigued by Black outlaws. I was an immediate winner with the Black students because I came from Harlem, an incontrovertible badge of Blackness, and they put me on a pedestal. Surprisingly, while I was away the newly minted "Black is beautiful" edict had become law, providing the first opportunity for dark-skinned cats like me to play with the pretty girls.

The student body was 10 percent Black, and most of them were bent on segregation. Although I gave them their due respect, memories of my Riverdale days flashed, and I was determined not to get sucked into a Black hole. I went searching for the cool White guys to balance my trip sheet. In those days, the place to find cool White boys was on the basketball court, because the game don't lie. Despite the fact that they were into beer and a bit more Gary Puckett and the Union Gap than was my pull, they were fun and could play. I was steadily losing my ability to make negative snap judgments on race. My White brothers at the home were changing my perspective.

On an early morning in April, Bruce and I came down for breakfast. There was something wrong with the atmosphere. Sadie wasn't torturing us. Bruce yelled into the kitchen, "Hey, what's the matter, Sadie, lost your voice?" We both heard an acute sigh and went into the kitchen. Sadie looked like she had been crying.

"What's the matter?" I said.

"You ain't heard? They shot Martin Luther King. He dead."

We ran up to Muchi Grasso's room, where the television was on and Dr. King was splattered all over it. As the day moved on, grief, anger, and hatred flooded the country, erupting into riots. I had never seen such a fireball of hatred from Black people against the White establishment. I watched decades of repressed rage power the bottles and bricks that were being hurled at all things White.

I was a King embryo, baptized in his philosophy, and understood that Black violence played right into the hands of those who hated our freedom most. The violent reaction to King's death was an embarrassment to everything he had stood for. This was not the time to incinerate hope and reason under the banner of his work.

Stack, Muchi Grasso's top aide, was particularly sensitive to my precarious situation. As I soaked in the events on television, Stack watched me closely, looking for indications of discomfort. My biggest concern at the moment was whether these White guys I had been living with were going to freak out over the Black missiles being launched at Caucasians. That day flowed like molasses. No one knew what to say to each other. Before dinner I spent some time with Sadie. She was in a state of shock. I sat quietly and watched her work in silence, gaining a small degree of comfort from her Blackness.

Later that evening, Stack approached and said, "We're going out."

"Where?"

"Just come." He told Bruce and four of my house brothers to do the same.

Stack pulled the van around front, and we all piled in. He turned on the radio. King's voice was on every station, highlights from his many speeches, so many of them about nonviolence. We cruised the heart of the Black section and discovered that Syracuse's sparse Black population was trying to do their part, adding their two cents' worth of anger and destruction. I stoically took in the atmosphere.

"Dennis, it's important to everyone in this car that you tell us what the hell you're feeling," Stack said.

"Stack, I can't explain this," I struggled. "I'm not angry. I'm sad. I don't think that Dr. King would want anybody to loot and burn in his memory. King going down doesn't affect how I feel about the guys in this van," I said. "So I hope this doesn't change things."

There was a contemplative moment of silence, until Bruce broke it. "I'm sorry they killed the guy. I didn't know who the hell he was, but the look on Sadie's face this morning told me that he must have been someone really fucking important."

We listened to the sounds of low-grade civil unrest as we circled the city. Stack told us stories about the Civil War. I don't quite remember the significance, except that it had to do with courage. He was preaching courage at a time when the nation was falling apart.

"Why did you do this?" I asked Stack.

"Dr. King was a hell of a lot more important to America than just civil rights. He stood for something that made the country a better place across the board. I didn't want you to feel isolated being locked up with a bunch of White guys."

"They might have killed the big guy," Bruce added, "but you're still here, and I'm with you one hundred percent." He put his arm around me, and the brotherhood we had developed over the previous months helped to extract some of the racial poison from this tragedy.

I would soon come to the end of my seven-month honeymoon with the legal justice system at the Ernie Davis Home, the greatest experience of my teen years. It was time for me to go back to my native reality. Four days after my return to East Harlem, I would be shooting heroin again.

Turning points in one's life are hard to predict. It's their gig to find you. After a few weeks back in the scene, I was juggling drug works at the old Benjamin Franklin High School. After scraping together enough money, my new best friend, Stinky, and I were racing toward a tenement building to get off. We scaled six flights in one breath before arriving in the small compartment that led out to the roof. We pulled out our product and paraphernalia, gleefully preparing for our day's first stab at nigger roulette. The morning's first hint of malfunction pierced our happy setup with the faint sounds of footsteps, activating our "uh-oh" meter. As the sounds grew louder it became apparent that someone was either going into a lower apartment or . . . ! Stinky and I looked at each other, answering the thought in harmony, "The po-lice!"

We broke for the door, anticipating the almost-as-scary-as-a-bust activity of roof jumping, the least attractive getaway option, but someone had nailed the door shut. The now-louder footsteps sounded like aggressive sandpaper. Trapped, we grabbed our cellophane deuce bags and threw them into the void of the spiraling stairwell, thinking in terms of a "not mine" defense. Looking down, we saw a strong arm outfitted in navy blue extend itself and turn its palm upward. Stinky and I added a few more numbers to our clad pectorals when we witnessed one of the cellophane bags flutter into the palm of the dusky hand.

Cornered like ghetto rats, we were soon confronted by a young, well-built six-foot African American, known on junkie paradise's morning beat as Mike the cop. With his broad chocolate smile out-widening his moustache, he patted the club in his hand and said, "First things first. I'm not going to have to use this, am I?" Stinky and I vigorously shook our heads in the negative. Suddenly we were trapped children without one street trick left in our bag.

Having both been just released from facilities, we'd been wound in thick probationary tape, so with our back sheets this bust could easily clear three to five. At sixteen, Stinky was in worse shape because he'd just crossed the line between juvenile and hard core: This was his first adult charge.

Mike ordered us to get against the wall with our hands held high. He then picked up the evidence before commanding us to face him. I startled him by breaking into a grand beggar's attempt at singing "Mammy" for his supper. I was gambling that a Black cat who rose to cop level respected higher learning, so I laid on poignant, informed, articulate bits of introspection with the fervor of the great Jolson on his best night at Broadway's Winter Garden.

"This will ruin any chance I will ever have at a successful life," I doubled-kneed. "I can't end my future today. That means forever, and I'm only fifteen."

I could feel Stinky's glare on my neck and his jealousy over Mike's extension of attention to my rap. His frustration burned over my secret weapon: education.

"Get up off your knees," Mike instructed. I obeyed. He said, "I'm going to take a gamble, and that gamble is that you got a lot more brains in that big head of yours than you have any idea." He took a deep breath, looking upward as though searching for a Devine tiebreaker, then barked, "Get out of here!" He jerked his head sharply in the direction of the stairwell. I bee-lined with Stinky trying to sneak into my draft, but Mike blocked his path. Stinky started screaming and Mike's tough-guy demeanor returned. I heard the echoes of Stinky being blasted with muscle and wolf tickets. I ran for four blocks before allowing myself to believe that I had been let out of a noose that would have hung me in the joint for the rest of my teenage years. I was lucky, but it was a good bet that by nightfall Stinky was on Riker's Island staring through wires and bars.

ELEVEN

I squirmed impatiently on my bed as I awaited the official word to split the hospital. It had been a cocoon that shielded me from the world for two months. The doctors assured me I would be okay if I stayed away from infected needles. Would I stay away? I didn't know. This was my last chance to beat back the two big blows that lay just outside the hospital doors—overdose and incarceration. I'd already used up seven or eight of the nine lives I'd been allotted. At sixteen, how was I going to survive the streets with only a couple of lives left?

The nurse entered with a wheelchair and insisted that I comply with the dumb rule of having to be wheeled to the door, but this was a droplet of annoyance next to the thought of facing hot concrete again. As I left the hospital, I was met by two guys: Fast Joey, a Puerto Rican dude and one of my best friends, and a guy I had never met before. The stranger was dressed in silk pants made by Mr. Tony's, the ghetto Calvin Klein, and some new Pro-Keds. He had to be a dealer. This was a good-hearted attempt to welcome me back into the nightmare. Joey wanted to take me to the cooker.

Belafonte was getting smaller in my mind's rearview mirror. The white lady stood before me in a new negligée with the scent of her poisonous thighs calling. Panic came to my rescue, and I spun on my heels and ran back into the hospital. I hid in the pavilion for a half an hour, hoping that they would get the message. After thirty minutes they were gone. I knew Joey couldn't sit on drugs for long without his habit spanking him. I took a different route home, making certain that no one saw me. I was intent on letting baby steps govern my entry into the black hole that awaited me.

The grapevine ran fresh reports of weekly overdoses and steaming teenage corpses. I stayed in my room and thought about how the world had changed around me. Dr. King is dead, Bobby Kennedy goes down, Alfred Lawyer dies. Who was Alfred Lawyer? A neighborhood hero I looked up to who was erased in the 'Nam. I struggled to stay clean for two months, rarely leaving my room.

My mother was beginning to beat her drum of impatience. "Greasy Black niggers can't hide," she would bellow. "You need God!"

That got me out of the house for short errands, mindful to walk on out-of-the-way side streets. It was a lonely time. Even my hero Sammy Davis was being diss-slapped. It was a bad time to be a one-eyed Jewish Uncle Tom spook. The Black Power Movement's ridicule of the little pioneer was the unkindest cut of all. Sammy had taken a series of savage psychological and physical beatings for his right to be. When he was booed at the PUSH Expo Event, it was the worst of a constantly carping Black judgment meter. Suddenly, we were eating our leaders. Roy Wilkins of the NAACP, Whitney Young of the Urban League, and other peaceful warriors armed with briefcases filled with civil dignity were being Tommed to death.

Chuck Griffin came by the house to pump me up. He told me that he had gotten new funding for the community center. He didn't let the fortunes of his neighborhood dream die with our drug madness, but managed to keep the ball in the air through an inexhaustible supply of energy. Chuck wanted me to play boy wonder to his social evangelism. He planned to start off slow, setting in motion an education initiative. He had hired a woman named Glynis Pierce to run his reading program and asked me to work with her.

I enjoyed working with Glynis, a peach-skinned Black woman in her mid-twenties. She was gorgeous. Glynis was too old for me and wouldn't give me the time of day, but I found it impossible to take my eyes off of her. She played against her beauty by obtaining her master's degree in education. Her down-to-earth humility was that of a woman eighty pounds heavier. She worked for Chuck because she believed in what he was trying to do, and injected an important amount of Southern-bred civil rights idealism into our efforts. Watching her teach the unteachable, the children who had been left for dead, inspired something good in me. It was a turn-on to polish diamonds in the rough. With Glynis's kindness and patience, it was easy to see that these kids wanted to learn.

One Saturday she offered me ten dollars to help her paint her living room. This was a delicate matter; ten dollars still translated into five deuce bags. I would have ducked her offer, except for the fact that I was interested in seeing what she was like during her downtime. As we mixed the paint, we talked about my isolation. I told her my fear of shooting heroin. She suggested a drug program. I refused. I wanted to hide, but I didn't want to run. I felt strongly that in order to beat this thing, I had to do it in the streets. Glynis pleaded with me to no avail, and I coaxed her into dropping the subject.

I asked her what she thought about all of King's Black-and-White-together business now that he was gone. "We have to do it together. I'm from the South. How can I honestly hate White people when my skin is this light?" The dream was certainly still alive in her. We lapsed into a comfortable silence as we began painting on opposite sides of the room. Glynis put on a record. It sounded different, almost hip in a cool White way.

"What's that," I asked?

"The Beatles," she replied.

"No shit!" Surprised, my memory ran to Barrett, "The Beatles are everything!" and I laughed out loud.

She told me to listen to the sitar.

"What?"

Glynis explained to me what a sitar was, and I connected with the sexy twang of the unusual instrument. She began to break down the music on the album *Revolver*. I fell in love; it was a seminal experience. One whiff of John Lennon's "Tomorrow Never Knows," and I was a different person. I'd found the keys that would unlock the doors of my private hell. I'd been shooting up to Black rhythms for three years. My cultural nourishment resided at the end of the radio dial, where the Black deejays kept shop. Heroin, Kool cigarettes, and soul music—these were the elements I associated with going to the cooker—and I was sick of it. As John Lennon chanted, "It is not living," I realized that I'd not been living. Where was the life?

I quizzed Glynis about these new Beatles, the cool ones, and she sensed that I was grasping. She educated me about the young White movement that was changing the country through music and politics. I got a kick out of the knowledge that so much beauty could come from an album named after a gun.

After we cleaned up and put the paint away, Glynis tossed me an additional treat. She took me to the Village to a club called The Bitter End, where I saw longish-haired White boys play acoustic guitars, singing their thoughts instead of their souls. This was great. The emphasis was on the words. There was little body bounce to their songs, so one's head was forced to do the dancing. I hadn't been this excited since viewing my first nude girl. Glynis provided me with the raft I needed to take off on a new adventure.

One night I ran into a drug-addict friend of mine named Bub. Bub's hustle was stealing phonographs from the New York City school system. He sold me a monotone record player for five dollars. I had to lie to my mother, telling her I'd borrowed it from the center, to squeeze it through her screening process. I locked myself in my room for months listening to the Beatles. I started reading about the "Summer of Love" and the Monterey Pop Festival. Otis Redding's success meant a lot to me. He'd been a ghetto superstar for years, and I was a big fan.

It was encouraging that White folks had embraced him. Lots of White cats fell in love with Black music and its culture, and I was going the other way. I dug the fact that it was the English boys who were feeding me the music. They were neutral when it came to America's race problem. Black music was being run through an English filter, and given back in this fresh and introspective way. The blues had arrived at the Waldorf. I heard that John Lennon wanted to visit the Apollo Theater right off when first arriving in the States. He was my man. I bought *Magical Mystery Tour* and soon became a walrus.

The *Magical Mystery Tour* album was my coming-out statement. I was letting my hair grow, and I bleached my jeans, which gave them a tie-died look. I bought a pair of sandals, and, finally, after a few hits of some good reefer, I went out into the block. People looked at me like I'd come from another planet. I was becoming an oddball phenomenon, a ghetto hippie. I darted around like a commando, eluding my home brothers, who still trafficked in violent treachery. Several of the boys inquired as to whether my hood had been popped in the joint, as though I were making a homosexual statement. They didn't know what to make of me, except for the fact that I looked happy, different, and relatively sober.

I listened to late-night FM radio. The Doors cooked, The Who slashed, The Stones burned, while Cream simmered. I took a shot at trying to match heads with Allen Ginsberg's and Jack Kerouac's rebel works. I'd formed a club of me. My mother was going crazy. One day, at the top of her lungs, she screamed, "I hate the beagles!"

The first time Chuck saw the new me he laughed, but he was an intelligent guy. He liked the fact that I was into something that took me away from the needle. He also thought that this new White angle would play great with the "good White folks." I told him that I was smoking pot to help my heroin cravings. He reluctantly conceded to the lesser evil. As we headed for a Little League ballgame in the neighborhood park, we talked about change. I was trying to convince him that all we needed was love. "Maybe, if you White with long hair, playing guitar for millions, then that love thing is all you need," said Chuck. "The niggers that we dealing with need education and a job."

When we arrived at the park, I saw Chuck's daughter, Gerri, standing alone, watching her brother, Kevin, play. Gerri was the neighborhood's princess. She was currently appearing in the groundbreaking musical *Hair*. Gerri sang one of the signature songs in the play, "Aquarius," and had actually met Dick Cavett backstage. She was cosmic. As we drew closer, I noticed her beautiful afro. She wore a denim jacket adorned with all kinds of hippie symbols. When Gerri turned toward me, I saw that a flower had been painted on her cheek. This was everything I'd been fantasizing about—everything I wanted to be. I brought it up to Chuck, who put the kibosh on it immediately. "She's the crown jewel. You ain't been out of drugs long enough to even think about it." I wasn't paying attention; I couldn't get that flower on her cheek out of my mind.

I wafted through the ghetto streets thinking about my Black hippie girl with the strains of Donovan's "Hurdy Gurdy Man" providing the soundtrack to my fantasy. I imagined that my neighborhood was Greenwich Village North as I carried several new albums wrapped tightly in a nondescript brown paper bag in order to conceal their identity. This had become a normal occurrence. Initially, I would buy the new music downtown, but my appetite for the sounds became so large that I wanted to create a neighborhood connection with my local record shop, Bluenote. I'd been a steady customer, and the owner knew me well.

"Hey, man, you hip to a group called the Doors?" I asked, mindful of being confrontational, keeping my Black chops up front. The merchant looked at me as though I were a foreign substance and said, "The Doors! This ain't no hardware store."

I asked him to order the record for me, and he agreed, but stipulated that if he were to order the music, I would have to carry it out of the store in a plain brown paper bag. Somehow he felt it might damage the store's soulful reputation if he were funneling what amounted to contraband. I agreed to his conditions, and we started our little undercover musical operation. He would subsequently soften about the music and even get into some of it, particularly when Jimi Hendrix came on the scene. Despite his new education, the brown paper bag remained mandatory.

When I arrived at my building, there were children playing stoop ball with gobs of people mulling about. In order to avoid inquiries about the contents of my paper bag, I dashed up the back stairwell. The normal rumbling sounds of activity echoed off the walls of the brick-solid encasement. Reality held its gun to my temple. I could smell the evils of a cooker; someone was shooting up. This was a semi-regular occurrence, and my game plan was to sprint by them, careful to keep my head down to avoid making eye contact.

As I accelerated, a familiar voice stopped me in my tracks. "Hey, nigger!" It was Alfred. I hadn't seen him in a while. He'd long since boarded the bad ship *Heroin*.

Alfred and three others were going through the process of injection. "What you got?" he asked.

"Some music," I said.

"Let me see what you listening to." Alfred took the bag, pulled the album out, and discovered it was *The Association's Greatest Hits*, with "Along Comes Mary" and other great tunes from the sixties. Alfred checked it out and gave it back to me with no comment.

"How was the hospital?" he said. "I didn't even know you were out." Alfred looked mangy and bore little resemblance to the person I had known in his prime. As two of his partners prepared their shots he asked, "You still hit it?"

"Look at me," I said, "do I look like I still hit it?"

"I guess not."

He thought a moment and then began to scratch his crotch in that patented, ghetto, Black-junkie way. "You know, if any nigger can beat this shit, you can, and I know, 'cause I raised you," he proudly stated. As I thought about the past friendship and wisdom he'd always provided for me, I focused on his handsome heroin-ravaged face, when his posture began to contract into the drug's signature characteristic, a tantalizingly slow nod into that other world. With his eyes closed, he muttered, "It was always you. It ain't never been nor is it gonna be me, but it is you."

"Alfred, you are the smartest person I've ever met, and yet you ain't," I whispered.

"Don't judge," he said. "I want to be exactly what I am. Now, get the fuck away from this cooker."

With the flashing focus of a cheetah, he noticed something wrong with the proportion of heroin being split up. He halted the activity and examined everyone's portion, making certain his shot was secure. Then, without even looking, he stuck his hand up and waved as if to say "Get the fuck out of here."

I continued to blow away time. I listened to "A Day in the Life," from *Sgt. Pepper's Lonely Hearts Club Band*. Lennon was becoming such an important part of my life that he began to rival both Sammy's and Frank's hold on my affections. I discovered that he was heavy into drugs, including heroin. That was a positive development for me; it brought us closer. I got a big kick out of the fact that I smoked my first joint well before Dylan turned him on during one of the early American tours. Lennon's defection from his English upbringing was exemplified by his selection of Yoko, a Japanese iconoclast who shook the Carnaby Street trendiness right out of him. He was beginning to receive flack similar to the headaches Sammy had experienced with his marriage to May Britt. The prince and the pushy Jap were too much for the Brits to swallow. Lennon's feet began to swell, bursting out of their golden slippers, wiggling clay toes for all of his startled worshipers to gnaw upon.

I was able to strike my first civil note with my father in years. He had written me off as a major disappointment, unable to figure out or stomach my heroin turn. I was a "no good Black pup." It was a frail, uneasy alliance. I did everything I could to stay out of his way, and he ignored me as best he could. A positive sign at our one remaining common intersection was the rumblings of the Miracle Mets. We watched the Mets beat the Cubs early in the 1969 season. The team that had become famous for turning losing into a profitable art form was becoming serious, but no one would dare consider them contenders. My father jabbed against convention and said, "Those Mets are gonna really do something this year." I welcomed the fragile bond we'd formed and refrained from answering, "Are you crazy?"

"Pitching is everything," he continued. "That Seaver can throw a ball through a redneck's trailer, and it would come out the other side without teeth marks." I didn't quite get that and thought the man had lost his mind, but the old bastard knew a thing or two about baseball, and over the next few months we watched the Mets begin to gel. My dad and I were on the bandwagon early, and the Mets rush to glory would be the last comfortable experience we would share as father and son.

My older brother, Robert, had hit bottom in his heroin addiction. One night my mother used her weight, strength, and will to crush him like a dried leaf after it became evident that he was stealing her few valuable possessions. This was a sad episode because Leola had a sensitive spot for her firstborn. She seemed to handle our heroin problems differently. She showed little sympathy for my addiction, using my early opportunities as a hammer. "Your brother ain't had the chances you had. White folks was good to you. There's a difference between lookin' in from the outside and bein' in and thrown out." I was on my own. She was a bit more apprehensive in her treatment of Robert. He was her most talented and sensitive child. His ability as a painter had emerged early, but he was blindsided by street-nigger dogma, where wielding a faggy paintbrush wouldn't cut it. This sent him careening into a black hole of burdensome reality. It would be a while before Robert would dig himself out of his drug-induced torment.

I was living from moment to moment, when my luck turned. I got a message from Chuck to come and see him as soon as possible. I went to his house, and as always, Chuck was sitting on the couch, resting in his boxers, with a ready blanket to toss over him should a female enter the room.

"Sit down, man," he said. "I got a job for you. The center is growing like a pregnant tit. I got the money, I got the building, I got foundation support with tons of White folks biting like fish in a crowded Mississippi pond. We are gonna have the best football teams East Harlem has ever seen. We gonna beat our chest as though Tarzan was Black. Restart the chorus and bring all our girls back."

"Is Gerri going to sing with the chorus?" I asked. Chuck detected an unusual amount of glee in my inquiry and said, "Un-ass the thought, nigger!"

"What?" I offered defensively.

"You just one pocketbook away from five years in Elmira. I suggest you think about dealing with that before you think about Broadway. Gerri is busy with the play, but I'm hoping we can squeeze a few star appearances when the situation calls for it. It'll have to be on a Monday because play folks don't work on Mondays. Now get your head out of Geraldine's ass because what I got to tell you is big."

"What?"

"I want you to whip heroin!"

"Where you been, man? Heroin whipped my ass, and I ain't looking for no rematch."

"Stop talking so goddamned much and listen, before I knock all that liver medicine out your ass."

"I have the right to refuse something if I don't want to do it," I protested in a moment of prideful insanity.

"Look, you little drug-addict motherfucker, for the next while I do all the refusing around here." I saw the old line in the sand being drawn, so I turned up my respect meter. "I don't want you to go out there and talk about how bad your shit is. That's typical weak, nigger shit," he said. "I want you to teach White folks about drugs, 'cause the shit is starting to blow up their children. I want the center to be out front in the fight against drugs, 'cause it's coming. Now, you either gonna be a live poster boy or a bruised ex-junkie."

A creepy, familiar feeling came over me as though Chuck was playing my mother in drag. I cut my losses and caved in big time. He took a step back and unballed his fist, comfortable with the fact that he had my willing attention. "I want you to start with the neighborhood," he continued, "try to clean up some of our niggahs. They'll listen to you; you been there. Then you go into churches and schools and build some local momentum. Then, when your shit is oiled, we'll hit the White folks."

"Hit them with what?" I asked calmly, fearful of reigniting his wrath. "Them motherfuckers usually do the hitting."

"Not this time. They gonna listen like anybody else. We gonna become the anti-drug motherfuckers."

"Chuck, I'm not sure I'm gonna be able to practice that sermon, 'cause heroin is still too real to me."

"Well, nigger," Chuck said, "you gonna have to be more real than heroin. Besides, if you go on record as being Mr. No Drugs, that will help keep you in line. We are gonna show that you don't have to shoot that garbage to be cool. Now, you done shot the shit, and as far as I'm concerned, kicked the shit. I ain't never met a nigger who can talk White folk and feel that shit like you do. You the perfect nigger for a very important thing, so in a sense, you been drafted."

The next morning I showed up at the storefront that Chuck would turn into his oasis, a plot of urban positivity that would float atop a sea of dangerous manure. The building was an old abandoned supermarket, a former part of the Safeway chain of stores throughout the city. The building was dank and more than a bit dusty that morning, but the construction workers were hammering Chuck's dream into reality. His chest extended the length of the huge, empty space that would become the site, where much of East Harlem's youth would share meaningful bits of themselves. An affectionate nickname that the guys had for Chuck was Black Nigger. It was a term of endearment and respect, like the one used for the great educator from New Jersey, Joe Clark: Head Nigger in Charge. Chuck's East Harlem Federation Youth Association was back in business. The official name was a mouthful for many, so it was called simply Chuck's Center.

The center was two floors and huge. The top floor would accommodate a successful reading and tutorial program, one of our jewels. In the basement the football teams would dress for games and participate in skull sessions, as well as provide a bonding chamber for young men. A portion of the basement was reserved for an archery range. Chuck brought in several bales of hay on which the targets would be placed. In the beginning, when Chuck introduced the sport to the ghetto, our archery knowledge began and ended with Errol Flynn's performance as Robin Hood. Over the next five years Chuck would train and shepherd two national champions, one male and one female. Chuck's freethinking was a boon to the neighborhood, and in his brilliance he authored what would become known as his gender-be-damned policy. He preached "Neither age nor what you have between your legs has any option on ability."

Everything was moving in double time, fueled by Chuck's irrepressible enthusiasm. Within weeks the chorus would be back together. It was predominantly female, thirty voices strong, which gave teeth to Chuck's gender-equity initiative. The chorus also acted as a drill team at football games and created and practiced sharp, exciting routines patterned after Grambling College's world-renowned marching band. The driving force behind the choral group was Anna, Chuck's wife and co–dream developer.

Anna Griffin was the first great New Age female role model to enter my life. She played chess, knocking off male competitors like the pawns she accumulated during a match. She became a very astute football prognosticator and could look at a play's design and analyze the action better than most men. Anna was the first Black woman I had ever met who earned her living seated behind a desk, allowing her brains to pick her cotton for her, while her hands remained smooth and feminine. An administrative whiz, Anna built and solidified the infrastructure of the center. Pleasingly attractive, her figure had been sculpted with heated tools. She had it all.

Anna was also a singer who had performed with many popular gospel singing groups. She and her partner, Bernice Coles, a storied performer who had sung with the great Sam Cooke before he jumped across that hot divide into secular music, were the musical directors of the choral group. With these seasoned professionals training the group, it would rise above the level of neighborhood activity and into the realm of serious entertainment.

Chuck quickly realized that the greatest advertisement for the new center was the wonderful voices that used the spirit of gospel to activate the most skeptical of hearts. He rented a bus and began to book free concerts at colleges. We hit one college per weekend, and in each instance left them dancing in the aisles. The group was helped considerably by the fact that the song, "Oh Happy Day," by The Edwin Hawkins Singers had hit big. At the end of each performance, Chuck would go onstage and talk about the value of integration provided it happened at what he called "eye level." The liberals just fell all over themselves. It was something to behold.

I accompanied the group on one of the earlier excursions, dressed in my hippie threads. I had added Glenn Campbell sideburns to my external visage. Campbell became my man after knocking me out with Jimmy Webb's "Wichita Lineman." I caught one of the chorus's Monday performances, hoping to steal the opportunity to rub elbows with Gerri. The gig was at Wesleyan University. Before departing Chuck made an announcement, "We're going out into the land of White folks. When we get there, leave all your nigger shit on the bus. Your job is to show the world grace, competence, and cooperation."

The excitement of it all blanketed the last strains of my heroin cravings. When we arrived at the college, the sight of the typically impressive New England campus unleashed my adrenaline. Once the show started and the first few numbers set the group's typical feel-good tone, Gerri stepped forward and took command of the stage. She was a gifted performer with that indefinable ingredient that separates those who are bigger than life from the mere talented. Gerri broke into an African song called "Jolenco," and with the easy brilliance of a Miriam Makeba, she rocked the house and hijacked my affections lock, stock, and barrel.

Gerri and I had first met in the second grade and made little impression on each other. In the same year that I was sent down South on my arson rap, she embarked upon her musical journey. Gerri was a gospel prodigy who made her first record when she was seven years old with the gospel titan James Cleveland. This set her off on a Garland-esque carpet ride. Like Judy, Gerri was immediately tagged as the little girl with a howitzer for a voice. She won four times on *Ted Mack's Original Amateur Hour*, the nationally televised talent show popular in the fifties and sixties. Gerri then tamed the unforgiving savage beast that was the Apollo Amateur Night audience by winning four times and receiving a professional outing on a bill topped by the great Otis Redding. Her climb through the business was swift.

By the end of the concert I had accumulated a healthy can full of wet-dream footage, which I played over and over in my mind on the ride back to the city.

TWELVE

After a few weeks Chuck had a one-hundred-foot banner painted for the center reinstating our battle cry: Number One on the Planet Earth. It hung across the wall in the main lobby for one to see immediately when entering the center. Chuck and Anna were surging, combining civil rights with athletics, entertainment, and education. The concoction had the charitable foundations panting. I started to have some fun in my sobriety. I talked to Chuck about how I should approach my drug rap. I wanted to strike the proper balance between street funk and discernible Whitefolkisms.

One day at Chuck's house I was surprised to see him listening to a folk singer. The singer's voice seemed to drip with the melodic anguish of a sharecropper's woe. He played an acoustic guitar like it was a banjo, pure rhythm, and sang an original composition, "Handsome Johnny."

"Who is this cat?"

"Richie Havens," he proudly replied. "I got hip to this cat in the Village."

Chuck told me that if I was really going to do this hippie thing, the Village was where all the interesting White boys were hanging out. He lectured, "If your shit is going to be wide, then you have to widen your shit."

I took that to mean that I should head for the Village. I got on the bus at Second Avenue and 116th Street and rode all the way down the avenue until I got to Eighth Street. I felt as though I had run away and joined the circus. This was right after the coffeehouse boom busted. These funky little potholes, where great artists like Havens, Stephen Stills, Odetta, John Sebastian, and Jimi Hendrix made their early coin, had run out of gas. I was about two years late for those guys, and the scene was just beyond its peak, but there was still a hefty amount of colors, drugs, music, and interaction.

I nervously entered a hippie-stocked club on Bleeker Street. By comparison, I looked like an uncool tourist from Harlem. The only thing I shared with them was my fresh love for their music. A few guys approached. One of them had an acoustic guitar, and we got to talking about music and drugs. I told him a bit about my background and the fact that I was just coming off of a heavy heroin hit, which stroked their fascination and seemed to accelerate my acceptance. The musicians onstage were playing blue grass mixed with a few Buffalo Springfield tunes. Someone asked if I wanted to go on a trip. I was still short on my understanding of the lingo.

"What?" I said.

"Mind expansion, man, a journey. Where you land is up to your destiny."

We left and went up to someone's tiny apartment on Ninth Street and Third Avenue. In the apartment were a couple of women and a few guys. We sat down in a circle, and I was given a small orange tablet. So small, in fact, I couldn't get a good tonguehold on it, so I gulped and it disappeared.

I got up to go to the bathroom, looked in the mirror, and discovered that there was a red spot on my tongue. As many have spoken in the past, I said, "Is that it?" One of the hippies replied, "Don't worry about it, just sit back and relax." They opened up some beers and put on Bob Dylan's *The Times They Are A-Changin'*. I listened as they grooved to "Only a Pawn in the Game" through "The Lonesome Death of Hattie Carroll." The sharp twang of Dylan's early strains dominated the tiny apartment.

After a while, "The Ballad of Hollis Brown" came on, and the weight of its words and music became a crushing force. I was underneath the song, pushing back, trying to regain some balance because it was so heavy. "I can't get up from under the weight of this music," I said to the suddenly comically contorted faces of my companions. I started to smile and laugh and giggle. One of the cats told me, "Close your eyes, think calmly, gather all of the wonderful colors, and use them to fight off the paranoia. This is about freedom, the only kind of freedom that you will ever experience. Let your mind be a room to create and amplify the vibrations of your feelings."

Whoa, I clung to his every word, trying to reinflate my collapsed perceptions. I swung my arms and saw a trail of multiple hands go before my face. I wanted to reach out and touch my friends, hoping that my hand would go into their bodies, grabbing hold of their hearts. We then all partied to the Beatles' *Rubber Soul* album, which I had never heard before. I played a silly game with a pretty hippie girl as John sang "Norwegian Wood." It felt like it went on forever.

The one thing that I liked about LSD was that it was a self-sufficient drug as opposed to the others that needed continual replenishment. Acid worked a strong twelve-hour shift. Long after the others had paired off and retired to rooms unknown, I stayed up and listened to every record they had. At dawn, as I neared the end of the record collection, I came across someone named Tim Hardin. I put his record on and listened to "How Can We Hang On to a Dream" and "The Lady Came from Baltimore." I was never as happy or enlightened as I was that sun-filled acid dawning. Heroin addiction, racial problems, and all of the other harsh obstacles that the time period trafficked in were downsized into mere speed bumps.

I sped up the construction of my new image, that of a Black John Lennon. I was no longer interested in any particular racial affiliation. I wanted to belong to the world. Chuck called a meeting with me about finalizing the details of the drug-talk tour. When I arrived, to my surprise I was reunited with my old good buddy, Noel Velasquez. Noel had just been released from this relatively new establishment tool, the drug rehabilitation program. The early rehab programs were about ridicule and debasement, the theory being that one could shame an addict out of his evil ways.

Part of Noel's shame package was the alteration of his appearance. His hair was cut really low in a time when afros held the property rights on cool Black heads. This took three inches off of his height, diminishing his street-fierce aura. Noel was no longer the emaciated heroin atrocity I'd last seen, but a stocky, compact canister of nitroglycerin who did not take ridicule easily. He was self-conscious about being Puerto Rican. In those days Puerto Ricans were often at the bottom of the butt of derisive ethnic humor. He enjoyed using his antagonists' epithets as motivation to prove them wrong by rubbing their asses in their own vitriol. Noel's quick mind and facile wit enabled him to field all comers like a fullback picking off blitzing linebackers.

Noel came from a large family. Unlike many other Latino immigrants, the Velasquezes learned English and assimilated quickly. Unfortunately, their pigment quotient rose above acceptable White entry levels, so the only brand of Americanism at their disposal was the rich Black culture. This handsome olive-skinned family presented themselves well. Noel's older brother, Barry, was particularly bright. I first became aware of Barry during my Boys Club days. He was one of the first prep-school phenoms and acted as a prime role model and spokesperson for the initiative. Barry was the guest speaker at the first orientation dinner after my selection as one of the "chosen." His speech was eloquent, reflecting all of the tools of the educated White boy, enhanced by the sweet flow of a Latin dancer. Barry was as polished a neighborhood gem as I had ever witnessed.

Noel and I met on Chuck's first football team. He was a smallish, round, fleshy, cheeky terror on the defensive line. It was not a glamour position, but his tenacity and surprising athleticism made people take notice. He was a year and a half younger than me, so he was on the outside looking in on the elite portion of that team. Despite our entrenched classism, I had to admit that even at the age of ten, Noel was the team's most talented defensive player. He would have been a big star the following year, if the funds hadn't dried up at Chuck's door. Noel and I lost touch with each other, until we met again several years later at one of my more popular places to renew old friendships, the edge of a heroin cooker.

Every morning we would meet in front of Benjamin Franklin High School, adoringly known as "junkie paradise." Noel and I put together ten sets of works (drug paraphernalia); each package contained an eyedropper, needle, cooker, and cotton. We rented the package whole to junkies who wanted to hit quick, eschewing the hassle of carrying and maintaining works. The early session began at 7:30 A.M., and Noel and I would pick off all of the thirsty addicts whose bodies were aching.

When Chuck approached Noel asking if he was interested in teaming up with me on our Just Say No campaign, he jumped at it. It was important for him to get his dignity back, and he was smart enough to understand that chasing that white lady was no longer the way to do it. Chuck formally introduced the idea of "The Boys Who Came Back" tour. "I want you two motherfuckers to rap passionately about drugs, 'cause everybody's listening."

Noel and I enthusiastically embraced recovery and were articulate enough to carry the flag praising the merits of sobriety. We would touch lightly on marijuana, because White parents had a bug up their asses about it, so we couldn't sell our honest belief that the weed was more antidote than hindrance. The sexiest part of the drug scare was heroin, and Chuck knew we could cook on that subject. It wouldn't be long before we would put together a successful presentation that smoked every audience we would appear before.

After that meeting Noel and I went on a long walk around the 'hood. We walked to 116th Street and Lenox Avenue and stood in front of the recently constructed temple and main headquarters of the New York chapter of the Nation of Islam. We had both been well educated on the Nation and its mission. Any time you were incarcerated, the influence of the Nation of Islam was there to draw a clear distinction between good and bad, offering you the opportunity to choose the former. I had Noel rolling with laughter as I told the story of me and a couple of other dope fiends copping heroin in a spot on 115th Street, west of Lenox. In order for us to get there, we had to pass the temple. At the time, a small, red, dynamic, turbo-rapping brother would speak to people outside of the temple. To maximize his impact, he pointed at my boys and me, citing us as examples of what this country had done to its lost Black souls.

"Look at them," the dynamic orator exhorted as we shamefully picked up our pace, seeking to outrace his pointed finger. Malcolm had been dead for several years, but this brother was cut from the same quality of cloth. The power of his rap rattled the walls of one's soul with each fiery blast of protestation. "They're searching for their souls!" The Nation of Islam's conservative, disciplined doctrine made street niggers nervous, so we started to run. We had no clue at the time that the man I was talking about was the young minister Louis Farrakhan. This brother's brand of Black pride would someday cast its influence over a million men.

Throughout that walk Noel and I talked about the new dream Chuck had laid at our feet. We decided that this time we would spin heroin before heroin spun us. It was a great conversation. We almost felt like kids again, with something new and positive to be excited about. The high rivaled that of heroin's, tipping the scale with its newness. As we headed east toward home, I decided to take the big leap and tell Noel about the changes I'd been undergoing, using Lennon as my Geiger counter in the search for a new me. Noel was fascinated as I told him about my undercover conversion and the Beatles effect. Surprised and befuddled, he stated, "Last time I saw you, you was ready to throw a nigger down a flight of stairs, 'cause he was fucking with your shot. What happened? How'd you become Dick Clark?" We laughed our asses off as we moved further east, passing the solid mass of hard-drug addicts nodding in various still poses. We wove our way easily through the fright museum, empowered by clean energy.

Noel's pivotal contribution was his declaration that if we were to play with the hippie shit, it had to be done balls first. We agreed that we had no interest in fucking with the "White boys' 'no war' bullshit." If LBJ felt that America had to put its foot up somebody's ass other than ours, we were with him all the way. The anti-military movement never made it uptown. Black folks had spent two centuries trying to get into the army; it was a step up. But aside from that, the hippie White-boy game was live. It would play an important role in the success of the "Boys Who Came Back" tour.

At this time Chuck met and developed a relationship with a cool White cat named Jerry Brandt. Jerry had caught our choral group wreaking joyous devastation on an audience and was knocked out by them. He thought they had potential, and at the time Jerry's gut reactions were influencing the entire new music scene. Jerry was a Sam Cooke–Abe Lastfogel production—a former William Morris agent with a genuine Black groove. He built the new music scene's pipeline to the Morris Agency. Jerry somehow sold the old guard on the potential of representing a young blues band from England that was practicing Neanderthal cool. After viewing the group and listening to the music, the Morris power cats, with clothes pins firmly secured on their noses, gave the go-ahead for Jerry to introduce the Rolling Stones to America.

Jerry convinced other talented young agents to move in his direction instead of hanging around NBC's studios thirsting for a tumble from the likes of Bob Hope, Lucille Ball, and other establishment icons. One of his Morris Agency protégés, David Geffen, would become an important coauthor of the how-to book for the new age of a higher sky. After leaving the William Morris Agency, Jerry opened The Electric Circus in the East Village on Eighth Street, a cutting-edge palace in which the likes of Hendrix and Sly and the Family Stone played.

On the day we met Jerry, he had come into the center with a guy with long blond hair wearing hippie attire. The cat was shy to the point of docility, and, because of his long hair, completely unrecognizable. When Jerry introduced him to us as an actor named John Voight from the freako movie *Midnight Cowboy*, we were impressed. It was pure Jerry Brandt to make his initial splash with an Oscar-caliber card in his desk.

Jerry spoke easily about his relationship with the great soul singer Sam Cooke, and how he had learned the tenets of true integration and harmony at the feet of the man he described as magic. Unfortunately, after a legendary stint in gospel music, where his great voice and God-given soul wiped out all comers, Sam's career had taken a wide secular turn into fame and fortune, subsequently careening off course into tragedy. An enraged woman shot him in a shitty motel under dank circumstances. The loss was incalculable. Nonetheless, Sam Cooke injected Black proteins into Jerry's DNA, greasing his smooth passage into the 'hood.

Jerry was hot to make the choral group stars. He made the bold move of booking them at a fund-raiser for Mayor John Lindsay that was to be held at Tavern on the Green. The host of the event was the Black crossover star Pearl

Bailey. The choral group had begun to add elements that would mature into some serious gospel-rock, a mixture of traditional church stomp-'em-up with insightful contemporary lyrics. They brought the house down that night. Noel and I were proud to share a peripheral attachment to our conquering brethren.

After letting it all hang out, White folks untangled themselves and cleared the aisles. Pearl Bailey came onstage and said, "I think that these kids are just fantastic!" After loud applause, she said, "It would be a shame if these kids didn't have an opportunity to take their music on the road." More applause, and the chorus just went giddy with excited squeals. Bailey, exhibiting her blessed comedic timing, turned to them and deadpanned, "I wouldn't go packing my bags just yet." The audience and choral members responded with a harmonious laugh.

The choral group's new fortune proved a boon for the center's health, acting as a turn-on to those who counted. Foundations, city agencies, and other prime do-givers descended upon the center as though it was a hot new IPO. Despite the addition of Jerry Brandt's savvy, it all came back to Chuck. Once White folks saw that he didn't bite unreasonably, they viewed him as uniquely cool and independent and danced excitedly to his rhythm. Chuck was also hitting the bull's-eye with our "Boys Who Came Back" tour. It catapulted Noel and me into some rarefied air. We came off like grizzled old street veterans who had seen the light. Noel and I played schools, churches, and homes throughout the tri-state area. We waxed poetic, dressing down our horrible experiences, while being careful to inject enough titillation to elicit amazement and buckets of sympathy.

I never thought that you could bullshit substantive people into petting a rattlesnake, but I was wrong. We were always careful to remain focused and not let the adoration jar our discipline. Once, in a high school cafeteria, somewhere in a White slice of Jersey, Noel was on a great roll, with everyone hanging on each word, when he slipped and said, "Despite how good it all felt, we knew that the White lady had to die." Dead silence in the room as the loving faces transformed and the warmth of the crowd hit a cold patch. I feared the scent of vigilantism would turn our cute little movie into a version of Henry Fonda's film. *The Ox-Bow Incident.* I stepped in and meandered through a touchy explanation for the usage of a White woman as a metaphor for heroin seduction. We had broken our cardinal rule: Don't say anything that might force the benefactors back on their heels.

As time went on and we got more of these gigs under our belts, the shtick subsided and was replaced by honest, thought-provoking sentiments on heroin's destructive effects. At the tour's peak we would go off on these gigs by ourselves. Chuck's warm parting sentiments were, "If you two niggers fuck this up, I'm gonna shoot both of you." Heartened by his vote of confidence, we immediately went buck wild. Who could have predicted that the hard life of heroin addiction would lead to the soft life and quasi-celebrity of talking about it?

Our first gig alone was at Bridgeport University in Connecticut. Because this was the first college we would speak to, we knew we had to be hipper. We tossed ideas back and forth, trying to come up with the proper balance that would turn kids on while not turning their adults off. After a strenuous, unsuccessful attempt at coming up with a satisfactory balance, we said the hell with it and decided to play to the adults, because they were the ones who would furnish the great food and ass-stroking we'd grown accustomed to.

We hooked up with three color-blind hippie girls and a guy. They took us back to their dormitory. As we approached the living quarters, the gentle, sardonic melody of the Doors song "Crystal Ship," from their first album, scored the exotic vibe that hung in the air. We went upstairs and entered a room that was loaded with guys and gals who were stoned on their asses. Apparently our message would take a while to settle in. We both downed a dose of white mescaline, and the shit was on.

"This ain't one of those bullshit street highs we've been dealing in. This is an experience," I said. "If you hit any scary spots, roll with it." Noel smiled and floated across the room and dove on the bed between four people, losing himself in their playful sexual silliness. Soon I would find myself nude atop a naked woman with two long braids that seemed to go on forever.

White youths immersed in hippie counterculture were the perfect soul mates for emerging former Jim Crow victims. It was a significant tradeoff. The hippies wanted our freedom of expression, and we wanted access to the main gate. The youth culture made stars out of twelve-dollar-a-night shit-bucket groaners, pumping out Black misery in faded blues clubs. If Muddy Waters was dependent upon Black audiences, who already knew how to move their mojos and had little interest in the pain, he'd have starved on the chitlin' circuit. Somehow these old rogues were perfect for the World War II generation's children. Postwar noveau White growing pains flooded the fifties with a sterility that tasted like castor oil to many of the pubescent boomers, leaving a void that only three chords and a howl could scratch. White parents from the period nobly sought to give their children the advantages they'd missed out on during their Depression-influenced childhoods, but unfortunately they had no antidote for the underdeveloped mojo.

The birth-control pill was an early license to steal sexual favors from women who had yet to catch on to the more important benefits that came with having control of their reproductive capabilities. During this time period, male sexual larceny was the crime *du jour*. White boys who didn't want to fight the war and White women who no longer wanted to live under the pressure of their male companions' thumbs seized upon the spirit of the civil rights breakthroughs, creating a momentary platform from which we all stood and yelled at the ruling class. At the sound of the decade's starting pistol, the race was on to share music, ideas, and sexual gratification until you dropped. It was a grand ball, and we danced through countless sunrises.

The party lasted only a few years. White kids would soon grow up and become more tolerant of White supremacy. Many of the old Jim Crow divisions would reappear, as the former war hollerers and the kitchen criers blew past their Black coconspirators. By the mid seventies the issue of communal integration had fallen from sight like the Strawberry Alarm Clock.

THIRTEEN

Fresh off of our successful tour, Noel and I had carved out a cool and quirky brand of stardom. The tour was helping draw funds to the center. Chuck's dream continued to expand to the point of his introducing falconry to our array of unusual activities. Chuck was able to buy two falcons that sat atop perches hung from the ceiling of the center. With their little leather hoods over their heads, they blinked incessantly as they peered down upon our merry party of madness. Under Jerry Brandt's management, our newly named choral group, the Voices of East Harlem, were the glitter stars of the center. They were doing a benefit at the Felt Forum, which was a part of Madison Square Garden, for our go-go Clintonesque mayor, John Lindsay.

John Lindsay had developed strong ties with the Black community, always careful to lend an ear if not a hand. His courageous, unifying walks down the streets of Harlem presented an important image for the illusion of integration. Lindsay had become particularly interested in Chuck, who was building his miracle a mile or so away from Gracie Mansion, the mayor's official residence. Lindsay took an interest in the program, and when his people saw the Voices of East Harlem and their scintillating brand of hip Gospel, it was a relationship made for the times.

The Voices did their normal wall-melting performance representing the best of Black youth—talented, forward-thinking young people who valued education and held an innocent desire to move people with their music. The gospel element helped in this effort because White audiences were assured that there was an old-fashioned, Black Christian base beneath the group's modestly scented Black-power message. The Voices had shed their conventional orange blazers and black pleated shirts, adorning working-class jeans and dungaree jackets with red, black, and green fists, a symbol of the Black Power Movement, painted on their backs. Lindsay's people put them on the A-list of their entertainment fundraising initiative. They never failed to loosen the hips and groins of the Kennedy, Johnson, and Clayton Powell Democratic operatives.

"That shit's like gold in the bank," Chuck would counsel.

That night in the Felt Forum was an entertainment bonanza. Everyone was there: Barbra Streisand belting out, "On a Clear Day"; the great Tony Bennett; and a young, dominantly attractive master showperson, Merv Griffin, hosting the affair. Noel and I had a field day sopping up celebrity gravy with delicious bits of our drug tale. As incredible as all of these stars were, Noel and I were the standouts in the green room. There was so much food that I took four bags of cold cuts and other things with the people's full encouragement. We wore our best Black kids' smiles, which really moved these cats. It was a dizzying experience, scored by a hit song of the times, "Give a Damn" by Spanky and Our Gang.

Viewing this mix would become an important memory to me—a visual snapshot of evidence that it was possible for the race and class differences to mix well if stirred unself-consciously. Streisand was young and gracious, with no apparent Nigraphobia, which was impressive because she was the new, undisputed queen of entertainment. Surrounded by Black folks lifting glasses in admiration, she jammed like real people. My favorite personal memory of the affair came when a scrawny little guy did his "woe is me" standup-comedy routine. The comedian said that he had been screwed up from birth because his mother had breast-fed him through falsies. I fell off my chair, both from the humor and the shock of someone being witty and clever enough to civilize vulgarity. This neurotic little fellow, named Woody Allen, was on to something, and I made a mental note to like this guy.

It was a great night for Chuck, as he held his own among the evening's power wigs. I learned a lot from watching him that night. He later explained his success away airily by stating, "There is no such thing as a place called there." This alluded to his firm belief, often stated, "There are no places, only moments. You can play even up with anyone because oxygen is free." Philosophy is one thing, but watching a virile, dark, powerful man, who was literally run out of Mississippi, back his words up with performance, was awesome.

That night I met my first press agent. He was one of Merv Griffin's troops. He told me that his job was to make celebrities seem bigger than they were.

"So, you guys are professional bullshit artists?" I replied respectfully.

"You got it, kid," was the response.

On another occasion, Noel and I made an appearance in one of the citadels of rich, White, quasi-liberal money at a private party given by a prominent stockbroker. It was a huge tented affair on the grounds of a mansion in Greenwich, Connecticut. The Voices of East Harlem performed and had the many stockbrokers and their wives out of their seats stomping in the aisles. Plaid pants and madras jackets were the odd threads for White males in the dough. The women were thin and beautiful, sporting their luscious frailties that seemed to bank well for them.

As usual the Voices blew the doors off of the event. Equally reliable was the reaction to Noel and me. Anonymous rich White folks were the easiest lay in the bordello. Chuck got up and gave a short speech, and the house, which had not yet settled from its choral quake, offered up props generally reserved for a messiah. It was madness. After the excitement subsided, Noel and I wanted to know who the hell owned this joint. "The cat's name is Brokaw," Chuck said, "a White cat with a legitimate street game. I like him because he's got the kind of balls that would put the average nigger in jail. But I guess that's the way it works with White folks."

Later Noel and I were approached by a man in his late forties who was ecstatic from a potent combination of music and vodka. We introduced ourselves, and he smiled and put one arm around Noel and the other around me. Though I didn't know it at the time, this was a wing I would reside under periodically for the next ten years.

"You kids are pretty good kids," he said. We nodded, trying to suppress our urge to laugh at the way he slurred his words. His grip tightened around our shoulders as he continued, "You wanna go to Hotchkiss?" What the hell is a Hotchkiss? We dutifully nodded in the affirmative, figuring it was a good bet that Hotchkiss was not another correctional facility. After giving us several playful, tough punches on the arm, he repeated, "You wanna go to Hotchkiss?"

"Sure," I responded as though receiving a dare.

"Good, you're going to Hotchkiss."

Upon hearing the music start up again, he half-danced, half-waddled back to the other stockbrokers-turned-gospel-stompers who were heating up for another dose of choral magic. Noel and I didn't give the drunk's odd invitation much thought, assuming that gospel music and vodka had flipped him out. We went over Chuck's way and were surprised to discover that our daddy figure for the night owned the joint. We'd been jiving with Bill Brokaw. Like Doberman pinschers with a burglar in their sights, we felt our ears stand up straight.

Noel and I later cased the premises and were blown away. The only reference point we had was Jed Clampett's joint, but Brokaw was no hillbilly. Because of his cool hospitality, we promised each other we wouldn't steal anything. In those days we engaged in good-sense self-policing, avoiding fuckups. We entered a bedroom and, like kids, jumped on the huge beds as if they were trampolines. As the opulence flashed brighter and brighter with each room entered, we fantasized about our future. In the midst of all that positivity, a rare moment in our lives emerged. Without a trace of illegal chemicals in our systems, we were tripping on life.

The community center chose to reward itself with a flashy banquet honoring the close of an unbelievably successful year. The boys wore tuxedos and dinner jackets, and the girls shimmied into evening gowns. It was a joyous event. Each of the center's many activities was honored with trophies and certificates for outstanding achievement. Our football teams won four out of five championships that year, and were feted continuously with a steady stream of affirmative hardware.

Chuck, the master showman at the height of his powers who could have talked P. T. Barnum into being his office boy, unveiled a new award that was not on the program. I had been told about the award minutes before the presentation. Chuck had come up with the idea of rewarding Noel with a trophy inscribed with our tour slogan, "The Boy Who Came Back."

"Didn't I come back?" I asked, my teenaged selfishness readying itself for takeoff.

"Noel needs it more. You got a jump on him in all this shit. Let him catch up some."

"I think that's bullshit," I whispered.

Chuck whispered back, "Do you think I care? We're all here under a bigger plan than any single individual. So, if you don't want 250 people to see a trophy protruding from your ass part, play ball."

I played ball. He was right. Noel had had a harder climb through this new terrain, having to learn on the fly many things I had been injecting into my veins since early childhood. Deep thrill lines sculpted Noel's facial expression as he approached the podium to accept the award. He relished the fact that he had been singled out for this very special accomplishment. We shook hands and hugged, and I felt great for him. It was the last award of the evening, and flashbulbs popped as Noel and I, dressed in our classy night threads, mugged for the camera. The ham in us baked under the extraordinary attention. Noel would become the neighborhood's number-one symbol for having beaten the scourge that had laid so many of us to rest.

Jerry Brandt was there with a pack of happening White cats that picked up the groove immediately, crossing over with aplomb. Jerry announced that everyone was invited to the Electric Circus on the house. Excitedly, I rushed to my date to ask if she was game for the trip. And my new girlfriend, Gerri, was with it.

Weeks later Noel and I and several of our peers were sitting around with Chuck engaged in an ideas free-for-all about how we were going to approach the summer months. We were interrupted by a call. "Yo, D and Nell, somebody called Brokaw is on the phone." After an initial puzzled glance at each other, our memories kicked in and we both lit up in remembrance of our drunken power player. Noel certified our conclusion. "The White dude with the Jed Clampett–sized crib. You talk to him, D, and freak it off with some smooth White shit."

I happily accepted the assignment and took the call. As it turned out, it was not Brokaw; it was his secretary, and she made an appointment for Noel and me to go downtown to Wall Street, where Mr. Brokaw wanted to see us. I accepted but was left in the dark as to what the old man wanted. I returned to the group and told of the invitation, and a swirl of possibilities was fired at Noel and myself. Chuck, being the voice of reason, said, "It could be anything. The deal is they callin', and your job right now is as easy as it gets, which is go down and see what the man is talkin' about." Noel and I chose Chuck's calm route, which was to hop the iron horse and head for the Taj Mahal of coin, Wall Street, circa 1969.

William Brokaw had met Chuck on the local community fund-raising trail. Brokaw had done extensive charity work for the Boys Club of New York and developed a keen eye for good people in need of help and support. When he discovered Chuck's work, they were an instant groove. Brokaw loved the fact that Chuck was a no-excuses, be-the-absolute-best-you-can evangelist. They would discover after exchanging props through a short period of tough-guy jousting, that their philosophies about pride, compassion, and balls made them mates. Brokaw felt that those who were left out of the American miracle deserved a chance to compete on a level playing field, and his principles about these issues were laid in concrete.

The early consensus of the center brain trust was that Brokaw was a gangster, if not in deed than in spirit—and we liked that. Brokaw had a rough truthfulness that you rarely found in White folks with good intentions. Tough, meaningful confrontations between the racial factions, where honesty and positive disagreements might have produced longer-range solutions, were often thwarted exposing a lack of depth at the core of these overly hyped dalliances.

Brokaw's ribs had too much rock in them for that kind of nonsense. I would describe him in the language of today's oft-touted oxymoron—a compassionate conservative. His edict that competition among all of our human resources made for a stronger America was 99 percent bullshit-free.

Decades later, Yankee uber-owner George M. Steinbrenner would reach out to two troubled Black superstars, Dwight Gooden and Darryl Strawberry. They had both drenched baseball's good graces with cocaine. Black drug addiction viewed through White lenses flash criminal as opposed to medical, so much of the press and fan base beat the drum earmarking these radioactive brothers for a toxic-waste facility. Steinbrenner bulled through that stereotype, offering a genuine hand with a clear warning that read: Don't fuck with me or you'll be scraping your kneecaps off the pavement. Raw, straight up, and racist-free sandpaper philanthropy, a page right out of Bill Brokaw's playbook.

As Noel and I rode the subway to our meeting with destiny, we were very much like two Curious Georges on our way to see the man with the yellow hat.

GRAY LIFE

Only a dark cocoon before I get my
gorgeous wings and fly away.

—**Joni Mitchell,**
"The Last Time I Saw Richard"

FOURTEEN

Summer 2001

I've decided to go back to my old neighborhood for a memorial basketball game. The James Weldon Johnson Housing Project in East Harlem is holding its twenty-fifth annual block party commemorating the premature death of one of the project's special sons. The Al Murph Memorial Basketball Tournament is being held on 115th Street and Lexington Avenue. Al Murph died in his early twenties, peaceably, while riding his bike in Central Park. In an attempt to avoid a pothole, he lost control of his bike, hit his head, and by sundown had met his maker. He was a man who took his future seriously, ducking drug addiction. His oldest brother, Olaf, was the neighborhood's outstanding entrepreneur who built a solid sporting goods operation. Each summer he sponsored the event, and it slowly caught on. The occasion grew to the point where most of the project's residents, past and present, would attend.

I head for the heart of the festivities, where each building has its own barbecue going. The great, well-seasoned food Puerto Ricans and Black folks are famous for dominate one's nostrils. It has been a long time since I have seen this many Black people in one place. As I approach the court my attention is captured by a breathtaking basketball move by one of the young bloods. I get caught up in the show-time basketball, one of the ghetto's most endearing American beauty marks. I envision my young self running on the same court, playing my guts out against tough competitors like Al Murph. My daydream is broken by the sound of a familiar voice.

"Hey, man, you came!"

It is Olaf. We embrace.

"Here, man."

He hands me a T-shirt reserved for the founding brothers and gives me a deep Black handshake before putting his arm around my shoulder. His actions scream "Welcome."

One of my few remaining live brothers from the center's original core approaches. It is Stephen Brown. Stephen was the center's golden boy who mastered football, archery, and the preparatory school, Tabor Academy, with an ease that surpassed any of us other private-school attendees. He was a couple of years younger than me, and I was something of a protective big brother to him, an easy task because Stephen was pure light. Unfortunately, Stephen baffled us all by getting caught up in the neighborhood's train wreck. Illegal substances led to several incarcerations. He has just finished his most recent stretch in hell dressed in bars.

Stephen looks great and is as bright as ever. After a near-tears reunion, we hop in my car and tour the perimeter of the neighborhood, enlivening our memories. We pull up to the corner of 115th Street, and, standing in front of a liquor store, is a beaten hulk of a man begging for spare change. Initially, he is unrecognizable, another cancerous polyp on the body ghetto, but upon closer inspection, we recognize him. It is the great Herba Lee, one of the most influential men from our past.

Thirty-five years ago Herba Lee was the neighborhood's self-appointed guardian. Although he was the toughest, most courageous individual among us, he had a heart of gold. Herba Lee, who was a few years older, took it upon himself to strong-arm all of us young twelve-year-olds through our basic training for ghetto survival. Stephen and I both immediately recall many instances of Herba Lee coming to our aid when older neighborhood slugs sought to intimidate us. He had taught us how to fight hand-to-hand combat, as well as supplying us with the verbal bullets needed to defend ourselves against the ghetto's oral assassins. He would also kick our asses if we did not account well for ourselves in confrontations with our peers from rival neighborhoods.

We pull the car in front of the liquor store, and I yell, "Herba Lee!" Initially, there is no response, and I shout again, "Herba Lee, it's me, Dennis!" This seems to penetrate. He turns in our direction, and the sight I see is enough to make me ill. His great athletic body is bloated beyond recognition. As he approaches the car, his face reveals an ugly, lengthy scar that defines his overall disfigurement. He has difficulty speaking, I later learned, due to damaged vocal chords.

"Is that Dennis Watlington? Oh shit!" he croaks.

Herba Lee was an exercise in contradictions. He made sure we went to school, even though he had dropped out. He'd lecture, "Never trust niggers more than books." He was a gun-toting, street-scorching proponent of integration who preached, "The White man can't hurt you with hate until you hate yourself. As long as you can meet White folks with your head up, they'll have to deal. But it's up to you."

Herba Lee's tactics had been effective. If you didn't heed his words, he would beat the shit out of you. During the heyday of the Herba Lee doctrine, I probably got the most ass-whuppings, for two reasons. One, I had the biggest mouth; and two, he was particularly fond of me. By the time I was in high school, Herba was sliding slowly down the heroin-greased pole, but he still preached, "Nigger, if you don't take all that big brain power of yours and do something with it, I'm gonna kill you." When I was going through my heroin addiction, the person that I avoided the most, aside from Chuck, was Herba Lee. Even though he was hooked himself, he was a strong proponent of "Do what I say, not what I do."

I get out of the car and hug Herba Lee, who smells like a cheap wine distillery. It take all the strength I have not to cry, because ghetto niggers don't cry in public.

"What you niggers doin' here?"

I tell him I am tripping down memory lane.

"You look healthy," he says. "Real healthy. I heard you been doin' some serious shit with yo' life."

I catch him up on my recent past and he says, "You married a White girl?"

"Not only did I marry a White girl, I married a cop's daughter."

He delivers a belly laugh over that one, and the smile on his face reminds me of him at the height of his powers.

"How did your life get away from you, man?" I ask.

"Shit, it's always hard out here," he says. "I'm just another nigger who can't pull the trigger. But you is me, and you doin' something good. And I raised you, so I can't be all that bad."

We go into the liquor store, and I buy the biggest bottle of cheap wine on the shelf. Along with the bottle I give Herba Lee twenty dollars. "I'll never be able to repay the debt I owe you," I tell him. "I've carried a piece of you in me wherever I've been." Herba Lee is so happy that his bent posture becomes erect for the first time. He shatters the speed record for unscrewing a bottle cap, takes a huge hit from his poison, and says, "You'se mine. If you fuck up yo' game over bullshit, then I'll kill ya."

After we depart Stephen and I talk about how things became so bad in East

Harlem. As we patch together our pile of broken dreams, Stephen comments "Look, at least there was a time when we had it all going on."

"Yeah," I answer. "We corned the market on hope."

"And friendship," Stephen says proudly as we trade old-fashioned palm-up fives.

1969

Noel and I sat in the reception area of Brokaw Capital Management waiting for our surprise package to be unwrapped. The office workers moved briskly, doing business. Secretaries' fingers raced across the keys of the latest electric typewriters. Men were dressed in their war clothes, conservative suits with well-appointed ties placed firmly beneath stiff no-bullshit collars Noel and I adorned our normal street kicks; our faded dungarees looked out of place in this smudgeless land of precise action.

We were ushered into his office and greeted by a clear-eyed, steel-jawed, sober Mr. Brokaw. There was none of the swiveled-hipped gaiety that had marked our first meeting. We'd never met a White man with Nixonian characteristics and LBJ's agenda. He didn't string things out with pleasantries but got right down to brass tacks. Mr. Brokaw pointed his finger and ordered, "I want you young men to go to Hotchkiss." His exhortation was delivered with Westmoreland-like authority. It was as though we were being sent off to war.

"Mr. Brokaw, what is a Hotchkiss?" Noel timidly asked.

"One of the finest preparatory schools in America," Brokaw replied.

Noel unconsciously blurted out, "School!"

He covered his mouth with his hand to restrain himself from speaking further. My mind shouted, "Uh-oh!"

In our haste to run off with our imaginary millions, we'd forgotten that odd Hotchkiss name that Brokaw had tossed around that night. Mr. Brokaw talked of Hotchkiss's long list of prominent alumni—national power figures and captains of industry who meant little to us. I began to recoil with fear and disappointment as I thought, "Here we go again." On the other hand, Noel was excited. I scratched my head, befuddled, and mouthed the words to Noel, "School!" He shrugged his shoulders as though this was a minor detail.

Brokaw took great pains to point out that he viewed us as assets to the school. "You're going to be as good for the school as the school will be for you. You'll offer a social kick in the ass to all the privileged kids who are being shielded too much from the real world." Noel responded well to the assertion that we could be proactive influences, veritable ambassadors from a foreign country called Harlem. The fact that Noel and I had long since pissed off school was a minor detail glossed over like the fine print that usually sinks a something-for-nothing enthusiast.

On this day the big guy had all the answers. He acknowledged the fact that we were barely educated in the ways of the well-schooled, privileged, top-drawer White kids but blew it off with the ease of Ralph Kramden, declaring that very important detail a mere "bag of shells." His next surprise was that he wanted us to take a series of tests. I froze, and the joy in Noel's face vanished. Brokaw detected our apprehension and explained that these would not be regular tests of math and science. They would be administered by a psychiatrist. The goal was to determine whether or not we had the aptitude and IQ to think with the White boys.

"Are you sure you know what you're doing?" I sputtered, trying to be honest without blowing the deal. "You know that we were hooked on heroin?"

He ran my question through his I-can-do-anything rich-White-guy mind and asked, "You kids have any problems now?"

"No," we both stated proudly.

Noel then added additional assurance. "We've been clean for months."

Brokaw said, "Good, that's behind you. It's time to move on."

As simplistic a dismissal of heroin addiction as I would ever hear. Mr. Brokaw then introduced us to another man who identified himself as a psychiatrist. He was a doctor sans stethoscope, but he did have a briefcase filled with an odd set of cubes and cards. After a few head-patting pleasantries, he announced that he was going to test us. The doctor pulled out his toylike gimmicks and began to ask us questions of the common sense variety. We relaxed and answered confidently. His smile indicated that we were doing well.

Finally, he pulled out a set of cards that had weird splatterings of ink on them. He explained that he wanted us to respond to what we saw. Noel's first answer to the doctor's first card was "spilled ink." We all laughed, and the doctor explained that he wanted us to form real images. He flipped another card over and asked, "Tell me, Dennis, what do you see?" After studying the pattern for a moment, I replied, "A donkey." The doctor was delighted, smiling affirmatively. I smiled back, thinking that this was some silly shit. Noel responded to his pattern with more time and deeper study, concluding that he saw a bazooka. Again, judging from the doctor's reaction, we felt as though we were so intelligent we could skip Hotchkiss and make a beeline right for the Ivy League.

After the test was concluded, Brokaw and Dr. Strange Tools huddled as we waited. I began to express my doubts about the process. "How the fuck can they tell if we can add or subtract by ink spots that look like donkeys? White folks are confusing as hell. If you would have told the police that you saw a bazooka, they would have locked your ass up."

Noel laughed and said, "Rich White folks always have some rhyme to their reason. We just learnin' their game. You could tell why so many of them is in high places,'cause their tests is so easy."

After that profound discovery, Brokaw and the doctor came back and delivered their verdict. The doctor sermonized, "It's obvious that you young men are very bright, and I see no reason why with disciplined application you two shouldn't be able to hold your own at the school in Lakeville."

"What?" we both said.

Brokaw chimed in. "That's the town in Connecticut where the school is . . . and . . ." He broke into a big smile, offering a glimpse of the face we had met in Greenwich. "The town that will be your new home-away-from-home!"

"Does that mean we're in?" Noel asked.

Brokaw replied, "You bet you're in. You two kids are going to make us all proud."

We would soon discover that Brokaw wasn't just an enthusiastic Hotchkiss alumnus; he was the head of the board of trustees, the big cheese.

Noel said, "Yeah!" I remained silent. I didn't want to say what I really thought, which was "Hell no!"

Noel and I were dazed as we left Brokaw's office, he hurdling toward exhilaration as I straddled the bar of disappointment. I would wonder out loud intermittently, "School?"

The next day Noel announced to Chuck and others that we were going to the Hotchkiss School. After a few moments of cautious contemplation, examining the angles, Chuck asked, "You mean they gon take you two criminal niggers in right off the streets? What did y'all do, give the man some of that heroin?" Everyone laughed, as Chuck continued. "You two niggers gonna be our pipeline to the White kids oil fields. I told you that something good was gonna come from this. Wasn't long ago you two niggers wasn't worth twenty dollars apiece on a good day. Now you getting cut into a chance to make White-folks dollars."

Noel was jazzed. I told Chuck, "I have a problem with this." Everything froze. "Chuck, I don't want to go to prep school."

"You don't what?" Chuck said.

"I don't want to go to a place called Hotchkiss."

"Let me see your arms," he said.

"What do you mean?"

"You must be high off that shit, because it's the only way you could possibly tell me that this man is gonna drop something in your lap this big and you talkin' shit. You gots to be back in your cooker. You the best nigger out of the heroin pile to deal with this high-powered White-boy shit, so you'se been drafted."

"It ain't all that it's cracked up to be," I said. "Rich, competitive White folks is a bitch 'cause they don't stop. This shit ain't about education, man; they want to rule the world. I know shit you don't know, 'cause I lived with them."

"We need nigger rulers too, motherfucker!" Chuck shouted. "This is about dreams, nigger. You ain't stealing televisions and radios now. You gonna be burglarizing them classrooms for knowledge."

"I ain't going!" I challenged.

He grabbed me up by my collar and threw me into a chair. Then Noel let go with a flurry of verbal left hooks. "D, you got to be down. This is the joint. You told me that if we did this shit, something big would happen. You was the leader, and I followed your shit. You'se the first nigger I ever did that with, and we made it. Let's ride this motherfucker out."

"This shit is the wrong way to go," my insanity shouted as I stared the big man in the eye. I had this bad habit of allowing gumption to paint me into a corner. "Once them White boys rope us in with their bells and whistles, we gon' wish we was in Rikers. Fuck this!"

Bam! Chuck hit me with a wicked right hand to the chest, momentarily disconnecting me from my senses. He yelled, "You going!"

"No!" I screamed, immediately wishing I could take it back.

He yanked me out of the chair, and I threw my hands up in a fighting stance. Bad mistake. This was not the best time to assert independence I had yet to acquire. Chuck was once a top-flight boxer in the navy, and he opened up his whole bag filled with rights, lefts, upper cuts, and straight leads. I went flying. He stood over me with his hands on his hips, exerting maximum intimidation, and said, "You going! This ain't about you, and it ain't about today. This is about the future of niggers." I couldn't take any more of his blows; they were getting harder with each exhortation. I succumbed and agreed to go. Everyone celebrated my decision but me. I kept my eyes on Chuck, who was still snorting fire over my reluctance.

Shortly, Noel and I would begin a tour around the neighborhood, accepting goodwill and cheer as the "boys who came back" and were now moving forward. This all struck me as painfully similar to what I'd experienced the last time I was designated to save the Black race. Noel basked in it all, reveling in his virgin undertaking of this absurd responsibility. No matter how hard I tried to nail my brother's feet to the ground, he continued to soar.

Since we were taking the big dive into Whiteness, we proceeded to have the longest, freakiest farewell-before-prep-school party ever. Over a two-week period, we held the first hallucinogen-drenched, rock 'n' roll bash in ghetto history.

Noel and I enticed many of our heroin boys and girls to try acid, mescaline, and peyote. Once they started tripping, we would whack their consciousness with the song "Good Morning" from Sgt. *Pepper's* and go from there. A common refrain would be, "Damn, them long-haired English motherfuckers is bad."

Our party was responsible for a brief Black-hippie trend that swept the neighborhood. For a precious few seconds, introspection and depth replaced anger and suspicion. The outrageous thought replaced the outrageous act. This experience taught me an important lesson about the races. Black people didn't dislike White people because they were White. It was rarely the color that rankled. White folks with authentic do-it fluid were welcome in the ghetto.

Noel and I closed out the summer's party stuck in traffic for four hours trying to get to Woodstock. On the car radio deejays were flipping out over how the Woodstock Nation was overwhelming the tri-state area. We sat lodged in an old green Volkswagen van that Chuck had lent us, in a sea of hippie freaks for as far as we could see in either direction. The peace signs flashed back and forth, bonding our prefab, temporary, auto nation, a brief alliance committed to the practice of sticking its tongue out at Eisenhower's America.

After a whiff of our generation's greatest weekend, Noel and I were catapulted into New England's gold-encrusted learning fixtures. The sixties, however briefly they shined in the ghetto, were gone and so were we.

FIFTEEN

A factor in our uneasiness has been a surprisingly delayed reaction to the infusion of disadvantaged blacks in the school. This year, we have three or four new black students who are much more desperately educationally disadvantaged than any we have had before. They are also much more dynamic and therefore much more highly visible in almost every way. For the first time we are hearing about double standards, lowered standards, and threatened standards. For the first time we are talking about special treatment. Predictably the reaction is not uniformly enthusiastic.

—**Albert William Olsen, Jr.,** headmaster,
The Hotchkiss School, May 1970

New Years Eve, 1970

I stood outside rock impresario Bill Graham's Fillmore East stage door vibrating to the hysteria going on inside. This was the hottest slab of rock 'n' roll heat ever produced: The great Hendrix was performing with his Band of Gypsies. As luck would have it, the Voices of East Harlem were opening the show, an incredible gig. I looked forward to the usual front-row seat and backstage access, but I was thrown a tough-breaking ball in the dirt that exploded at my feet. Chuck was forced to lay down an airtight edict that no one but the Voices and their handful of paid associates could see the show. The concert was in such demand that Graham put a headlock on all comp tickets. It was a stunning blow to my star trip. I was left to shuffle my feet in the late-night cold, with only the strains of music that seeped through the cracks to keep me warm.

Hendrix was the man! He had cultivated his musical chops on that gifted Black caravan of the early sixties, playing behind great Black novas like Little Richard, King Curtis, and the Isley Brothers. The Apollo Theater and other jump-out joints on the chitlin' circuit had been Hendrix's teething rings. He was among the last Black musicians and singers whose art had benefited from Jim Crow segregation. The Jim Crow laws were so tight that Duke Ellington was as limited in his movement as Pigmeat Markham, the great, balloon-lipped. Apollo house comedian. There was little distinction made between ballroom caviar and pool-hall pig knuckles. Black folks were all the same in the eyes of the law. A Black entertainer on the road, regardless of fame or fortune, was forced to truck to the outlands at the end of the day, where segregated facilities awaited them.

The beauty of this forced cohabitation was that the greatest of the old and the greatest of the young were able to rub experiences intimately. Hendrix absorbed every precious trick in the Black entertainment handbook, playing with or learning from the best collection of American artists ever assembled, all courtesy of Mr. Crow himself. These facilities to Black artists on the road were little hothouses laden with cross-pollinating geniuses. A decade later the integration breakthrough would allow the elite Black performers to spread their wings, depleting America's strongest cultural reservoir. Integration would sentence the fertile Jim Crowed chitlin' circuit to the same cold front that claimed the Negro baseball leagues.

As I endured eighteen-degree temperatures, Jimi was tearing it up inside. I stayed on in the off chance that someone would open the backstage door and let me in. I lit a Marlboro and continued to shuffle from one foot to another wishing Noel was there. His Hotchkiss trip was turning sour, and divisive droplets of estrangement had begun to fall on our relationship. Noel was having a tough time making it in the world of the privileged White, a predictable occurrence given the absurdity of our endeavor, but we started out like a house of fire.

A few months earlier Noel and I had been world-beaters on our way to early football practice at the Hotchkiss School. Our close friend and sergeant at arms. Red Machine had come up with a broken-down battered car that barely coughed its way up New York's Route 22. Red tried to navigate, while Noel and I knocked out a bottle of Wild Turkey and laughed through a haze of pot smoke as we told street-war stories, our way of preparing for boarding school. Red Machine kept getting lost, so the three-hour ride stretched into a six-hour party.

We entered the sleepy town of Millerton, New York, around midnight, and the quiet began to sober us up. Everything was so still that it looked like an empty film set. We pulled up to a bait-and-tackle shop. Noel and I got out and looked in the window, while Red fought another round with his map.

"Where the fuck are we?" asked Noel.

"Where you wanted to be," I laughed.

"Hello out there!" Noel shouted, getting off on the echo that carried through the empty streets. "Hey, D, we could rob the whole town before anyone wakes up."

I laughed. "This is a different world, man. They don't do that shit around here."

"Bullshit, every place got thieves."

Red Machine started to grumble, ordering us to get back in the car. He'd figured out that we were a few minutes from our destination. When we crossed the Connecticut line and rolled into the little town of Lakeville, Red said, "This is it," pointing to the road sign. "Lakeville, whatever the fuck that is."

We laughed as we cruised through this four-blink town, and Noel asked, "Where do people hang out, man?"

"You askin' all the wrong shit," I counseled. "Look in front of you." He glared out the windshield. "What do you see?"

"Nothing," he answered.

"Look to each side, what do you see?"

Again he answered, "Nothin'."

"You startin' to get the point."

Noel squirmed a bit and said, "Yo, Red Machine, hurry up and get us to the motherfucking joint."

When we arrived at Hotchkiss, the quiet was unnerving. The car's bad muffler sounded twice as loud as we pulled through the great school's vaunted brick pillars. The campus was well lit, and as we drove a narrow path to the main building, there was a sense of higher calling, demanding the kind of reverence one feels approaching the Lincoln Memorial.

"This motherfucker is too clean," Red Machine tossed, shattering the silence. "Noel, how the fuck you gonna survive in a place this clean."

"You callin' me dirty, man?" Noel inquired unthreateningly.

"No, I ain't talkin' about yo ass. I'm talkin' about anyplace this clean don't have a lot of loopholes to it, and you the kind a nigger who need loopholes."

"That's bullshit, right D?" Noel asked beginning to squirm again.

Sensing his discomfort, I let him down easy. "Don't buy into that shit, man. These joints are a lot dirtier in the daytime."

The place was dead and pulling someone out of bed past midnight and showering them with Wild Turkey breath was a sure way of getting off on the wrong foot. We decided to fend for ourselves. The three of us walked around aimlessly, before gathering the courage to enter one of the dormitories. We crept down the corridor, discovering that there were several empty rooms. The student population had not arrived yet, and the players for early football were sprinkled all over campus. Noel and I unloaded our few bags in one of the rooms, figuring that we would crash for the night and check in in the morning. We offered Red the opportunity to crash with us, but he chose to split. He insisted on getting out because the place gave him the creeps. His parting shot, "You niggers are going to be living in an old White museum. This ain't my speed."

After seeing Red off, we went back to the dorm. Noel stumbled upon a big room with a television and a sofa. We would learn that this was called the Common Room. He flipped on the TV, and a Jimmy Cagney movie, *Angels With Dirty Faces*, was just coming on. After our long, tiring day, this was the perfect way to unwind. I dashed back to our room to get the last of the Wild Turkey, and we watched Pat O'Brien and Jimmy Cagney tame a pack of street toughs before passing out.

Several days later Noel and I were seated on the grass beside the front entrance in a wide-eyed trance. We silently watched the Mercedeses and Porsches file through the brick pillars and pull up the drive. After a while we moved closer to the dormitories in order to sharpen our lustful focus upon the parents and students unloading oodles of expensive stereo equipment, luggage, typewriters, you name it. It was a bizarre situation for Noel and me to be in—two still-wet criminals in a palace with no locks. The well-coifed, amply moisturized mothers doted over their prized offspring. The males were classy Noel Coward–types, who looked like they worked the levers of power and fortune comfortably. The endless procession of stereo equipment fascinated us. It was the first time we had ever seen the word Sony. This was the major leagues.

Noel dug his nails into my arm so deeply it felt like a shot and said, "Damn, D, you mean we can't steal nothing?"

I repeated Chuck's last and most forceful edict before we left. "You two criminal, junkie niggers have to check your ghetto shit at the gate. If you take that shit across them lines, you'll kill it all."

"This shit is torture, D," Noel said, "like a naked lady in your bed and you can't touch her."

One of the mothers, an older Sandra Dee–lookalike who was aging gracefully, focused upon us in passing and offered her best. Fresh-Air-Fund smile. We smiled in kind. "These are some serious White folks," I whispered through the corner of my mouth, "rich and delicate, with top-of-the-line doctors and dentists."

"Their butlers probably polish them right along with the crystal," Noel joked, and we laughed heartily. From that light moment emerged our permanent and respectful nickname for the Hotchkiss elite—crystal White folks. They were void of any visible scuffmarks, residing in the penthouses of advantage, shielded by impenetrable security systems. We were awed by our naive perception. Noel brought it back to our home field, whispering, "I bet none of these White boys get no pussy."

"I bet there's a lot of things we have over these White boys. We just have to find them."

"I'm sure they all shit and piss like everyone else, you think?" Noel quipped.

"I hope so," I tossed and we shared a confidence-stabilizing laugh.

We needed to pump each other's gas because we both sensed that we were in over our heads. But we had advantages as well. We were hardened, slick, quick-minded, quick-tongued, seasoned criminals. Noel and I talked about how we would play these White folks. Should we stay to ourselves, having already witnessed the nauseatingly juvenile immaturity that passed for White-boy fun among the ball players? Noel's aversion to goosing and towel-snapping in the locker room was profound.

"I don't have a lot of stomach for that short-haired. White-boy silliness," he moaned.

"I didn't come here to be with a handful of niggers," I asserted. There were fourteen Black students and over four hundred White boys in the school. "If you put fourteen drops of chocolate in a gallon of milk and stir, the chocolate would disappear. I don't want to disappear. I want to play the game on their level."

"Does that mean you're going to turn White?" Noel asked.

"No," I responded thoughtfully, "but the nigger game won't play here."

I was assigned to a dormitory named Dana. It was the newest and most modern dorm on campus and, unfortunately, the farthest from the main building. Sub-zero early morning jaunts to class would provide bone-chilling discomfort. Dana overlooked the school's golf course. Rolling greens framed by beautiful trees defined the course's boundaries, while the mountainous Berkshires acted as chaperone. I later discovered that the dorm was named after a rich patron of the school. It was a lesson in how rich White folks constructed their immortality— brick by brick.

One of the many school rules was the mandatory attendance of chapel most mornings. After breakfast and before classes we were to absorb White folks' words of wisdom and inspiration sweetening the start of our day. There was a dress code, which consisted of blazers, ties, and khaki pants. I owned a ratty blazer, two shirts, and two pairs of dark pants. Noel didn't have a blazer and wore a bomber jacket with a shirt and tie. After the ritual we bumped into the headmaster, Mr. Olsen, a tall, distinguished, blue-eyed gentleman with the polished aura of a U.S. senator. His presence, like his cologne, reeked of refinement. Noel and I were heartened by his demeanor, which was that of a rich White uncle oozing benevolent vibes. Knowing the answer beforehand, he gently asked if we had the clothing needed to fulfill the dress requirement.

"Which requirement," I joked, "the one that says you can't run around naked or the Hotchkiss requirement?"

His sense of humor emerged in his reply. "Wise guys answer questions with questions. Smart guys provide straight answers. Which are you?"

"A wise guy who provides answers." We both laughed.

Then Noel said, "If you want us to look the part, you're gonna have to come up with the scratch."

Bemused, he answered, "Well, we'll see what we can do about coming up with the scratch." We all laughed heartily. It was the beginning note of a fruitful, difficult affair.

Later that day we were summoned to the administration offices in the main building, where we were greeted by guardian-angel number one, Bill Brokaw. In his take-charge way of doing things, Brokaw said, "We're going shopping." Before we knew it Noel and I were cruising in his green Porsche on the way to Caanan, Connecticut, a small town that housed the closest clothing store. As Noel and I stood outside ogling the display in the store's window, we heard the big man's commanding voice order, "Time to shop." We danced to the Motown sound of our White dad's credit card. Noel and I went crazy, buying so many articles of clothing and accessories that we could hardly carry them. The small trunk of the Porsche brimmed over with White folks' duds. Our spirits were soaring faster than the old man's propensity for exceeding the speed limit.

Brokaw proclaimed, "You're not poor kids anymore, you're Hotchkiss kids." If only our fairy godfather's magic wand could strengthen the tremendous lack of fundamentals in our educational background.

This was a golden time for Noel and me; we were glued together in harmony. Noel was my anchor; he had heart for days. It was his autumn to remember. He was nestled in the most scam-able blanket an ex-sting artist could imagine. People left their doors wide open with their valuables in full view. As Noel once said in those early heady days, "D, I'm in heaven. You can even take they shit, and if you lie well enough, they rich enough to let the shit go." I warned him about White folks, "They'se part squish and part piranha. Play them straight up, as real people." The liberal segment of the establishment was stroking his ass too soothingly for him to hear me.

We tried out for varsity football, but the style of football these guys were playing was a bore. It was a regimented game, devoid of imagination or risk.

Noel and I came from a tradition in which pressure, speed, and power created action. It was a style that would change how the game of football was played. I was a quarterback, and in those days Blacks were discouraged from playing that position. It was a position I had played for years, winning over 90 percent of my games. I had a choice of sitting on the bench or changing positions, which would have been easy enough, but Chuck had made me a quarterback. I opted for playing the position at the junior varsity level. Noel was more than capable of starting at running back for the varsity. His football gifts were tremendous. In my opinion he was one of the most talented running backs in the school's history. But the regimentation on the varsity team was something he felt he could easily delay. We decided to go down to junior varsity together and have some fun playing ball. We figured that I had three years and Noel had four, so if we put in a good performance we would be able to move up to varsity the next year on better terms.

I began to make friends with my teachers. My corridor master was Rock Coughlin, a young, energetic soccer and swimming coach, a good man and straight as Geronimo's arrows. He was a guy who really cared about his students. Rock would invite you into his apartment at the end of the hall for pizza and then put you to sleep over tales of his Outward Bound excursions. He was not my cup of tea, but I respected and admired the fact that someone so different would extend himself to the point of honestly trying to connect. Of course, it would never quite work. Neither of us would ever understand the other's version of the real deal, but his heart was easy to commit to.

Rock had a charisma problem that marginalized his effectiveness, but there were others on the school staff capable of seizing your attention. The man who emerged as my biggest hero on the establishment side of the Hotchkiss landscape was Blair Torrey, the dynamic warlord of the English department. Blair was a football and hockey coach, a rah-rah, hard-on Princeton Tiger from the fifties. His nose had been broken so many times on the grid iron that it was intriguingly misshapen and hung on his face like a neon sign that blinked "Don't fuck with me!" Yet he was an English master who loved and appreciated literature.

Blair was the literary son of Dick Gurney, the outgoing English department chairman. In 1969, Gurney appeared to be a thousand years old with a stud-tinged voice of gravel, the work of a trillion unfiltered cigarettes. He held great influence over both Blair and Bill Brokaw, two of his individualistic, rough-and-tumble, Hemingway-spooned students of Hotchkiss past. Gurney challenged them to be "good men," a phrase that defined the margin of your net social worth in the Gurney-Torrey-Brokaw universe. I was deeply impressed by their two-fisted approach to the expression of English literature.

Blair would perform his literary lessons with the nimble ferocity of a sensitive blue-collar mine worker. He struggled, reaching for the right phrases of expression as his battered beak fought for oxygen. Blair had been an offensive lineman in college, an undersized warrior who fought to open paths as his teammates ran to glory. This discipline nut took his quest for opening holes into the classroom, clearing paths of enlightenment for his students to dart through. No one ever blocked so hard for my young mind.

I had always loved words, but up until that point I had hated English classes. In my experience, literature had been taught in a boring haze of awestruck reverence, and that wasn't learning to me: It was praying to the gods of Shakespeare and Fitzgerald. But the Gurney-Torrey style took the great literary masters in the ring and sparred with them. Witnessing the phallic joust between Torrey and Hemingway was the most absorbing classroom experience of my life. Making literature physical struck a deep, artistic chord inside of me. I wanted to be one of Torrey's "good men." This added an additional layer to my confusion as I compiled mentors and influences faster than I could sort them out. A Northeastern baked, tough-White-guys club had me secretly yearning to join their ranks. I couldn't have sold that notion back home if I offered free heroin with it, but they taught me as much about freedom as Chuck Griffin.

The one disappointing area in the "good men" philosophy was its woeful race ignorance. Gurney earned a pass because in his heyday of the thirties, forties, and fifties in Hotchkissland, he had come in contact with Black people about as often as he rode a camel. But Blair was a much younger man, and the way he skated across the civil rights era wearing blinders was inexcusable. He leaned on his idealism, synthesizing all men's experiences into one size that disingenuously trivialized legitimate Black pain. Admittedly, I believe this was largely an inadvertent act, but role models aren't afforded the luxury of hypocritical lapses.

For example, Blair and I engaged in a holy battle over Mark Twain's perverted humanism in *Huckleberry Finn*. He wore the notion that the relationship between Huck and Jim conveyed an important message of racial harmony and understanding. Where the hell had he been the previous ten years? My contention was that the book was racist and, in those heated times of racial transformation, historically embarrassing. The thought that a grown Black man, Jim, was subservient to a White boy, Huck, trumpeted that Black men were boys, the ugliest stereotype in the pile. That painful notion was unacceptable in the post-King world, no matter how sensitively Twain stirred the tale.

Blair was shocked; slapping Twain was almost like slapping his wife. It was the first time I had gotten into the ring and dueled hard-ons with him. Blair's failure to contend honestly with the racist weaknesses inherent in his White brethren damaged his credibility, putting him in conflict with America's most romantic axiom: all folk are created equal. Inexplicably, he closed the drapes, choosing not to witness the consistent, unconstitutional ass-whippings his Black stepsiblings routinely suffered. He issued himself a blind pass, clinging to Twain's outdated, simplistic, patronizing racial blather. With the exception of daddy Porsche, there was very little Black social dirt under the fingernails of the members of club "good men."

As far as I was concerned, Blair was standing on a raft shakier than Huck's when defending Twain's novel, but in the heat of battle Blair's flesh-and-blood humanity began to play tricks with my own racist stereotypes. When he made the awkward inclusion of Piri Thomas's ghetto-tough memoir *Down These Mean Streets* to the reading list, upon my recommendation (a book he hated), it threw me for a loop; Blair had actually been listening. This took the edge off of my nigger-yelping for recognition, dissipating into new and enlightened questions. After waving the flag of discrimination and demanding inclusion, was I as unforgiving a doorkeeper? Was my signature cry for the right to be judged for my content as opposed to my exterior a one-sided proposition? Short-haired straight arrows like Blair Torrey had always been fair game for countless lashes with my Black whip of prejudgment. Blair taught me that White guys didn't have to have long hair and a fractured Black street rap to have credibility in the new war of ideas. My ghetto shell was softening, exposing a disorienting vulnerability. Tackling this social calculus would embody the heart of my education at Hotchkiss far more than the math and biology that was piled upon my desk.

While my life was being enriched in Torrey's English class, Noel was descending into a barrel of hell. He was assigned to the prep dorm, where the first-year students lived, a wet-nosed lot of thirteen- and fourteen-year-olds. The joint was a nursery: the sheltered, rich backgrounds of the inhabitants made them nine-year-olds in street years. Their games of Cowboys and Indians in the corridor, using their fingers as weapons, shocked Noel. Was this anyplace for a guy who had been involved in god knows how many armed robberies? This constant game of "bang, you're dead" had him crawling the walls of his tiny room. Noel's most legitimate effort to tackle the academic curriculum was marred by the distraction of the air-shooting preps. As the prepubescent gnats had a ball, Noel became obsessed with the task of finding an effective swatter.

Predictably Noel's fuse gave out, and he took matters into his own hands. During one of those Cowboys and Indians adventures, he came out of the room and screamed at the top of his voice, "If you don't stop all of this bullshit, I'm going to get a real gun and shoot all of you! I've had a gun and shot at people. I liked shooting my gun at people and will blow all you little motherfuckers away if you don't stop it." The baby crystals were frightened, and Noel's outburst made it to the faculty powers that be. What did they do with a student who threatened to rub out the freshman class?

They came up with a two-pronged solution. The first order of business was to get Noel out of that dorm and into one with the older students. The second was to assign him an adviser who would subsequently become a key figure in his life: Leif Thorne-Thomsen, or TT, as we called him. He was a baby-faced young master of Greek and Latin, but he moved with a fluid, hip jangle that you saw on the streets of Greenwich Village. No one would have mistaken him for a Hotchkiss master, and yet he was one of their finest. Leif was a six-foot blond bombshell with an undergraduate degree from Princeton. His graduate coat of varnish had been applied at Cornell University. The former NCAA national champion cyclist had arrived at Hotchkiss in the early sixties with a new wife, Sarah, and a gut full of rebellion, albeit smothered in ivy.

Initially Leif tried to play the Hotchkiss game according to its house rules, following the straight up and down "good man" edict. But a revolutionary lurked beneath Leif's surface, and it was painfully dredged to the forefront in 1967, after his brother, Carl, a Harvard student and tremendous athlete, answered his country's call in Vietnam, where tragedy struck and he was iced in the line of duty. This incident ripped the isolated tarp off of Leif's sheltered Hotchkiss existence, and the social radical emerged with a passion. His brother's death had a profound effect on the way Leif challenged life. Two years later, when Noel and I arrived, we would find a determined advocate for the underdog, a label we wore comfortably.

When it was decided that Leif would be Noel's adviser, his pent-up social flame found its frying pan. He understood that Noel was worthy of respect and that his valuable experiences merited consideration. Leif believed that Noel's contributions to Hotchkiss would be greater than Hotchkiss's ability to reciprocate. On a common-sense street level, Noel was as bright as any student in the school, and helping him carve out new turf in the Hotchkiss universe became Leif's great challenge. He lobbied for Noel to have a room on his corridor. Once he moved to Leif's floor, a smile emerged on Noel's face that would remain for a while. Leif made sure that Noel honored his commitment to work with the elaborate set of hated academic tutors that he needed so badly. This was never easy. Noel reeked of rebellion, but the leather-bomber-jacket, punk side of Leif's character harmonized well with Noel's street anger. Unlike most of the elite White males of the time, Leif knew what cool was. As a teenager he had drawn on a healthy dose of the Brando-Dean variety of fifties' angst. He recognized and appreciated those impulses in Noel's behavior.

With Noel feeling better about himself, the school became fun. We recovered our sense of humor and this enabled us to wade through the land of the privileged accumulating a multitude of laughs. An early example was our first social mixer. The school invited ninth- and tenth-grade females from Ethel

Walker, one of our sister schools in the area. Given their youth, the mixer was the beginning step for many of the students on the road to relationship Armageddon. The object was to pair the students off, where they could begin, under highly chaperoned circumstances, to exchange nuggets of adolescent sexual confusion destined to grow larger in time. When Noel and I arrived for the big event stoned out of our minds, we looked more like red-eyed bouncers from the Electric Circus than classmates. It was a laugh. For better or worse we were both seasoned pussy hounds, and it had been a long time since we had been around this many training bras.

One of the poor teachers who chaperoned the mixer had the awkward job of pairing us off, finding two baby chicks for two old sharp-toothed wolves. Noel and I joked with each other about our opportunity to scope out and impregnate the richest of them all. When it came to our turn to be hooked up, the teacher looked at us with fear and embarrassment in his eyes. His face read: What the hell am I going to do with you two grizzled criminals? Without saying a word, Noel and I laughed. Initially the teacher was puzzled by our actions, until I pulled him aside and said, "Hey, man, don't worry about it. We understand."

Another interesting development occurred on parents' weekend. It was also alumni weekend, and the class of '54 was having a reunion. There was a big varsity football game, and Noel and I watched the first half. At halftime we decided to split, and as we walked along Route 112, which led us to the main campus, we were feeling particularly good about life. It was a beautiful fall day; the pageantry that accompanied the weekend's festivities was colorful and gay. The previous night a wonderful bit of Lebanese hashish had found its way on campus, and a taste of that Middle Eastern magic helped to accentuate the good vibes that surrounded us.

In the midst of this good groove on, a car came roaring up behind us. We jumped to the side, when someone stuck his head out of the window and yelled, "Get out of the road, you goddamn niggers!" It was a car full of juiced up alumni. Noel and I chased the car for a few steps before giving up. We didn't know whether to laugh or get pissed off. We knew that there were racist thorns in even the best-kept White folks rose garden, so there was a degree of humor in the reminder that despite the locale, niggers are niggers all over the world. But ever the con persons, we figured we could use this hefty dose of racism to our advantage. In other words, whose shoulder could we cry on and what could we get from it all?

When we arrived back on campus, we bumped into George Norton Stone, the head of the math department. We vented our trumped-up anger, delivering a calculated dose of "woe is me." Mr. Stone pondered our dilemma as though he were analyzing an algebraic equation, then spoke with his trademark lisp. "What class did you say these guys were from?" I said, "Class of '54." Mr. Stone again did his pondering thing and said, "Well, look at it this way, if it was the class of '44, they might have run you two over." Noel and I looked at each other and just broke into hysterical laughter. George Norton Stone's deadpan humor hit the right note. The old man of numbers handled the situation with deft calculation, endearing him to Noel and me forever more.

When the football season began, my coaches, Chris Getman and Jimmy Marks, men I was very fond of, played the typical ignorant White man's card on me. It read Black athletes were too talented physically to waste on the quarterback position. The feeling was that most Black athletes with ability could excel at several positions. The quarterback position was one of leadership, and the American White perception of Black leadership, was just short of nonexistent. Despite the fact that I was clearly the best quarterback on the team, I wound up playing the accepted "good nigger" positions at the time, free safety and wide receiver.

Coach Getman was not a racist. He didn't have to be: the practices that were administered embodied the status quo. In his White coach's wisdom it made perfect sense that I would be more comfortable playing a position where I didn't have to think too much, only react, and that imposing instinctive concoction of power and speed would best serve the team. I accepted this because Noel and I were having fun getting stoned and kicking ass on the practice field, so I easily relinquished my rightful tour of leadership. Fortunately, Chuck didn't see things that way.

It was the first game of our season, and Chuck and Anna drove up to witness our coming-out party in prep football. After the opening kickoff, when Damon White, one of the coach's sons, trotted out onto the field to assume the quarterback position, Chuck went nuclear. "What is this shit! What the fuck is this shit! Whoa! White boys pulling shit!" Standing ten feet from the team on the same sideline, Chuck's anger continued to raise its volume. "That boy been a quarterback since he was a motherfucking baby!" he shouted, dying for those that matter to hear. "The boy throw the ball out the motherfucking arena." Getman and his coaching staff and other sideline onlookers began to squirm. Noel and I, knowing Chuck's A-list explosions, relished the opportunity to watch the show. "Four hundred years!! Four hundred years of this shit! Ain't gonna be no more. This is 1969. Niggers died all over the South to stop bullshit like this!" At this point his large afro and poncho-like dashiki began to grow as he waved his arms, casting the most unusual dissenting presence in Hotchkiss's history.

Where most of the White men remained uptight and quiet as Chuck rained upon them, old Dick Gurney let out a proclamatory cry. "Chuck Griffin is full of shit!" he rasped through damaged vocal chords. Chuck replied, "Who is that old motherfucker?" Masculine jaws tightened to a skin-piercing level as Chuck ranted on. "White folks ain't shit! Don't matter how much money you got. Don't matter how many diplomas you got on your wall. It's the same old shit!" Much of the attention left the playing field. Those who tuned in seemed to be aware that they were witnessing history. Anna cried, "White ain't right!" She repeated her assertion excessively.

Meanwhile, we were losing the game, and old Damon was having his ass handed to him on the field. At halftime, Getman made the decision to put me in at quarterback. We were down by two touchdowns, so I am not certain that Getman folded under the pressure of Chuck's tirade. Coaches hate losing, and given the respect I had for Getman's manhood, I'd like to think that his choice was made thinking I could pull the game out. Chuck had calmed down, having made his point. The other White males on the sideline remained a bit shaken, having witnessed an unsettling preview of what people twenty years later would come to know as the Al Sharpton treatment.

We won the game easily, as I led the team to several touchdowns and took over the emotional leadership of the team. We proceeded to become a junior varsity juggernaut, trouncing any school that dared play us. After Chuck's performance, one might have expected the school to place him on its nigger-non-grata list, but this was the late sixties, and colorful dynamism seemed to trump exclusion. Coach Getman accepted Chuck's challenge to play the East Harlem Chargers, mine and Noel's old team. Chuck lurched at the chance to take on Getman, as well as several other prep school coaches on the junior varsity circuit. He brought the Chargers to schools like Canterbury and Gunnery, trashing them by obscene scores like 54-7 and 42-0.

Our Hotchkiss team swept our first four games with a swagger. It was a brilliant little moment in time when a bunch of gutsy, crystal preppies quarterbacked by an authentic street nigger would braid respect and affection into wire that provided the juice empowering our oddly hip foxhole. As we approached the confrontation with the Chargers, the impending battle between the chosen Whites and their raging Black ghetto brethren would be more exciting than anything that would happen on campus in the fall of '69. It was probably the only time in the school's history when a junior varsity team would generate more memorable heat than anything the varsity had to offer.

The week before the game, Getman, a big man of six-foot-four, with an athletic pedigree that demanded respect, gave us a pep talk, attempting to rev the team up against the unknown. Black folks whose prodigious athletic mythology preceded them were coming to town. "This week we're playing the Chargers, Dennis's and Noel's old team from Harlem," Getman preached. "We expect to treat them just like any other opponent and whip the hell out of them."

Despite his mushrooming boredom with rich White boys, Noel decided to step forward. "Coach, this rah-rah stuff ain't gonna make it happen. The only way to beat a ghetto team is with blind ghetto. This week, if we gonna win, our guys have to become ghetto."

Getman, mindful of the racial sensitivity that made this game unique, said, "I don't think I quite understand what you mean, but I sure as hell love the spirit of it. You guys pay attention to Velasquez. He's got the right attitude. Now hit the field."

After practice I asked Noel about his surprising behavioral change, and he responded, "They scared, you can see it in their eyes. They ain't used to being scared. You know Chuck gets his dick hard kicking White ass, and he comin' up here with five busloads of Black motherfuckers who want to turn this place out. Now, that's niggers plus. If Hotchkiss have any chance of playing a good game, its gonna be 'cause we led the way. There's something important about that. I want to win this game."

I knew the warrior in Noel would play hard against the Chargers, but there was something bigger going on.

"White folks don't rule the world for nothin', right D? So big Sprol and Lefond and Hart, they come from that same White folks, kickass, choke-anything-in-front-of-them shit, right?"

"They'se one and the same," I said.

Noel laughed, "We can't make our guys niggers in a week, but if we can at least bring the White cop out of them motherfuckers, that could be enough to get the job done."

I put my arm around Noel and said, "This is the first time since we got here that you're playing as big as you really are. That's the Noel we need."

"I didn't think you needed me for nothin'," he challenged. "Since we got here, you been getting Whiter and Whiter, wrapping hippie beads around everything."

His statement irked me, and I replied, "White folks is a big part of America and I don't see no fuckin' reason for bein' in this motherfucker if we ain't gonna try to play their brand of ball. When you was parading so hard for us to come here . . ." I trailed off not wanting to dampen Noel's thrust.

"I hate almost everything that's White about White boys, except in this case they'se my niggers, so I gotta go down with the shit. I still hate this silly rah-rah shit. It gives me a headache. But this is one of my few chances to kick some ass without books."

Noel's attitude during the week of practice leading up to the confrontation was that of a man on a mission. He often did the unimaginable: led the team in the exercise drills. His earnest commitment to the lengthy distances the team's conditioning regimen required was an inspiration to our White teammates. They worked extra hard as Noel fed their penchant for ferocity.

On game day, as the team readied for battle, dressed in our conservative navy blue jerseys and White pants, Noel stood before the group and delivered an intense pep talk. "Look, I know you dudes may be scared,'cause brothers is scary, especially since none of you dudes know what a nightstick feel like. But we can do this. Me and D have known these guys all our lives, but today you'se our brothers. I'm with you, so don't bitch up on me. We gonna play street ball."

After one of the more unusual pep speeches in the annals of New England prep football, our White boys were fired up. When Getman approached the team he was pleased to see that he had a group of tigers on his hands. He delivered a short bombastic message straight from Frank Leahy's handbook. When we took the field for our warm-up calisthenics, the ghetto foe had just arrived, unloading from four charter buses lining the field. They dominated the small playing area with the jingle-jangle of street-Black fluidity. A soulful groove began to transform the atmosphere, overwhelming the ivy doctrine of comportment. The predominantly Black and Latino crowd gathered on what would be their sideline for the day.

Twelve gorgeous, buxom cheerleaders led the crowd with an intimidating chant. "Chargers on the warpath, woo, woo!" They repeated this chant while performing Motown-savvy gyrations usually reserved for inner-city high school basketball games.

The Chargers were dressed in shiny gold uniforms trimmed in black. The ballplayers divided into two lines and ran deep-pass patterns. The first glimpse of superior Black speed jarred White onlookers. The Chargers quarterback, Chito, a movie-star-handsome Puerto Rican with a rocket arm, hummed the pearl as the Black crowd went nuts with each reception. The Hotchkiss team watched the Chargers perform, its resolve chipping away, moving toward a fatal dose of impotency.

"Don't watch them," Noel exhorted. "Come on, we got business to do. It's easy catching those passes when nobody's hitting you. But we can hit. We're undefeated. Let's go!" He led the team in a spirited series of jumping jacks. "One two three louder, one two three after me, they can hit, we can hit."

It was a beautiful American moment, as common goals trumped race and class. The team responded to Noel's leadership, burying fears, eschewing the notion of there being a switchblade in each Charger's jock. For the next two hours, the wealth of Lake Forest, Illinois; Darien, Connecticut; and New York's Park Avenue would connect with two street-scarred ex-heroin addicts. The battlefield had been leveled to the point that the poorest of us was asked to lead. The school had liberaled itself into a ghetto majority for the day, and our White players had to go into battle on their home field and be jeered by an effervescent Black crowd playing from the Apollo Theater's Amateur Night rulebook. The Hotchkiss sideline was far more sedate, intimidated by the constant refrain of Black people on the warpath. If I were to translate their faces into words, they would read "What the fuck have we done!"

Fortunately, our teammates had jumped the broom with us. There was no discernable sign of cube shrinkage. During the coin flip, I gave a look over to the Charger sideline, and there stood Chuck, hands on his hips, wearing blue jeans, boots, and a huge woolen red poncho, breathing fire. It was odd. I'd never played a game with Chuck on the opposite sideline. I wanted to kick his ass, knowing that he would be disappointed if I thought otherwise. I then looked over at my sideline and saw Coach Getman, a striking physical presence in his own right, and a guy who had spent an inordinate amount of time trying to make me the best football player I could be. The White game was different, more slam and less dance. Having both styles at my command was an empowering, unforgettable moment in my life. I had narrowed the distance between the two worlds down to a hundred-yard patch of grass, and I would be representing both.

The Chargers won the coin toss and chose to receive the ball. On kickoff the Black cheers were so loud it felt as though I was in Harlem at the Rucker Tournament. Our guys reached deep into their Hotchkiss "good men" bags and came out with game faces, locking eyes with the ghetto fervor. Our aggressive defense stuffed them, forcing a punt. This was huge for the Hotchkiss team. They took a significant swipe at their own fears of Black athletic dominance, alerting the Chargers that they were in for a ball game. On our third offensive play in the huddle, I called an off tackle run for Noel and looked to my football buddy-for-life, big John Sprole, and told him, "You have to blast that motherfucker off the line. We don't win this without you, big man, so give it up. Noel's coming right behind you." At the line of scrimmage, I took the snap and handed the ball to Noel off our right side. Big Sprole threw a block that would have evinced the gap-toothed grin of the great Lombardi. Noel saw daylight and went seventy-three yards for a touchdown.

The Chargers sideline was stunned. During their New England prep school ass-kicking tour, they had never been behind. Noel and his band of trust fund beneficiaries had humbled them. Our sideline was swelling in numbers and confidence and began to cheer loudly. The Black sideline responded with louder voices. "Chargers on the warpath, woo, woo! Chargers on the warpath, woo, woo!" Students from other parts of the campus heard the uproar and were drawn to the sounds. For the many that came, it would be their first and only experience in a Black neighborhood in their lifetimes.

Anna let loose a passionate wail that will always amuse me, when she screamed, "Kill 'em, kill 'em, if they play for the White man, kill 'em!" It was a gas. I looked at my teammates who were listening to all of this, trying to avert their eyes, not wanting to test my loyalty under the waves of persecution. Noel and I cracked up laughing and assured our teammates in the next huddle that we were Hotchkiss blue all the way.

At the end of the first quarter, it was Hotchkiss 7, East Harlem 0. As we neared the end of the first half, I ran a sweep from the quarterback's position, got a good block, and made it up the sideline. As I was coming to the end of a forty-yard-touchdown run, five yards before reaching the end zone, a White cat with a bomber jacket and a cool black tam was suddenly running beside me on the sideline. At first I thought it was some nut, but as I focused closer upon him after reaching the end zone, I discovered it was TT. He came into the end zone, slapped me five, and gave me a hug, and I said, "You're a bad motherfucker!" We slapped five again, and he split. On this insane day, one could call a Hotchkiss master a motherfucker and see him welcome the complimentary expletive as would a brother on the corner.

Things were getting desperate—Hotchkiss 14, Chargers 0—as we neared the half. An upset loomed. Few things hurt more than White boys kicking Black ass in the world of sports. If the White boys have genuine chops, then they are respected and often admired, but when a bunch of geeky pearl gems do it to you, it hurts. With their pride up against the wall, the Chargers got the ball and began to move it with determination. Several big plays in a row put us back on our heels. The cheerleaders were going crazy as they ran down the sideline, following the team and screaming encouragement. The Chargers quarterback threw a deep pass. The wide receiver had beaten his man, caught the ball, and cruised into the end zone for a touchdown.

The Chargers sideline exploded, and ours sagged as though we were being forced to watch file footage of the Watts riots. In the hysteria few noticed that the referee had thrown a yellow flag. When he signaled that the Chargers were offsides, nullifying the touchdown, it was time for the Chuck Griffin show. "Offsides, offsides, my ass! That was a bullshit call!" The referee approached Chuck, seeking to explain his decision.

"Bullshit. Don't come over here. It's a bad call. You're stacking the deck. You been blowin' calls all game. You cheatin'. If they beat us, that's one thing, but you gon' make sure they win. You cheatin'. I gave you my two best players, and you still cheatin'. Do they teach cheatin' in this motherfucker!" The referee had his fill; he blew his whistle, tossed his flag, and penalized Chuck fifteen yards. Chuck's afro was about to blow clear across the campus. "You robbin' us," he yelled to the crowd. "Slavery's over, it's dead!" He then waved his poncho with a sweeping motion like it was a defiant flag and shouted, "Everybody back on the bus!"

An avalanche of people from the Chargers sideline stampeded toward their buses. The Hotchkiss crowd freaked and began to run for cover. It was chaos: The melting pot's contents had turned to lava. As people were running every-where, Coach Getman took a stand and ran behind Chuck, who was marshaling his troops back on the bus, and yelled, "What's the matter, Chuck, are ya chicken?" Hotchkiss folk within earshot prepared to witness a murder, as Get-man again challenged, "Chuck Griffin, are ya chicken?" Chuck froze in his tracks and spun around, and, with everyone awaiting his reaction, he blasted, "Chicken! Who you calling chicken? I'll show you who's chicken. Everybody back on the field. Let's get 'em!"

The Black crowd reversed course and, filled with fire, ran back chanting their war cry. The Whites reversed field and returned to the Hotchkiss sideline as though their lives were in the balance. Somehow order was restored and the game resumed. The Chargers had the ball and scored before halftime. As we took our breathers, it was Hotchkiss 14, Chargers 7.

The second half was a defensive struggle. The teams refused to give an inch. The hitting rose well above the JV level. While covering a punt, Noel knocked the punt returner head over heels with the most vicious hit of the contest. Late in the fourth quarter the Chargers scored another touchdown. The score was 14-13. As we prepared to defend the extra point, both sidelines were delirious, cheering madly. There was an interesting meld of the Chargers' warpath chant competing against the less rhythmic but equally intense Hotchkiss cheer: Go! Go! Go! White fists were now pumping defiantly with unabashed virulence, let-ting it all hang out. It was exciting; it was funky.

Down on the goal line before the all-important extra point that would tie the game, we huddled. The Charger crowd was chanting. "Beat the traitors. Beat the traitors!" Chuck called a time-out. Noel spoke to the team. "They're going for two. If they get it, they win. If we stop them, we win. You guys played your asses off. We deserve this win. You earned it, so let's wrap this motherfucker up." As we broke the huddle Noel whispered to me, "You know, D, our White boys ain't the pussies they look like."

We assumed our positions, Noel at linebacker and me lined up behind him at safety. I cupped my hands and shouted through the intensity of the moment, "Skin and heart are two different things. One you can see, the other you have to weigh." Noel swung his head around and gave me a big smile.

The ghost of Douglas MacArthur visited Noel's body for one play as he commanded his troops. "They ain't gonna pass, they gonna run. You linemen, Sprole, y'all better cave that shit in up front. Me and D will finish it off. This is our win."

Both teams took their stances, head-to-head, breathing heavily on each side of the ball. The Chargers ran a play off left tackle, handing the ball to their best runner. Sprole and the boys up front got off quickly and closed the Chargers' ability to penetrate. The halfback bounced to the outside, where Noel and I both strung the play out and combined to bring down the running back for a five-yard loss. The ref indicated no score. The clock added the final sting, abandoning the boys from the ghetto, leaving history to proclaim the result: Hotchkiss 14, Chargers 13.

Right after the game, the team gave Noel a special cheer. "Let's hear it for Noel, a hell of a football player. Hip, hip hooray! Hip, hip hooray!" Noel responded tongue-in-cheek, "Thank you. I will never forget my first White-boy cheer." He was enjoying his well-earned visit in the spotlight. Chuck and Getman shook hands heartily. The two warriors showed their class and respect for each other in simple but meaningful terms. Getman said, "Excellent game, Chuck, let's do it again." Chuck's response: "You got it, man." They again shook hands, and the most unlikely confluence of characters in Hotchkiss's storied past drifted back to their uneven fates.

As the buses were about to leave, Noel and I, still in uniform, spoke with several of our friends through the window. One friend said, "Noel, you can't come back to the block no more. You got that vanilla in you."

"Ain't no vanilla here," Noel responded, "it's D who got that cream fillin'"

"Yo, D, you usin' that Vitalis on your afro yet?" another friend teased.

I needled, "All I know is that we whupped your Black ass."

Chuck approached, put his weary arms around us both and whispered through a scratchy, overworked voice box. "Good job, I'm proud of you."

He got on the bus. As the buses pulled away, Noel, wearing a sad expression, continued to wave until the caravan was a tiny spot in the distance. "I would give anything to be on the bus," Noel said, choking with emotion.

"That the past, man," I pitched. "This is the future."

"It ain't my future, man. I'm counting the minutes until Christmas vacation."

"I'm not," I said to his surprise.

"Come on, you're bullshitting me, right?"

"No," I challenged, "When was the last time you lived in a place where you didn't have to look over your shoulder?"

"Don't you know these White folks will cut your heart out?" Noel protested.

"Look, I'm learning that White folks are people like anybody else, good ones and bad ones, like good niggers and bad niggers. I want to learn how to tell the difference."

"Man, your shit turnin' squishy right before my eyes," he mourned.

"I'm tired of kill or die."

My statement was met with a chilly silence.

Right after the Harlem-Hotchkiss game, Noel and I were approached by a young journalist named Gail Sheehy. She had gotten news of Chuck's heated heyday in East Harlem and became intrigued with his story. Gail had ridden the bus up to Lakeville with Chuck to pursue her interest in the story about an elite prep school interacting with pure street genes. After the game, her mind was blown, having been pelted with an afternoon full of astounding contrasts. She told us that she was interested in writing about us. As if our heads weren't swollen enough, Gail's enthusiastic interest in our lives pushed our egos closer to the edge.

The school powers gave us a pass on the obligatory pain-in-the-ass extracurricular activities, allowing us to wax street poetic in a series of interviews. Gail would drive up to Hotchkiss with her two-year-old daughter, Maura. Noel and I would dinch our pot roaches, hop into her rented car, and do the Connecticut countryside for hours at a time. This recently divorced young White woman who approached the Harlem streets with a swagger was a pure hard-on. Gail was Anna Griffin–like smart, with hot legs that thrived beneath skirts that rose slightly above the knee. Noel and I gladly double-humped the lure of her ever-present tape recorder.

Gail passed the Jerry Brandt test for White cool, when she turned her head as Noel and I introduced Wild Turkey into the sessions. Our booze-pinched tales of embellished pain and anguish poured into the time-freezing device. Her special listen provided the first opportunity anyone had given us to express our strengths, weaknesses, and confusion about all that had happened in the previous year and a half.

Gail would subsequently jar our groin-swelling view of her, when dribblings of fear and insecurity began to pierce her exterior. As elements of her own pain and confusion spilled out, we would come to realize that she was in a tough spot. Gail was on the shaky turf of the single mother. Divorce was still veiled in tabooism, and Gail was fighting to maintain her balance in a culture where the old White mores still dominated much of the social topsoil. Added to that difficult task was her attempt at fostering the unlikely prospect of infiltrating the White male locker room mentality that dominated the game of journalism. Fortunately for her, the double-X-chromosome explosion was right around the corner. With the term "women's liberation" beginning to bubble up from the grassroots, Gail quickly found herself on the fast track of her generation's upgrade in female opportunities.

Little Maura acted as chaperone, snuggling and comforting us all when we would lapse into sorrowful exhortations about our fear of falling on our asses in our respective overwhelming environments. As we wove our way through the Berkshires during those jam sessions, Gail would emerge as a special person in our hearts and minds.

In late November we played our final game against the last-place team. The conditions were horrible. Sleet pulverized the frozen field, rendering a meager kickoff to the start of the game. The only attendees were the sacrificial lambs who moved the yardsticks. After our Harlem victory, we remained undefeated and felt like the coolest junior varsity team ever. Overly souped up with nothing to prove, we attempted to mail in a final victory. Despite the horrible playing conditions, we moved the ball pretty well, running up a 13-0 lead in the first half.

Suddenly our coach began a descent earmarked for pumpkinville. Noel blew out a knee trying to make one too many cuts and was carted off to the locker room, relieved to have found a noble exit from the horrible conditions. A few plays later I aggravated a season-long ankle injury and followed Noel's exit with equal satisfaction. It was determined after halftime that Noel and I would sit out and nurse our injuries, while Damon White, the second-string quarterback, whom Chuck's tirade had pushed out of the picture, would mop up the victory. Noel and I were left alone in the locker room to baby our mud-stained injuries and reflect upon the latest of our string of improbable locations.

As we peered through a narrow window, watching the second half from the locker room bathroom, Noel said, "Ain't this a bitch, D."

"What?" I said.

"Where we at. A year ago we didn't know what the fuck any of this shit was, and now here we are two niggers alone in a very White locker room. Don't it bug you that we're at where we're at?"

"There ain't no places," I chirped, covering a song from Chuck's catalog. "You belong wherever you'se at."

Noel shook off my bromide and said, "This ain't fun, and it will change us before we change it. You have to be White or wanna be White to get off on this lame shit. My problem is you seem to be slurping this bad boy up."

The comment was another in his growing refrain of my selling out to the seductive lore of White might, and it pissed me off. "I'm for sale, man, 'cause I don't want to be a nigger for life. That's nine parts pain, one part gain. The one thing this joint can't teach us about is being niggers. We got that down pat."

I took it to the fist-balling stage, and Noel backed up. His respect for my hand speed still gave him pause when a trip to thump city was in the offing. We both calmed down. He pulled off his football pants, revealing a swollen black-and-blue injury on his right thigh. Noel touched it softly and winced. "How far are you going to go with this White thing?" He deadpanned, "What's next, square dancing?" We laughed. Noel's dead-on joke resuscitated our sense of humor.

In the midst of our guffaws Noel caught a glimpse of the game through the window and discovered that the team was having its problems. Noel and I started to get nervous. We didn't want to end our season with the taste of a loser in our mouths. Ultimately we would have to live with a 13-13 tie hung from our spotless record.

At the football team's awards party, I shared the T. J. McDermott Award with one of the White players. The McDermott acknowledged the team's most valuable player. It wasn't the Heisman, but I took great pride in the honor. I'd happened upon a batch of quality White folks who were making progress in the undeveloped practice of giving a Black man his colorless due. It was a feel-good oddity, but I had to be cool because Noel's glare of alienation intensified with each slap on the back that I received from my White teammates. The accolades were nails in a coffin that contained our shaken brotherhood.

Thankfully, the holidays arrived, and Noel and I took a well-deserved breather from each other. My budding relationship with Gerri provided more than enough excitement to occupy my time. She was performing on the same bill as Hendrix, and I was in the clouds. As I froze my ass off in the last hours of the decade, the cold ground outside the Fillmore East stage entrance had me dancing. My spirits were buoyed by the sounds of Hendrix. As the clock wound down and the tune of "Auld-Lang Syne" came from the master's blaster, the door opened and I sped through the unattended post. I made my way backstage, careful to duck the Voices, not wanting Chuck to think that I'd defied him. When Hendrix emerged for the backstage worshippers, the humble icon reflected a mysteriously integrated presence, a Black, Indian, European concoction, American cross-breeding at its best. I used up my privileged gawk allotment and split.

I rumbled uptown by subway car surrounded by drunks who were still hanging on to the old decade. The new decade was up for grabs, and I felt like I was running out of hats from which to pull my rabbits.

SIXTEEN

If there is a single factor which contributes most strongly to the unrest among our black students it is a feeling of isolation. The more disadvantaged the background of the black student the more intense the feeling of isolation. An easy solution would be a retreat from our present policy of accepting hard-core black. I for one feel that such a move on our part would be a betrayal of all that is best about Hotchkiss.

—**Albert William Olsen, Jr.,** headmaster,
The Hotchkiss School, May 1970

It didn't take long for the brushfires that would characterize the seventh decade to begin. Two weeks into the New Year, Chuck and Anna broke up. Mom and pop of our thriving mom-and-pop enterprise had tossed in the towel, and like most of our initiatives, it did not happen quietly. I arrived at the center on a Friday night, and moments later I was summoned by Marvin Griffin (no relation), one of Chuck and Anna's top lieutenants, to pick up the phone. On the other end was my beloved Anna shouting at the top of her lungs, "Chuck Griffin is a no good, lying Black motherfucker!"

"Okay," I replied, "What happened?"

"He ain't shit, he ain't never gonna be shit, and all those flunkies around him that kiss his ass ain't shit either." She slammed down the phone. My plan was to take Gerri to a movie and relax, but it was a pretty good bet that when I went to the house to pick her up, it would be anything but relaxing. I immediately ran to the basement where Chuck was practicing on his makeshift archery range. "I just talked to Anna. What's up?"

"I walked out on that lying gorilla-butt bitch," he replied heatedly.

"Come on, man, you don't mean that," I coaxed gingerly.

He put down his bow and ordered me to look him directly in his eyes. His pupils were in flames when he said, "If you ever see me walk in the direction of that woman's home . . ." He paused to let the power of his no-bullshit glare scare the shit out of me. "Shoot me!" he blasted as though firing a shotgun.

Chuck wanted me to swallow hard and accept that my family of choice had been blown to bits. Gerri, who loved her mother and adored her father, was shell-shocked by the suddenness of the announcement. Chuck and Anna both shared my heart, but my love for Gerri was the tiebreaker, and Gerri lived with Anna. I had to walk a skinny tightrope, dodging Anna's rage-filled grenades. Her pain had the impact of a daily whacking with a two-by-four, and the resulting unhappiness found her in bed with Johnny Walker Red. Johnny W. became her pimp as she strolled Desolation Row, trying to contend with losing all that she had worked for. Fortunately, time and her internal resources would enable her to put Chuck and the center in the rearview mirror, when a move to Mobile, Alabama, fueled her recovery and successful Third Act.

The free-loving seventies were heady times and Chuck's big splash gave him a case emperor-itis. In his early forties and exhausted, he had spent Sharpton-sized energy on his ghetto activism. As fatigue set in, the adulation that came with his brilliant accomplishments found its way to his gonads, which were heavily wired to his ego. Chuck's occasional roving eye had sighted new prey.

"It's the scent of young pussy. It's got to be pussy," Noel lectured. "What's the one thing Black nigger ain't got." He cupped his hands around his mouth and shouted, "Young pussy. I'll bet you some young bitch done opened up his nose."

It was true. Initially, we weren't savvy enough to tie Chuck's sudden loss of thirty pounds, stylish new clothing, and (horror of horrors) Cesar Romero–thin mustache to a younger woman who was repairing the cracks in his bell. Dorothy Raven, Chuck's new wonder woman, had once been a friend and colleague of Anna's and had used her inside knowledge and fresh, wholesome, kittenish beauty to slice Anna's throat. Anna's feminine game had been schooled in the garter-and-girdle academy for women who came of age dancing to the Lindy Hop. Chuck's mid-life crisis placed her on the grill, forcing her to compete in an age when skirts had ascended to new heights. It was an unwinnable proposition.

Anna's dignity and maturity had been especially assaulted when the wonder woman inspired Chuck to buy a Mercedes-Benz. It was the first time we had ever seen a Benz in Harlem. Chuck cruising down Second Avenue with his woman in the passenger seat for all to see set off a war that tore the center apart. Anna left the center and took the Voices of East Harlem and the center's organizational discipline with her. Our female members lost interest when the Voices left, following them out the door. In their absence the testosterone levels became alarmingly high, as the partying, drugs, and machismo snaked forward. The great dream's nasty hangover was in session.

When we arrived back at Hotchkiss, Noel's struggle in the land of ivy was bringing out his inadequacies and insecurities at an alarming rate. The regimentation sapped his confidence, enabling him to care less and less.

In our first weeks back, he and I were virtually estranged. I decided to break the ice by visiting him in his room. I wanted to play him a new album I was crazy about. At this point he had discarded any pretense of following the rules. His room was a cloud of cigarette smoke, with butts spilling out of the ashtrays all over his school books. I broke into a conciliatory pep talk that fell on deaf ears. His pain had mugged his purpose.

"I can't fuck with this," he said. "White people is a bitch. I would love to get these motherfuckers in the streets, see how they deal."

"You have to give in to the shit. You can't fight it. You gotta get down," I coaxed gently. He fired a snarl that played like an expletive. I felt like McCartney trying to persuade Lennon to put on the cute no-collar suit one more time. My efforts only fostered his growing mistrust.

"You're becoming soft!" he screamed while flicking cigarette ashes on the floor. "You runnin' around with these pussy-faced White boys like they happenin'." I lit a Marlboro as he sang his rant. I wasn't sure whether to hug him or kick his ass. I did neither, choosing to elude the burnt aroma of his defeatism. He turned up the temperature, bellowing, "I want to tell these motherfuckers . . . !" Noel didn't finish. His voice tapered off into a cacophony of inaudible, seething half-tones of anger. The mechanics of the White power machine were grating him into shavings.

"Yo, man, try to pull your shit back in," I stroked. "I told you these was tough motherfuckers. This level of White folks built they shit with concrete. With Barry as your brother, how the fuck don't you know that?"

"Barry's oatmeal, he's fucking lost his mind," he screamed. "That motherfucker lost his mind. He ain't come out the house for years." Noel let the weight of his words hang.

Shaken, I asked, "What happened?"

"This shit turned the nigger into mierda. What chance do I have?" The moment was memorable. It would be the only time I would ever see Noel cry. Barry was the standard. My brother Robert used to call him the golden spic. "He lost his motherfucking mind," Noel wailed. His words broke me into pieces. I approached to console him, and he pushed me away. "While you're running around sniffin' Whitey, I'm dying, nigger! Whoever thought I'd be jail-fucked by Charles Dickens!"

He threw a copy of *Oliver Twist* at me. I hit the ground because Dickens's books are thick enough to kill you. "You crazy, nigger? Don't make me start throwin' shit back." My counter outburst calmed him a bit, and he withdrew his tears, embarrassed by his lack of cool, and fought to play out the remainder of his meltdown peaceably. As I watched Noel writhe in silence, he demanded, "Leave!"

"What?" I asked.

"Get the fuck out! You ain't the shit no more!"

I wobbled on whether I should do battle or go quietly. I chose the latter. Before leaving, I decided to play my album, Neil Young's *After the Goldrush*. Young's demented soul music celebrating isolation ("Oh, Lonesome Me") only encouraged Noel's harsh leap into his own shit. This song for pity-grabbers seemed to massage the troubled toreador's cry spot. "See you tomorrow, man," I said. Defiantly, he whacked me with a non-response, and I split.

At the time, I was going through my own social-racial reconstruction. The frigid winter conditions forced students indoors, activating an inadvertent integrated interaction. As color consciousness dissipated, our shared youth provided a bond that placed old Jim Crow into detention. My dormmates and I would sling our teenage realities in bull sessions, framed in acid and pot, sharing experiences that zoomed from Darien, Connecticut, to Harlem's 125th Street and back. I was impressed with what young American freedom really looked like up close. Their privileges provided a confidence that fueled a wide open, well-financed blank canvas for them to dream upon.

Once during a first listen of Pink Floyd's debut album, we shared notes over the fact that many of us had been raised by Black women. My buddies were shocked to discover that their biscuit-warm mammies were capable of beating the shit out of their own kids. I pointed out that their families were cash cows, helping to keep people like myself in cheap sneakers. Mammy warmth was a salable commodity; much of Beulah's kind stroking was a part of the gig. But Beulah's act played for White audiences only.

"No, they did not love you," I tossed on the campfire. "Your parents were sorely needed paychecks, and you, by extension, were pay stubs." I suspect that this revelation left some of my crystal cats a little downcast.

That spring I emerged from the dorm with a color-be-damned playbook. The new familiarity slayed much of the racial ignorance I had been fed. These experiences convinced me that racial differences were a false concoction easily vanquished by honest discourse. I was high on White-boy dream juice and determined to throw the ball deep against any force that stood between me and the integrated freedom I now craved.

* * *

Irod Daly was one of fourteen Blacks among Hotchkiss's 440 students. From this paltry lot he managed to cull a Black resistance organization, the Brothers of Umoja, whose main purpose was to work the guilt levers of a naive administration. Irod was a middle-class West Indian kid from Brooklyn who rhapsodized over self-determination and Black-owned businesses leading to ultimate political power—on its face an admirable initiative. He pleaded with me to join his efforts to inject a dose of Black militancy into the school's consciousness, but our approaches were at odds.

"White folks are only going to wear our boot in their ass but for so long," I argued. He balked, and I told him to go fuck himself, reasoning that it made little sense to accept the school's largesse sneering from beneath a dashiki. I liked Irod. At five-foot-seven, this bespectacled little gnat was intriguing, a Black Dilton Doyle with an attitude, but he was selling the ferocious artistry of the Last Poets, while I was hung up on the heroin-induced sensitivities of "Sweet Baby James."

He began to take me on in public. At the weekly school meetings, I spoke of my beliefs on integration and praised the positives embodied in my crossover journey. Irod weighed in with a flaming rebuttal to my rap, painting me as a misguided purveyor of soft Negro compliance. I seethed as his angry, articulate oration came down on me, earning hearty applause from the Black peanut gallery. Noel, seated a few seats away, stood up and pounded his hands in support of a philosophy he often ridiculed.

"What the fuck are you doing, man?" I challenged.

"I don't give a fuck about this Black Power shit," Noel said, "but somebody has to stop your shit.

Irod continued to backbench me with potshots, rarely missing the opportunity to take shots at my Blackness. I decided to peel off from the school's Blackstream.

Blade Brokaw, Mr. Brokaw's son, was a freshman at Hotchkiss. Blade smuggled in his record player, keeping it in my room because freshmen weren't allowed to have one. We agreed that he would come down and listen to music in my room whenever he wanted. In turn, I could listen to tunes on a good system. This deal initiated a brotherhood that would shadow the breadth of our lifetimes. The music box was a godsend. I did a straight line from my room to class and back, spending much of my time wallowing in Brian Wilson's *Pet Sounds*.

One day Noel paid me a visit, and, after making his obligatory disparaging remarks about the Beach Boys, he surprised me with a peace offering.

"I know who you are and what you done. So I ain't Tommin' you up. To me, it's about the streets, and all you have to do is dig your street shit out of the closet." He screamed, "Bring that motherfucker back out, man,'cause that's who we are!" His face soured as though he had taken a swig of lemon concentrate, and then blasted, "Why do you listen to this shit?"

"Because the good Black shit still reminds me of heroin, and I can't fuck with that. If I go back to the cooker it will kill me."

"I can dig that but what about the rest of your shit?" he asked compassionately.

I mulled Noel's offering around in my mind as "Caroline No" purred. His accusations rattled my pigment cage. I'd been softened by Irod's Uncle Tom pressure, and the confusion over my identity forced me to clutch my ghetto shawl tightly, fending off the suddenly frigid crossover winds. It was time to turn my blue eyes back to brown. Noel and I talked for hours as the music changed from the Beach Boys to a very young Al Green, who filled the air with the gospel-soul we could both commit to. I shunned my best instincts and strapped on the old psychological street gear. It would be my last shot at self-niggerization.

I began riding shotgun with Noel, and the predictable mayhem that followed was regrettable. We focused on Clark Billings, an innocent biracial puzzle. Noel and I first met Clark when we were trying out for varsity football. Noel had an itching suspicion that there was more to him than White light and became irked whenever we'd see Clark in the hallways during class changes. He would taunt, "Hey Clark, you the almost White boy!"

In the early months of 1970, Clark Billings became a bulls-eye for Noel's anger. "That motherfucker is counterfeit," Noel would say, suggesting that Clark was passing for White. I thought Clark was White because he seemed comfortable wearing his faintly tanned skin on the White side of the street. To me, it was a bogus issue: African Americans are biracial by design. Black folks come in twenty or more skin flavors because of all the European gene play. If Clark wasn't White, he turned White when departing the cafeteria and coming face to face with Noel's verbal blast. "Hey, fake nigger! That's right, fake nigger!" Clark sped up, trying to create distance between himself and the taunts, but Noel and I accelerated to keep pace.

Noel silently mouthed the words, "Let's get him." We cornered Clark on the stairwell and proceeded to kick his ass, while peppering him with racist epithets. "You're a Black man!" Noel and I shouted intermittently, until Clark finally screamed, "All right, all right, I'm Black!" There was an astounding amount of pain in that moment. And it wasn't the beating. His exhortation released an agonizing wail as though this contentious issue had stalked him for years.

The hallway mugging of Clark Billings was Noel's and my greatest sin against Hotchkiss. An excellent athlete, he could have put up a better fight, but he was defeated before we laid a glove on him. In my hate-filled racist ignorance, I'd whipped the ass of someone as American as Thomas Jefferson. Clark Billings's pain had a profound effect on me. He and I would become civil acquaintances after I apologized, but the incident haunted me, and it was a long time before I could forgive myself. Noel also felt bad but summed it up by saying, "Maybe we were wrong, but White folks is wrong all the time, so let's move on."

Later that day Noel and I and several other Black students were gathered in Irod's room burying ourselves in our Blackness, until one of our favorite pastimes broke up to the powwow. At 1:00 p.m. before the commencement of our athletic commitments, we would ogle the minister's wife as she walked the main campus square dressed in tennis whites on the way to her daily game. In an all-male school the sight of a marginal beauty strolling across the main green in a tennis miniskirt was an erectile experience. We crowded at the window, up to eight faces vying for sight turf, to get a glimpse at her wonderful, faintly cellulite-challenged thighs. Noel and I were uncomfortable having sunk to the level of drawing wood over such questionable goods, but her sexy jaunt was one of the few major hard-ons the school's meager menu had to offer.

Irod began to whine, protesting the ritual, again singling me out to admonish for the sin of White lust. This tripped my wire, and I decided that Irod was in need of a dose of real Black reality. I opened the window, then broke for him, grabbing him by the throat and slapping him silly before hanging him from the window by his ankles.

"Umoja your Black ass out of this one, motherfucker!" I screamed.

This put an end to all of the Uncle Tom bullshit, and oddly enough, it set the stage for what would become a wonderful friendship. The following year, after his departure from school, Irod revealed to me that he was gay and that his confusion over his sexuality was a factor in our earlier tussle. He was in the throes of coming out of his closet and asked for my understanding and friendship. After jostling with my naive homophobia, I committed to the pain in his heart, and we subsequently fell deeply into like.

After regaining my individuality I returned to Abbey Road, and Noel's hostility flared. "Fuck him!" was our mutual sentiment, and I went back to playing the Hotchkiss game. It was clear that Noel was dead meat, but no one wanted to be the executioner. Political correctness turned into administrative constipation, leaving Noel to twist in the wind.

The incident that pushed Noel and me beyond our breaking point was a relatively innocent development. My relationship with Leif Thorne-Thomsen was growing. TT's endless patience acted as a life raft for the off-centered students' desire to express themselves. His magnet lured a band of interesting, talented misfits. One of those misfits was a young man who would become a life long blood worthy friend, Jim Sadwith. Jim was a beleaguered, creative sort, constantly ducking crap flung at him by his fellow seniors who had mistakenly consigned him to their nerd list. He was an intellectual, non-athletic, small-framed Jewish cat, bright and organized enough to hone his Hotchkiss experience into Harvard acceptance, just the kind of person Noel hated and I found interesting. Noel couldn't see that Sadwith wore his cool flashes on the inside.

Jim was one of Leif's disciples, and it was at TT's table that I heard him speak of his plans to stage a theatrical adaptation of *The Catcher in the Rye*. I'd read the book in the Peddie School and had been woefully unimpressed: Old Holden's disturbed-White-boy angst left me cold. But Sad was on to something more interesting. His intent was to interview the stud of the "leave me the fuck alone" literary club, J. D. Salinger, the book's reclusive legendary author. Jim's unpopularity courted a hailstorm of skepticism, but I thought that Sadwith's quest was the coolest thing I'd witnessed at Hotchkiss to that point.

Jim would complete a search filled with mystery and lucky breaks, ultimately connecting with the old bastard. He scooped the world. The details of the interview have faded from memory, but the size of the whale he'd bagged from a dormitory room was irrefutably hip. Unfortunately, Jim couldn't enjoy his score. His knucklehead detractors drove up his insecurities to the point where he wrapped himself in aloof gauze.

Noel and I argued over my interest in the nerd with the golden quest and started to level me with jibes that wouldn't stop. "After that motherfucker gets out of Harvard, he's gonna remember you, offer you a nice gig as his chauffeur."

I doubled him up with a low blow. "You just an angry, self-hating spic that couldn't turn a trick." Noel hated any disparaging references to his Hispanic roots. That was the straw that spanked the camel.

"I hate you, motherfucker!" he exploded. "You better watch your back!"

The shit was on. Several days, later, during a class change, Noel and I passed each other in the hall. I had a lead pipe in my jacket sleeve that I allowed to slide down to my wrist, revealing its nose. Noel held his hand tightly on his breast pocket revealing the imprint of a bowie knife. We shot each other street-real looks, trying to gain the intimidation edge. A few days later Noel and I came upon each other at the student mailboxes. We shared kill-filled glares, and Noel made a move toward me. I let the pipe slide down my sleeve into my hand, ready for battle. With a blinding motion Noel's shank appeared. A handful of students were in shock.

I yelled, "Split!"

"Are you guys gonna kill each other?" one asked.

"Cut out!" I ordered.

Suddenly we heard a rush of footsteps coming down the stairwell. Noel barked, "Let's take it outside."

We went out of a side entrance that led to the golf course. Once we were standing on the green, Noel yelled, "Kill or die motherfucker!" I turned on him and swung my pipe and missed. Noel ducked and sliced my jacket sleeve with his knife. I jumped back, avoiding serious injury, and challenged, "Let's put the fucking weapons down and fight like men." We both agreed but hesitated waiting for the other to toss his weapon. Finally, I took a few steps back, making sure I could run if Noel reneged, and tossed my pipe to the ground several feet away. Noel flung his knife, and it landed in an adjoining sand trap.

He and I squared off, and that son of a bitch grabbed the flag pin out of the hole and swung. I dodged the pole and grabbed hold of it. We got into a tug-of-war. Noel wrestled it from me and jabbed me in the stomach. I bent over, feigning hurt. He came toward me to assess my condition and I let loose with a roundhouse right that caught him flush on the jaw. Noel fell back, and I jumped on him. We rolled on the ground until we tumbled down a slope into the sand trap. We shouted obscenities as we jostled for the upper hand.

"I'm gonna kill you, motherfucker!" I threatened.

"You ain't got enough dick left to kill me!"

Noel and I rumbled to the point of exhaustion. As our efforts began to peter out, insult was added to this injurious oddity, when a golf ball came flying in our direction and landed between us. "Well, they sent us here to upgrade our shit," Noel said. "Instead of fighting on the streets, we'se fightin' on a fucking golf course." We both couldn't help but laugh. Noel then became serious, declaring, "You ain't my big brother no more."

The "Boys Who Came Back" would end their first Hotchkiss year with a permanent bruise on their friendship and the disturbing realization that White folks glitter ain't necessarily gold.

SEVENTEEN

That summer I hung out with Gerri. We were surfing the first wave of what would be a very long affair. The Voices were preparing to tour Europe. On their itinerary were stops at the Albert Hall, an appearance on Tops of Pops, then on to the Isle of Wight. The Harlem invasion would conclude at the Olympia Theatre in Paris. Noel and I good-naturedly avoided contact whenever possible.

Every day felt like the Fourth of July. I couldn't wait to get up in the morning and see what would come my way. I hung out in the Village a lot and caught most of the greatest classic rock artists in their prime. I felt a powerful sense of vindication for having chosen the path I had coming out of the hospital. This was the summer that Chuck's throne began to crack beneath him. He had reached icon status in a forty-block radius. He was a powerful figure, and I was his spoiled New England–prep-school brat. I basked in the aura of his popularity and respect, but when the king starts fucking the wide-eyed handmaidens, the castle is in trouble.

As the summer moved on, father and son would face a stern test. One day I was heading to meet Gerri. As I approached her building I noticed that she was standing with four people surrounded by a pile of film equipment. One of the people was an oldish, balding guy who looked like a public school teacher. Gerri introduced him as Bruce Davidson, a noted photographer, who

had the assignment of doing a short film for television on the ghetto phenomenon that was Gerri.

Bruce Davidson shook my hand, pulled me to the side, and said, "I want to
broaden the scope of the film I'm doing."

"Huh?"

"You're really important to her. I was thinking that we might be able to do
something with you and her together. You know that little patch of grass not far
from here? It would be great if we could get you and her together, holding
hands, talking to one another. I hear that you go to prep school and you're a
pretty accomplished fellow in your own right."

He searched for my response.

"I'm listening."

He asked, "Well, what do you think?"

I mulled his offer and then laughed out loud. "Are you crazy? You want me to
be in movies? Man, brothers would laugh me out of the projects. Look, leave all
that stuff to Gerri. But me, forget it."

He seemed disappointed, annoyed over the pinprick I had delivered to his
vision. But then his eyes lit up. He pulled me a little farther away and delivered
a second proposal. "If you do this for the film, I'll give you fifty bucks and
lunch."

"Where do I stand?"

In those days a legal fifty dollars was a fortune, and the moment Bruce mentioned the price I broke and ran, searching for an afro comb. I wanted to look
good for my introduction to the world of film. While the crew set up, I mingled
among them. A White cameraman and his Latino assistant were fussing over a
huge camera, and I wandered over to the aforementioned patch of grass. Seated
on the ground cross-legged, hippie-style, was a girl with a large taping machine
in her lap.

"Hi, my name is Dennis."

As she looked up, her long, straight dark hair parted and her face emerged
from behind its curtain. Squinting into a noon-day sun, she said, "Hi, my name
is Barbara."

"What ya' doin'?" I asked.

"Sound."

She immediately returned to concentrate on her task. Clad in attractive hippie garb, her dark features were intriguing, sparking instantaneous, involuntary
wood. The crew under Davidson's direction shot Gerri at play in the projects. I
was quickly introduced to how much waiting there is in this film game. Bruce
became irritated with my constant nagging questions.

"When are we going to do this thing, man?" I bugged continuously.

Bored out of my skull, I started to pick the brains of the crew members. The words "pain in the ass" began growing on my forehead. To my relief Barbara came to the rescue by inviting me into her world of sound. I was drawn to Barbara because it was clear she rated zero on the scale of Nigraphobia.

"What's your last name?" I asked.

"Kopple, Barbara Kopple."

"Kopple? I was thinking you would say something more Pocahontas-like. You know, Indian."

"I'm not Indian." She laughed. "I look like an Indian to you?"

"Yeah, the long dark hair, the clothes, the comfort level—White girls usually freeze up when suddenly tossed in the 'hood, so I took it for granted you were something not White."

She laughed, stating, "I'm from Westchester."

Finally, Gerri and I were told to sit down beside this anorexic, pathetic excuse for a tree, as though we would ever consider sitting on ghetto ground just passing the time away. Another quick lesson learned about movies: It's all about bullshit. Gerri and I got into it. We caressed and even got off a speck of innocent teenage fondling. At other times we were instructed to strike a more serious pose. After several takes, we finally pulled it off to Bruce's satisfaction. The experience reminded me of football and how the crew was a team and the director was the coach, and if everyone pulled together and there was enough talent in the lineup, you could win.

I was lit up and offered to take Gerri to dinner and a movie. On our way to Second Avenue to catch a cab, we stopped for a moment at the center to see Chuck. He was in the basement practicing for a big archery tournament. With about four arrows left in his quiver, we watched as he stared intently through the focusing site on his bow and planted arrow after arrow in the bulls-eye circle. He put his bow down to take a short break, and Gerri and I, bubbling over with excitement, told him about our day in the movies. His reaction was much less cheerful than we expected, and he began asking detailed questions about the film's operation.

"How many niggers on the crew?"

Surprised, Gerri and I looked at each other. I said, "There's only four people."

Chuck pressed, "Out the four, how many?"

"Chuck, this is a really good thing," I responded. "They good people."

"How many?"

I stalled and mumbled. "Well, there's a Puerto Rican."

"That's cool," Chuck nodded.

"And there is an older White guy who runs everything. He's a photographer with a big rep. And there's a pretty girl, and she's real nice . . . Right, Gerri, real nice?"

"Right, daddy," Gerri said, "real nice."

"And she's an Indian."

Chuck liked that and responded, "Indian motherfuckers can play. We on they turf. That's three."

"And the cameraman," I said, "is a regular White guy."

Without hesitation, Chuck stated, "He got to go."

"What do you mean, he got to go?"

"If they want to come up here and film, then everybody who can be Black will be Black."

"Why you making such a big thing about this?"

" 'Cause that's the way it's got to be. White folks ain't givin' up nothin' you don't take from them."

That was a puzzling response from a cat who had built his jam from dealing amicably with White folks. We may have earned what we'd gotten from White folks, but we certainly hadn't taken it from them. I couldn't figure out Chuck's point. It seemed that he was battling a bad case of power-itis.

"I'm going to talk to them motherfuckers tomorrow," he said as he picked up his bow and got ready to shoot another round.

Gerri and I slinked out of there, bummed to the point that we canceled our dinner plans. I was really angry, because I was used to making racism work for me, not against me.

The following day Chuck whacked Davidson with his bizarre ultimatum. It all came to a head when Davidson invited Chuck to see some of the raw film footage. He was aware of how fond Chuck was of me and hoped that the positive images of his daughter and his right-hand boy would bring the big guy around. Bruce, Barbara, Chuck, Gerri, and myself met at the offices of the renowned filmmakers, The Maysle Brothers. Everyone was cordial as we assembled in the screening room. The lights went down, and onscreen were Gerri and me lying in the grass talking about our bright futures. Our large afros and high aspirations oozed from the screen as the onlookers swooned over a tiny patch of grass surrounded by project apartment buildings. We were playing a bleeding-heart liberal's fantasy of a young Black couple.

When the lights came up, all White faces focused on Chuck, as Gerri and I squirmed in hopeful anticipation. I could see that the formation of his face was indicating a quick No!

"I ain't moved," he uttered, pooping the party. "White folks are invited guests in the neighborhood, and no matter how welcome a guest they is, you'se a guest. You can't be running nothin'. My word still stands. If you don't have a Black crew, you'se through," he stated with a quiet intensity.

Gerri and I sat quietly and watched as the filmmakers fired every argument in their quiver, only to have them bounce meekly off of Chuck's steel-belted racism. He stood and raised his arms, imposing his signature wingspan on the room, and restated his edict, "If niggers don't run the crew, you'se through!"

My budding manhood lurched forward, and I spoke. "You're wrong, Chuck!"

"What!" he fumed.

"These are good people, and we're in a movie. Are you crazy, man?"

The group looked on, conveying a glimmer of hope, as I continued to surprise myself. I had crossed over to the other side in full view. Gerri was caught in the middle, leery of going against the family line, but I was feeling no pain. The intergrationist in me was firing and misfiring all over the place.

"Chuck, how we ever going to move forward if we don't all do it together?"

Chuck looked at me like Michael Corleone looked at his brother Fredo in *Godfather II* after issuing the kiss of death. It chilled me to the bone, but I held my ground. Dumb move. Chuck held firm, and the project was quashed. I'd become Chuck's pariah of the month. After sobering up from one too many testosterone cocktails, I had to contend with my fate.

Chuck hurled me out of East Harlem like an afro-tipped javelin, and I landed in Barbara Kopple's loft in the East Village. Our bond during the struggle had grown to the point where she sort of adopted me, inviting me to come and live with her and her man for a while as I licked my wounds. Chuck loved me and was my de facto father, but his behavior was against everything I'd come to believe in. I could no longer play the race game. Color turns irrelevant when the complexity of personalities and common interests come into play.

Barbara was good tonic for what ailed me during the tail end of the summer of 1970. Smoking pot and looking out on Fourth Avenue and Twelfth Street from her loft-apartment window, I reveled in my principled stance as I watched the colorful freaks parade before me. I stood tall, took the heat, and wound up in hip exile.

EIGHTEEN

At the end of that intense summer, Chuck lifted the ban on my presence and all was forgiven. He gave me his collard greens version of the Godfather's warning to his son: Never go against the family in public . . . ever. Chuck's rap was clear and direct. "No matter how fruitful America might be to you privileged niggers, don't confuse right and wrong with blood and skin. Nobody else in this country does."

Noel and I met at Port Authority Bus Terminal for the ride back to Hotchkiss. The only thing that kept him in school was his respectful fear of Chuck's bruising left hook. The wheels had come off the experiment. His attitude was "fuck it!" His only interest on campus was in developing a financial stake in its drug scene. He was a walking time bomb that would detonate in the Stalin wars.

Gunner Stalin was soaked in privileges and peers with diplomatic immunity that came in handy when smuggling quantities of cannabis into the country. Gunner's connections gave him a lofty position for a relatively nondescript schmuck. Noel's association with Stalin was a dalliance of convenience. "That little bone-nosed White boy gets on my nerves," he would say. Stalin let Noel know that he was smuggling in a shipment of hashish and promised that he would give Noel a substantial amount to sell back on the streets. I was hands-off on the deal; it smelled too much like street shit.

When the hashish arrived, Stalin, for reasons I could not fathom, decided to renege on his offer. When Noel went to collect his bounty, Stalin lied, saying that the deal had fallen through, but Noel had gotten the word off the grapevine that the dope was in. Stalin couldn't sell this jive line and 'fessed up, but chose to remain steadfast. They argued heatedly, resulting in an ugly stalemate.

On the other side of campus I was on an exquisite acid trip, doping out in colors to Hendrix's *Axis: Bold as Love*, when Irod broke into the room and announced, "Noel and Stalin are going at it, and it's getting out of hand." I was out of my colors and into a pile of Black and White ugliness. When I arrived at Stalin's room, Noel shouted, "Stay out of this, D. This motherfucker is trying to beat me out of our deal!" I tried to reason with Stalin, urging him to honor his commitment. Stalin declared, with the determinative balls of a Patrick Henry, "It's my right to share with whomever I want to." I roared with laughter. Through my tainted lenses, he looked like a little pickle-nosed rat debating from the floor of the Senate. But this was street law, and he was arguing his case in the wrong court.

Tripping unmercifully, I stepped back and listened to the sounds of Hendrix that were still scoring my vision. I made one last plea to Stalin, but he stood his ground. Blue blood was tougher than I thought, because his resolve was impenetrable. I stepped back, accepting my impotence.

"I'm gonna take this motherfucker off, D," Noel warned.

"No man, this ain't the place," I uttered, suppressing my desire to laugh. Suddenly Noel whacked Stalin in the thigh with a powerful right hand. The pain caused Stalin to grab for his leg, thus putting himself into a position that allowed Noel to roundhouse him with an open hand. It was mesmerizing, balletic violence.

"Turn the lights out!" Noel ordered Irod, who complied. Then Noel unleashed a series of carpet bombs on Stalin's skull. Stalin took the ass-whipping. When the lights went back on, he still resisted. "I'm not scared of you," he shouted. "I'll stand up for what is mine."

Noel ordered the lights out again, and the fireworks continued as he dropped his next assault on Stalin's body. I dove in and separated Noel from Stalin and ordered Irod to turn the lights back on. "Gimme my shit," Noel shouted. I was becoming pissed at Stalin, wishing he would just fucking surrender, but with the conviction of a Mississippi Freedom Rider, Stalin shouted, "No!" Frustrated, Noel accepted defeat, realizing that only homicide would separate this tough little bastard from his principles. Stalin, who would probably hate American Black people for the rest of his life, quivered in a heap of brutality. He had no way of knowing he had passed the toughest test a street nigger ever faces, by holding on to his manhood in a cell beat-down.

The Stalin affair destroyed any of Noel's remaining feelings of goodwill toward the school community. The following morning, after his umpteenth Discipline Committee meeting, Noel came to my room while I was asleep and kicked the bed.

Startled, I yelled, "Whoo!"

Noel was standing over me. "D, I'm cuttin' out. I can't cross this White folks highway, man. The cars move too fast. I met my match. Nothin' ain't never kicked my ass like this book shit. These White motherfuckers are tough. In the streets, I understand the enemy." He took a deep breath, his face reddening. "I'm doing the bird, man, over the wall."

It was only a few days before the Thanksgiving holidays, but he was adamant. Later that morning we stood in the lobby of the main building waiting for a cab to take Noel to the bus station. The large picture window acted as a movie screen as Noel and I quietly watched a gathering of light snow swirl. He put his arm around me.

"We did this shit together," I said.

He smiled, resting his head on my shoulder before whispering. "I was never a part of this. I'm just glad that I made this move before I really fucked something up." We sighted the cab as it came toward the main building. "There goes my shit, man," Noel said, and we grabbed his suitcases.

After depositing them in the trunk, we gave each other a hug and a brother shake. As the cab pulled out, I watched it disappear through the gates. It cut deep. I guessed it made sense that I would have to go it alone, because I was the one who wanted this life.

After Noel's departure Hotchkiss turned gray. Many of my special Black privileges had been taken away. Whitedom would no longer bend. Hotchkiss wasn't a school to me; it was a stage. The producers had decided to close the show, and I descended to the bottom of my Hotchkiss experience. My interest waned, and no matter how much acid I did, the colors that had once stimulated me faded.

I took one last shot at relevancy when I decided to compete for the class presidency. Initially, the idea was drummed up by one of my favorite classmates, a picturesque red-headed nerd named Harvey Neville. He convinced me I could win. I needed this challenge because I had given up on the classroom side of life. Harv's brainstorm lit a fire under me. Once my ego fully grasped his proposal, I was off to the races. James Carville and Paul Begala had nothing on Harv, as he wound me up properly and pointed me in the right direction. I ran on the potent issues of upper mid (eleventh grade) smoking privileges and an additional weekend home. We kicked ass, and I won decisively.

There I was—momentarily king of the high-tax-bracket White boys. I was the first Black cat to be so honored. The headmaster Bill Olsen used me and my unusual distinction well, assigning me to give campus tours to potential students and their parents. Announcing my presidency became a genuine kick for him.

Winning the presidency topped off my end game at Hotchkiss. I had achieved everything I could have imagined in the ivy White world. I came to Hotchkiss looking for America, seeking to prove my equality. With my inferiority no longer an issue, my Lennonist, integrationist principles strengthened. With a year and a half left in my commitment, I was ready to graduate. It had been an exhausting ride from my hospital bed to Hotchkiss's unyielding atmosphere. With little of the fanfare that had accompanied my arrival, I split Hotchkiss at the beginning of winter term.

In the winter of 1971, at age eighteen, I landed in a Harlem very different than the one I had left. Everyone's life had moved on. After leaving Hotchkiss I had convinced myself that when I got home I wouldn't be just another nigger. But it was in a different disco now. I was neither a good enough athlete nor musically talented enough to shine among Black people, and as quick as you could say Martin Luther King, the neighborhood had junked social optimism like an aging copy of *Ebony* magazine. Without the power of my White folks, I was again a second-class citizen on first sight.

Noel had filled the vacuum that Chuck had left during his major drift away from the kingdom by injecting the new street agenda into the curriculum: drugs. The center had quickly turned into a facility of unsupervised delinquents. The house of a thousand options was becoming a dark sanctuary for street hustlers.

My old friend, Reverend Collins, found me a job as a gardener at the Union Theological Seminary in Upper Manhattan, near Columbia University. This has-been shit at eighteen was a drag. I was gardening by day and dodging street pitfalls at night. In a flash of desperate artistry, I had my friend snap a picture of me lying in a pile of garbage. A gross act for sure, but it defined my descent accurately. I had the picture developed and sent a copy to Gail Sheehy, with a note attached that simply said "SOS."

As always, she responded to my plight and invited me to her new apartment. I hadn't seen her in a while, and her new prosperity was stunning. The vulnerability she had showed during our interviews had been replaced by a toughened confidence. Gail was one of a group of talented Young Turks who were falling like leaves from the branches of the many defunct newspapers, such as the *Her-*

ald Tribune and the *Journal-American*. The new hot magazine in Manhattan that was snaring the best of them was *New York*. Its talented troops included Breslin, Steinem, Hamill, Wolfe, Greene, and others whose work would define the tidal wave of change that the country was engulfed in. Gail established her space on the masthead, developing a role as an instinctual courier of the social psyche, helping to shepherd the "me" phase of White boomers to water.

After a quick dinner Gail proposed that she use her influence to get me a job in the magazine's mailroom, and several days later she delivered. Almost instantly my horrible trip through irrelevance was over. *New York* magazine was a stone cold rehabilitative gas. I got to know everyone by delivering their mail. There were mother figures like Ruth Gilbert, who edited the entertainment listings, and big-sister role models like Ellen Stock, who handled "Best Bets." She never hesitated to pass down promotional copies of new albums and unused comp tickets to just about everything in town. Ellen was in friendship with young Ron Delsner and other concert promoters, so big time rock 'n' roll was back in my life.

I was a six-foot-one, slave chiselled athlete, a hip Black pet, an exalted position in early-seventies liberal land. At that time liberals were strong believers in tokenism, and I was the only token in the small brownstone on East Thirty-first Street. Rarely were there many Blacks among the liberal elite, but the few they chose got a fun ride out of it. I brought good vibes and my Hotchkiss tag, signaling that I was comfortable with rich White folks. It was the best island an emergency parachutist ever landed on.

Renewed with the spirit of privilege, I quickly reconciled with my dilemma over Hotchkiss, and, in relatively short order, I decided I wanted to go back. This would be no easy task, having left under such murky circumstances, but I was determined to rejoin the starship.

NINETEEN

In the winter of 1971 the Voices of East Harlem did a musical gig in Ghana that would subsequently make a fine documentary called *Soul to Soul*. The Voices were a part of a larger show featuring Ike and Tina Turner, Wilson Pickett, Roberta Flack, and Santana. The experience had a profound affect on Gerri. Her love of Blackness was cemented by the great reception that the real Africans offered. Gerri's trip included an audience with the king of one of the oldest villages. Surrounded by hunky tribesmen, she was in heaven. They were ten days that shook her world. The temporary merger with her natural people gave rhyme and reason to Gerri's instinctual African sensibilities.

When she touched down at Kennedy Airport on a cold early March morning, she was still walking on air. She arrived home wrapped in an evangelical overcoat. I was freaked and thrilled to see her newly acquired African hairstyle. She had her hair braided, and then each braid was wound in black thread and connected artistically in a bouffant structure that was indescribably beautiful. It highlighted her broad Negroid features that were too often left off of the Western fashion mavens' drawing boards. Gerri was so excited that she took me by the hand, pulled me into the bathroom, closed the door, and locked it. She announced that she wanted to give me my gift.

I immediately thought that it was something sexual, and after ten days apart I was hot game. She took off her coat and then removed her sweater. The door was opening to a sexual African fantasy. My mind was racing, considering all the possible angles. She then opened the top of her jeans and reached into her private area, producing a leather pouch that she had bought in Ghana. I went into rapid deflation when Gerri opened the pouch, revealing a handful of red dirt. She offered the most spellbinding smile and said, "Africa!" Despite the diminution of my tropical fantasies, her revelation warmed me. The picture of her pride in her possession provided the most natural African American moment I'd ever witnessed. Gerri had smuggled her feeling of ancestral oneness back from the masters.

The downside was that for a lengthy period of time everything was seen through African lenses. I had a big afro and let Gerri talk me into allowing her to cornrow my hair into an African style. It took hours, as I fought the pain that came of having one's scalp pulled every which way. The next morning, as I was about to take the braids out, I looked in the mirror and liked what I saw. Decades before New York Knickerbocker basketball nova Latrell Sprewell made cornrows popular, I rode the 6 train to work, watching people stare as they tried to negotiate my seemingly gay hairstyle with my football-hardened upper torso.

The hairstyle was a hit at work, and my fashion statement caught the eye of a very special person who worked at the magazine, Joni, an attractive White woman in her mid-twenties. Her compliments were pointed and profusive. I was young but far from stupid, and I could see in her eyes that she was crossing the line between benevolent White person into the land of maybe. I was turned on but regarded her attention as little more than mind candy for future bathroom sessions. Joni was playing for bigger stakes.

All my inner cool was suspended as the "gee golly" part of me began to spill all over the place. Every morning, when I dropped off Joni's mail, I would try to come up with the most mature, perceptive anecdotes I could muster. My comfort level increased when it became apparent that anything I said was gobbled up seductively. I could sense that I had the upper hand, as Joni fed me all of the lure signals, but I was hesitant. What would a smart, sexy package of adult White snatch want with a Black kid? It didn't add up enough to turn my red light green. Joni visited me in the mail room and suggested that we go to lunch. My knees knocked. I feigned cool but was burning inside, crazy with anticipation and confusion. I had to carry my inflated head around the building in a wheelbarrow.

That evening I went into the projects to cop some weed. When I hit the park where everyone hung out, I ran into Noel. He approached, handing me a joint, smoothly conveying the body language of a peaceful truce. Noel was selling coke, developing a clientele of mostly heroin guys who were getting off on speedballs—a sweet, deadly concoction of heroin and coke. I told him about my Joni fascination, and he joked approvingly. "Pussy don't got no color,'cause yo dick's eye can't see." We laughed. This droplet of old times felt good. As we puffed on the joint, Noel's demeanor beamed rays of his old confidence.

"Watch your back in that White world," he said, " 'cause niggers die two ways with Whitey—once from expectations, the other from reaching those expectations."

On that bizarre note, we parted.

The next day I arrived at an outdoor plaza of a housing complex on Thirty-first Street and Second Avenue. Joni had chosen a low-key setting and brought along a slew of high-priced deli foods. The plaza smelled of progressive energy, as the beautiful summer fashions wore their Clairol-treated White babes with distinction. Throughout our meal very little was said: I didn't want to fuck things up by talking. I could feel her looking past my youth as she carefully placed shrimp in my mouth. The light between us turned green when she reached over and kissed my forehead, saying, "I'm sold."

That evening I tracked down the only person I knew who had a genius for being human, Jerry Brandt. I told him my crossover fears about Joni. He pondered my dilemma before saying, "Don't be a schmuck and take this shit so seriously. She might be older than you, but she's White and doesn't know shit about Blackness. It's your game. You're the fucking star!" He brought me back to earth by slapping the "Oh, God!" wuss-filled drama queen right out of me.

Meanwhile, Gerri and I had begun to drift apart. Her stardom induced insecurities leading me to the conclusion that I was not in her league. Gerri's desire to commit to my constant flights from our pigment-rich reservation was waning precipitously. I didn't want to be as Black as she did and was becoming weary of closeting my White side. Gerri had exhibited a great deal of patience, but after my four hundredth assault on her sensibilities with *Led Zeppelin II*, she began to loathe White popular culture. These problems became the recipe for a relationship on the wane.

Joni and I were still limited to heavy panting, unable to find the right lay place. We played out the early part of the affair on the subway platform at Park Avenue and Thirty-first Street as countless trains sped by. After hours of enjoying each other, she would catch the PATH train back to Weehawken, New Jersey, where she lived with a roommate. During our subway romance, Joni introduced me to pop art and the world of Andy Warhol, encouraging me to think in a variety of colors. I taught her about the streets and painful fun. She loved my dramatic street anecdotes, and the more I articulated, the more she purred. Her auburn hair and green eyes joined a small contingent of freckles, embellishing the youth in her smile. On the days that she wore dresses, her shapely legs reeked havoc upon my self-control. The combination of her attributes were a luscious buffet.

Joni was an athlete at a time when beautiful female athletes were rare. Somehow she was well versed in the male aggression that framed the world of competitive sports. This became evident when we played together in pick-up softball games. When her juices got going, Joni could rift all the salty language that came with being a ballsy athlete. This widened our comfort zone, and I began to quiz her about her colorful behavior.

"What is your thing for Black guys about? That's a sure way for a White girl to win her tramp button. My Uncle Womp used to say, 'The only thing a White woman can do for a nigger is put money in his undertaker's pocket.'"

"Your color is beautiful to look at," she stated simply.

It was?

"Don't you love mahogany?" she asked.

"What?" I mumbled, not having a clue as to what she was talking about.

"It's a beautiful piece of rich brown wood. It's warm and comfortable color reminds me of you."

She didn't just tolerate my skin color, she celebrated it? That night on my way home, I went through a spate of embarrassment. I realized that I was still screwed up over the color of my skin. I had looked past my color, never choosing to draw any inferences about its beauty, too hung up on its way of hindering my movements.

Late that evening, as Gerri and I walked though Jefferson Park, I asked, "Do you know what mahogany is?" Gerri was a wealth of information about such things and went into a dissertation on the subject.

"A girl told me I looked like mahogany to her."

"That's a compliment. Whoever the sister is who said that has her head in the right place."

"Think so, huh?"

"She must have it together because she understands how beautiful Black is. Who is she?" she quizzed as her thoughts turned to interrogation.

"Oh, just a girl I met at a party. There wasn't much to it other than the mahogany thing."

She rode my answer, never suspecting that the sister she praised looked more like Jane Fonda than Jane Pittman.

The roar of the trains provided an exciting urban soundtrack as Joni talked about a woman's desire for equality and freedom. I marveled at her attitude. Only Anna Griffin and Gail Sheehy had given me glimpses of a woman who had punted the conventional woman's play book. I was amazed to discover the many similarities between the Black struggle and women's. I didn't know much about feminists, until Joni declared herself one. Her exhortations about the equality women sought rose above the noisy screeches of braking vehicles. During our quieter moments, lust piled layer upon layer of groin pressure on our fixed gazes. I suggested that we go to her house when her roommate wasn't there, and she froze.

"Does your roommate have a case of Nigraphobia?" I asked.

Joni paused for an inordinate amount of time and then disclosed, "It's not that." She paused again, and I became uncomfortable. "It's not a good time," she concluded.

Her smile returned. She took a little carton of strawberries from her bag and began to feed me. The strawberries set off sexual alarms, as the rumbling of the trains turned the wooden bench into a makeshift vibrator. I was learning the artful pleasure of extended foreplay, but its luster was waning as the pressure of non-consummation continued to grow.

We began to go to the movies a lot, finding privacy in the darkness of theaters. She turned me on to a new actor whom she described as the offspring of Dustin Hoffman's one-night stand with a chicken. The movie was *The Panic in Needle Park*, and the actor was Al Pacino. He played a heroin addict. The portrayal was so real that I was moved to tears watching heroin drain the color from the character's life, leaving him in a puddle of gray. Joni asked me why I was crying, and I told her, "I don't know who this cat Pacino is, but he's serving up my hard past on a fucking platter. That's the first time I ever saw on-screen how fucked up my shit was." Joni began crying over my reaction, and through the tears, she invited me home.

Several days later, on the way to Joni's crib, I got lost. Having misplaced her phone number, I was left with the task of searching for a needle in Weehawken's White, middle-class haystack. I could feel the bull's-eye growing on my back as I crept along gingerly, trying to be as inconspicuous as a full-afroed, six-foot mahogany power symbol could. Suddenly, I heard the call of a joyous auburn-haired siren. Hanging out of a small apartment window, Joni shouted, "With that afro, I'm surprised you made it!" My body was pumping heat as the clock ticked down.

The closer I got to the building, the hotter Joni looked. I ran up the stairs, and when I got to her door, she greeted me with a hug and invited me into her smallish two-bedroom apartment. She wore cut-off jeans and a torn sweatshirt that exposed one unself-conscious nipple. Her recent boyishly short haircut allowed her face to send heated androgynous signals of a sexy tomboy well above the age of consent. I was mad for her. Itching with thrust and want, I made my move, but she stopped me cold.

"What's this shit? Are you crazy?" I roared.

She chumped me off, pulled away and sat on the couch studying me. I was flabbergasted. Her quick change jammed all systems. I had been taught to go full throttle once given the green light. I was supposed to be in charge from this point on.

"I don't want to be eaten alive," she said.

"What?" I shrieked in a whiny tone.

Since when did the woman have a say after the consent decree had been issued? It was there that our ages and maturity differences became apparent. She was a woman into subtleties and nuances; I was a boy who was still doing it standing up in uncool places. The tent pole in my pants withered, and we both watched the collapse of the denim canvas.

"You're much better than that," she said.

"What?" I belched, feeling five years old. I was a mass of jelly in her petri dish.

"Guys think that sex is their creation," she softly instructed.

"Why the fuck did I come here?" I shouted.

She approached, looked me in the eye, and said, "Come with me."

She led me to the bathroom, where there was a walk-in shower, and asked me to undress and forget everything I'd ever learned. I was weighing whether to tell her to stuff it, but intrigue trumped indignation and I complied. When the water flowed, it flattened Joni's hairdo, eroding her makeup, revealing a face bent on mischief.

Joni lathered my body slowly, reigniting my impulses. I wanted to pounce, but her hands moved so slowly beneath my waist that I was trapped between excitement and frustration. I pressed her against the shower wall, but the slipperiness produced by the lather enabled her to break free. My confusion ruled as I pleaded, "Come on, baby, I have to do something with this thing." She laughed and then leaned against the shower wall, pushing the lower half of her body forward and asked that I come and hold her. "Let the water work," she whispered.

The water cascaded down, rinsing our bodies, enhancing the traction of the embrace. She continually whispered, "Go slow. We'll both want it more." I was inspired by her wisdom, instantly and all at once, as our thighs locked. She played both the aggressor and the pursued. I'd never been with a girl who knew how to ask for what she wanted once her clothes were off. It was my first experience with a woman who wanted sex as much as I did. Joni's bold approach broke all the rules on my sexual docket. We completed our shower, and I was hot for the bed.

She kissed me and simply said, "The next time. I want you to think about the difference between a boudoir and a racetrack."

"Next time?" I jabbered.

"The only way to experience sexual freedom is through equality and trust. Women are superior sexual beings," she teased. "You have to incorporate the skill of a musical conductor directing my multi-orgasmic orchestra."

She'd turned sex into art, opening a door that allowed my clumsy male ignorance to escape.

I discussed my new relationship with Chuck at the risk of ridicule. I was ready for a lecture filled with wisecracks, but as was often the case, he surprised me.

"Eat the pussy!"

"What?"

"That White gal know something. When you fucking her, it's your thing. Eat the pussy and everybody walks happy." This was Chuck at his best. "You playing way off Nigger Island with this one. Be careful, and remember the only thing that is for sure is that you ain't White! Hold on to that fact, and you should do okay."

After my initial visit to Weehawken, Joni had picked up signs that people in the neighborhood didn't take easily to my kind. I wouldn't leave the apartment until three in the morning when Weehawken's set was empty. The indignity that went with this covert behavior seemed meaningless at the time. I was too juiced.

On one of my visits everything came together for us. I had never seen a woman have an orgasm before, and it was a humbling experience to discover what a satisfied woman looked like. Joni taught me that there were sexual pleasures above the waist and below the knees. After a marathon episode, we lay in bed. Silently, I focused on what a really sexually satisfied male felt like, but like most slices of human heaven, my euphoria was short-lived. The sound of a key entering the front door's lock changed everything.

Joni dashed from the bedroom, leaving the door open. In walked her roommate carrying two suitcases. When they hit the wooden floor, it sounded like gunshots.

Joni's surprised and flustered voice bellowed, "I didn't think you would be home until tomorrow." She then blew me away when she meekly ended her statement with the word "honey."

"Honey?" I shouted.

The sound of my voice brought the roommate into the bedroom. She stood over the bed glaring angrily at me and asked, "Who the hell is this?"

"Who the hell are you?" I fired back.

The roommate quickly left the room, slamming the door, and began to read Joni the riot act. Her voice could have peeled the paint off the wall. I could hear phrases. "How could you? After all I've meant to you." I was finally getting the notion that Joni was a lesbian, at least part of the time. The only lesbians I had ever known were so definitively dykes that part of their survival depended upon their ability to out-man men. But a woman as beautiful as Joni, why the hell would she want to be a lesbian?

As their argument subsided, I dressed quickly and entered the living room. Joni sat in the corner, the chastened, obedient girlfriend. Her partner was extraordinarily macho, stockily built with a tight, bulging ass stuffed into a pair of black jeans. She wore a short-cropped, boyish hairdo and no makeup. The power she held over Joni seemed as oppressive as that of the males Joni eschewed.

"What the fuck are you doing in my bed?" she shouted. I looked to Joni, who avoided eye contact. Her lover continued, "I don't want to ever see you around here again!"

I began to wise off. "She's in love with me, so you can kiss my ass."

This set off the bully in her, and she got into my face, nose to nose, and threatened, "If you don't get out of here, I'll call the cops."

"I'm not scared of you," I told her as I backed up.

"You better be," as she inched closer to me.

"Joni, what the fuck is going on here?"

"It's complicated," she eked, coming up major weak when the jets needed firing.

"Leave her out of it," the roommate demanded.

I jumped full street and said, "I'm not going to let you butch me off of my woman."

Poor choice of words. During that period in the ghetto, the word butch meant someone was trying to intimidate you. I had forgotten that the word was also a lesbian slur. Lovergirl started screaming about my defamation of her sexual orientation. I tried to explain but to no avail.

The roommate never got the opportunity to call the cops. The neighbors beat her to it. The Weehawken police came knocking and asked me to leave. I was dazed, confused, and embarrassed. Before leaving I pulled a young, dopey B-movie stunt: I grabbed the silent Joni and kissed her in front of everyone. This enraged the roommate and sickened the cops, who then hustled me from the apartment. All eyes in the immediate vicinity were on me, as I skulked forward under police escort.

I had gone from ultimate bliss to abject humiliation. When I arrived at the PATH train, to my surprise Joni was there waiting for me. We rode back into the city together, and she said, "I thought I was through with men, but our attraction took me by surprise. It was too powerful to pass up. Everything we experienced was different than my other heterosexual relationships. Maybe it's because I'm older or maybe it's because you're a special guy, but you were never threatened by who I was. I loved that."

"I never knew who you were," I sighed.

When we reached the city, we found a late-night pizza joint. As we ate I said, "Your girlfriend is a tough motherfucker."

"She needs work, but she has been good to me." Then she laughed and said, "If she had more of your sensitivity, we'd be better off."

"What about us?" I asked.

"You're going back to school."

"So?" I said.

"There's not much more we can do without repeating ourselves."

"You going back to your husband?" I blurted out sarcastically.

"Don't be hurt. I'll always love you."

I felt the curtain coming down around us, and I didn't know what to say. I wanted to stretch our last moments, so I ordered another slice of pizza. When our pizza jam ended, I walked her to the train, held her as long as time allowed, said my good-byes, and hopped a cab back to Harlem. Ironically, by the nineties, the qualities embodied in Joni's makeup—she was independent, educated, beautiful, athletic, competitive, and feminine—would define the quality woman. Her lesbian-authored independence was a model for future heterosexual women.

I would never see Joni again.

TWENTY

Lime Rock, Connecticut, Spring 1972.

The dull roar of the electronic bumblebee disturbed the silence of the beautiful New England town. Lime Rock was the home of a world-renowned auto racetrack. The sound of an early-morning test run was murder on my hangover as I awoke in a small apartment on the property of Leif Thorne-Thomsen. Leif had bought a home in the town of Lime Rock, five miles from school. It was a huge house on several acres of land. On the property was a carriage house with three apartments. Leif had given me one of the apartments to live in.

I pulled myself out of bed and fired up my album of the moment, Elton John and Bernie Taupin's *Madman Across the Water*, then made my way to the bathroom, filled the sink with cold water, and dunked my face repeatedly until my hangover froze. I dressed quickly in the blue-collar garb of the area—construction boots, jeans, and a faded khaki shirt. I went to the refrigerator and reached for an old Hellmann's mayonnaise jar filled with Tanqueray and grapefruit juice, took a huge hit of the liquid, and shuddered from the impact of strong alcohol in the early morning. I sealed the jar, placing it under my arm, grabbed a jacket and tie, and left.

My 1960 Pontiac cost a hundred dollars and was bought from a company called Fitch Inertial Barriers. The car was once used to test new safety barriers on the highway. The Pontiac had been beaten up so badly that one could never count on its performance.

I drove west on Route 112 headed for Millerton, New York, leaking transmission fluid. Tanqueray and breakfast in a funky shit-kicker's diner had become routine.

The diner was half filled with local farmers and others whose hands wore honest dirt at the end of the workday. I hit my favorite booth, and a warm, friendly waitress approached with a pot of coffee. She ran off my usual order of three eggs over hard, bacon, and toast, and I nodded in agreement. She offered another smile that brightened my disposition, poured me a cup of coffee, and left. I stared at the java through a bleary-eyed buzz-on and tangled with my mind's confusion.

My senior year at Hotchkiss was a big mistake. Given my weak academic record and irresponsible departure, gaining readmittance had been a tough sell. After all of the trouble with Noel and several other Black students, much of the school's hierarchy was intent on burying my era. Headmaster Bill Olsen and his folks deserved a lot of credit for ignoring the obvious in order to reach out to the criminal element, but it was a good bet that Black and Puerto Rican kids with spotty formal education and recent heroin-coated rap sheets were not a good fit at the Hotchkiss School. I would later discover that Bill Brokaw had used his power to squeeze me back into the fold after fighting off a barrage of objections.

My relationship with the big man had become strained. Brokaw wanted me to do things the old, traditional way, and I had my own ideas. More often than not his adult experience was right, but who gave a damn. He wanted me to study hard, play great football, and follow in his footsteps to Princeton. I learned from my Hotchkiss experience that I didn't want to continue down the ivy path.

Brokaw's son Blade reacted more radically than I to sipping the ivy potion. He decided junior year that Hotchkiss wasn't his thing, and despite the old man's pressure, he split. He struggled with the school's regimented, heavy-handed academic curriculum, gave it the big try, but his thoughts were in working and creating with his hands. He was a budding carpenter in rich boy's clothing, so he turned his back and said, "So long."

Blade's academic indifference led many to think that he was confused, but he was out in front of us all. Somehow, he acquired the rare gift of accepting truths about his inner self. I had bumped into Blade several months earlier, and he had told me a story about an experience he'd had on the West Coast. While driving, he noticed a desperate hand emerging from the brush on the side of the road. He pulled off to investigate and discovered the errant hand was attached to a homeless bum. After absorbing the bum's sob story, Blade decided to dust him off and take him out for a meal. At the restaurant the bum ordered a steak. In a time when it spelled lunacy, Blade had become a strict vegetarian. Nevertheless, the joy that the bum exhibited after his first bite of steak inspired him to honor the bum's pleasure by ordering a steak for himself. When I asked him why, he said, "What else could I do?" Blade dealt with life right between its eyes. It must have been tough on the old guy watching two of his Hotchkiss plants wither.

Black coffee and Tanqueray sandwiched a fine breakfast, and I was fit for another school day. As the waitress tallied up my score, she teased me about my bloodshot eyes. I flirted half-heartedly. As my Hotchkiss career wound down it was securing its place in my rearview mirror with its image shrinking. My return had been riddled with anticlimactic bullet holes. I was out of control in both my attitude and drinking, and many school appearances were tinted with volatility.

The year's saving highlight was the growth of my relationship with Leif. He never ceased to dazzle my imagination with his ability to quote usable pearls of wisdom obtained from the loftiest perches of the Greek and Latin classics, and yet he was able to get down and dirty with the street hards in the ghetto on the occasions when he would come to Harlem. Dressed in clothing that the old Andy Griffith sitcom's Barney Fife would have pulled from his closet on a Sunday morning, Leif strolled the hot pavement with an ease that suggested his threads were the work of a hip drug dealer's tailor. The consensus opinion on the block was "TT is a bad motherfucker!" Leif neither drank nor smoked at a time when abstinence deemed you a pussy, but he could play in any ball yard. He encouraged me to read and provided a list of books that were challenging. My favorite was Nathanael West's *Miss Lonelyhearts*, an ode to displacement.

I came back to Hotchkiss because I didn't trust the streets. Their rapidly dissipating magic spelled turmoil. The winds were blowing out in 1972 Nixon's America. A reshuffling of the deck dealt the spent civil rights movement out. Black anger had put White liberals on notice to back off. The ghetto was devolving into an open Black bitch fest and the chaos was mounting. Fistfights and blades were being replaced by pistols and death. Respect for human life was on the wane.

Living off campus made it difficult to grasp the better parts of Hotchkiss's attributes. Unless you were one of the corpuscles that flowed in the institution's bloodstream, you were relatively inconsequential. During the year I'd morphed into a townie with a particular fondness for Lakeville's Juicy Lucy's Roadside Bar, which had little formal educative value, but it sure taught me a thing or two about slurping the sauce. Shooting pool with the rank-and-file boys nuked my desire to study my senior curriculum scriptures.

Later that day, after several additional belts of gin, the dark cloud that followed me throughout the year shanked me. Drunk as a skunk, I brandished a toy gun in the assistant headmaster's office, scaring the hell out of everyone. After finding me passed out on the floor in one of the dormitory shower stalls, Bill Olsen decided that enough was enough, but his benevolence was still in evidence when he offered me a deal: the school would assist me in getting into New York University, and in turn, I would vaporize quietly.

I was at an impasse. To quote Bob Dylan, "There was no one even left to bluff." As the sand hit bottom in my Hotchkiss hourglass, I had little desire to return to the ghetto. But with the ink drying on my banishment decree, I was homeward bound.

When I arrived home from school, Noel was waiting for my bus at the terminal. After exchanging pleasantries, I asked, "What are you doing here?"

"You my man," he said. "Now that you've finished your tour of duty, welcome home."

I picked up my bags, and we walked inside the Port Authority Bus Terminal building to a waiting room. I lit up a cigarette and asked, "What's up with all of those cheap shots you've been taking at me, calling me a White toy? Do you really believe that shit?"

"No," he said, "but I had to go after your ass."

"Why?"

"It took the weight off me. I didn't want motherfuckers to think I failed, so I played it like the school failed, and them failin' meant you failed. It might not be the truth, but the shit worked. But that's old news, because a whole bunch of new shit is happenin'. Besides, I've been talkin' you up again, talkin' good shit." His smile belonged in that small group of smiles that were impossible to stay mad at.

I softened my deal and said, "So what's up, nigger, what you got on tap?"

He told me that over the previous ten months a large teenaged gang population had emerged out of thin air. Suddenly, it was gang season. Over twenty groups were sprinkled throughout East and West Harlem bent on making their presence felt. Noel had this brilliant idea to start our own gang. As he imparted his grand design, I learned that he had already jumped into the fray, naming himself the president of the Slum Lords. He'd already gained a foothold in the gang world's hierarchy. Noel was a master at mixing savvy with savagery, a perfect prescription for gang leadership.

Another smart decision Noel made was naming Checko as vice president. Checko was Noel's and my princely heir. He was younger by four years but had joined our fraternity early. In those days he was a cat-smart eleven-year-old who would act as our watchdog when we shot up in the project stairwells. Checko was now fifteen years old and had grown into a powerful physical specimen whose dark, handsome face often wore an endearing smile. Despite his youth, we afforded him A-group status.

Checko was following in our prep school footsteps, only to turn his back on a firm commitment when he saw Noel and others come back pitching stories of the stinging horrors that were prep school life. Checko was pointed in the direction of *Abbey Road* after turning on during our acid summer of '69, sinking a sizable chunk of his groove quotient into potent Eastern philosophers and *Sweet Baby James*. But the streets were draining these initiatives, leaving the cold, jutting edges of its brutal reality.

Noel challenged me to be the Slum Lords' war counselor. The offer surprised me because my criminal instincts were buried in rust. I was a devout John Lennon disciple and believed in giving peace a chance—loudly. But I couldn't turn a deaf ear to the changes in social attitudes that were sweeping the streets. I didn't have the cubes to live in the ghetto and swim against the tide, so I accepted Noel's offer with one condition: I would determine when we fought and what weapons we'd use. We shook on it.

"You still have that White boy acid shit in your system?" he laughed. "It'll be interesting to see how flowers go down in a rumble."

Within hours I was uptown attending a meeting of several gangs: Satan Spades, Renegades, and others. They wore colorful, distinctive insignias that represented their particular gang. Noel brought me in and introduced me to the other presidents as his war counselor. His intent was to develop a coalition of gangs to increase our strength. Noel gained the sworn confidence of each gang leader, and soon he would be elected president of the newly minted Third World Party. In the middle of our meeting two younger bloods came dashing into the center shouting, "There's a rumble on 118th Street!" After quickly discerning the details, Noel and the other gang leaders put together a plan of action.

I was six hours out of Hotchkiss and standing in the middle of a street gang controversy. One of the presidents tossed me a chain. A big chain! As I tried to figure out which end was which, Noel shouted, "Let's go!" We ran up Second Avenue toward 118th Street. I was trying to hide my chain under my shirt, and as God would have it, we ran smack-dab into my mother. I screeched to a halt as the others continued onward. My mother shouted, "You, boy!" I tossed my chain under a car and began to act as though I were just out having a nice walk.

"When you get home?" she asked.

"A few hours ago," I said, respectfully adding prep school affectations to my demeanor.

"What you doin' out here runnin' like a fool?"

"There's a big basketball game up in Wagner Projects, and everybody wants to get there before it starts."

She looked me up and down and seemed to buy the bullshit, but she left me with these words. "Remember, boy, you gettin' too old to be young and stupid."

I agreed with her profusely and she went on her way. I retrieved my chain and tore ass to catch up. When I got to 118th Street, there was a wild fight going on. Noel and the Satan Spades president, Peleu, were battling against some other gang warriors. After spotting me Noel shouted, "Get down, D!" I swallowed, reached into my street gut, and came up swinging. I was now officially a war counselor.

After the fight that day, I instituted an anti-rumble policy. Instead of these suicidal missions, each president of a warring gang would choose his best fighter, and we would put them in a circle. The idea emanated from memories of cock-fights I'd seen in my southern days. The adversaries fought to the point of near death. It was brutal, but it saved lives.

I did a lot of acid trying to contend with the depersonalization that came with senseless balls-ripping violence, but my altered pupils accentuated the drab colors and discordant squeals, producing a psychedelic horror show. The times weren't just a-changin', they were under assault. The Beatles had broken up, Hendrix, Morrison, and Janis were dead, and Noel and I were again street detritus.

There were perks that came with the position of war counselor: power, mounds of respect, and lots of girls. My relationship with Gerri was solid, so I wasn't much interested in the girls part. But the power certainly went to my head. The gang issue was big news that summer, attracting a load of nonsensical attention that the press showers on its hot topics. Every time they asked a question, expecting a street grunt, Noel and I would provide a sophisticated prep-school response. Taking the bait, they would ask more intelligent questions, and we would lace them with the hard street stuff. I would experience a nose-to-nose joust with the legend-to-be, Barbara Walters, on her show *Not For Women Only*. It was a gas.

Our gang folly peaked when we organized an outdoor summit of the entire Third World Party on the basketball court in the middle of the projects. Sixteen different gangs showed up, all under our colorful party banner. Noel, Checko, and I, along with other gang dignitaries, gave horse-shit speeches about taking over our neighborhoods, taking over City Hall, and what the hell, for good measure, taking over the world. We had created harmony between many warring factions, and they were all there to honor an imaginary purpose that no one could define. Much of our lofty rhetoric espoused protecting our environment from the influences of drugs and violence. Admirable goals for sure, but the truth was we would soon become the perpetrators of the unwanted mayhem. The sense of power that came from the approval of hundreds of gang members was a bittersweet experience. Obtaining power over a group is a lot easier than knowing how to use that power effectively. In truth, Noel and I were the proprietors of a confused, psychotic frat house.

Checko led the operation on the ground, enhancing his street reputation immensely. Days before his sixteenth birthday, he peacocked one of the most powerful positions on the streets of East Harlem that summer. Noel settled for savoring his ability to do the impossible, which was bringing all of these weapon-wielding concrete urchins together under his hand.

"That was a lot of people out there," he said after the event broke up.

"Yeah, man, you pulled it off. Now what?"

He smiled and said, "Drugs. That's the future. Niggers living in shit gots to get high."

As the fall approached, the gang thing was becoming a bore. After your umpteenth human cockfight, the thrill dissipates, so we decided to tone down the rhetoric and distance ourselves from our positions of authority. Noel and I had been pampered enough in prep school to have whiffed the other side of life, and we knew that gang-banging was a dark flag to nowhere. Like the Woodstock festival, our gang summit was the last true note of passion for the unified front we espoused. The peel-off would soon begin. As I planned to leave the active streets again, Noel concentrated on leading his remaining loyalists into the dope game. The Italian grip on the neighborhood's smack flow was loosening, thus creating an opportunity he was hell-bent on exploiting. After all the chain-swinging bullshit, I was ready to do some spiritual gardening in Strawberry Fields, hoping to deflect the violent images that still resided in my head. Noel's dream of drug kingpindom was dead in my water.

At the end of August I stumbled upon the opportunity to go to a goodwill civil rights convention in Golden, Colorado. A wealthy White woman from Hotchkiss offered me the chance to be a representative at this liberal hoedown. I was interested in the offer because it provided my first opportunity to fly in an airplane. After an unforgettable charge that came with my first liftoff, I didn't know whether to be frightened or excited but loved the feeling. By the time the plane touched down in Colorado, I wanted to turn around and fly right back, but I was committed and played through. A kind, attractive, middle-aged White woman and two large White men clad in cowboy hats and boots met me at the airport and were as warm and accommodating as fine people get. We chatted about my background. I played my Hotchkiss card, and the woman was duly impressed. The cowboys were laid back, much like the ones I had seen on television shows like *Bonanza*—amiable, hospitable, and sturdy. I asked the woman about the itinerary, and she said, "This evening, before the entire delegation, Martin Luther King's former aid, Jesse Jackson, will be speaking."

My hosts led me to a comfortable dormitory room at a local junior college. I was directed to a large auditorium on its campus. The SRO crowd were well-intentioned southwestern White believers who still saw King's vision for America as a plausible option worth considering. I was in a fog, far more impressed by the gorgeous mountains I had seen on the way to the campus. I had been raised on this civil rights stuff, so it felt a little passé. It was rare that these gatherings produced anything positive anymore, but to some it was still feel-good stew. There would be a Black gospel choir punctuating the rousing speeches.

As the uncertainty of Black-White relationships loomed larger in the post-King era, good White folks craved these outings. That's why the arrival of Jesse Jackson—a minister with a dynamic speaking style who was lobbying for the cavernous job of advancing King's legacy—so excited the masses.

Jackson had recently organized a charity concert held for his new organization, Operation PUSH. During the concert, a history-challenged pack of Black yahoos booed the great Sammy Davis, Jr. Mr. Bojangles was brought to tears in his sanctuary, the stage, when his people assaulted him with their ignorance. The throng was still stinging from an unfortunate burst of exuberance Sammy had displayed when he joyfully hugged President Nixon at the White House. Lost in their assault was the fact that Sammy had enjoyed a robust relationship with Nixon since the fifties. Richard Nixon, the president who had signed off on affirmative action, was portrayed as the Black man's nemesis. Whether or not Nixon deserved his bulls-eye was questionable. Ten years earlier Sammy's public embrace of a president would have been landmark stuff that would have pumped the majority of Black people's pride meters. Sammy had loved and suffered for his people far more than the majority of Jackson's ignorant jury had.

When the public ass-whipping severity dials hit the red zone, Jesse stepped forward to lend Sammy some onstage support. Sammy didn't duck and run. Instead he chose to sing his huge heart out. This diminutive social treasure delivered a crowd-quelling rendition of one of his standards, "I've Got to Be Me." The lyrics of the song defined his lifelong desire for individual rights and liberties—the African American's Holy Grail. The Black Power-indoctrinated younger generation had developed the habit of tossing our best and most honored pigment pioneers overboard. Sammy would not be the last of the great Black heroes who ate shit raw while fighting for our freedom, only to fall victim to misguided militancy.

The compassion-filled liberals in the arena had their sleeves rolled up and veins batted down awaiting their King fix. Jesse who at that time had a large afro and was clad in a dashiki, took the stage. Under the lights he was the embodiment of a beautiful ebony prince. The audience was geared for one of those outdated, hand-holding singalongs that King had made famous, but the great one was gone and so were many of his rituals. Jesse launched into a stinging diatribe about White America's ills. His oratory was harsh, divisive, provocative, and disturbing. The crowd turned ugly, no longer King's compassionate devotees, now more like White folks after the O. J. Simpson verdict. They felt cheated and betrayed, and their reddened faces flashed embarrassment. I was reminded of something Mr. George said. "When White folks turn red-faced, clear out."

After the speech, Jesse made a beeline for a waiting vehicle, ready to hightail it to the airport. I ran him down trying to meet him, but he bulled right past me. It wasn't a snub; he was focused on his immediate future, which might have included a noose if he didn't haul ass. These White feel-gooders had bent over backward to be gracious hosts to the handful of Black attendees, but after Jesse jammed his thumb up their asses, the crimson-necked throng were fit to avenge the Alamo. Instead of perpetrating King's legacy, Jesse had debunked it with his self-serving diatribe. I spent three more days in Golden, Colorado, and was careful to spend my time in the dorm, avoiding activities. I didn't receive a single inquiry from my hosts.

Over the years I have come to admire Reverend Jackson tremendously. Through his presidential campaigns he honored Dr. King's legacy as dutifully as did any African American to come after the great one's fall. He managed to up King's mountainous ante. If Dr. King gave us the vote, Jesse's two presidential campaigns gave that vote character. In my book he's a legitimate twentieth-century-America Hall of Famer, but on that late summer evening in Colorado, I was not a Jesse Jackson fan.

As the affable cowboys, who had been so hospitable upon my arrival, sat waiting for me in the cab of their pickup truck for my trip to the airport, they wore menacingly stone-faced masks. I was scared shitless. These guys looked as though they had been mainlining the speeches of a pre-incapacitated Governor George Wallace. At one point during the drive to the airport, the driver turned off the main highway, and we wound up on a dark back road. My projected lifespan was dropping precipitously as my ass made its way to my throat. If I could have gotten my hands on Jesse at that moment, I would have torched his dashiki, but all I could do was pray. Expecting the worst, I held my breath, squirming nervously, fighting off my urine's desire to vacate my bladder.

Finally, we came to a point where I could see a slew of headlights. Thankfully, we were back on the main road. When we reached the airport, the cowboys gave me a muted farewell, which read, "Get out of Colorado, nigger!" I suppose, in retrospect, it was a bold move for Jesse to separate himself from his mentor's perceived passivity. That strategy marked the beginning of Jesse's long, unyielding position as the poster boy for the right White wing's Blacklash.

•   •   •

In September I attended New York University on scholarship as an education major. I decided that I wanted to be a schoolteacher. In my experience to that point, schoolteachers were the brightest, least corrupt, dedicated group of public servants I had ever come by. Leif was my role model, and I wanted to follow in his footsteps.

Gerri also attended N.Y.U. as a nursing major. She was playing on two levels—Florence Nightingale by day and a budding Sarah Vaughan by night. Despite my desire to teach, I couldn't get past the boredom that school dished up, and I often found my way to the Loeb Student Center lounge. It became my home away from home. I would tell people I was attending Loeb University. There was a great setup at Loeb, where a student could requisition albums and gain entry to a private booth. There you could listen to the music of your choice. I spent much of the semester listening to the entire Beatles catalog over and over. This activity comprised the bulk of my college groove, except for English class.

My professor was a very attractive no-nonsense Black woman who encouraged me to write. I had been taught well by the Hotchkiss English department, and my fundamentals in writing were strong, but it wasn't until this English course that I learned to turn the written word into a power tool. The professor was the first Black teacher I'd had since my southern childhood. That eliminated 80 percent of my well-honed bullshit, because you can't manipulate a Black teacher with guilt and flash like you can a White one. She was a strong, gorgeous, red-black-and-green sister who took educating people seriously—particularly Black ones she thought had ability—and she demanded that I work my ass off. She compared parts of a paper I had written to Shakespeare, and that was all the helium I needed to take flight in her course. I worked the writing into my unofficial major, Beatle absorption. Music and writing would soon feed on each other. In my other subjects I played a good game of squeak-by.

Gerri was beginning to do a number of solo gigs in Greenwich Village, so I dropped out of the ghetto and did most of my hanging in the Washington Square area. Noel would leave messages for me, seeking to chart our next move, but we were a philosophical canyon apart. He was laying the foundation for the New Jack generation, while I reclaimed my seat on the magical mystery tour. No amount of arguing or cajoling could bring us to an agreement, so he went off to do his thing and I bought an acoustic guitar. I hid behind the skirts of Gerri's peaking aura and practiced until my fingers bled, pouring gobs of passion into butchering songs, like Harrison's "Here Comes the Sun."

•   •   •

On New Year's Eve of 1973 I invited Noel and one of our Slum Lord comrades, Black Pierce, to the small tenement apartment Gerri and I had recently rented in East Harlem. We were there to watch the Sugar Bowl between Notre Dame and Alabama. Noel and I were at soft odds, continuously sparring beneath the surface. As we awaited the kickoff, one could feel that there was going to be some hard rocking that night.

"Silly acid White boy shit!" Noel shouted belligerently. I ignored him, choosing to concentrate on the game.

"Crimson Tide is going to kick Notre Dame's Irish Black ass," I needled.

"The hell with those crackers!" shouted Black Pierce.

"They have brothers on Alabama," I said.

"Not until Notre Dame started taking brothers down there in them bowl games and kickin' they ass," Pierce challenged.

"Pierce, calm down, you're not a nigger anymore. We've been freed," I teased.

"Says who?" he laughed.

"Don't listen to that shit," Noel said. "Dennis has been John-and-Yoko–ed. He's lost his mind. It's that acid. Snap out of it, man." He then cupped his hands to his mouth and shouted, "It's over."

The bug that was making its way up Noel's ass was his inability to deal with my growing aversion to street shit. Our respect for violence had brought us together, and my distaste for violence was driving us apart. I was careful to show Noel enough street heart to maintain his respect. I had reestablished my former, well-touted ability to turn deadly on a dime during our gang episode. This kept him from heading down Stupid Street on me.

Noel and I had called a truce for the holidays, but as we sat before my irresistible combination of a Sony Trinitron television and its pristine reception as a result of this new thing called cable, we sniped at each other constantly. We watched a great game as Notre Dame beat Alabama late. Noel and Pierce gloated as we settled into a bowl of pot sprinkled with Noel's new product, cocaine. As we got high, I put on David Crosby's first solo album. Noel started in on me about the choice of music, and we tore the cover off of our truce.

"Turn off that White shit!" he barked.

"Fuck you!" I replied.

"Them California White boys are a bunch of dope fiends. You should stick to Black music," he exhorted.

"This is Black music; all American music is Black music. Crosby's shit is a poetic musical charm bracelet."

"Fuck Crosby!"

"Why do I have to stick to one kind of music?" I challenged.

Noel and I eyed each other warily as David Crosby and friends sprayed acid-laced musical notes over our uneasy alliance.

"You ain't got no Earth, Wind, and Fire or Marvin Gaye?" Noel shouted. He proceeded to do four hits of coke. "That White shit is played out."

I acceded to his wishes and put on Sly and the Family Stone's heroin-dipped album *Riot*. The room turned into a blue funk, and we rode that mood to a New Year's Eve party.

A female friend I'd met somewhere on the Black bourgeois trail invited us to the Lenox Terrace. The Trump Towers of Harlem in the early seventies catered to the Black elite, like Lionel Hampton. The party was a prime smoker. Noel and I met two hot, sweaty women who dominated the dance floor. We lured the women to an open corner and created our own little party.

In the middle of our bliss break, Noel said, "See, you still Black. Black women, Black music, Black neighborhood. Come back home, man."

"I'm looking for something that's coming from both sides," I reasoned, "like an Eric Clapton guitar solo. You know, White craft, Black heart. That's my station, man."

Exasperated, he threw up his hands, and we laughed. We decided to concentrate on something we could agree on: how to get these women into bed before sunrise. Several hours later the four of us left the party in a great mood. We hit the street, laughing and joking, when suddenly a Black woman came running toward us, dressed in colorful African garb. Her elaborate headdress sat crookedly on her head; she was frantic.

"You've got to help me. Somebody hurt my husband. Please!"

Noel and I followed the woman as she ran toward the scene. When we got there, lying in the street was an old, professorial-looking White man. His head was bleeding as he lay in the gutter. I reached down and pulled the old man to his feet, but he was too dazed to stand on his own and collapsed. His wife became hysterical.

"Noel, hail a cab," I said. "We can take him to the hospital."

Noel assessed the situation, and after a moment of study said, "Fuck him."

"What do you mean, fuck him!" I yelled as the woman continued to cry.

"If she was dumb enough to marry this little White man and bring him up here, then she got what she deserved." He turned and walked away.

The hard line down the middle of our road had become indelible. Anger and revenge had driven humanity over a cliff. Integration, goodwill, and civility were in the gutter twitching spasmodically as the African queen wailed. The heart of King's legacy had been smashed to bits, like a discarded beer bottle thrown from a moving car. I hoisted the old man on my shoulder and headed for Lenox Avenue as his Black woman with the crooked headdress limped closely behind.

*   *   *

After watching Gene Tenace of the Oakland Athletics blow up the Cincinnati Reds in the '72 World Series, I came to the decision that I was going to be a professional baseball player. I had always been a very good ball player, with power and above average speed. I had played the game all my life, so why not? I locked in to my baseball dream and put together a killer regimen of exercise and weight training, and devoured the great Ted Williams's bible on hitting. With a Hank Aaron–model baseball bat and several weighted donut rings, I began to develop a swing that was so smooth and powerful I could demolish a building with it. My biggest problem was finding someone to throw batting practice. Most of my friends thought I was crazy. Noel went as far as to question whether I was going down the same route as his brother Barry, succumbing to the pressure that came with taking the White world too seriously.

I ignored my detractors. I wanted to hit home runs like Hammerin' Hank. The one person I could count on to throw batting practice was Bobo Motion. Bobo was one of our community center offspring who had come along a few years later in the scheme of things. I'd coached him in football and befriended him off the field because he was one of the brightest, most charismatic people I would ever meet. He was seventeen years old at the time that I coaxed him into pitching three mornings a week at our local field.

Bobo had big plans for his life. He didn't know exactly what he wanted to do, but he did feel and express repeatedly that there was greatness in his future. He had been a student in the Hotchkiss Greater Opportunity (GO) Program, a summer school that Bill Olsen and Reverend David Kern designed for ghetto kids from Hartford and East Harlem. They spent six weeks studying a truncated version of the young White dreamer's play book. Bobo had a great sense of humor as well as a surprising amount of sensitivity and perspective for a kid who had grown up on scorched pavement. He was beating the temptation to dive into the muck of the streets. It was clear this kid was going places.

Thwack! was the sound as I sprayed line drives around the rock pit that moonlighted as a ball field. Bobo had pitched in the Boys Club Little League and had decent stuff. My intense training, diet, and study prepared me to take some lethal cuts at his mediocre off-speed slop. Bobo talked another favorite protégée of mine—the notorious, enigmatic Barker—into helping out. Barker was the complete opposite of Bobo, having accepted the notion that he was born to die in the streets. He reminded me of my old buddy, Willie Leach, a wonderful, kind-hearted kid, earmarked for self-destruction. He was a gifted athlete who was short and thick with unusual strength, much like Mike Tyson's. Barker's athleticism and a clear path would have probably taken him to the

Major Leagues, but his disdain for school and his love for the streets trumped that possibility. He threw the ball close to ninety miles an hour and was just wild enough to keep you on your toes. After a few pitches that were so fast I could hardly see them, I got my rhythm together and began to turn Barker's heaters into line drives. That was encouraging. I figured if I could hit Barker, I was headed in the right direction.

Bobo and Barker enjoyed my impossible quest. After our last session, as Bobo and I walked through the park with our spiked shoes scratching concrete, he said, "You ain't gonna make no major leagues, but you a bad motherfucker for tryin'. That's what this shit is really about to me."

I quarreled with his assertion, stating that I intended to make it. He stopped and said, "I don't care if you make it or not. Niggers ain't supposed to do shit they can't do, and you don't believe that." He smiled and put his arm around me. "Now, buy me breakfast."

Unfortunately, Bobo was a prophet. After all my effort, I garnered a few try-outs from the local professional teams. The most I got out of the experience was about twelve good cuts in the batting cage, one of them a screaming shot off the right centerfield wall at Shea Stadium. In the end I was basically told to get lost. Like many of the losers, I felt that I hadn't been given a serious opportunity. One of the coaches who helped run the tryouts said, "You probably swing that bat better than ninety-seven percent of the people your age, but unfortunately it's that three percent that matters, and you're not quite good enough to crack that group."

Momentarily crushed, I dreaded having to go home to the neighborhood and admit that they were right about my hardball dream. There was one significant event that came out of the experience. My relationship with my father had been on thin ice for a long time. He never got over my junkie-criminal phase, and de-spite subsequent accomplishments he dismissed me. When the New York Mets organization called my house to notify me about the tryout, my dad took the call. You would have thought I was Jackie Robinson and he had just spoken with Branch Ricky. I can't do justice to the exhilarated look on his face when he gave me the word that the Major Leagues had called. Then, to my surprise, he of-fered a handshake. It was the first overture of this kind in a very long time.

When I arrived home and told of the bad news, his deflated body language sharpened the lines in his tired face as he mumbled, "What can ya say—at least you got to be king for a day."

I think my father was speaking for himself.

TWENTY-ONE

After the death of my baseball dream, I was twenty-one and again washed up. Stephen Stills had scared me off of the acoustic guitar. After playing for several years and rising above mediocrity too infrequently to feed my ego, my music dream went down for the count when I saw Stills on a great night blow the house up with a version of his acoustic blues gem "Black Queen." That was lights out for me. I would have to be at least as good as he was to feel relevant, and that wasn't going to happen. Gerri was so talented that it seemed as though her destiny was hiccup-proof. As long as she could stand on a stage and unleash her gift, the world's embrace was hers for the taking. With nursing as a backup, her life's plan was solid.

I was a devout self-importance junkie who was tapped out of dreams and schemes. It was time to panic. I'd wasted enough of the university's money and didn't want to rob someone more deserving of the opportunity, so returning to college was a null set. My anxiety found relief when a thirteen-year-old street kid named Spooky showed up at my door at 3:00 A.M. with nowhere to sleep. He was a relative of a friend who had told him, "Try D's. He got some of that candy-hearted White folks' charity in his shit." When the kid repeated my friend's statement, I laughed so hard that I had to invite him in.

Gerri and I lived in a studio apartment with two holes in the wall that acted as a bathroom and kitchen. Despite the tight conditions, we were also living with Gerri's current heartthrob. All her life she'd had this odd, persistent desire to own a Great Dane. Our finances were good, so she dipped into her prosperity and bought Katari, the biggest dog in the world. When he stood on his hind legs, he could rest his front paws on my shoulders. I was six-foot-one, so that was a lot of dog dominating our matchbox, but I relented to her insanity because Gerri loved this behemoth with all her heart. We played through a nearly impossible situation. Katari slept right beneath our couch pullout, and I would invariably trip over him in the middle of the night on a leak run. He was hung like a horse and would set up in the corner producing extreme wood. My ego was being pummeled from all sides.

We were in no position to accommodate house guests, but one look in this kid's frightened face made the decision a no-brainer. I made a comfortable pillow and blanket bed for him on the floor, and Spooky slept beside Katari, who took to the kid and continually licked his face with a tongue as big as a washrag. Despite my recent spate of mediocrity in most things I had attempted, I was an expert in this kid's pain. I decided to do something about it.

Chuck's quasi retirement had left a vacuum in our neighborhood that was filled with bad intentions. Spooky inspired me to follow in Chuck's footsteps by attempting to revive hope for kids in his predicament. "Good idea!" everyone cheered, when I announced my plan to bring the community center back to prominence, but most of those who offered their good wishes did so on the move. The enthusiasm was a mile wide and an inch deep.

The neighborhood was in limbo waiting for something to happen. Young kids coming up who had missed out on Chuck's miracle were listening to the foul melodies that were imposing themselves upon the environment. The hallways and streets were robbing thirteen-year-olds of their opportunity for an education. There were no books on ghetto corners.

A heightened mistrust of the police hastened the collapse of the pavement's respect for authority, altering the street nigger's view of the cops from necessary intruder to mortal enemy. The postwar White flighters had passed on the precincts and firehouses to their suburban sons and daughters. This generation had inherited little of the street savvy that their Depression-toughened parents had experienced. Old-school White cops who walked the beat knew what the streets were about, having grown up on them. One of the biggest problems that hurt the neighborhoods of color was the decision to bus the cops in from a different culture. The objective shifted from protecting residents to taming them. This horrible clash between the two groups would provide ugly New York headlines for decades.

My decision to take a shot at running the center was good news to Chuck. It was decided that I would officially take the reins in September of 1973, but over the following four months there was a lot of prep work to be done. Chuck and I formed a *Godfather*-style setup, in which he was to be the don in semi-retirement and I was to run the day-to-day operation. The building was under the threat of darkness. Chuck had been doing a song and dance with Con Edison for ten years, and the bill rivaled the national debt. In our heyday the notion of turning off the electricity in an urban community center would have sentenced the utility company to liberal purgatory, but the times had changed and there was a new set of White folks in town. They weren't ruthless or evil, but they meant business. Sob stories were out, and the focus had moved closer to the bottom line. After one last collective plea to Con Ed, they issued their final decree: Lights out!

Starting off my run in the pitch black was empowering. When you can't see your hand in front of your face in your place of work, there is nowhere to go but up. Fortunately, I was a member of the African American pool of instinctual resourcefulness: turning pig guts into chitlins was a large part of our gift. Drug and thug activity flowed through the center, and the joint was ripe for a bust, but the police remained hands-off. Chuck's big bang in the neighborhood, along with his willingness to reach out to the cops, held the blue boys' respect. I shut down the center at night for a month, and the rumbling sounds on the street coagulated into an eardrum-shattering nigger shout: "D is fucking shit up!" I was intent on taking the program back to its basics, which was football and education.

City and private funds had dried to a bone: Fewer and fewer outsiders were interested anymore. Poverty-program veterans who thought that the LBJ gravy train would flow forever failed to do their homework on the new White folks. Black folks in the poverty game saw government funds as an entitlement. The orgy of the sixties overestimated the depths of White guilt, so when the tide changed and the new White folks began to mix a few "Fuck offs" into the stew, the poverty pimps panicked. The decision to dredge up the tools of the sixties by taking to the streets with rallies and marches fell flatter than Olive Oyl's bra. Sequels rarely live up to the original, and we sadly discovered that the Vietnam War and the length of the lines at gas pumps had replaced nigger angst on the national pop charts.

When I went back to the center, there were only three salaries on what was once a paid staff of eighteen. The only thing that the center was rich with was kids looking for direction or, as my mother would say, "Good raisin'." The football program was the only tradition left in our organization's once-bulging catalog. Our five teams had dwindled to two: a peewee team of kids between eight and ten years old and an intermediate team for ages eleven to fourteen. I could barely come up with the money for the league entrance fees, but the teams were the key to reviving the center's esteem. It was incumbent upon me to find a way for Chargers football to kick somebody's ass.

It was great fun putting together my fall game plan as I stumbled through a candlelit spring. After a while things began looking up. My biggest goal was to change the public's perception of the center. People either thought it was a house gone wrong or it was defunct. I promoted my new message of hope like crazy, and my influence in the moneyed White folks world began to pay positives. A friend gave me five-hundred dollars for football equipment, while another Hotchkiss crony set up a good deal so that I could buy supplies for an all-important remedial reading program.

In the early spring I began scouting the basketball courts looking for football talent for the upcoming season. I was working off of one of Chuck's rules of thumb: "Criminal niggers make better football players." I searched for these purported incorrigibles with a ferocity that blew them away. Football was an easy sell, but what was most important was my ability to successfully pitch a quirky remedial reading plan that simply stated, "If a nigger could talk, he could read." My intention was to have them write their own compositions, utilizing their own vernacular. We would then do a grammatical nip-and-tuck hoping that the basic fundamentals of reading and writing would emerge. They were somewhat intrigued. Whenever a kid bought into my rap, I immediately paid a visit to his parents. Many of them were aware of my neighborhood reputation, and I promised that if they gave me a free hand, I would look after their boys. Most of the kids were the products of single mothers living in heartbreakingly inadequate conditions, so when I arrived as the bronze, sober do-gooder, they swooned.

Chuck and I began a new phase in our relationship. I was twenty-one years old, and after several dances with the Grim Reaper I had managed to elude his sickle. Chuck took great pride in the person I'd become. His acceptance of me as a peer was instantaneous, and his confidence in my judgment was strong. He liked the hard work I was pouring into the new dream. There was only one problem: I had to deal with Noel. We'd kept our distance as he grudgingly held his fire over my nigger-less nighttime center policy. We'd never officially squared with how the center was going to be run. My early work had given me some leverage on the center's direction, but Noel was an heir too. So despite his drug activity, Chuck sought to draw the line between us fairly when he called a meeting at our favorite *cuchi frito* restaurant.

Noel and I both were wearing our street game faces, unwilling to show our hands. Chuck blew that away by producing a bottle of J&B, saying, "Before we eat, you niggers need a drink." After a few slams the hardened looks faded and we both loosened up. Several weeks earlier Noel and his love mate, Linda, had

had a beautiful baby named Lynnel. Unforeseen maturity buds were sprouting as Noel expressed his joy over the birth of his daughter. His concern for his little girl's welfare had widened his perspective.

"I've been hearing around the neighborhood that you been doing some good shit," he said, "and I think we got to bury our beef, D." Surprised, I held my tongue and we eyeballed each other. Then he said, "I know you have problems with what I'm doing, but folks out there want cocaine, and there's a lot of money to be made supplying it. I hold the line at eighteen years old. Most kids younger than that can't afford coke, so you take care of the kids and I'll do my business out of their way. I'm glad the center is going back to its roots, and you the only one who can do that. No offense, Chuck."

Happy over the positive vibes, Chuck smiled and said, "None taken."

Noel continued, "You got my help, and I got your back. You got mine?"

I was thrilled over his conciliatory gesture. I got up from the table and summoned Noel to me. He complied, and I said, "You'se my always nigger." We hugged as Chuck beamed, reveling in the completion of our rapprochement. "The drug game is hard, man," I said.

Noel smiled and replied, "Easier than Hotchkiss."

When June arrived I was forced to take a summer gig in Brooklyn because my center salary wouldn't start flowing until fall. My job was inspecting day-care facilities in impoverished neighborhoods, making certain that they were complying with sanitation regulations. The drawback was that I had to travel two hours to get to work. On the day before I was to start the job, I was hanging out with Chuck and his new love, Terry. Not since the early days of the now-vanquished Dorothy Raven had I seen Chuck cooking up such a positive strain of love. It was a happy period of calm storms.

Chuck brought his hay bales and targets up on the center's roof for his archery practice, and he was firing away preparing for an upcoming tournament. Terry and I adored each other and chatted it up as Chuck zoned out everything but a tiny circle thirty yards away. Suddenly, we heard frantic footsteps coming up to the roof. It was Stephen Brown. He was out of breath as he shouted, "It's Noel! Something's happened to Noel!"

We dropped everything and tore ass. Thirty minutes later Chuck and I were in Flower and Fifth Avenue Hospitals, where we met Noel's family. Noel's love mate; Linda, was immobilized in a state of shock. Stevie, Red Machine, Checko, and many others were huddled in the waiting room. They filled us in on the grim details. Earlier that afternoon Noel had hit the streets with a half-pint of Bacardi rum to get his motor going. He was standing on our drug corner at 115th

Street with a nice buzz on, talking to people, when a young lady had approached him. She was one of the debs—gang groupies—of the Satan Spades.

During his presidency Noel had dived into this perk with relish and had kidded me endlessly over my unwillingness to sample them. The deb who had approached Noel was distraught and fearful, with several visible bruises showing. Despite our distance from the gang scene, he was still dipping into the frantic young lady's well. She told Noel that the cruelty had been inflicted by the Satan Spades' president, and that she and Noel's liaison were responsible for the ass-whipping. Her heavy tale of woe angered Noel, and with the Bacardi acting as motor oil he decided to defend this young woman's honor. With artillery that consisted of a silver one-shot, pearl-handled derringer, he was intent on squashing the beef. When Noel arrived at the Spades' hangout, he quickly discovered that the woman was lure bait. His last conscious moment offered a view of shotguns and pistols waiting in ambush to blow his nineteen-year-old body to bits.

At the hospital Noel's life hung by a thread. I managed to catch a glimpse of him as they wheeled him upstairs for surgery. I ran alongside the speeding bed and asked the doctor, "Come on, Doc, don't bullshit me. Give me a percentage. What's his chance?" The doctor slowed his pace as the bed sped forward and said. "Less than ten percent." I froze as the bed continued onward, becoming smaller as it neared the end of a long hallway.

The following morning I had to get up at 5:00 A.M. in order to take three different subway routes to get to my new job. Distressed by Noel's incomprehensible odds, I bounded around Black Brooklyn aimlessly, from Red Hook to Brownsville, checking the refrigerators in which children's lunches were stored. The kids may have eaten bad cheese that day because I spent the time praying for Noel's life.

When I arrived back in Harlem, I made a dash from the subway station to our favorite hangout bench, where a group of friends were gathered. The overwrought crowd sent a punishing jolt of angst through my body. It was obvious that my long prayer vigil had been for naught. I discovered that Noel had died fifteen minutes after I left the hospital. He was gone forever. My friend Pierce said, "I'll be damned if death ain't a final motherfucker."

Initial anger fueled countless revenge schemes. The question Who could we kill? was the talk that accompanied our sweaty hand-wringing. When Chuck arrived on the scene, he was as cool as a cucumber. I was confused by his serenity and asked, "What's up, man? Why do you seem so aloof?"

"The price for living is dying," Chuck said. "Death is something you don't really have to think about because it's a certainty. The only way to fuck with death is to celebrate the fact that the nigger was once here, because everybody gonna go." Noel had been a virtual son of Chuck's, but he knew that all of his boys walked a tightrope between life and death. "Lord knows, I'm sorry to see that boy go," he said, "but life is about breathing. Those of us who still are is what it's all about."

Chuck's philosophy about death was one of the biggest gifts he ever gave me. Over the next few years, I would go through innumerable personal death experiences with Chuck, including the loss of his son, and never saw him mourn a moment. Although I never mastered his philosophy, it often came in handy. By the time of my twenty-fifth birthday, I had lost more close friends than your average octogenarian.

"Street niggers have to factor death into their daily game plan," Chuck counseled. "That's what makes nigger life sweet. It don't come cheaply for us."

Noel had the biggest funeral I had ever witnessed in East Harlem. The church was packed and spilling outside onto the sidewalk. During the service we all walked by the open casket to pay our last respects. When my turn came, I took solace from the fact that at the time of his death our coexistence agreement was flourishing, and for the first time since the early days of Hotchkiss there was unencumbered brotherly love flowing between us. The fluid boys had served him well because he looked good.

Inexplicably, a bemused sense of jealousy came over me. Noel had made an indelible street statement, and it was frozen forever. He'd gotten the last word on our sibling rivalry, because he wasn't stuck with having to live with my death. As I studied his face for the last time, I read a smile that seemed to say, "Well, D, now what?"

TWENTY-TWO

The painful loss of Noel was evident, but a positive result from the tragedy was that the gang nonsense was put to bed. I was on my own and loved it, but the work was just beginning. With September quickly approaching, I was intent on turning twenty-five incorrigible thirteen- and fourteen-year-old street urchins into the best Charger football team ever. I understood these kids and knew how much they wanted someone to care about them, proving that there was something special about the gift of life. Again I reached for Chuck's playbook, knowing that I would have to "whup about ten niggers' asses to get their attention." Banging several heads together would subsequently provide the opportunity to apply hands-on love.

I challenged their sensitive intellects developed from the profound awareness ghetto life sharpens. They were expected to fail, so when they came upon an adult who eliminated the possibility of failure, it turned them on. My routines on the practice field were brutal. The objective was to burn all of the excess testosterone right out of those little fuckers. All drills were tests of discipline designed to push them further than they had ever gone, and then some.

The leader of the team was a Puerto Rican kid named Toro. His ability to run the football was phenomenal. Next to Noel, he was the best Charger football player I'd ever seen. Toro was a genuine game breaker, but early on in the process he was intent on breaking balls, challenging me on every front. Predictably, he began disrupting practices. I would shout, "Do I look like one of them pussy-hearted White schoolteachers you been fucking over?" I called him out in front of the team, goading him into blocking me, one-on-one. After he took the bait, I would obliterate his little ass. I once embarrassed him so severely that he not only threatened to quit the team, he went on a pistol search with the intent of busting a cap in my ass. He was playing into my hands. I again employed one of Chuck's theorems: "Whup the baddest nigger's ass, and the rest will fall in line."

It was a gamble because I really liked this kid and didn't want to lose him. After that blowup I didn't see Toro for several days. His teammates were in a sullen mood, acting as though the team's head had been severed from the body. I made a little speech. "I know you niggers are upset about what's going on between me and Toro, but I want you to give him a message." Their focus was zeroed in on me, searching for signs of resolution. "Tell Toro I whupped his ass because I love him." Initially, my words fell flat, and they looked at me as though I was queer. "Tell him exactly what the fuck I said. Now line up for drills."

The following day after practice, as the team undressed by candlelight, Toro entered carrying a flashlight. I looked at him, and he blurted out, "Fuck candles!" I laughed. Oddly, he ran to the back of the center, and I followed his light. He huddled in a barren corner, and with everyone out of earshot he started to cry.

"What the fuck are you crying about, man?" I challenged. Through his tears I could see the tough part of him falling away, revealing a confused thirteen-year-old. At that point I was careful not to break his spirit.

"I want to play," he said.

"I want you to play too," I responded.

"Then why you fucking with me!" he shouted. His flashlight was pointed at the floor, casting an oddly shaped shadow. "You tryin' to make me look stupid in front of everybody."

"Bullshit! You one of the best football players I've ever seen, and I ain't the one who is going to ultimately lead this team, you are. You my nigger, you'se the engine. But the engine got to work. We in the motherfucking dark, and our football jerseys don't even match, but we have the heart and the talent to win. If you want to play, then I'm gonna squeeze every ounce out of you, and if I have to whup your ass to do it, then that's where I'm gonna go."

I let my words hang and left him to his corner, gambling on the strength of his character. I either had my leader or I didn't.

The next day at practice, Toro was early and in pads, and I never said a word to him as I prepared that day's practice. Once the whole team was dressed, I made Toro run laps for the practices he had missed until his tongue hung out. I was thrilled that something had clicked between us. He put his balls to the wall, accepting the challenge with vigor. Ghetto kids have tremendous pride. The oversharpened instincts that are forced upon them creates a powerful competitiveness, which is often overlooked. The incorrigibles, who scare the shit out of the public, are in truth vulnerable, confused, and needy.

After he ran what seemed to be his one-millionth lap, I demanded that he stand before the team and apologize for letting them down. This was the moment of truth. The success of the entire fall initiative lay upon the shoulders of this thirteen-year-old hunk of street matter. The worst thing you can ask a young ghetto sprocket to do is to reveal vulnerability to authority in front of his brethren, but I was searching for character, and I have a profound belief that street niggers are loaded with untapped character. I was surprised by the depth of his mea culpa. He concluded his luminous apology by stating, "The big nigger knows what he's doing, so I'm gonna follow his shit. And you niggers follow his shit too." That was the first sign that the community center was back.

The team took off as I drilled them on a steady diet of "Young niggers' minds are fast! Young niggers' hearts are strong! Young niggers' brains are big! Young niggers matter!" That was my mantra on the practice fields of Jefferson Park as I injected my troops with psychological steroids. Their confidence was developing visible biceps. I called them the "ragtag candlelit gang," teaching them to wear their disadvantages like a badge of courage.

The league we were in was a citywide venture. At the end of the season the two top teams would play for the city championship and be honored by its sponsor, the New York *Daily News*. After two months of my calculated ball-busting, the ragtag candlelit gang was ready for battle. I started out with forty-five kids and through a process of attrition settled on twenty-five solid ghetto-warriors who would make East Harlem proud. A half hour before our first game, they were all gathered in the center when I approached them carrying a list. On the list was every single one of their school reports. I clicked off each of their names and put their shitty grades out front, creating lots of laughter that covered an encouraging amount of embarrassment.

"This is your free game," I told them. "This is the game you get to play for dealing with six and a half weeks of my foot up your ass. Now I'm gonna check you little street motherfuckers' grades once a week. Whoever I get a report on that says they ain't tryin', ain't playin'! So go out and have fun, because if you don't intend to keep your school shit in check, this could be your last game. One thing I know we all understand is that I mean what I say. I won't settle for you young motherfuckers being anything but champions, and that doesn't mean winning, it's the way you win that buys the day. Only a fool fucks over school, and I ain't in the business of coaching fools."

From the outset, I trained my warriors to chew on adversity. We won the game by three touchdowns, but we were sloppy and made a number of mistakes. Had the team not been in supreme physical condition with overpowering talent at the skilled positions, we would not have fared so well. After the game I employed the wisdom of one of my greatest influences, the incomparable Vincent Lombardi. Upon entering the locker room, I went completely off. I was beside myself with feigned disappointment, pointing out errors in execution that were the result of mental lapses. The great Lombardi would often administer his most blistering diatribes when the team had won, but performance that did not pursue perfection was unacceptable. They were shocked and angry, but they got my message: winning on a bullshit tip was no win at all.

The following game was against a team of the sons of the Coast Guard that were stationed on New York's Governor's Island. As the ferry pulled into port with my ragtag bunch, we were greeted by a welcome wagon that whisked us off to their cafeteria where a great lunch awaited. I had to watch them carefully, so that their gluttonous instincts didn't destroy our basic initiative.

The Governor's Island team was coached by the players' fathers and their militaristic egos. I overheard one of the coaches say to another, "What do we do if these kids become discouraged after they are forced to cope with a real football program?" The Governor's Island team had beautiful uniforms and all of the best equipment. Their well-manicured football field and working electronic scoreboard were intimidating.

I gathered my team together and spoke to them. "The other team thinks they're going to whup your ass. Superficial White folks' bullshit has been intimidating niggers forever, but that football field is an equal opportunity motherfucker. Now, you guys, despite what you look like, got superior training. First of all, I picked most of you motherfuckers because you were potential criminals. To me that meant you had active minds, coupled with adventurous hearts. You come from the best raw talent base in the country—the ghetto. Y'all know about Hotchkiss, the school that me and Noel (whose younger brother, Patrick, was one of the quiet stars on the team) went to. You niggers been fed high-level White-boy discipline and focus, Hotchkiss prime rib, and I bet my money on White-boy-trained street magic any day of the week. That's your edge."

Toro led his juiced-up teammates out on the field and put them through a spirited warm-up. The Governor's Island team kicked off to us, and our return man fumbled the ball, recovering it near the goal line. We had ninety-three yards ahead of us. On the first play Toro took a pitch right and went ninety-three yards for a score. Toro's big play opened the floodgates, and when the dust cleared the scoreboard read: Chargers 55, Governor's Island 0. We demoralized Governor's Island that day and in two subsequent games. The cumulative score was Chargers 163 to Governor's Island 7. Their painful lesson was that we weren't inferior, just woefully misunderstood.

The team was brilliantly quarterbacked by a long-headed colt named Kevin Druit. He was the only studious, well-parented, independently motivated player, and he led his offense to an overpowering undefeated season, culminating with a win in the city championship game that garnered local news coverage on the back page of the New York *Daily News*. In the interim, a true miracle occurred: They all improved their school performance. My love-dipped ass-whuppings had hit their mark.

During the sixties we were successful in telling White folks what they could do for us, subsequently becoming ensnared in the illusion of entitlement. The Toro group asked not what benefactors could do for them, but what they could do for themselves. It's a bizarre thought, but one of the best ways to train the underprivileged to compete in mainstream society is to convince them that they are superior. By the end of our football season our success convinced the White folks that be to turn the lights back on. One of the great thrills occurred when a party of eighty waited in the dark for the moment when the electricity went on.

Now that we could finally see each other, we revived the tradition of our annual awards banquet. I insisted that we follow the model from our heyday and instructed the boys to rent tuxedos and the girls to wear formal gowns. Several of the grateful parents, thrilled with the progress their children had made, pitched in by cooking all of the food and cleaning the center until it was spotless. Chuck was excited. Several hours before the festivities, Chuck and I sat joyously slamming Wild Turkey and talking about good times past. We recalled the banquet at which I had given Noel the award for the "Boy Who Came Back," ducking the sadness that his demise evoked.

Gerri's gracious behind-the-scenes effort convinced the Voices of East Harlem to come back home. Nostalgia abounded as the group tore through several of their most popular numbers. After the Voices fired the evening's opening salvo, I stepped forward as master of ceremonies to face a room drunk with hope. Having been something of a one-man band, I was intimately involved with each award winner. The most gratifying aspect of the event was that there were as many educational awards distributed as there were athletic. The highlight of the evening was when I gave Toro a special award for Outstanding Leadership. My reformed hellion looked great in his white dinner jacket and tie, evoking memories of Noel past, and I fought back the tears when handing him an award similar to the one that once honored his spiritual predecessor. I gave him a big hug and thanked him for reviving memories of Noel's legacy. After my emotional bluster, Toro leaned into the microphone and simply said, "Thank you. This is the greatest anybody has ever thought of me." On that note the house drenched him in applause. It was a night of a thousand hugs.

After the glow of accomplishment began to wane, an alarming sense of exhaustion set in. The task of leading a neighborhood away from an impending collision with drugs and destruction was tough work. Angel dust was making its initial house call, severely debilitating the process. The dead wood was piling up much faster than my efforts could combat.

Sadly, the banquet would be the center's last hurrah. The erosion on the streets summoned a darkness so pervasive that I was stymied, and this time there would be no ConEd to lobby.

TWENTY-THREE

At twenty-two years old, I was in a constant state of growth and change, stalking new monsters to slay. As the glow of the banquet dimmed, I was left with the thought of doing it all over again. I didn't have the stomach to live my life as a twenty-four-hour-a-day hotline for the crumbling ghetto psyche.

One afternoon Gerri and I were listening to the radio: WWRL, a Black station that was forced to sit in the back of the dial. An advertisement came on for an acting school—Black theater in the heart of West Harlem. I was attracted to the bite, which extolled the virtues of the acting profession. Over the next few days my acting itch broke out into a rash, and in classic "what the fuck" form, I ran with the advertisement's promise. I soon found myself in the world of the bombastic, temperamental genius of Ernie McClintock.

Ernie was a gay whirling dervish with an acerbic wit that would have impressed Truman Capote. On the first day of class there were forty new students. The breakdown was twenty-five women, fifteen men. Ernie swept into the room with the theatrical ebullience of Carol Channing's hairdresser and proclaimed, "Y'all have no idea what's in store for you. Artistry and freedom are synonymous: you cannot achieve one without the other. First we're going to focus on freedom, which will provide the opportunity for you to measure your artistic impulses accurately."

He used his hands so beautifully when expressing himself that his rhythmic flare was captivating. Ernie then fired his first strategic nuclear blast by ordering everyone to strip naked. The class immediately dropped by half, as most of the females hightailed it out of the room to demand a refund. We were now down to thirteen guys and six women. Ernie scoffed at the weak-willed, applauding their departure. I was of two minds. Stripping didn't bother me, but I wasn't sure if there was any real method to Ernie's apparent madness. Was this a search for freedom or a gay giggle?

The clothing came off slowly, until we were all standing before him in the nude. Ernie walked among us inspecting our bodies. His light seemed to turn green over the male anatomy and red for the female. He made playful, disparaging comments about unseemly bulges on the women, while offering colorful evaluations of male genitalia. His comments were direct and uncompromising because he was intent on chasing the thin-skinned away. Before the males put their clothes back on, Ernie hit us with another one of his freedom-inducing brainstorms. We were handed pantyhose and ordered to put them on for a jaunt up and down 145th Street through reams of sweaty, July-baked heroin addicts. This move lopped off five more males.

Those of us who passed the test gained passage onto the provocative ship *McClintock*, set to embark on a voyage to his island of creativity. I was intrigued by Ernie's antics and wanted in. After innumerable bizarre acting exercises, he gave me my first role: Walter Lee in *A Raisin in the Sun*.

Despite my growing respect for his brilliance, it was only a matter of time before our wills would clash, a confrontation I couldn't resist. He and I fought endlessly over the interpretation of the role, but he also was forced on occasion to admit that I had ability. The thrill I felt from the slightest affirmative nod of Ernie's head rivaled that of scoring five touchdowns in a championship game. Petulant, dictatorial aggressiveness was at the heart of his technique. His vindictive wisdom haunted me unmercifully. "Trust your right to be free," he asserted with his patented arrogance. I fought off my homicidal urges, allowing Ernie to teach me the art of acting.

The six-week course flew by. My Walter Lee drew appreciative raves from everyone, except Ernie who only would say, "Not bad for a pain in the ass." At the end of what was a transformative experience, Ernie was to decide which of us would be accepted back for the following semester. Everyone was required to perform a monologue for Ernie and his staff. My classmates were damn good, and spirits were high. My monologue was comprised of selected passages from Jim Morrison's poetry from the Door's album *Soft Parade*.

When I was back there in seminary school,
There was a person there who put forth the proposition
that you can petition the Lord with prayer.

Ernie thought a Martian had descended. Everyone else had selected Black pieces to work from, so when I introduced the Doors and praised Morrison, Ernie said with a hint of admiration, "You crazy, nigger!" I was again combining my two Americas to their best advantage. Morrison's poetry was like a comfortable pair of gloves, and I nailed the audition. We were told that we would be notified within the next few days about our future. I was confident that I had gained a second act under Ernie's tutelage.

In true show-business fashion, a week went by and I didn't hear from him. I called the theater under some pretense to try to get some information and was blown off. My embarrassment turned to anger, fueling a determination to prove that Ernie wasn't the only show in town. A friend of mine had told me about the American Academy of Dramatic Arts. I discovered that they were auditioning potential students, so I booked an appointment. I reached for Joni Mitchell's red hot album, *Court and Spark*, and chose the cut "Same Situation" for my audition piece.

With heaven full of astronauts and the Lord on death row,
With a million of us lost and lonely ones, I call out to be released.

Mr. Cuttingham, the director of the school, immediately stamped me a potential talent. The Academy was a five-story structure on Thirty-first and Madison. It was equipped with three theaters and all of the accoutrements that McClintock's joint lacked. It was famous for shepherding young actors to the stage and screen. Its graduates included Robert Redford and Don Rickles.

Three days after my White audition, still no word from Ernie. I received a call from the Academy offering me a position in their fall class, and I accepted. Ten minutes after I hung up, the phone rang again. It was Ernie. He explained that he wanted me to sit on the skillet for a while to teach me a lesson that he thought would be of great value to me. He then extended a gracious invitation for me to return. I declined his offer, allowing my ego to opt for the prestige of the Academy. Ernie seemed stunned, and after a long pause he left me with these words, "If you choose to go with the White folks, don't let them ruin you, because there ain't been a brother like you in a long time."

I felt many pangs of regret over that decision over the years, because there was only one Ernie McClintock.

• • •

In early 1974 a good friend from my Hotchkiss days, Charlie Schultz, rang me up. Charlie was a fun soul with incredible wealth. I told him of my new acting fetish, and he informed me that his brother-in-law was working on a screenplay about basketball in the ghetto. His brother-in-law was a filmmaker named John Ballard.

John took me into his working quarters, where there were several assistants typing away at his four-hundred-page screenplay, *Champions,* but it didn't quite cut it.

"That's what I need you for," he said. "Can you fix it?"

"What do you want me to do? I'm no writer."

"I just want you to tell us when we're going off track."

I pondered the thought before deciding that this wasn't my scene. I waited for the opportunity to make a graceful exit, but lunch hour's arrival changed everything. Soon a luscious platter of thick, mouthwatering sandwiches was placed before me. My second gargantuan roast beef and Swiss on rye bought me in.

John and I hit it off, forming and older brother–younger brother bond that would survive many storms and soak up its share of rays. After weeks of processing the rudiments of screenplay construction, I stepped off into an adjacent room and took a crack at writing a scene. That was the easy part. The hard part was showing it to John, expecting him to dismiss my amateurism. He was floored by it, and soon pulled me into the process, gradually giving me more responsibility until I was a fully accredited writer on the project.

John's had hired a small crew to film the city's double Dutch competitions at the New York Coliseum. Double Dutch was a true urban gymnastic art form. The youthful ability to dodge two jump ropes simultaneously was a mainstay in female playground activity. A once Euro-ethnic city art form had been taken over by female African American teenagers who elevated the tradition with their physical creativity.

When we arrived in a gymnasium the size of an airplane hanger, where various rounds of competition were being played out, John began to interview people supporting the various teams. I was taking sound and wandered off to capture audio for later use. When passing the judges' table, I heard a voice that said, "Hey, you!" When I turned toward the voice I saw that the wide smile of Mike the cop had found me again.

Mike summoned me over to the table and said, "You are that kid who I let go uptown on the East Side, right?"

"Yeah, that's me. That was about five or six years ago. I can't tell you how many times I wanted to thank you. But the question in my mind has always been why me?"

While he thought, we were interrupted by a scoring decision. I hung on my question until Mike came back and, without missing a beat, said, "Why you? Because it was your argument that made the most sense. Your verbal tap dance convinced me that someone had put some polish on your Black ass, and I couldn't terminate your life at fifteen. Scared the shit out of me, and for a long time after that I kept a sharp eye out for your ass, determined to take care of business if I saw you out there."

"If you hadn't made that gut decision, I wouldn't be here working on a short film, in possession of a fine education, with the opportunity to become a screenwriter. Without that difficult nod of your head toward the stairwell, my whole ball of wax would never have rolled. Great cop work, my man."

We hugged, and he said, "Almost none of you guys from that time made change stick. Congratulations. I'm the happiest man in the world that you were one of the exceptions."

He laughed through a cloud of relief, continuing to look me over. It was as though he had to assure his eyes that I was who I was in the flesh.

For several years Gerri and I had been ensconced in a period of golden love. We moved in together against the conventional wishes of our elders, except Chuck, who financed our initial house play. With this step came a stronger commitment to each other, and I discovered that I liked living with her. Despite the hectic pace her career generated, Gerri always had time to love me. At heart she was a basic homebody who enjoyed the security and order that a committed relationship provided. I'd put my past indiscretions in the dustbin and swore devotion to this extraordinary woman. We drew from a mutual core of oneness, with our groove providing reams of satisfaction. My film gig with John and acceptance at the Academy provided a nice résumé in her world. We were cooking as a young Black power couple.

I embraced my beloved with dreams of holy matrimony dancing in my head. Filled to the brim with self, I assumed that her acceptance would be a formality, but my ego suffered a serious flat when she rejected my proposal. How could this happen? After the blowout she tore my ego off its rim by alerting me to her sudden lust for infidelity. Gerri had fallen hard for one of her touring band mates and informed me that she had grown tired of us and wanted to cut back on my dream. I was poised to announce the upcoming nuptials of the Prince and Princess East Harlem, and *thwack*—it shattered.

I had taken my eye off the ball, misreading clues to the distance growing between us, choosing to chalk it up to artistic temperament. Again I had cut too deeply into Gerri's conservative sensibilities. Too many spins of Dylan's "It's Alright, Ma (I'm Only Bleeding)" had wreaked havoc on her soulful, uncomplicated insights.

"Dennis, I have to find myself," she said. Gerri soon hit the road for Boston. With her lust and lover in tow, she would try on her new freedom.

Director Eve Packer from the American Academy dabbed at my tears as we stood in the wings minutes before the curtain was to rise on a production of *The Chalk Garden*. I was in a white jacket and other servile togs that dressed the character of Maitland, an effeminate manservant, minutes from opening the show with a comedic bit intended to draw a crowd-warming laugh, but the pain of rejection was clouding my concentration. Through the dramatic, alcoholic fumes of a face-to-face encounter, Eve told of the first of her countless husbands who'd dumped her the night she was to debut as Othello's Desdemona on the London stage. "There is no lover more demanding than the theater," she consoled, "and no lover's pain rivals the horror of a rotten performance." Despite her efforts, heartbreak toxicity had wiped me out, but somehow I nailed that first laugh and the audience's subsequent enjoyment of the show pulled me through. Once the generous ovation dissipated, my thoughts turned back to my empty bed.

My earlier behavior had included its share of side runs, so I didn't begrudge Gerri her desire, but it hurt like hell. Surprisingly, I was discovering that heartbreak was my most intense vulnerability. After a week of anguish, I received a call from her loaded with regret and disappointment. She asked for my forgiveness, and we decided to put the incident behind us. The following day, seated in the bus terminal awaiting her arrival, I was a happy man with a good attitude. When her bus arrived, she wasn't on it. I waited through the next several buses and no Gerri.

The following day I was a zombie. John Terenzio, a close friend from Hotchkiss, and I were to go and see a New York Giant exhibition game at the Yale Bowl. On our way it rained buckets, giving my tears a run for their money. It was the first time John would see his tough-guy hero break into little pieces. Finally, we turned around and went back to the city, where I hightailed it to the Port Authority Bus Terminal and counted buses from Boston. After my fifth bus and no Gerri, I became enraged. With my pride on fire, I decided to check out on her and into a flea-bitten hooker hotel on the Upper West Side.

My raging assholeism set off a comedy of errors. When I entered my "suite," a battalion of roaches greeted me at the door, welcoming me into their all-night party. I never realized how gross a pool of self-pity could be. There was a full-length mirror on the door, and I stared at myself and hated the sad-sack reflection that was coming back at me. I became fixated on my moderate afro and discovered that the light penetrated my 'fro to the skull. What the fuck was this! After hours of inspection from every conceivable angle, the verdict was in: the light bore through to the dome. I was going fucking bald! Game, set, and match.

Dancing with roaches to the tune of automated hooker wails was the worst way to calm an inaugural obsession with a newly discovered deformity, so I bolted. Back on the neighborhood barstool I packaged my tales of woe in generous tips and dumped them on a Puerto Rican bartender's patience, until he leaned over the bar and nose-to-nosed me, saying, "You know, bro, your shit's fucked up. I can't help you no more." I wobbled off of the barstool, onto the streets, into a major surprise. Standing before me was Irod Daly, my old Hotchkiss nemesis/friend. I couldn't make heads or tails of this hallucination, until he revealed that he'd moved into 1199 First Avenue, a new housing development. We were living with less than a city block between us. Somehow we exchanged information before parting.

At home I continued slamming my blues with booze, until my consumption authored a dash through a huge thunderstorm through the streets in my underwear. With Irod's crumpled, wet address in hand, I sprinted to his home. The next thing I remember was being in my apartment in bed with Gerri lying beside me. I discovered that after I passed out, Irod had somehow gotten me home. When Gerri arrived she walked in on Irod and me in bed. She was seized by guilt, fearing that her wanderlust had made me gay. Seeing no chance of reviving me, she woke Irod. "Girl, you better take care of that man better than this!" he said as he hopped out of the bed. While dressing he needled, "Don't worry, he's nothing more than a drunk, broken-hearted heterosexual who wants you."

I awoke, squinting through tomato eyes before going into convulsions, puking until the heaves became stabbing jolts to my rib cage. With nothing but bile pouring forth, it was my demolished ego coming up. The baffling curve Gerri had thrown buckled my knees. Humiliation and defeatism was a new pill for me, and it was a tough swallow. Her genuine flurry of apologies inspired little more than little. My shame had taken over, and the only salve for shame was anger. I exploited her repentance by again proposing marriage, and she quickly accepted. I wasn't sure if the proposal was out of love or the desire to repair my shredded self-esteem.

The wedding took place in New Jersey at the home of Gerri's sister Cynthia. Gerri and I threw away the rulebook, writing our own ceremony, a marginally popular custom at the time. We decided to get married in jeans and our newly acquired Fry boots. As the folks streamed in, the diversity represented a high point for the America I'd gathered. Black, southern, devout, grandmotherly God freaks mixed with drug dealers from the neighborhood wearing wide-brimmed hats. Hippies along with the hip rolled with Blacks and Puerto Ricans, as rich and poor got down in a joyous pigment-rich groove.

John Terenzio's family made an appearance. I had gotten to know them well through my friendship with John, so my nuptials rang true for them. John's father had recently been the commissioner of hospitals in Mayor Lindsay's administration, and his family's participation was a pleasant leap across many lanes, when for one day they put aside the disturbing connotations that wide-brimmed hats wrought.

There were three social rooms: one for the old church folks in their seventies who viewed God as their drug of choice; another for those in their late forties with alcohol nudging the Lord to the perimeter; and the last room for our contemporaries was awash in cocaine. Joy won out over incongruity, setting an odd harmony asail.

Despite my many close relationships in the house, it was fitting that Leif would be best man. Our friendship had continued after Hotchkiss, and I maintained a residence on his property. With the school's training wheels off, we became closer in adulthood. Leif's two young sons, Eli and Carl, were toddlers who bounced around, getting into different forms of mischief, bonding with similarly aged, darker offspring. Even my mother was happy. She liked and trusted Gerri's strong Black gospel roots, figuring that Gerri had the best chance to bring me to God. Illness prevented my father's attendance, but he liked Gerri as well. Chuck rolled with our request to drop the father-up-the-aisle bit and was bursting with all things good, watching his daughter and adopted son tie the knot.

The eminent Reverend Norman Quick presided over the affair. Like most Black ministers he was a conservative but took pleasure in the group's diversity and surprised the throng when announcing that in the spirit of good-natured unorthodoxy, he was removing his tie and, for further emphasis, unfastening his top button. Well-timed laughter loosened the room. I was parked in nirvana staring into Gerri's eyes. Leif stood by my side flashing a perpetual grin. His youngest son, Eli, the spitting image of Hank Ketchum's Dennis the Menace, insisted on standing beside Reverend Quick. The Reverend acquiesced, tussling Eli's hair adoringly. After a prayer Gerri and I recited our personal vows to each other. Then Leif spoke his piece, followed by Gerri's maid of honor, Lamay, her NYU roommate.

After Reverend Quick declared us husband and wife, there was a confused silence. In the family's first wildcat wedding, no one knew what to do, so big Drey led other street bloods in an applause that picked up in intensity, generating a shower of extended hand music. Gerri and I grabbed each other's hands and walked through the applause. Someone flipped a switch on the stereo, and the joint broke out in funky music following Gerri and me up the stairs. The party exploded with good vibrations.

Shortly thereafter, someone made me aware of the fact that a number of White women had had trouble seeing the ceremony. Apparently, Leif's wife, Sarah, John Ballard's wife, Sidney, and Ballard's sister, Joan, had been buried in the kitchen. When they first arrived nervousness triggered their high-grade social protocol to kick in, and they made a beeline to the kitchen to offer their help. What they did not understand was that Black folks didn't read quite as much between the lines, more apt to take people at their word. The Black women doffed their aprons, handing them over to their inexplicably generous counterparts and joined the party. Through quirk-filled race-ignorant happenstance, the situation bulged with irony. This had to be one of the few Black weddings with rich White domestic help. My first righteous act as a married man would be to liberate all the Caucasian women from the kitchen.

This was Gerri's and my day of days, with all of the positive systems maxing out. Anticlimax stood in the shadows wielding a two-by-four.

TWENTY-FOUR

The first two years of our marriage was a fragile fairy tale spoiled by gifts and opportunities far exceeding the average Black American's grasp. Gerri was establishing a solo act and was becoming the object of adoration on the old Judy Garland circuit. With good management supporting her, success seemed inevitable. Meanwhile, I was about to take a paid educational carpet ride through Hollywood's film machine.

After completing the script *Champions*, John Ballard, his new top aide, Josh Silver, and I set off for Hollywood to pitch our project. Josh, who had the look of a Hollywood baby mogul with the smarts to match, and I would develop a friendship that bordered on brotherhood. We had received good buzz on the script and had meetings scheduled at every major studio. The likes of uber-producers Robert Stigwood and George Roy Hill would become relevant figures in our lives for a moment of delusion or two.

Going to Hollywood with John Ballard was quite an experience. John booked a luxuriously appointed room for the three of us to share in the Beverly Hilton Hotel. On the night of our arrival the American Film Institute was to induct Henry Fonda into its cherished ranks. The Fonda crowd at that time represented one of the final acts for Hollywood's greatest generation. Virtually every movie star I had ever seen on *The Late Show* entered gracefully before me as I sat in the lobby and peered from a corner. Heston, Quinn, Peck, Stanwyck, and Davis— all the monsters from that era—wore their photogenic professional smiles as they moved through the onslaught of flashbulbs.

The following day we set off on our appointments brokered by Marty Bower, John's agent at William Morris. We had to take on the insurmountable task of convincing the big boys to invest millions in a Black movie. I followed John's lead as a lounge act providing street-Nigra blasts of forced titillation to enliven the pretenders. Marty Bower spit the bit, and we were cut adrift in a sea of Hollywood cruelty.

On our final day, once the trail went cold, we got a hopeful dab of salve from a small independent film company, and we used that to declare victory over several rounds of martinis at the Brown Derby. I had witnessed the Hollywood illusion as well as Hollywood's hard truths. My early conclusion was that the Hollywood crowd was a fast-thinking, game-popping group of street-wise hustlers with swimming pools. I was hooked.

I tended to my wounds by soaking them in the industry's booby prize for the rejected: lies and exaggerations. Blessedly, Gerri had scored one of the lead roles in the road company of a successful Broadway musical, *Bubbling Brown Sugar*. She had the big closing number in the show, singing Billie Holiday's "God Bless the Child," cinching the loudest ovation every evening. I glided from acting at the Academy to center business before going to my paid job as a screenwriter. My ghetto standing was solid because of the work I had done in the center. I had it all for a minute.

Gerri's career was managed by a man named Lewis Friedman. He owned Reno Sweeney's, a popular nightclub in the West Village, and, like most people, he fell in love with Gerri's talent on sight. Lewis was gay, and thanks to the degree of intimacy he and Gerri shared, I was introduced to the world of open homosexuality. After my experiences with Joni and Irod, I considered myself progressive, even while hiding behind a "don't ask, don't tell" phoniness. In truth, I felt guys popping guys was a freak show.

Lewis's nightclub was staffed by a contingent of proud closet-escapees who served a predominantly straight clientele. His gay band of workers emitted a hip sense of androgyny that rarely failed to excite the atmosphere. Lewis was in his thirties, standing about five-foot-two in platform shoes. This intrigued me because I had never seen a man that small commandeer an effort so large. Lewis didn't flit; he darted. This mini person was a powerful force and a stalwart pioneer in the early struggle for gay liberation.

One time, in Lewis's apartment, I watched him make out with his boyfriend.

It bothered me, so later I said to Lewis, "I was being cool when you were kissing your man, but it's weird." He sought to look in my eyes by bending his head back to the point where he was staring straight up and said, "Your knowledge of gay people is tied to sex, and it's damn insulting. If I get three good hours of sex a week, that's a lot, so obviously I have to live the rest of the time, and it's who or what I am in that vast amount of time that matters. It's like dismissing you because of your skin color. That would be a pretty dumb thing to do, wouldn't it?" After a definitive deadpan look, he laughed, flashing the satisfied grin of a chess player who had made quick work of his opponent, leaving me to chomp on my homophobia.

Access to Reno's provided a number of perks. One of the biggest was the opportunity to see the great Peter Allen perform. Liza-free, he was doing some of the greatest live music a club has ever contained. During one of his notch-above-everyone-else performances, he whipped a predominantly gay and female audience into a frenzy. I'd brought some street brothers down, and Lewis set us up at a good table, but the mist of gay freedom was too heavy for them and they fled. Coincidentally, their departure afforded me my first experience as a straight practitioner in an audience one hundred strong of happy-to-be-homosexuals. Slowly one's comfort level heightened as the odds of a barroom brawl breaking out plunged.

Several afternoons a week Gerri rehearsed at the club. This gave me an opportunity to get to know many of the staff members. One afternoon I was seated at Lewis's table observing the workers tend to the task of setting up for the night's run. Hints of femininity in their brisk, organized movements added a wisp of grace to the grunt. What separated the gays from the heteros was a keen passion for detail. I focused on two young, well-conditioned guys moving a piano, a major undertaking, and they had the strength to move it handily, passing the macho, physical part in a breeze. They then took the process one step further, reaching into their bag of feminized sensibilities to artfully place the piano perfectly. "Wow!" I thought, "This is some evolutionary shit. They could be superior." This observation vaporized my homophobia.

Freedom from bigoted judgment is a gift, and little Lewis jabbed my ignorance until I clasped the importance of other people's freedom. Despite the many thrills he and Gerri shared, their relationship would miss their SRO target. More crushing was the fact that Lewis would become one of the early AIDS victims. This very big man in the small body suffered a horrible death, but his legacy of helping to make mid-seventies New York urban life a little larger will never be forgotten by those of us who rocked to the early notes of the gay dawning.

•   •   •

In 1976, Gerri was in Chicago for an eight-week run of *Bubbling Brown Sugar* at the Shubert Theater. I stayed in our new apartment that overlooked the East River. It was a glorious ride through bicentennial summer, where money, connections, and a twenty-three-year-old groin made living a privileged experience. I was poised for the credits to roll.

Unfortunately, life's movie has its own writers. I suffered a crushing blow when I received a phone call from Leif Thorne-Thomsen. He asked if it were true that Irod was dead. I'd just seen him and thought it was a rumor, but I told Leif I would check it out. I sprinted the half block to his building and stepped off the elevator into a homicide investigation. Apparently, Irod had been killed by a lower-than-shady sexual partner.

I returned home and called Leif, confirming the rumor. I got off the phone and bolted from the house. Just as I was stepping from my apartment building, I looked to my left, and running up the block toward me was a man whose fear had increased his speed. Behind him was an angry gun-wielding brother in pursuit. I was in the crossfire certain that I was going to join Noel and Irod in the Dead Black Hotchkiss Alumni Society. I took a deep breath and a step backward into the tiny foyer and waited for the shooting. After watching them both pass by the building, I slumped to the floor realizing that the pressure of living in the war zone was becoming too much.

Sound the alarm, an unexpected newborn was on its way. Gerri's and my first child would arrive in the world to a lot of love, but the timing was a mean left hook to our lives as we had known them. Gerri's pregnancy forced her off the road, and although she would continue to be paid her salary for several months, the forecast had changed. I had to put an offer from the Tisch Film School at NYU on hold, figuring I needed the year to help settle the baby into the world. Gerri went ultra-maternal, a side I had not witnessed before. It was as though she was relieved to be out of the mix after fifteen years of attention. This shook my insecure roots. Suddenly, the family's financial future was threatened, in body and attitude.

The sneaky, dark fear that plagued me was that if Gerri stopped being Gerri, three-quarters of our privileged life vanished. To my surprise, she was unconcerned with the obvious. Gerri was happier to focus on a supplementary diet of brewer's yeast, spinach, and carrot juice that someone named Adele Davis convinced her to drink by the gallon. Gerri's pregnancy soldiered on the prenatal care war front, and we were a part of the early Lamaze craze. The classes were a comforting step for first-time parents that was essentially built on the subtly inferred bullshit that they could help make natural childbirth less painful. The myth lasted until the woman gained the post six-centimeter Holy Ghost—then all bets were off.

All of a sudden, I was at a door with a mat that read WELCOME TO REAL LIFE, and I wanted no part of that. Gerri began to talk about future stability and the curtailment of dreams. That was not the script I'd signed on to play. I held down my disenchantment while playing by the conventional book, not wanting to spoil Gerri's stint with childbirth, but the unwanted changes were running over the edge. Gerri's commendable effort to remain totally healthy during the baby's gestation period made my drinking and drugging play louder. Our new lifestyles called for rest, peace, and quiet, which clashed with my "Live at Leeds" impulses. In short time, rent payments that were mere formalities became problematic. I concentrated on the community center more in order to hold on tightly to my now-vital paycheck.

On April 31, 1977, Gerri and I welcomed Avery Dylan Watlington into the world. The poor kid narrowly escaped being named Avery Lennon as I flipped a coin between legends. He was a healthy, special baby, and all was well. The arrival of new life in a family often creates an uneasy truce with a short shelf life, and my experience was no different. I resigned myself temporarily to the horrible fate of growing up.

I kept my hat in the acting game. My career consisted of the stomach pains that came from the response of "all clear" in reply to my ten answering-service inquiries a day. I was being weaned off my lust for bigger things, when an opportunity snuck up on me. Joan Hyler, an agent for International Creative Management, was a good friend of Lewis Friedman's. She'd taken me on as a client after seeing me in a screen test, where I played a character opposite the great Black pearl, Earl Monroe, the gifted guard for the New York Knicks. She got me an interview with a casting person named Sis Corman who was working on a film called *The Deer Hunter*. As luck would have it, Sis was taken with my game and insisted that I meet with the director, Michael Cimino, and the film's star, Robert De Niro.

I was a De Niro fan and admired him as a craftsperson, but he was still in a period of being drowned out by the voices of Hoffman, Pacino, and Nicholson. My lucky streak continued when I was given a small part in a major motion picture. My introduction to flying first class and big per diem fees recharged my high-voltage dreams. Hallelujah was my buzzword as I nestled comfortably into my first-class seat. I was headed for Pittsburgh, where the cast and crew of *The Deer Hunter* stayed. The hotel was forty minutes away from the film's location in Weirton, West Virginia.

Several months before I was to report for *The Deer Hunter* shoot, I received a call from Gail Sheehy inviting me to dinner and a show. At the night's end we taxied up to her new joint on Fifth Avenue. Gail spoke of a surprise she wanted to give me. Nestled in her glowing prosperity, I was pumped for climax. She reached into a manila envelope, pulled several pages from it, and started reading out loud a chapter she had written about Noel and me in her soon-to-be-published book.

My initial reaction disappointed her. My virginal ears winced when they heard an inaccuracy. Her desire to turn the story of our Hotchkiss experience into a chapter in her book was more than enough to win my appreciation, but my facial expressions fired blanks. I couldn't grasp how important this material would become. In swift order that book would wind up on more than half a million coffee tables. Gail's monster bestseller, *Passages*, unleashed a wave of self-introspection that engulfed Baby Boomer sensibilities.

When I arrived on *The Deer Hunter* set, many had heard of the book. My notoriety enabled me to duck the "just another nigger" tag, which on a major White film location can make for a lonely go of it. I was whisked to De Niro's trailer to rehearse our scene. I played a cab driver who brings De Niro home from the airport after his Vietnam War duty. In the scene he changes his mind and decides he wants to avoid the welcome home celebration that awaits him. There are three or four lines tossed between us. It was a simple scene, but I got lucky. The scene was shot at dusk, so the amount of proper light available was scarce. This was in the days when De Niro took the smallest scene and broke it down through multiple takes. The process dragged on for about eight days with several schedule days thrown in.

The scene we played was set in the wintertime, despite ninety-five-degree heat. We were huddled in a taxicab, dressed in heavy winter clothing, with the windows rolled up. Each take we perspired like steamed pigs. The makeup artists would descend upon De Niro, blow-drying every pore, ignoring me as my woolen scully started to drip. De Niro said, "Take care of him too," and they responded immediately. That little gesture of back-watching made me feel like a million bucks. I put my hand out, and the young Don Corleone slapped me five.

De Niro, Meryl Streep, George Dzundza, John Savage, and John Cazale would all ride in a van together as we went back and forth between the hotel and location. Streep was involved with Cazale, who had played Fredo in *The Godfather* saga, and she cuddled close to him as he told stories about the theater, past movies, and plans for the future. I was the pup in the pound and stayed on my best behavior, removing the cotton from my ears and placing it in my mouth. Cazale's personal charisma was extraordinary. The notion that six months later I would be in Joe Papp's Public Theater, where the flags were being flown at half-mast over his untimely death, was inconceivable during his van raps.

A-list film privileges were great. Fans and wannabes were crawling throughout the hotel bar, and if you were a legitimate film production participant, no one ever let you buy a drink. In the late night, when riding my booze high down, I wrestled with my picture in the conservative portrait that was becoming my life. The picture didn't play for me. During the shoot I was influenced by Desi Arnaz's autobiography. The creative street savvy he had used to build his television empire was inspiring. If a Cuban refugee who spoke fractured English could make it, then so could I. When I got back to New York, I had gained back most of the hop in my step.

Unfortunately, on the night of my arrival, the vibe in the city suffered a crushing blow. Shortly after I discarded my luggage, I decided to go to the supermarket and buy up a feast. Upon my return, with a shopping cart filled with goodies, I summoned the elevator for my eleven-flight trip. The elevator arrived, the door opened, and then everything around me went dark. A New York City blackout was upon us. I carried the groceries up eleven flights and huddled with Gerri and the baby in candlelight. We sought to emulate the great experience of goodwill and sharing that had been the prominent theme during the previous blackout in the Lindsay-led sixties. But this blackout would be very different.

It seemed to signal an act change in city life, bringing down the curtain on post–World War II White flight, slamming the door on its urban roots so the pride in the community was in transition. On this black night, the vacuum was filled with violence as sirens blared and street soot rioted and looted with blind purpose. When the lights returned, New York City's face had changed forever.

Much of East Harlem had been wiped out. The liquor store across from the center was run by a warmhearted old Jewish cat, who had been a staple in the neighborhood for thirty years. The children of his customers slashed, robbed, and burned his joint to the ground. The community center no longer had the muscle or the will to put forth the effort to make a discernible difference. The asshole rioters had turned the last of the area's diversity to ashes. The '77 riots officially kicked off a period where Whites had decided the only way they would be caught in Harlem was searching for better drugs.

Chuck gathered his inner circle, and we mourned the disfigurement of our neighborhood, but there was little we could do. Mayoral candidate Ed Koch launched an exploitive campaign that inferred he would get tough with the impoverished Colored community. The city's shaken young White Boomers responded heartily to his get-tough approach. The embattled mayor, Abraham Beame, and his gentle liberalism were deemed impotent. The center became a graveyard, housing a few stragglers who fed off of the moments before the guillotine arrived. City funds for the poverty programs dried to the bone.

I think a part of the destructive behavior that the younger cats unleashed on their neighborhood was the result of the introduction of the most wicked, debilitating drug to find its way on to the hood's menu—angel dust. It turned a simple joint into a stick of unpredictable, hallucinogenic dynamite. The drug introduced the neighborhood to psychotic delusional behavior. When angel dust hit, the older guys saw it as a teenage goof and paid little attention, but reports started to pile up of bizarre shooting incidents and other reckless acts of daring that made little sense. Dust exacerbated suicidal impulses in the Black ghetto teenager, and with aging schools built for the immigrant crowd crumbling around them as the former inhabitants wagged their fingers in disgust, the metastasizing time bomb was as clear as the nose on Mayor Edward Koch's face.

These kids were born to die, ditching school early to prowl the streets in search of life's only equalizer: instant gratification. Their Black church roots fell victim to rot as young single mothers, too immature to provide a moral foundation, allowed the meaning of Black Sunday morning to slip through their fingers. Many were drug addicts and dust heads as their out-of-control offspring turned schools into houses of fear. Does this movie look bleak? It gets worse. These kids arrived after the party was over. With the King escapees narrowly beating the drawbridge's retraction, a new file stamped NO PLACE TO BE SOMEBODY would fill up so fast that anyone under the age of nineteen was perilously at risk.

One day I was on the corner of 115th Street and was brightened by the sight of my Hall of Fame running back, Toro. He was standing on the corner opposite me holding a can of beer, when I shouted his name. He didn't answer. Crossing the street to get closer, I continued to call his name, but again no response. Toro lifted his can, stared at it menacingly, and began to scream at the label.

"Toro, it's me," I shouted again. "Your coach."

He paused and looked at me closely, sizing me up. Recognition seemed to drain the anger from his face. I extended my hand, and he conferred with his can of beer, "Who the fuck is this?" He left me hanging as he resumed his argument with the maker of Old English Malt Liquor. My heart fell out of my ass because this was the greatest kid I had ever coached. It had been four years since he had been the most valuable player on the city championship team. Now, he was waging war with inanimate objects. There's a lot of pain on this field of battle.

A stark difference of opinion between Gerri and me defined itself with a red hot blade on a late Sunday afternoon when the Dallas Cowboys were playing the Denver Broncos in the Super Bowl. The setting was perfect. My large-screen Sony with its cable reception placed the game in my living room. Gerri had taken the baby to church, and I was all by my lonesome. After the coin flip, I hovered over my shellacked, wooden coffee table, a handmade gift from my buddy Blade Brokaw. The table was lined with all my choice pleasures—pot, booze, and food—a recreational junkie's picnic.

After an exciting first half I was geared up for the second-half kickoff, when a human figure stepped in front of the screen. It was Gerri. The sight of her provoked an impulsive response. "This is the fucking Super Bowl, baby. You blockin' the shit."

She wouldn't move. Gerri was clutching a bible, and with divine seriousness she said, "Dennis, I have to talk to you. It's important."

As I maneuvered to see the screen, I said, "What's the matter, something with the baby? Somebody die? Because anything else can wait."

"No," she demanded, "we have to talk now."

"What?" I whined.

"I've decided to give my life over to Jesus Christ," she said.

I didn't quite get what she was saying initially and replied, "Good, is that it?"

She then became evangelically inspired, flooding the apartment with holy lava before concluding, "I got saved, Dennis."

Alarms of my mother went off. "You mean, saved, like saved, saved?"

"Yes, I want to serve the Lord. He is my salvation."

This got my attention. "You mean, saved like the folks who get the Holy Ghost in church. That kind of saved?"

She didn't answer, but her divine look with her head tilted upward told me she was now one of Lord's winged soldiers. I didn't see it coming, and in itself it wasn't a bad thing, but it sure as hell wasn't me. I missed much of the third quarter as my life changed forever. Self-consciously, I removed my contraband, and with the compassion of a Bing Crosby film's nun, Gerri uttered, "Dennis, I would appreciate it if you didn't swear in the house anymore."

That was it! I exploded, "Damn, woman, you just cut out half of my motherfucking vocabulary!"

That episode put our relationship on life support. I couldn't serve God, acting, and cocaine at the same time, but Gerri's decision was a solid one and she was determined to show me by example how God would be the best choice for our union. Our life began to resemble a scene from the film *Arthur*. "A good woman could help you stop drinking," Arthur's fiancée tells him as he finishes off a Scotch. "It would have to be an awfully big woman," he answers.

Gerri on her knees in church and me falling to my knees off of a barstool made for an insoluble dilemma.

Over a four-year period I had studied at a variety of acting schools, including Lee Strasberg's joint, and was growing bored with paying for the opportunity to perform. One of the last scenes I performed on the "you pay to play circuit" was at Herbert Bergdorf Studios. I'd written, directed, and acted with a fellow classmate a scenario that climaxed with my simulating the act of shooting heroin on stage.

I was so far out of circulation that I didn't know where to get a legitimate hypodermic needle. Someone suggested Alfred Mealy. Alfred was still shooting heroin. His years had turned into a trough of pathetic, self-destructive decisions. The magnificence was torn from the bone. Once one of the only people who had the presence and charisma to wear a cape and monocle in the ghetto square was petrified wood. The broken man whose pieces could give Humpty Dumpty a decent run grabbed me by the arm.

"Damn, nigger, I can't believe you'se a full man. I always knew you'd make it somehow," he rasped as he stood on the stoop of a well-known shooting gallery. "What you want with a spike, nigger? You ain't fucking with that shit, is you?"

His words tumbled off his deep nod. The growing heartache that was the seventies ghetto disconnected one's tear duct apparatus, numbing the brow. I shook Alfred and said, "Wake up, man, I ain't fucking around. I'm an actor and I'm doing a scene. I'm going to the cooker onstage."

He let out a laugh and said, "Any other nigger I know say some shit like that to me I would certify it as bullshit, but you was always the kind of nigger that would wind up doing some shit like this. Besides, you look good. You still with Gerri?"

"Yes," I answered. "But you know something, man, she got saved. She in church four days a week."

He let out a belly laugh, and a flicker of the old Alfred came through when he said, "Living with a saved woman, there's a good side and a bad side. The good side is she'll calm your shit down, so you'll live longer. The bad thing is, unless you find the Holy Ghost, you'll hate every fucking minute of it."

We laughed. He took me a few blocks over, and we entered a dark building, where we scored from a guy who was dishing spikes. The untainted goods were professionally packaged, just what I wanted. I gave Alfred fifty dollars when ten would have done. His eyes widened, and he asked me, "Why you givin' me all this man?"

"Because I want your drugs to feel good to you tonight," I said. "You will never know how much you meant to me, and I love you." I kissed him on the forehead. "Even though we both know you gonna die."

Alfred pocketed the money, and we slapped five. His mangy yellow hand felt cold. I stood immobilized and stared at Alfred as he scurried off into the distance, pumped up over his good fortune. Several months later I heard on the grapevine that the great Alfred Mealy was dead.

I was twenty-four years old, and my neighborhood had turned into a community of ghosts. Gerri was kept very busy singing at funerals of friends. The outside world understood little about the pain of burying so many young loved ones. My thickened hide was badly punctured when the news arrived that Bobo Motion had been killed in a street shit episode. Bobo had been my baby brother. At his funeral, all I could see was the kid who pitched to me in my effort to become a major leaguer. Bobo was a combination of human tools that should have taken him anywhere he wanted to go in his life, but the streets ate him. This kid's indefatigable optimism was a gift snuffed out before his twenty-first candle.

I couldn't face the neighborhood after Bobo's death. I sought isolation in my house, mixing Minnie Riperton with Pete Townsend. The amount of numb needed to stomach the ghetto had tapped out. Going down like my boys felt like a done deal, so I was intent on picking my own poison.

TWENTY-FIVE

In the early days of Anne's and my togetherness, she would hold my hand as we walked down the New York City streets, oblivious to everything other than her new blast of important love. I was nervous, always on the lookout for the late-night drunk who might make a run at us. Our first home was on Ninety-second Street on the East Side of Manhattan, between First and Second Avenues. This once tough Irish-German neighborhood lingered in the fading scent of Jimmy Cagney's Yorkville hell-raising days, where the White ethnics sharpened their bite during the Depression. The bulldozers were driving these people out, building and renovating apartments for the well-off. In the late seventies, the scraps of the old mick guard were left behind to suffer a nigger's fate of displacement and confusion.

When Anne and I moved into our newly renovated duplex, there were a good number of unemployed, crime-prone Irish street niggers on the block. They hung out at Reif's Bar, just off Second Avenue, heading east, a great little empowerment shack, where the cynically depressed went to grow their balls. In the shack the patrons mixed alcohol, deprivation, and bravado into an elixir that provided a few hours of relevance as the final pillars of their lives disintegrated.

One morning, shortly after 2:00 A.M. as Anne and I turned the corner of Ninety-second Street, we ran smack-dab into a drunken spill-out of the falsely empowered. The sight of their menacing appearance scared the shit out of me. Their leering perception of Anne's beauty flashed like a lantern, etching angry lines in their faces. We picked up our pace on the molten turf as taunts and intimidating snickers singed the air. Two of the Cagneyites came after us, mouthing off. We ignored them until they gave chase. I grabbed Anne by the hand, and we accelerated. The punks made an abrupt stop and puked racist invective through haughty laughs. Once safely behind closed doors, Anne was in a state of disoriented relief, not quite knowing what to make of this game of combustible street poker. I ran to the kitchen drawer, and behind the utensil rack was my old shank knife. I grabbed the shank and headed for the door.

"What are you doing!" Anne screamed.

"Trust me," I shouted and dashed out the door to hit Ninety-second Street. I hid my shank beneath my sleeve turned in. I was hoping things wouldn't go deep enough to spread red, but this was a presence move I had to make. I didn't want to play street, but it took street to deal with street. I had to show these albino niggers that I understood what kill or die meant or they would run me off my woman.

As I approached the bar, my heart doubled the speed limit. I made a splashy move, assaulting one of the Cagneyites that had chased us. I punched him in the chest, careful to avoid his face. After impact, I jumped back and drew my shank. My adversary ran into the bar and came out with a stool. I waved my shank, and he fended me off like a lion tamer. He was drunk and less fit than I, so I easily danced away from his clumsy thrusts while flashing enough knife to keep his boys off my ass. The Paddy boys still took pride in nose-to-nose combat—even their lowlifes had trouble stabbing you in the back. If I had pulled this stunt in front of an Italian or Puerto Rican bar, I would have been quick casket fodder. I was talking deep, loud street shit when the police came swinging around the corner, and everyone fled. The whiff of blue provided the perfect opportunity to gratefully bow out with dignity.

When I returned home for my successful warrior's welcome, things didn't go as smoothly. Anne was furious; she read me chapter and verse from the civil White people's doctrine for good behavior. She saw none of the honor or daring that I'd experienced, but her background and gender carried the day, and I was dutifully chastened. My instincts were in for some serious reprogramming.

Shortly after the incident I started a fence-mending effort with one of the combatants, Duffy, a good dude who had the respect of the neighborhood. Our mutual street chops played harmoniously and the word in the block found my favor, earning me a nigger exemption.

Over the next decade, as the block was being purged of its White niggers, the nigger in me would follow suit.

At the end of a decade that had offered such promise, the new Mayor, Ed Koch, came to the ghetto and confronted the angry Colored faces, declaring that he was going to cut the jaded poverty programs' windpipe. This added the letters *ph* to the center's epitaph. I decided to white out the pain by taking the advice of an old Hotchkiss master, Bob Haiko, who said, "When all else is screwed, hit the gym."

I joined a YMCA in midtown Manhattan. One day, after a workout, I decided to walk home. When I reached Eighty-sixth Street on the East Side, I came upon a little health food store. I peered through the window and saw a very attractive woman performing the duties of an oddity called a juice bar. She was a White woman in her early twenties who wore big glasses. She removed them for a moment, and the sexual transformation was powerful. These delightful little fantasies were dancing in my head as I entered the store and stood in line for a go at this juice bar.

While waiting I focused upon the rows of new miracle supplements that lined the shelves flaking for the dawn of New Age commerce. When the woman in the glasses turned to me, I laid a lot of fake symptoms on her to lengthen the engagement. As she pondered remedies, I focused on her beauty, discovering the incandescent light that resides behind the smile of an Irish woman. I had recently adopted Frank Capra's autobiography, *The Name Above the Title*, as my official show business bible and thought of how the great director must have felt when shooting his first meaningful closeup for his heartthrob, Barbara Stanwyck.

In the following weeks, after my umpteenth lame reason for showing up at the store, I summoned the will to ask if she would have coffee with me—in the daytime, in a public place. I wanted my proposal to be confessional-booth safe. She one-upped me with an invitation to her apartment the following evening.

When I arrived at Anne McCormack's apartment on East Eighty-fourth Street, I was petrified. I knocked on the door lightly until she answered. She had just come out of the shower. Absent Clairol and Max Factor's touch, I saw that Anne was a member of that small grouping of the Maker's best work. My courting tools of choice were Barry Manilow's second album and Crosby, Stills and Nash's *CSN*. The Barry Manilow surprised her. She hadn't figured me for a lame sentimentalist. This intrigued her.

Anne McCormack was a fascinating, innocent, middle-class White Boomer.

She had grown up in fifties America, where the Beaver and postwar security had upstaged real life, but beneath the suburban Valium, the world had been stewing. Anne had left home after high school to do a stint of confusion at Hartwick College in upstate New York. After a year she left school and decided to travel the islands of the West Indies, landing in St. Thomas. She was in search of a balm that would ease her discomforting uncertainty with her postwar, middle-class baptism. In St. Thomas, Anne met and fell for Gerhard Hofmann, a German whose age lapped hers by decades. He was a Hitler survivor who had combined a wealth of European cultural knowledge with a tireless work ethic to achieve part ownership in the Hotel 1829 on the island. Gerhard was the perfect teacher, and Anne warmed to his guruship, which consisted of German pain tendered by the arts. She rode Gerhard's cloud until he began to let other young female pupils on board. Anne's disappointment brought her back to the States, where she settled down in New York City. She found a job through friends in the health-food business, joining the early legions of single self-sufficient city women.

After a comforting laugh at my expense over the syrup that poured from Manilow's "Mandy," conversation seeped in, exposing common perceptions on cultural and political issues. We discussed the recent East Coast blackout and the rioting that had followed. Anne had been out of the country and was shocked by the swift change in racial attitudes that she had picked up on after her return. She spoke of White acquaintances' racially tinged hostility over the Black and Latino communities and felt it was excessive. She condemned the criminal acts without smearing the race. It was endearing. Anne was what Neil Young at his perplexing best must have meant when he crowed, "I am just a dreamer, and you are just a dream." I was holding dynamite in my hands, a White American female with color-blind intensions.

I was careful not to offend her food sensibilities. I was relieved to realize I had been mistaken in assuming her chaste occupation was an indication that her social habits were vice-free. I was pleased to discover a fifth of booze atop the refrigerator. Eureka! My angel had a taste for scotch. After adding booze to the groove, our damn of reservations crumbled. The phone rang, reminding Anne of a later date she had made. My visit was intended to be a simple meet-and-greet deal. Upon her return, she told of her decision to delay the date for an hour. Anne sat beside me and spooned a few moments of sweet silence into the mix. Her eyes offered new hope for my crumbling emotional infrastructure.

I told her that I was in mourning over the death of my street brother, Bobo Motion. I was a bit of a freak to her, a young man talking like an old soldier whose past is embedded in cemeteries. Her instincts led to a gentle embrace, and I felt a rush of adrenaline.

"Drink up. I want to show you something," I said.

She complied, and we hit the streets. I tried to hail a taxi, and after several cabs galloped by, she asked, "Why won't they stop?"

"You really are from a different world."

"Don't tease me. I want to know."

I stepped back in the shadows and said, "You try."

She raised her hand, and two taxis screeched to a halt. She opened the door, and I raced to the cab, entering behind her.

"A Black man can't get a cab heading north."

"Why?" she questioned.

"Because the closer you get to Harlem, the less your citizenship is worth."

"I don't believe that," she challenged.

The cab driver was a brother, and I asked, "Yo, bro', do yellow-cab drivers like to pick brothers up?"

The cab driver shot back, "It's a rule. I can't even get one. Where to?"

"Harlem." The driver did a double take, fixing his stare on Anne. "Don't worry, man," I stroked. "I'm just giving her a taste of my old neighborhood. Look at her, she strike you as somebody up to no good?"

On the ride uptown, I told Anne of my Hotchkiss past. "I guess that explains Barry Manilow," she teased. Her laughter activated several of my dormant feel-good impulses. Anne was different, yet unafraid, but a larger test was in the offing. When we hit my neighborhood, I gave her a tour of the crevices where scenes of my life had occurred.

"That's where another friend of mine was shot by the police."

"My father is a cop."

I gulped. "Oh, yeah?"

She smiled and said, "He's a good guy."

I gulped again. "If you and I make it beyond tonight, how would this play with him?"

"I don't know. I'm not sure how many Hotchkiss guys who quote Joni Mitchell he's ever dealt with." She laughed as I swooned to the music of her sounds.

Still in the cab, we cruised the neighborhood. I showed her the community center and its surrounding ashes from the riots. It didn't look like much at the time, but I assured her that the building held important memories. As the meter continued to gobble money and the driver's eyebrows began to arch, I assured him that there was a big tip on top of the number. This freed him to enjoy our ghetto-lit romance. We passed by the drug corner on 115th Street and Lexington Avenue. One of my soon-to-be-deceased center kids, Little Stevie, came to the car window.

"Yo, D Wat, I got the shit," he bellowed.

"D Wat, I like that. Can I call you that?" Anne asked.

I answered her with a kiss before copping three trey bags of pot.

"Hey, man, that's your woman?" he asked.

"I hope so."

Little Stevie gave me my change and slapped palms with me. That would be our final goodbye. Days later he would be smoked off the count. I rolled a joint and asked the driver if I could light up.

"Put the windows down and pass it."

We puffed up and took one more spin around the neighborhood. We turned on 112th Street and First Avenue and came upon Jefferson Park. I told the driver to stop. Anne and I got out and walked the sacred turf on which Chargers were taught to bleed for a win if they had to.

"This is where Bobo Motion used to pitch to me when I was trying to break into professional baseball." My emotions mugged me, and I choked up. "I love living in the rhythm section," I croaked. "It's a gift of sweet survival. We're masters at turning chicken shit into porterhouse steaks."

Attempting to beat back the sentiment, I began to walk off the field. Anne caught up to me and extended her delicate hand. I clasped it and mumbled a Neil Young lyric.

I remember the good old days, stayed up all night getting crazed.
Then the money was not so good, but we still did the best we could.

Anne pulled close to me and we walked off the field together.

Back in Anne's living room the phone was ringing off the hook. It was her date. I could hear her making apologies as she closed her bedroom door, leaving me to Stephen Stills and his ode to the "Dark Star." Anne came back into the living room, and her look told me that she was mine. Her emergence from the shadows into the light offered an image so filled with excitement that it would nourish my fantasies henceforth.

She leapt into my arms, clasping hers around my neck and her legs around my waist. We remained in that position as she rested her head on my shoulder.

Several months passed as we flirted with the volcanic implications that lie along the racial fault lines. The rapid growth of our commitment was nudging us toward introductions to family and important acquaintances. Anne chose her younger sister, Ellen, as the first family member I was to meet. Only two years apart, the sisters often jousted over sibling differences, but I quickly learned that their occasional moments of volatility counted for little when blood loyalty called. Ellen would be our first read of the family's pulse as we built toward my official Sidney comes to dinner move.

The encounter played out at a friend's Upper West Side apartment. On the morning of the meeting, Anne had had several wisdom teeth extracted, and the right side of her jaw was swollen and black-and-blue. When I answered the fateful ring, Anne was standing behind me, barely visible from Ellen's vantage point. As I reached to shake her hand Anne stepped from behind her pillar, offering an enthusiastic greeting. Instant steam emission heated the room as Ellen fixated on the bruises. Her Irish eyes went from languid to ninety in a blink, exchanging soft feminine features for Sonny Corleone's glare before riddling me with a round of stinging presumptive bullets. I ducked for cover as Anne assuaged Ellen's fear of domestic battery by injecting the simple truth definitively. Her rap managed to hose down the flames gushing from her sister's nostrils, and a warm embarrassed smile emerged on Ellen's face. Its sweet innocence provided the perfect background for large, wondrous brown eyes.

I had Ellen by the short hairs. The harshness of her instant judgment created a window of opportunity. I could screw it up by playing an indignant hand, or I could reach out and pull her back from the edge of defenselessness. Ellen's body language wore her humility appealingly, making my call to let her off the hook an easy one. A conciliatory gesture was warmly received, and we clicked, allowing for an immediate ditching of the speed bumps that slows the bonding process. Like her sister, Ellen's heart was too instinctual for Nigraphobia, and our racial barrier thinned on sight. I would learn that she was quick to eschew Irish Catholic reserve, wearing an out-loud laugh on her sleeve that packed a Black wallop. This emotive characteristic would entwine our rhythms around a single heart for decades.

Having gained sister Ellen's confidence, we chose to broaden operation pigment splash, which is how I wound up seated at the McCormack dinner table in my first official proclamative nudge for Anne's hand. Jack and Ellen McCormack were an attractive couple in their early fifties who lived in Merrick, Long Island. Jack was in his patriarchal prime time, alongside of his wife Ellen, a movie-actress-pretty devotee, whose charm cut between Jean Tierney's allure and Donna Reed's value system. They were middle-class, middle-aged, mainstream advocates for the American way, reminiscent of the families in the sitcoms of the early sixties.

After our meal Jack invited me into the den. He was a pleasant man, and we quickly leapt upon the best common denominator Black and White men have—

sports. We glided into a discussion about the Mets that led to talk of Gil Hodges, the former Brooklyn Dodger and only man to lead the Mets to a World Series championship at that time. The Dodgers were one of Jack's favorite passions, and he was delighted with my intimate knowledge about the exploits of Jackie, Campy, and the Duke. All in all, we enjoyed our initial feel-out quite a bit, and never did my intentions toward Anne come up for discussion. For the time being, the multiple ways of cherishing Sandy Amoros's brilliant series-preserving catch securing the one Series title the Brooklyn Dodgers would ever win, enabled Jack and me to mail the blood-swapping issue third class. I was playing well as a lounge act, but could I make it on the main stage. My criminal background ignited a neurotic fear of the police. The thought of a White cop accepting his daughter's large Black stud drawing the milk for free was beyond my ability to grasp.

Anne and a close friend, Jacquie Davis, rented a newly renovated duplex apartment, setting the stage for our seven-year honeymoon. At the time, I had just completed the last of my Ballard-Hollywood ass-whippings. I was too much of a young schmuck to realize that I had experienced an education in the game that was priceless. After talks of two- to four-million dollar budgets wound up amounting to nothing more than wasted time, I wanted to hone my skills in a vocation that demanded little more than talent and work space. I decided to write a play.

Before the writing began, Anne and I wanted to define a philosophy that our still-young relationship could point toward. We came up with the name People's Neighborhood Theater for the company we hoped to realize. It was an effort to brandish our ideas of what we felt diversity meant. In these increasingly divisive times, the goal was to put our vision of the human hearts that lay beyond racial and sexual stereotypes on public display. This was particularly exciting after my many years in the White theater, which was as pigment-challenged as the U.S. Senate.

The plan was to write a one-act play and cast it from one of the city's richest, cheapest resources—its horde of actors. I created two characters by splitting myself in half, pitting my White self against my Black self, rounding out each half's fictional self through creative invention. The depth of conflict that came with my serious biracial intentions forced self-examination onto the page. What emerged was a Black Democrat opposing a Black Republican. The initial plot was for the Democrat to beat the hell out of the Republican. I now had to find the right scenario to stage a mugging. I was feeling pangs of guilt about my Blackness, given the blindingly White moves I was making, so I hid behind artistic cowardice, using art to boost my flagging Black esteem by flogging my White self in public.

After a number of unworkable settings, I hit upon an experience I had had in lockup. I was once busted after a street blowup with a close friend and heroin junkie who sold Gerri's beloved Great Dane for drugs. Several days after the incident had been forgotten, three policemen literally dragged me out of my living room where I had been watching a Yankees game. They took me down to the Tombs, a holding facility in Lower Manhattan. In the cell adjacent to mine was another perp, with whom I struck up a conversation. We couldn't see each other because our cells offered only a forward view, but we shared cigarettes and talked for the better part of the night.

The next morning I met my neighbor. He was a six-foot-four, 250-pound Jim Brown double, who happened to be a transvestite. Draped in a cocktail dress the size of a tent, his day-old stubble clashed with a blond, crookedly placed wig. It was a shocking visual. I made quick peace with our differences, fearing that if I angered him he might kick my ass. He was a sucker for flattery, so I paid his legs a cautious compliment.

Eight of us were lined up and handcuffed to a chain that was twenty feet long. We were then led to a paddy wagon. In those days the inside of a paddy wagon was made of wood. The wood rattled and shook as we made our way down to the courtrooms at 100 Center Street. My transvestite friend was on one side of me in the handcuff chain, and on my other side was a very sick heroin junkie. The rattling of the paddy wagon made the junkie sick, and he threw up all over my shoes. Normally, I would have gotten angry, but he was in such pitiful shape that, despite the disgusting bile dripping from my lower extremity, I felt sorry for him. When we arrived at the courthouse, they herded us into a holding area called the bullpen. Unlike the bullpen in baseball, where pitchers await their turn to perform, this pen was a dank gray cell overcrowded with the worst layers of the criminal community stacked upon each other.

During my wait to see the judge, the transvestite and I took turns calming the sick junkie lying in the corner, sweating and whimpering as withdrawal tied him into knots. We spent hours tending to the pain-filled droplets of sweat that never stopped. When I was brought before the judge, he released me on my own recognizance. It was my luck that my victim had been a Black junkie with no rights, and my good standing in the community subsequently melted the charges.

I decided to set our play in the bullpen. Carl, our Republican Black, was educated in prep school, graduated with honors from Yale, and scored a high entry-level position in the world of banking. Avery, the Black Democrat, had been offered several opportunities in the opportunity-rich sixties and blown them all. He was now living the life of a numbers runner, nursing the dream of becoming a successful actor. I had to come up with characters to surround and instigate the slugfest. The first was a Puerto Rican named Loco who was culled from my old

buddy in Spoffard. The next character was a blue-collar, tough-ass White cocaine dealer named John Lanigan. I had always admired this kind of White cat.
He was a reminder to me that poverty and street pain could turn anyone into a
nigger. The next major character was fashioned after the junkie who had thrown
up on my shoes in the paddy wagon. This poor, pathetic figure was so lost that I
often fantasized about his life and background, ascribing all sorts of noble accomplishments to his past. I turned the junkie's character into a fifty-year-old
dejected former civil rights activist. The last important character was the prison
guard who represented White paranoia and confusion that came with the thank-
less job of a low-level societal lion tamer.

I relished the opportunity to pin the tail on the Black Republican donkey. As
the characters marinated, Anne and I went off into an extended period of absorbing Marvin Gaye's *I Want You* album, and a funny thing happened when I
began writing. Despite my best efforts to make an ass out of the Republican, his
voice kept fighting back. Carl's conservative values and perceptions screamed so
loudly that my pen succumbed to his dignity.

During this period Anne's support inspired me artistically in a way that I had
never experienced before. Her young White energy and vision of unlimited options provided the wattage that helped me over the hump. Uptown, many of my
Black friends of the same age were beginning to experience a precipitous decline
in their youthful belief in the American dream. Mortality reality had blown away
any illusions they may have harbored in their youth. Anne blew new clear winds
through my inclination to succumb to Black frustration. Living with someone
and witnessing the White sunny-side-up view of America was fascinating.

Anne and I developed the play from scratch. I was a napkin and brown paper
bag writer. I would write anyplace at anytime on any surface, subsequently
bringing piles of scraps home, where Anne would bang out my words on an old
manual typewriter. The seductive mixture of love and creation drove me to try
to impress Anne with my ability to nurture our first literary child. When we were
ready to look at the entire play, we invited several friends: Kevin LaFond, an old
Hotchkiss classmate, and Alan Harris. Alan was also a writer, and, despite the
fact that we fought incessantly, my respect for his knowledge and sensibilities
had few boundaries. I did a one-man reading on tape, and the evening drew an
encouraging response.

Armed with my tape and filled with nervous anticipation, I invited Chuck
over to listen. He listened and laughed in places that I had not anticipated.
Chuck's consistent laughter changed the context of my intent. This taught me
that the best way to communicate serious issues to an American public was to
wrap them in comedic gauze. It became my motivation in subsequent drafts.
Chuck was thrilled, and pleasing him was a huge step forward.

We were now ready to see if we could get the play produced and caught an immediate break when John Ballard's wife, Sidney, became a board member of a new theater called the American Theater for Actors. She gave the play to Jim Jennings, the artistic director. The venue, located on Fifty-fourth Street between Eighth and Ninth Avenues, wasn't much of a theater at all—just several empty rooms in a building that the city had given Jennings at low cost. Jim was a theater rat who lived and died for the live performance. He immediately snapped the play up, and a week after submission *Bullpen* had a home. Jim was a writer himself, often directing his own work in defiance of that taboo. He encouraged me to direct my own work.

With the help of my old Hotchkiss buddy, Charlie Schultz and his brother Peter, whose coin toss banked the effort, Bullpen was set to sail. Anne and I began to cast the play: Bo Rucker, Otis Young-Smith, John Salemmo, Frank Martinez, and Gunter Kleemann filled the primary roles. There was one character that was very difficult to cast: Charlie Herbert, the old junkie with a past. The pickings were slim in this age bracket.

I called Richard Ward, a very accomplished actor I'd met when we both worked on a sitcom pilot for Rupert Hitzig and his partner, primo comedian, Alan King. It was a takeoff on *Amos and Andy*. As we had waited for our shot on camera, groups of brothers and sisters were practicing antiquated, stereotypical, "honey chile" Negro affectations. It was a time when it was often an embarrassment to ply the acting trade in Black. I contacted Richard and sent him a copy of the play. He was complimentary about the work, but his dance card was full. With my other viable choice, Joe Seneca, committed to a project, I was running out of time.

Robert Abrams was making his initial run for the office of New York State attorney general, and Chuck and I attended one of his political fund-raisers at an old steak joint called Gallagher's. As the political bullshit filled the room, Chuck and I were fit to get looped. The drinks flowed as Carl Nesfield, a prominent anti-poverty merchant who coached our hated West Side football rivals, the Browns, visited our table. Carl and his son Junior were our competitive counterparts. We both had tweaked a running beef throughout the years of which duo was the most accomplished. Junior was incarcerated at the time, so Chuck and I had the decided leg up. Fueled by demon sauce, Chuck was ragging Carl about his wayward son.

"My nigger has got everything it takes to be great," Chuck crowed. "He's twenty-five, and he's getting ready to do his first play. The sky is the limit for my nigger. There ain't a nigger on earth like my nigger."

We laughed and rubbed it in as we got drunker, and I in an elated state put my arm around Chuck's shoulder and said, "Shit, matter of fact, I got this role that I'm trying to cast that was modeled after Chuck. Fuck looking for other actors, I'm gonna cast Chuck." I had not meant that! I figured Chuck had no interest in acting. Wrong! He leapt upon my words and nailed them to my ass by accepting gleefully. I was stuck.

The following day an excited Chuck called, declaring himself ready for duty. He was persistent, and with time running out he became my consolation choice for the role. What at first appeared to be my biggest mistake turned out to be a coup for the play. But it wasn't easy. His first day ever in a theater was the first day of rehearsals. Chuck and I worked hard during private sessions, and the biggest obstacle was convincing him not to act. But he was a quick study, and after falling on his ass with a stilted Clark Gable impression, he began to get it. Imbedded in every charismatic social activist is a truckload of ham. Once we forged a direct line between Chuck and his inner ham, he delivered the bacon.

On October 9, 1978, as John Lennon celebrated another hermetic birthday, Robert Watlington, Sr.,'s oxygen entitlement expired, gaining him passage into the unknown. It had earlier been discovered that he was born with one kidney, and that organ was washed away by explosive blood pressure levels. He'd been sentenced to a dialysis machine for the last several years of his life. It put a damper on the joy that preparing the play was providing, because I had a lot of unfinished business with my dad. My most haunting memory of his final days took place in a hospital. He was in a state of delirium, cursing White America, lashing out at its treachery, screaming, "Those White motherfuckers robbed me of my life, robbed me of my turn. Those motherfuckers, I hate them motherfuckers! I hate them!" I was speechless. Baseball was the only thing we ever shared. Without the game to make things all right, I was helpless, with no angle from which to comfort him.

It's tough medicine watching a Jim Crow survivor gag in the final days of his private hell. On a slow walk to the bus stop, my heart bled for my father, a man whose dreams and heartaches had battled to an unsatisfying standstill. I was hoping against hope that the words in our racial treaties from the sixties hadn't been written in pencil.

On the fall day of Robert Watlington, Sr.,'s funeral, the Yankees kicked the Dodgers' asses 11 to 1 in the World Series. Fortunately, he died a Steinbrenner guy, and this news would have made him happy. As all the men gathered waiting for the cars to show up to take us to the funeral, my mother's brother, the great Womp, showed up to pay his respects. He was drunker than hell, a noisemaker in a pool of solemnity. At the church, people were crying, and my mother was enshrouded in dignified sadness. Womp livened things up when a Lifesaver lodged itself in his throat. He started to cough and gag so loud that the whole proceeding was disrupted. People took turns whacking him on the back, trying to dislodge the candy as he gagged and coughed. Everyone was trying hard to suppress their laughter. Finally, someone hit pay dirt, and the lifesaver came flying out. Everyone looked at the minister for guidance, and he said, "Let us move on." To the very end, my old man had had time called during his turn at bat.

That night I went to an East Side bar alone to drink and cry. I played Judy Collins's cover of the Steven Stills composition "So Begins the Task" over and over again on the jukebox as I wrestled with my father's love. I hadn't understood him, but I believe he loved me while understanding me even less. The America I was born into was a foreign country to my dad. He had passed long before his death certificate was filed.

Bullpen was to open in January 1979 for a three-week showcase run. On the day of the opening, Anne and I were shopping for a pin-striped suit for our Black Republican. We were thrilled by the final rehearsals and flirted with the warm feeling that we might have produced a winner. With our work done, there was nothing left but to wait for the child's arrival. That night the play sizzled before a packed house. Chuck was magnificent, and all of the actors fed off his energy and shared in his bath of rousing ovations. It was a once-in-a-lifetime dividend.

The play had pushed Anne and my relationship from the level of possibly serious to definitely serious, setting the stage for a real-life production titled *The Unchartered Territory of Biracialism*. After the encouraging reception to our work with *Bullpen*, there was a lull. As the well-wishing and back-slapping faded, we discovered that the shelf life of a Black dramatic play was as long as that of milk left out in the sun. We found reality through the regular jobs that found us.

Anne worked as a waitress, and I worked in a group home for retarded male adults. My duties entailed spending four nights a week taking care of the needs of twenty residents. The pay was lousy, but I came to love and respect these men tremendously. After my delusions of grandeur about the theatre were shattered, the simplicity of emotions and instincts that my beloved retards offered was tonic that balanced the soul. Their inability to express themselves dishonestly provided a psychological oasis in a storm of bullshit that seemed to be a way of life for those of us with more IQ points to juggle.

It became a suitable respite to end a decade on. I studied a long list of the greatest playwrights in history and wrote my second play, while enjoying the seat-of-the-pants atmosphere that came with caring for adult children. I was a young man who was rested, optimistic, and raring to move forward, but the scent of the eighties offered a new, unfamiliar fragrance that would wreak havoc on pigmented respiratory systems throughout the nation. The man carrying the canister with the chemical gas was a warm, congenial former movie star and TV pitchman who'd won my worship as a child when he portrayed one of my favorite Notre Dame football heroes, George Gipp.

TWENTY-SIX

In the eighties the once-promising African American stock was swirling in the nation's toilet. LBJ's deliverance on his pledge that Black folks would receive a full portion of their legislative birthright now screened like an old black-and-white movie. The unintended consequence of President Johnson's gift certificate was the emergence of a Blacklash-fueled White party that thundered across the decade's landscape atop a herd of rambunctious elephants. The new hot stock surging was the conservative edict that a swift kick in the asses of the poor would cure the nation's sagging spirit. The White majority turned the social stock market on its ear, gobbling up enough shares to hand the country's management over to the "all things considered, I'd rather be White than right" contingent. Utilizing twin megaphones—one trumpeting the threat from an evil empire abroad and the other egging on the fortunate to slam the door on the poor—cleared a path for the elephant men to use our national treasury to starve both pools of evil into submission. These southern-fried policies would force an incalculable number of human beings into the bowels of a nightmare.

In the midst of honoring the terms of their eviction from the White House, President Carter and his wife Rosalynn submitted to an interview as they packed their belongings. The first lady said that the American people liked Ronald Reagan because "he makes us feel comfortable with our prejudices." Reagan's revolution pummeled the term "liberal" to the depths of "nigger lover," rendering it radioactive. All but the true-believing Boomers dropped their commitment to inclusion like a hot crack stem.

Our new president spun tales of the welfare queen who pled poor by day but drove a Cadillac by night. This vicious myth convinced a generation, whose parents had suffered the sting of the Great Depression, that it was in the nation's best interest to cane its poor. Though millions of Caucasians wallowed in the same pit of despair, Blacks came to represent in the public mind the newly indictable crime of receiving public assistance. Crossover Black folks, shaking in their entry-level boots, broke for their overcoats, seeking to fend off the chill from their White Boomer colleagues as they distanced themselves from the idealism that pigments depended upon.

I spent my final year in Harlem in 1981, and on many occasions when entering my building I would see a handful of Black teenagers making funny, rhythmic, farting sounds with their mouths. One of the young cats would be preaching through poetic street rants reminiscent of the improvisational Black group the Last Poets. Their torrid Ebonics arias knifed through the street's sirens, night after night, a disturbingly seductive sound with no melody, niceties, or compromise. The new doo-woppers were all percussion and anger. This early crude refinery provided the chemical process that produced high-octane rap music, which would subsequently morph into the internationally embraced hip-hop art form. The new fuel would fill the urban basins with a fresh language for expression. It wasn't music to me, but I respected their energy. I applied one of Chuck's standard mantras: "Never underestimate the creative instincts of urban niggers in pain."

These Black and Latino postpubescent live wires were Reagan's bastard offspring wailing from their disenfranchised playpen. Their combustible anger with authority blotted out America's promises. World War II's Black generation looked on hopelessly as their grandchildren mocked their hard-fought battle for inclusion. They cared squat about assimilation. Not since the bebop revolution in the late forties had an underground art form openly sneered at White convention. These urchins of disillusionment trampled upon the warm Black musical porridge of melodies in gospel and blues that fed the dance in America's step. Reagan's America was brutally honest with its bastards, offering incarceration or death as the primary choices in their alienation. If the urchins were going to have to figure out how to survive in hell, they would do it their way. So the most talented of Reagan's angry Black kids answered back in a syncopated, farting, rhythmic, revolutionary rant that spelled attitude.

All the while, the great John Lennon's voice was absent from the rankled discourse. After taking off for five years to bake bread, John Lennon was going to release a new album, *Double Fantasy*. Not since *Walls and Bridges* had there been any signals from *the man*. John stepped back into the spotlight to suggest that it was time to start over. What? After I had listened to the new record countless times, it began to make sense. I was approaching thirty, and all that I'd lived through had only provided passage to a spot at adult life's starting gate. Lennon was advising that we take a deep breath and reassess our generation's new challenges. The difference-maker was cranking up for another run.

Several weeks after my Lennon renewal, I awakened early in the morning in a sweat and didn't know why. I woke Anne and told her that I felt something terrible was going to happen. That day, as I prepared for a rehearsal, I played Lennon's new jam enough times to melt its vinyl. Later that night, when the shots fired from Howard Cosell's mouth on *Monday Night Football* that John was dead, blown away in an instant, my day of discomfort made sense. As Cosell did the hard news, Anne and I traded on our grief. I dug up the album *Revolver*, put it on the turntable, and joined the national mourn fest.

I was on duty at the home the day of the memorial ceremony for John in Central Park. In order to attend I had set up a field trip, taking ten of my charges with me. The park was packed. It was the largest, civil congregation of humans I'd witnessed to that point. My 'tards provided a wonderful sense of emotional support. The mentally retarded are vibes people, and they reacted to the love and sadness encouragingly, lending a comforting sense of credibility to the mourner's sincerity. When the people began to sing "Give Peace a Chance," the off-key 'tards added a touch of humor to the proceedings that John would have appreciated. My companions came through for me like the champs that they were.

Lennon's death drained the righteous Boomer pool of a portion of its conscience. He would no longer be there to point out when the big shots were full of shit. Fate revealed its true agenda when the Gipper beat his bullet while John never saw his coming. Intolerant conservatism filled the pool, and the sight of capsized wooden ships littered the edges of the drink. The mist of Kennedy and King, had now found the great Lennon, knocking our team out of contention. The resilient Gipper toughed it out to lead a brilliantly orchestrated effort to bring America back to the fifties.

Anne and I decided to launch another production of *Bullpen*, hoping to bottle the previous show's excitement. One afternoon I received a call at work from Anne, who was holding auditions for the new cast.

"I've got a couple of people you're going to love," she said.

"Oh yeah, tell me about them."

She began to describe the attributes of John O'Donohue, an actor who moonlighted as a police officer with the NYPD. Anne was impressed by the raging creative fire that simmered beneath John's blue uniform. Her vote was to cast him as the guard.

"Okay. Who's the other guy?" I asked.

She paused, "He's a cocky son of a bitch that you're going to love who's perfect for the Lanigan character."

"Can he act?"

She stated assertively, "He's the real thing."

The following morning, after my shift, I laid hugs on my 'tards and bolted. On the subway back to the main island, I had extra energy to burn after three days of inveterate responsibility. My head was as clear as a minister's when I hit the city and met my former brother-in-law, Kevin Griffin. On our way downtown to rehearsal to check out what our two new White boys could do, we hit the liquor store. After knocking back our first half-pint, we were fired up and decided to make a stop at a movie theater. I'd been hipped to a new film called *No Nukes*. Many of my favorite music guys—James Taylor; Crosby, Stills and Nash; Gil Scott-Heron; Jackson Browne; and Jesse Colin Young—had come together in protest, seeking to chip away at nuclear proliferation. Aside from the fact that one would have a better chance of sneaking Redd Fox into Nancy Reagan's boudoir, it was a noble effort. I'd given little thought to arms reduction, because unlike my idealistic White counterparts, I knew that the Reagan group was not in the business of reducing its might.

The film was a ball. We knocked back raw liquor at a time when you could still smoke in theaters. The husband-and-wife duo of James Taylor and Carly Simon performed the opening number, launching a film that soared. Toward the end the audience on-screen began to chant the word "Bruuuce." In short order, the people in the theater picked up the call, and "Bruuuce" filled the air.

"Who the fuck is Bruce?" Kevin asked.

"I half heard of him, but these motherfuckers sure know who he is," I responded.

The fervor of the chant grew, when on-screen came an indefatigable, Asbury Park powerhouse. There are few things that compare with an initial sighting. If you mixed Bob Dylan with Gary U.S. Bonds, clothe the body in Woody Guthrie's spirit, inject a few CC's of anabolic assistance, you'd have the picture of my first impression of a man named Springsteen. From "Thunder Road" to "The River," he sent my cheap booze high into orbit. I left the theater empowered by his force.

I hardly remember how I wound up in a tiny rehearsal hall in Manhattan's Little Italy, but I do remember that Kevin and I made spectacles of ourselves as we shouted repeatedly Springsteen's most potent refrain, "I'm a prisoner of rock 'n' roll!" We floated a boozed-up inquiry, "Where's our White boys?" I saw John O'Donohue first, and he outdid anything I had ever written for the guard's role. The fact that he was a cop was an asset for sure, but it was his talent and imagination that made the role stand up. He was perfect. Anne was batting 1 for 1.

The Lanigan role was more complex. While writing the role, my objective had been to answer the question. How would I have survived on the streets if I were White?

I approached Anne and whispered, "What's this cat's name again?"

"Bruce Willis."

I looked at Kevin, and we did another exhortation of our being "prisoners of rock 'n' roll," and Kevin chanted, "Bruuuce, Bruuuce!" Out stepped before us my day's second ruggedly handsome, well-built White boy from Jersey named Bruce.

Chuck sidled over to me and said, "That White boy look like he could whup somebody's ass."

"That's what we looking for, right?"

"Yeah, but you know how these live lookin' White boys have a way of coming up counterfeit."

We laughed. I introduced myself to Bruce, and he offered instant personality. This might have been the first and only time Bruce would ever audition for a drunken Black guy. He read a monologue from the play, and it blew me away. He had that Elvis factor—he could sing like a nigger. I was so taken by this cat that I immediately sought to offer both the role and friendship. Coincidentally, my next play, *Fifties and Forties*, was to have its initial theatrical reading later that month, and I offered Bruce the lead in that play as well. He had very little polish, but his get-the-joke energy along with an apparent absence of Nigraphobia was inspiring.

After a week of meet and greet, the new cast embarked on a road trip, answering an invitation from Brown University's theater program to come and expose their students to a work in progress. One early morning, after a tough day of rehearsing and a night's dance with Jack Daniels, our bloodshot crew made its way in a caravan to Rhode Island. Seated in the car with Anne and me was John O'Donohue, a tough Irishman from the West Side of Manhattan whose heart wore a gold seal.

John had rumbled around an impoverished youth, surviving a dad with an elbow that bent too many times for the good of his family's psyche. The O'Donohues were entrenched in the potato-nigger phase of New York's postwar

Irish-American evolution, gaining a foothold, like many others of Celtic background, by wearing the blue hats and the red hats of the city's first responders. After a stint in the navy and an early marriage to his life mate, Agnes, he scored a cop's job coated with civil service security. But John was an odd egg, with street smarts that were baked in the heat of Manhattan's mid-century Hell's Kitchen at a time when kitchen concrete grilled its Paddy boys extra tough. He'd earned his authentic bare-knuckle scuffs, and yet, somehow, John landed enough left hooks to win a decision over his preordained reservation at the Terry Molloy school of heartbreak. The theater enabled John to cash in on one of our most sterling White American virtues, the ability to dream away class restrictions. Multiple characters and study provided the key to John's trunk stuffed with his beyond, and he rode revelation like the wind. The fact that he and I had been seated beside each other on a mutual search for hidden soul bites behind curtains that rise and fall in darkness was another unique American gift.

In the twenty years that followed, John would become Anne's and my most trusted friend, godfather of our son—and minor human frailties aside—the closest thing to a pure spirit on the human highway.

After the road trip, we took a break, and I focused on the reading of my new play, *Fifties and Forties*. I was filled with curiosity as to what the other Jersey Bruce could do. We arrived at the theater, and Annie and I went backstage to see the actors. Everyone was fired up, except Bruce. His presence seemed to be shrinking. The reading got off well with all the early laughs and plot points holding up. Bruce's entrance late in the first act was set up for his character to go deep.

"Sit back, this motherfucker is going to eat this role up," I whispered to Chuck, who slapped me five.

Bruce's first lines were barely audible, and he proceeded downhill from there. I was astounded. Gripped by fear and uncertainty, he was a virtual no-show. Picture an ice cube on a hotplate, and you had Bruce's performance.

"What the fuck happened?" I said to Chuck.

"You never know how a White boy gonna dance under the lights."

That wasn't enough of an explanation for me. This guy had it all. After the reading, I went backstage and was met by a humbled Bruce who knew he had fucked up, but his angst seduced my compassion. Normally, in our troop, when you screwed up we would blast the hell out of you, but Bruce's disappointment in himself was so complete that piling more on would have issued a debilitating blow.

In those early months Bruce was one-third cool, two-thirds vulnerable. His cloaked history was that of a slow bloomer who'd taken his share of crap in his early life. An early age stuttering detect, was a hell of an acid test to snort, but he endured. Somewhere between sixteen and twenty, Bruce turned into a charismatic, musically talented stud. The *Bullpen* is where he began to construct the helicopter that would subsequently airlift him to international multimillion-dollarism. His topsoil was that of a Jersey tough guy who was fearless, and all that wussy intimidation that White guys felt in the company of Black people was beneath his cubes. His outstanding presence and comedic timing were evident from the beginning, but he went through hell harnessing his fear of being onstage. His show-stopping stints in rehearsal would desert him as the wattage surrounding the task increased.

Days after Bruce's ice cube impersonation we all settled down to the business of molding the new production of *Bullpen* into shape. Our biracial, bi-gendered, bi-anything caravan was in motion. After a rehearsal we would often huddle together, and, as the weed made its way around our inner circle, a family of troopers emerged. A cast of four Blacks, three Whites, one Puerto Rican, and two women rallied around the spirit of my incessant cheerleading and Chuck's street-spun charisma, sparking the illusive chemistry that breeds willing interdependence. This contingent was a Lotto-winning payoff on the America I chased, with its reality exceeding my mind's images.

Bruce's major contribution to the circle was his *Animal House* energy: good old urban White American blue-collar male pride embellished with flecks of fallen comedian John Belushi's sense of humor. Belushi's smash-mouth comedic artistry insured the eighties White age-comers their central impetuosity. Bruce's White juice had the rare opportunity to mix equally with genuine Black street genes, and despite conventional wisdom to the contrary, it was a good fit. Checko, ex-vice-president of the Slumlords, developed a tight bond with Bruce. "Bruce is on the up," he once told me. "I would hang with that White boy in a race riot."

John O'Donohue combined the acerbic poetic license often found in an Irish player with his many experiences on the runaway penal express. This infused the play with unforeseen energy, inducing a sharper sense of place that illuminated the absurdity beneath his fellow actor's grim embodiment. A watershed moment on the tour occurred when John was able to secure rehearsal time in his notorious Harlem precinct's lockup. The initial time allotment was an hour and a half, but John and I had secretly agreed to extend it. After several hours behind bars, the line between reality and make-believe blurred. By the three-hour mark, real incarceration had fed the actors a sense memory that burnished the raw holding cell's dark brand on their character's hide.

Chuck and John were developing a close bond, evidenced one evening as

Chuck and I splashed about in one of O'D's post-rehearsal Heineken baths. In a bizarre flash Chuck muted his gaiety, graying its colors with grim introspection. John picked up on Chuck's change and asked, "What's the matter, Chuck, your bottle's low?"

Chuck offered a warm chuckle before speaking. "John, I know we sitting up here having a good time, niggers mixing with White folks, and all that's real. But don't let your shit drop. Most niggers on the street don't know nothin' about this mixin' shit. Don't let our shit put you at risk, because some of these boys out there want you dead. Now it ain't like cops don't kill niggers too, but you can't let up if you have to blow a nigger away. I don't want to be visiting any of my boys in the morgue."

A Harlem icon raised on an early-century diet of Jim Crow dog shit was telling the White cop to protect himself from the horrible truth: "Niggers kill cops." It was a special moment for me, a colorless flicker of raw U.S. humanism.

It was good to have Checko as my sergeant at arms on the *Bullpen* scene, despite the glaring clues in his game that marked him for a one-way ride down Alfred Mealy Boulevard. Checko was trying to keep one foot on my turf while holding on to a drug dealer's death wish. A seasoned integrationist, he took a healthy shine to Anne and she to him. Anne paved a path for Checko back to his favorite White groove, James Taylor's music. His street-crusted persona had stored these sentiments in mothballs, but Anne's disarming Irish Catholic touches arrested his imposing front, inspiring the "Fire and Rain" enthusiast Checko secretly cultivated. Hearing the first chords of J.T.'s signature lament from the speakers, Checko wound down into a cross-legged pacifist.

Their relationship survived a big test when Checko showed up at our crib one night and asked the girl from Merrick, Long Island, for a favor. "Would you stash my gun while I take care of some business in a place I can't carry a piece?" On the surface, given the divide in their backgrounds, this was asking a lot, but Anne reached out and harbored the cold instrument of destruction. She came down on the side of her maturing street genes' credo: blood is thicker than caution. After a stiff lecture on gun control, making it clear that she did not want to make felonious risk a habit, Anne acknowledged that an occasional stint as a gun moll came with the territory. This interlude opened the door for Anne and Checko to solidify their bond for years to come.

Bruce, Anne, and John's melting-pot ability grooved their induction into our pigmented souls. Their inclusion completed our circle's unique composition. Together the troop covered so many of the social bases that an empowered rush of head freedom ensued. Our group oddity stumbled upon the fruits of positive-based, indiscriminate inclusion, whose nectar offered the best mind-altering high on the human market.

As the rehearsal period began to wind down, we secured our first gig with Theater for the Forgotten, a theatrical company that produced plays for prisons and drug-rehabilitation centers. We were to tour facilities in some of the worst neighborhoods in the city. The final week of rehearsals was moved to the center. We constructed the set in the basement's dank, musty flavor, ideal for a prison cell, then opened the door and shouted, "Come one, come all!"

Chuck and I were staging a miscreants' ball. If we were going to be on the road doing rehabs and prisons, it was important for this show to rehearse in front of people who threw things if you sucked. In addition, we wanted to test our White cats under real street heat. On the night of the first run-through, we invited forty or so noted prison alumni from the neighborhood for a midnight show. It was a drug dealers' cocktail party, a chill-down blast before their evening's after-hour club activity. As they sauntered in, Chuck and I stood in the corner, inhaling the pot smoke that dominated the groove.

"How do you think Bruce is going to do with all these niggers breathing in his face?" I asked.

"Don't worry, he got chops. There's a lot of heart in that stage-fright-dipped motherfucker."

The cast came out smoking, embracing the instant pressure that comes with non-diplomatic street hards adorning the nape of the stage. Cocaine emerged, and snorting sounds peppered the soundtrack. I listened to the audible chatter synthesize into positive reviews. "This shit is real!" articulated the crowds' stamp of approval as they jockeyed for better sight lines.

John O'D's performance was so powerful that each time he came onstage as the prison guard, brothers in the audience felt the tension. His portrayal was an exercise in savage stage mastery, evoking several advanced hoods in the audience to instinctively raise their hands in the air at each of his entrances. In Bruce's case, the up-tempo buzz that rose from the collective said it all. "That White boy bad!" He'd carved out his own turf in an oil-dark stronghold. Chuck fed the sweet ham from his monologues to the audience, mesmerizing the hometown crowd to a point where the sound of a pin hitting the floor would have clanged. The cast was becoming one with those they had signed on to portray, and my confidence rose with the rave reaction delivered by my home blood assemblage.

We were all winners that night, and an appreciative high fest broke out. Chuck, East Harlem's new Olivier, preened in the adulation. After several well-deserved victory laps around the scene, he joined me in my shadowy voyeur's corner and said, "We baptized our White boys, and they'se the real shit. I told you them boys would get the joke."

Bruce's White street power onstage always got the most attention from the small-time agents and managers lurking about. He was catnip to the ten-percenters, attracting a talent manager named Robert Tusher to our makeshift playhouse. Tusher was a handsome, charming, seductive theatrical character who entered our lives during our quick-lay period, when anyone White with a business card set off the illusionary bells of pay dirt. We jumped at the chance to invite him uptown to make us stars. I was impressed by the fact that he represented one of my favorite icons—the inimitable writer and wit, Quentin Crisp. My fantasies got the better of me, spinning comparisons between Tusher and Brian Epstein. In my scenario, Tusher would pluck us all out of our basement in Harlem, like Epstein did the Beatles from the Cavern in Liverpool.

Tusher arrived for one of our late-night street-patron specials and was seated within a few feet of the performance area. Bruce was the first character onstage and inexplicably slammed the play's rhythm with a two-by-four, coming apart before our eyes with a wicked dose of fright. I died right along with him, when slight hisses of confusion became audible as his fans wondered *Where's that White-boy juice?* When Bruce came offstage, he knew he had blown it. It was a delicate situation, because his problem had been stripped bare.

Before I could say anything, Bruce said, "It was Tusher. I couldn't do it in front of that guy."

"You playing out there in front of hard reality, and your shit's come up real," I said. "If you weren't a good enough actor to convince these niggers, they would have pissed on both of us. With that White street power you bringing onstage, cats like Tusher will spread them easily. If you can deal with your fear of White folks, then you'se the whole thing."

Despite Bruce's meltdown Tusher went wild for the play and agreed to manage the entire show. We set out to play multiple drug rehab centers at the dawn of the crack cocaine boom that was packing these inadequate dens of misery to the brim. The play was a smash with this hardcore audience, even though the message was one that contradicted popular opinion, speaking loudly for the abolition of welfare and the end of Black zero-accountability for our plight's depth. The in-your-face message struck a chord. The audience seemed to agree that many of their excuses for self-destruction were bullshit when they cheered raucously for Chuck's beat-down of their prototype. The purity of the bottom feeders' perspective was enlightening.

Hand-to-hand gorilla theater is the most satisfying art form I've ever experienced. Our band of dedicated, unpaid artists were young and enthusiastic enough to play a string of magnificent hovels and dives that rolled out their stained red carpets wherever we made the scene.

WHITE
LIFE

I fought with my twin, that enemy
within, 'til both of us fell by the way.

—Bob Dylan,
"Where Are You Tonight?
(Journey Though Dark Heat)"

TWENTY-SEVEN

Berkshire County, 2001

Brewer Hill Road is one of the many scenic paths that define the natural beauty of the mountainous Berkshire landscape. Anne and I are workout hogs, challenging the onslaught of our late forties with an obsession for tackling lengthy distances. Anne remembers when women feared tarnishing their femininity on the fields of athletic endeavor, but the great surge of the Rebecca Lobo–led U-Conn women's basketball team in the early nineties finally retired that perception, helping to make gritty balls-to-the-wall competitiveness sexy.

Over the years Anne has turned herself into a middle-distance gangster, making any pull of seven miles or less hers to eat. I coached her like a guy, mercilessly whacking away with my Lombardi stick until she got it. Early on she often wound up in tears challenging the steepest, lengthiest hills on the scape, but the strength of her Irish Catholic will aided her determination to jimmy the lock open on her cage of "can't do," eventually cementing the coach's mouth shut. Our locker-room-harsh breakthrough afforded us time out from the sexual poker game that gender differences invoke. After countless athletic teams and awards that I'd been a part of, Anne emerged as one of the toughest teammates I had ever had.

As we come to the midpoint of a run, we're cruising, taking in the sights. The fall season has bled the leaves to death, and gaggles of tiny red and gold coffins carrying the summer's green party to their resting place overwhelms the portrait. I can't imagine anyplace that does the autumn changes better than Berkshire County. The higher power was in Van Gogh's mood when it painted this patch. I bait Anne into sprinting an upcoming hill. She gnaws on the challenge and we haul ass. Part of my reason for the command is to watch the sexual energy pour from her red-faced grimace. I've learned that White faces can flush red for reasons other than rage. Seemingly benign revelations like these offer intriguing insights that blunt reflexive stereotypical perceptions. At the core of the biracial perk packet is a couple's ability to construct patios onto their root cultural predispositions. We've attempted to mix the suburbs with Harlem streets, Irish Catholic reserve with Southern Black Pentecostal exhibitionism, topping it off with White American female trading sweat with African American male. After years of stirring this can of contrasts, we've hurled it all against a bare canvas, surrendering to our new mural's depiction.

Normally, this would be a typical October gem of a day, but our nation has entered troubled times. A month earlier U.S. enemies launched an attack on the World Trade Center, using our commercial jets as the lethal weapons. The buildings collapsed like sand castles that met the backside of an angry shovel. I was on an early-morning drive to Manhattan when the first plane hit and quickly learned that this was no run-of-the-mill catastrophe when shock jock Howard Stern and his gang were doing hard news responsibly. The hit ruptured the nation's spine, and its impact was temporary paralysis. The globe listened to the fear-filled whine blaring from America's loudspeakers.

An underutilized news media performed admirably, taking advantage of a sudden pardon from the musty corridors of Congressman Gary Condit's jockstrap, proving that they still knew a thing or two about journalism. Our president, George W. Bush, faced the gut task of leading a nation spoiled by good fortune. We'd been weaned on the notion that we were impervious to a countrywide ass-whupping. The fact that the enemy had the audacity to go after two of our vital organs, Wall Street and the Pentagon, scared the shit out of us. The horrific tragedy of three thousand deaths and the pain of their many loved ones will always hold a piece of the nation's collective empathy, but the loss of three thousand anything out of 280 million is microscopic. America was tagged in its collective jaw by a sucker one-two combination. Our reaction will determine if we have a champion's heart or a glass jaw. When a champ gets tagged, he covers up and holds on, drawing on his superior chin and ringsmanship. After clearing his senses, he often knocks his opponent out in the later rounds. The impostor with the glass jaw panics and tries to flail his way out of his dilemma, exposing himself to a knockout.

As Anne and I scale a hill with an incline a quarter of a mile high, we suddenly hear the roar of a truck-sized vehicle eating up our rear. As it draws closer it seems like the driver is intent on running us off the road. We scurry to the side, and in his passing we notice that stenciled in fluorescent glitter on the window of the cab is an American flag and the words GOD BLESS AMERICA.

We never really experienced in-your-face racism in these parts, so we weren't quick to go there. When you factor in the country's segregated reality, much of White America has a slightly better chance of petting a piranha than coming into contact with an interracial couple. It's incumbent upon Anne and me to distinguish between curiosity and hostility when framing assumptions. American White people are essentially a kind, giving, religion-regulated lot whose instinct is to share capitalism in relative harmony with those in their communities. If you respect the basic white-flour tenets, you can't find a better group of people to live among. Unfortunately, they rarely respond well to two of the land's most exploitable commodities, ignorance and fear.

Anne and I continue our run allowing the scenic beauty to steer us back to optimism. Dusk wanes and darkness creeps forward. We are locked into our pace when the roar of a raging vehicle again shatters the postcard. Our overheated American has returned to flatten us. He accelerates, as Anne and I dive into the side brush, making our way into the woods. The muffled sound of the word *nigger* comes from the truck's cab. I catch another glimpse of the fluorescent flag glimmering.

The environment has turned my shade of black as we move cautiously, trying to avoid stepping into a hole or ramming a stump. Rays of light from tucked-away homes become our guide. We work our way to a cottage, settling in its backyard to soak our bruised equilibrium. After a distilled period of silence waiting our misguided patriot out, I begin to ramble on about my trip to New York on the twelfth of September, the day after the terrorist attack.

After wiggling my way as close to Ground Zero as was allowed, I came upon the sight of dazed young White people moving in slow motion. The dust from the collapsed towers had settled in their hair, graying them by decades. It was heartbreaking to watch one's countrypersons labor under the weight of their most powerless moments. On my way back to New England I stopped in my old neighborhood in Harlem. I entered another country. A jubilant vibe emanated as the excitement of Freddie Ferrer's mayoral campaign was peaking. A bus with multiple speakers protruding blared hot Latin music, increasing the bounce in the rhythm-prone denizens' steps. The possibility of the first Latino mayor far outweighed the anguish of the estranged mourners in the other nation a few miles south of them.

I asked a friend of mine on the corner what he thought about the attack, and his indifference was jarring. "They don't let niggers buy stock, and whoever did this was lookin' for the motherfuckers with stocks." With a whimsical shrug of his shoulders, he concluded, "Ain't our fight." Maybe the patriot missile driving the pickup truck pulls from the same manual of ignorance, agreeing with the word on the corner that it ain't our fight. If it ain't, then who the hell's is it?

Anne spears my ramble by asking, "You think he's gone?"

I check and the coast seems clear. Another of the perks of marrying across the racial line is the us-against-them rush you feel when jousting with the Black or White troops patrolling the racial borders.

We're back on the main road when I say, "You know what? I hope these ya-hoos learn the difference between an Arab and a nigger."

Summer 1983

My close friend Timmy Hitchcock was getting married in Salisbury, Connecticut, just a few miles from Leif's place in Lime Rock. Timmy had been a teenaged maverick when we met in the fall of 1972. I was taking a course at the local high school on assignment from Hotchkiss. A stranger on the scene, I was sizing up potential allies when I was introduced to Timmy, and we sparked. He was a blues man, and I soon learned that beneath his long blond hair was the soul of a country picker on the Mississippi Delta trying to sing some sense into life's complexities. This gave us a lot to talk about during the many hours we spent in my crib on Leif's spread over Muddy Waters and a fistful of music boosters.

After settling at Leif's, Anne and I took a walk before going to the ceremony. We wound our way down old Dougway Road, where we came upon a cemetery and sat on a stonewall that enclosed the deathbeds. Anne's disturbed demeanor flashed widely before uttering two of the most life-altering words in our language: "I'm pregnant."

The wedding was a New England beauty that took place in an old church with a rustic colonial feel. After the ceremony, a wild party broke out in a scenic spot straddling the Twin Lakes of Salisbury, Connecticut. Anne's maternal responsibility meter began its ascent, and she gravitated toward Blade Brokaw's wife, Eileen, who was nursing their baby. Eileen and Anne embarked on a Mamma-thon. Her instant transformation scared the hell out of me.

The new model of our existence set itself in soft cement on the night of Tim and Linda's bliss. The sweat was a-popping over my fear of another dose of fatherhood. Avery was all that I could handle, given the empty-refrigerator, fast-motion life my dream required. After five years of individualistic, bohemian cohabitation, our lives changed in an announcement. In the world of interracial America, the stork's arrival is where the rubber meets the road. A child creates a sea change in any relationship, but when the story is shot in black and white it's a different film. When I joined the family, it forced Jack and Ellen's social perspectives about race up against the wall, shining a piercing light upon their rich faith. Their Christian values won out, and I was granted a visa. But with their grandchild's blood engaged in a pigment takeover, I feared it would be a difficult pill to swallow for White people born decades before Jackie Robinson's first at bat.

Anne and I didn't make it easy. We weren't married. In fact, we had never seen the inside of a church together. Anne's parents tried to deal with our generation's accepted alternative of living together without matrimony, but the pregnancy and flaccid viability of my career choice as a struggling playwright was a gathering storm of red flags. Bringing a child into this brittle atmosphere was not ideal, but abortion was out of the question. My mother-in-law, Ellen McCormack, had been one of the pioneers of the right-to-life movement. In 1976, she had waged a legitimate campaign for president as a candidate for the Democratic nomination. Empowered by the unyielding strength of her principles, Ellen challenged Carter's bid for the nomination, an astounding leap for a game plan designed around her kitchen table. Despite the lack of popularity of her position among my friends, I came to know her as a loving person. I discovered that conservative matriarchal affection was as endearing as any other brand. We respected her passion for life, which rendered the choice of termination a non-starter.

My mother was dead set against my relationship with Anne. Leola put her core racism on the auction block allowing one bid—hers. After refusing a sit-down with my intended, she handed down a definitive statement in a powerfully worded African American shorthand. "I've seen good boys hang for that!" Her last word had the impact of the great Bo Jackson's bat driving a hanging curve ball. It was an honest, profoundly layered sentiment that deep pigment could understand. Old Black racism is heartbreaking, a rare condition in which venom's poison is cloaked in ambiguity, but it still lacks justification.

My core chaffing response to her edict: "With all due respect, Mama, its not you I want to sleep with." Leola Bradley Watlington exploded. Her storm produced a shower of every kind of low-class, trash, immoral word in her righteous pouch. "Mama, I won't trump love with color," I declared forcing her heat into retreat.

"You was always the one I had to leave in God's hands, because I could never understand how somebody so smart could be so dumb," she said. Once again the Lord conveniently alleviated my mother's responsibility for her actions.

These battles provoked my mother into staging a boycott. Her refusal to receive Anne dried up much of my children's Black roots. It was a bizarre situation because the stereotype would have suggested that the Black family would be more tolerant and the Nuevo White family would have freaked out. But racial madness is rarely predictable at close view. I spoke to my mother a handful of times over the next three years. The communication always resulted in huge fights over my perceived defection.

I had been pushing diversity hard, and now I had to belly up to my principles. The taboo-sharpened sword of interracial commitment had come for its pound of flesh. Measured stoicism was Jack's first reaction to the pregnancy. When we issued the official announcement at the family crib, I was so spooked by the pregnancy's racial implications I feared my camel's back would blow, placing its last straw at risk as it straddled the imagined line marked WHITE BOILING POINT. Jack and I talked a lot of sports that day, sidestepping much of the elephant lounging on the couch. I was embarrassed that I couldn't bring a concrete financial promise to the table, which any potential father-in-law had the right to expect. I'm sure Jack had doped out his limited grasp of the tightrope his daughter had chosen to walk. I was a bit of a puzzle to him, playing the Louisiana Purchase to his Meriwether Lewis. The new territory forced him to tinker with his bar of expectations.

My fears were unfounded. The unifying love that awaits a new member of an Irish Catholic family is immutable. Putting the sanctity of blood ahead of latent fears, the entire family embraced its new blessing. Anne's family's willingness to reach out and be a part of our lives, while my family stood on the sidelines, opened the door to a new world for me: White middle-classdom. I thought I was beyond culture shock, but watching Donna Reed from the other side of a television screen was a lot different than being cast in the show. Up to that point I could always count on retaining my outsider status when it served me. But my gratitude for the family's platinum acceptance of our child triggered a set change in my life. It was time to get up to speed on my corned beef and cabbage.

Jack, a World War II veteran, reminded me of my dad. The were both honed on Depression-era toughness and tangible common sense acquired in their youth inhaling the same city's concrete scent. They also had a penchant for hard-assed discipline, along with an unshakable loyalty to Brooklyn's Dodger blue. Their biggest difference was the least relevant human ingredient, pigment. I'd witnessed the frustrated version of the greatest generation because of my father's bitterness over having been Black-bitten. Although both served in the same war, Jack was on the side of the acknowledged victors who benefitted handsomely from their sacrifice. A World War II veteran, sans the handcuffs of pigmentation, was an odd thing for me to view up close. Jack's America loved him and he knew it.

Anne became more conservative around the edges, moving closer to her roots for support and guidance. I began studying Jack's patriarchal behavior. His fierce commitment to the family's welfare topped his list of objectives. Jack's grindstone-scraping consistency was in line with his stereotype, but his inordinate attempt to be fair during these awkward days was not.

The shit hit the McCormack fan one evening in 1983. Anne's sisters, Ellen and Kathy, were there with their husbands, Flip and Eddie. I had yet to gain my full in-law stripes, but the impending baby had secured me a larger role in the family circle. Flip and Eddie were great brothers-in-law, and after an initial feel-out we developed close relationships that I valued. They were suburban White guys, but we chucked our pigment and cultural differences aside and embraced our proximity.

Flip's parents, Phil and Jean, also attended the festivities. Phil was a bright, intense little man with a heavy booze flow. When all the men gathered in the den to watch the football games, Phil was knocking back the drinks. He was the only family member who drank more than I did at these occasions. As a part of my attempt to become responsible I was riding the wagon, so Phil's large run had no bookend. When the women sounded the dinner call, everyone moved to the dining room.

I was comfortable with the setup, enjoying the conversation, and was quick to contribute. After the meal was over, the women cleared the table while the men sat around and shot the breeze. Smoking was still the order of the day, and the room quickly filled with post-dinner fumes. Anne was six months' pregnant, and the extra pounds were beginning to weigh heavily on her every move. This exempted her from cleanup duty. She sat beside me, resting her swollen ankles on my lap, as the dinner chatter continued. Phil kept knocking them back, despite the sobriety-inducing meal's influence on the room. The contrast enhanced the shrill in Phil's rap.

Suddenly, he leaned toward Anne and me and asked, "What's a pretty girl like you doing shacking up with a nigger?"

His timing and delivery struck me as humorous, but the scene exploded. The *N*-word had invaded, and the *N* could have stood for napalm given the ensuing chaos. Ellen almost fainted, as Anne sat in stunned disbelief. Her sister Kathy yelled for Flip, who came running upstairs, hurdling a couch that obstructed the path. Within an instant, he was in his father's face chewing him out. I was astounded. I'd never seen this many White folks lose it so honestly. Jack eyeballed Phil and ordered, "Get the hell out of my house!" His command froze the room as though it had been muted at a seminal moment by a remote with inoperable rewind capability. The resumption of forward movement marked the end of our collective racial virginity.

Jack had known Phil for years; they were both products of the sixtyish Caucasian American male fraternity, so I assumed Jack would shift into neutral. But he booted the guy! In the spirit of Frank Capra's *Mr. Deeds Goes to Town*, with Jack cast in Gary Cooper's legendary role, he blasted the jade right off of my well-traveled attitude. From my station, Phil's soused barbs had had zero impact, as I had long been inoculated against the word *nigger*, but Jack would have none of it. Phil coated his inebriation with indignant strength propellant and bolted.

The incident quickly broke up the party, and as Anne and I prepared to leave, Jack offered to drive us home. Normally, a ride to the Long Island Railroad would do, but he wanted to take us back to Manhattan. As we sped along the highway, Jack didn't say a word during the entire trip. I was in the front passenger seat and spent much of the time staring at his profile, wondering what his mind was feeding him. Why did he break out the sledgehammer when a penknife would have done? He knew Phil had a booze problem and could have smoothed the issue over with the too-much-alcohol defense. But he seemed to be delivering a message, that if I was going to be a part of the family, I wouldn't have to put up with the *nigger* thing on his watch. I continued to sneak glances at his silence, trying to discern if he was what strength of character looks like.

At the end of our *Bullpen* blow-up-the-stereotypes integration tour, we were left with trunks of memories and no pot to piss in. With vaporized prospects and a baby's arrival careening forward, we made a dread-tinged choice to mount another production. My bloodied idealism tricked me into committing the theatrical felony of leading a tired property back to the post once too often. I'd opted for the pain of rejection instead of the numbing state of irrelevance.

We gathered our fifth production at the American Theatre for Actors. I arrived early for the first read-through and was met by an angered Chuck brimming with confrontation.

"Don't we blow up every joint we've played? People love this show," he bellowed. "It's because we've niggers! How long are you going to continue to hold on to the myth of fair play in this fucked up game?"

"Look," I answered, "I believe it's here for me. I got to."

"Bullshit! You the best young motherfucker out here," Chuck snorted. "How can you be so good and yet still have your face pressed up against the big window?"

"Lot of White cats noses is pressed up against that same window," I defended. "It's the fucking business."

"You ain't White, nigger." He exploded, "You ain't White, motherfucker! You ain't White!"

Chuck was so angry I thought he would have a stroke, when good fortune made a house call. His love for me got its hands on his vocal chords before the consequences of his verbal beat-down raised a lasting welt. Chuck chewed on his chamber's next bullet during a hasty beeline for the exit. Left with the shocking revelation that my skin wasn't White, I proceeded with my newly adopted ritual of numbing out before rehearsal. I took a few full blasts from the half pint of cheap vodka that was rooming with my back pocket.

Chuck reentered the room with his flames still showing. "I followed you even though I didn't trust these motherfuckers!" he jabbed.

"Look man, I'm tired," I said. "I'm just fucking tired. Have a drink."

I passed him the bottle, and he refused. He was in the process of reloading when the flow of arrivals interrupted the caning. Despite our frustration there was still a ball game to play, so we quickly adorned our smile masks.

Bullpen had begun to act out the woeful tale of the great bar band that knocks 'em dead live but can't get a record deal. We still attracted the now-annoying small-time guys pitching their near misses. The easy camaraderie that was our strength frayed, replacing spirit with booze and creativity with coke. During the final run, we shared a two-stage open-dressing-room hookup with an Australian play called *Knucklemen*. A young Dennis Quaid was one of the cast members. Fortunately, he and the rest of the *Knucklemen* players were wild enough to appreciate a dark party atmosphere when they saw one, because the consumption of cheap booze in the raw faintly concealed behind rumpled paper bags was our prime coping mechanism.

In this time-bomb atmosphere, Anne clashed with Lydia, our stage manager and Chuck's new bride. Lydia was an invaluable asset to the production's un-orthodox style and generally delivered the goods, but these were tough times. She failed to have our Republican character's pin-striped suit cleaned, and when Anne discovered the garment in a rumpled pile, she blasted Lydia over her mishap. Lydia blasted back, sparking an ugly, gloves-off confrontation dipped in racially tinged animus. Fortunately, the curtain was ten minutes from rising, so the blades were hastily withdrawn, but the clash would throw more pepper on Chuck's and my suddenly coarsened vibe.

People's Neighborhood Theatre was committed to a diverse assault on the humor beneath the surface of negative human stereotypes. We pelted those im-ages with pies before yanking the practitioners offstage with an old vaudevillian hook. Absurd revelations about race are considerably more effective than the an-tique moral argument. The wisps of pleasure that I'd won rolling integrated dice at the table were now frowning through a pair of snake eyes. Despite audiences' healthy clamor for the work, at the production's end we dunked the dream. Our hard-fought credo would serve many of us well in the future, but when the final curtain came down there was little to celebrate. Everyone hightailed it out of the tiny, dank dressing room, cloaked in apparent failure.

*   *   *

Anne and I were blessed with an uncomplicated pregnancy, but I still didn't have the slightest idea how I was going to bring another kid into our crazy, underfunded world. The night that Anne's water broke was a watershed moment. Two weeks before her due date she was cleaning a closet, when *pow*: the flow was on go! Each step that followed the warning salvo would be a physiological challenge. I played it cool, remembering that Avery wasn't born until eighteen hours after the flood.

We called the midwife, and she instructed us to sit tight and wait for the next series of signs. This offered little comfort for a first-timer as we squirmed and fidgeted through the evening. I don't think that a man's love for a woman ever flashes more poignantly than in hours before an impending birth. During the wait I dozed off as Anne watched the tube, firing intermittent verbal assaults at an awful production of Sam Shepard's play *A Fool for Love*. At 5:00 A.M. the contractions moved from whispers to shouts until the hospital beckoned.

I had saved the number of a Black car service for this occasion. I called and, in minutes, the car awaited us. The vehicle was so battered that the term broken-down heap could have sued for defamation, and the look of our driver would have resided comfortably on anyone's Most Wanted list. I squeezed Anne through a door that barely opened halfway, and we set off for the hospital. We drove through Central Park on our way to Manhattan's Roosevelt Hospital. The car rattled, emitting gas fumes that hung in the air like a poisonous mist. It became too much for Anne, and we had to pull over to the curb, where she puked her remaining guts out. I massaged her back in between heaves, assuring her that this was not a bad omen.

We finally got to the hospital, and after hours of anticipation the labor pains were gearing up for a powerful third act, with each contraction accompanied by an expletive-enhanced *Whoa!* It was at this point that our capitulation to our generation's whack-ball thirst for natural childbirth rivaled the purchase of an Edsel. We worked our Lamaze training and discovered, when trying to pass someone the size of a bowling ball through a narrow canal, that breathing exercises' impact on birth pain was only slightly more effective than aspirin for a gunshot wound. After ten hours of this rising and falling action, Keelan James answered our turbulent cue, squeezing into the world's pool of human imperfections. To our great relief, he was in perfect health. To my surprise, he was as White as an Aryan fantasy.

Keelan's debut cemented our commitment to one America. His arrival made us better Americans by default, etching our color blindness in stone. I immediately called my mother, hoping that her new grandson would melt old hatchets.

My enthusiasm hit a wall when my mother dismissed my plans for détente with an icy reply, "Ah, it's just another half-baked baby born in a bush!" With her eardrum-searing phone slam reverberating in my head, I was left to chew on Leola's clever two-pronged assault on biracialism and her generation's definition of a child's legitimacy.

My happiness rebounded quickly the moment I held Anne's hand. The exhausted extremity induced a moment of awestruck humility. Her physical endeavor exposed me to new levels of strength, courage, and stamina, with its climax offering the kind of pain that would have thrown the bravest of men's knees into a wobble. But after a woman enters the ninth-centimeter home stretch at which time pain and exhaustion reach their crescendo, the will to keep punching is the only alternative nature provides. Anne had earned her rest, and when she drifted off my adrenaline bowed to exhaustion. Before I knew it, a cab driver was waking me up in front of my apartment building, and I broke for the sheets. When my head hit the pillow I was the happiest man alive. Before my eyes forced themselves shut, I secured the Lord's promise that he would speed up the next sunrise, opening the gates for my well-deserved sire's victory lap. Exhilaration blotted out the fine print in my lifetime contract with Murphy's Law.

The following morning Anne called and was beside herself with angst. "Where were you? I tried to call you all night," she screamed. "What the hell is wrong with you?"

Surprised, I said, "What happened? Everything was so beautiful."

Anne proceeded to tell me a startling tale. I had left the hospital around 4:30 P.M., and shortly after my departure the hospital staff changed shifts. At feeding time, when they brought the babies from the nursery to the new mothers, everyone had their child but Anne. Disturbed, she got up and hobbled to the nursery, where she saw a group of doctors huddled around Keelan's crib. Fatigue and worry overtook her as she approached the doctors and discovered that they were concerned over blemishes that had sprouted on his body. They feared that the kid had developed an infectious skin condition that might warrant special attention. This freaked Anne out, and she tried to reach me with countless phone calls that my slumber had fended off. As the experts huddled around her bed, doping out the worst-case scenarios, they concluded that the problem had them stumped. Ultimately, their decision was to transfer Keelan to another hospital, where he might benefit from a new set of whitecoats.

Just as they were ready to ship the kid, an Indian doctor asked the only question no one had considered, "Is your husband Black?"

"Yes," an exasperated Anne replied.

The doctors became wide-eyed over the taboo-smeared curveball Anne had tossed them, before their collective lightbulb turned on. Keelan was perfectly fine. The poor kid's pigment was just fighting its way to the surface. The unsuspecting staff's American dictionary had no definition for someone as fair as Anne birthing Black babies. The manual's omission led them on a search for any explanation other than miscegenation. Race ignorance in America is boundless, and this malady brought our son within minutes of paying the price for our nation's segregated instincts. Keelan's first day out of the womb ensnared him in a controversy over his racial composition.

Welcome to America, son.

Keelan was comfortably settled in the world for five months when Anne and I decided to marry, and like most things on our biracial excursion, this was not a conventional experience. There was friction as the marriage drew near. I was in a tenuous situation with my mother-in-law, Ellen. She welcomed the idea of Anne and me hooking up legally, but there were problems for her with our sought-after legitimacy. Ellen's angst wasn't racially motivated. A running joke was that my rap sheet was so filled with no-no's that Blackness didn't even crack the Top Ten list. I was divorced and had a child with another woman and had an unstable profession, not to mention no religious affiliation. To a conservative Catholic mother, I had liability written all over me without nary a rosary bead in sight. But her Catholicism taught me that at the base of her religion was a well of compassion, and despite her inherent misgivings, there was no tightening down the screws on matriarchal access. The warm flow of her interest remained intact.

Our marriage was performed at New York's City Hall before a justice of the peace. We knew how difficult this antiseptic atmosphere would be for Ellen, so her absence was absorbed by the collective's good vibe. Anne's sisters, Kathy and Ellen, accompanied us and provided moral support, with Jack and Keelan bringing up the rear. We sat in a room among fifty or more couples waiting their turn to tie the knot. The circumstances were reminiscent of a ghetto hospital's emergency room. When we reached the justice of the peace, Kathy and Ellen stood with Anne and Jack beside me as Keelan gurgled in his stroller. I was moved beyond perception when Jack consented to stand up as my best man. I chuckled over the thought that despite the many occasions I would race across his pain-in-his-ass monitor, he had stepped forward to validate my inclusion.

Anne and I had our new marriage and baby, with few people left to lobby. I got a gig as a phone dispatcher for a messenger service and practiced the wail of an exiled artist. It was my way of preserving the tiny amount of creative ego I had left. Frustration uncapped tensions between Anne and me. The fact that we were in our early thirties with so much new responsibility sucked. One day I got a call from Anne at the messenger joint, and she told me she had just seen Bruce in a promo for a new show called *Moonlighting*. It had been less than a year since our last *Bullpen*, and Bruce had done some Sam Shepard work Off Broadway, but his face coming through the television screen was startling. It was great for him and *ugh!* for me, turning up the depression dials on my predicament.

An unexpected ray of hope descended when two producers sought me out to write the book for a musical they were preparing, called *Rainbow*. After several meetings, I came up with a scenario that was inspired by Keelan. It was the story of a biracial child being pulled in opposite directions by his show-business parents who has to contend with a common malady that afflicts biracial children, the throbbing internal gut-check exam: What am I, Black or White? Drawing wisdom from the teachings of Martin Luther King, the child's fight for his identity forms the crux of the plot's fiber. The work came easily, and the producers were satisfied.

After a successful backer's audition, at which several songs and important bits of story matter were displayed, the financial folks said all of the right things, as the participants sipped champagne and ate major league shrimp. Over the following three weeks, all news was positive, and a go seemed in the offing.

During these heliumated times Anne and I were invited to a surprise birthday party for her mother. The extended family had gathered in Bellmore to close another of Ellen's calendar cycles. The party's gaiety was bolstered by everyone's opportunity to lubricate before the honoree's arrival. I enjoyed Anne's extended family. Jack's older brother, Tom, had seven boys, a cache of young, handsome, rambunctious Irish livewires who electrified a party's fun with their brand of blue–collar, Kennedy-esque energy.

Anne's uncle, Jack Sheehan, was a particular joy. His thick glasses and thick answers to any question offered a visage that was a cross between a grizzled retiree and the long-ago TV schoolteacher, Mr. Peepers. Oddly, he was the family member most felt likely to put his foot in the racist section of his mouth. But from the moment he'd heard I was one of my generation's Brooklyn Dodger afficionados, he had viewed me as an important historical carrier. His affection for Brooklyn's magnificent former ebony sticker fueled over a decade and a half of family jams: Sheehan and I would go a few good rounds of hearty tribute to the '55 championship "bums." He would describe, frame by frame, Sandy Amoros's Series-preserving catch against the hated Yankees. I told Sheehan of my father's love for the Dodgers as well as his service during the big war. Both of their young-adult lives had been largely consumed with the Dodgers beating the Yankees and the Yankees beating the Nazis. Their generation's incontrovertible commonality whipped our racial horse's ass, igniting an startlingly interactive groove. I was learning to reach for my grain of salt when old White guys were stamped racist often for little more than being old White guys. If Sheehan's politics swung that way, it was irrelevant. I had enough Robinson in me to break the Sheehan color line.

Many years later Sheehan was at death's door with only the beam of his curiosity left to battle a dementia-laden group of illnesses. His beloved wife, Kay, of fifty years passed, and there was a question as to whether old Sheehan's health would be up to the task of giving her a proper sendoff, as it was his patriarchal responsibility to do. When Anne and I entered the Catholic church, Jack Sheehan was on his feet front and center, greeting and consoling loved ones, gifting his beloved with an endnote of gutsy clarity. When old Sheehan stepped to the plate in his last official public at bat and took the ceremony deep for his family, I was aglow. Watching the bespeckled enigma's effort clear the fence made me feel pretty good about my Irish Catholic visa.

Amid the family's gradual acceptance of me and Broadway melodies on the horizon, my thoughts were soaked in promise with the end of my exile in sight, when I received a phone call from one of the producers. The instant paranoia that accompanies a show-business psyche kicked in when the first words he spoke were cause for alarm.

"Dennis, there is a bit of a problem."

"What?" I asked, trying to beat down my fatalism.

"You know how much of our story reflects the spirit of Martin Luther King?"

"Yes."

"Well . . . We discovered that Sir Richard Attenborough is preparing a musical about Martin Luther King's life. You know how financial people are."

"Yes," I gulped.

"The moment they heard that such a heavyweight was doing a story with a whiff of similarity, they folded."

"No, no, fucking no!" were my last words before the producer rushed his condolences and hung up.

I was beyond stunned and when I told Anne the news, her dejection quickly rivaled mine. Resentment immediately poisoned the water. I'd over-hyped the project's viability because I wanted it so badly. It killed me that Anne might have gambled away her prime White girl card on a loser. The value of the cutting edge we'd fostered was plummeting precipitously, ultimately bottoming out alongside Tiny Tim's discarded ukelele strings. This loss opened the trapped doors beneath the noose, plunging me into a vat of stinkin' thinking.

It all bubbled over, and I completely flipped out one night at a small music joint in the Village, the Bitter End. I mixed booze with the amphetamines,

Black Beauties, and the combination of the two acted as an anabolic steroid empowering my bitterness. I heckled the master of ceremonies, and the confrontation turned ugly when I ran up on the stage attempting to ring his neck. Before I knew it, I was being chucked from the club by two bruising bouncers. I topped my performance off by lying in the street, daring a bus to run me over. My immature assholiness landed me in Bellevue Hospital's psychiatric emergency room, the infamous "Tank."

In my drug-drenched drunkenness, I convinced them that I was hearing voices and prone to suicidal behavior. When I awoke the next morning and discovered that I was in the freak tank, my renewed clarity hit like a brick. I got up to go to the bathroom, and one of the attendants followed me. I was getting ready to take a leak, and the guy was standing within a few feet. I discovered that this cat was following me because he'd been charted to think that I might piss myself to death. Obviously, I'd stepped in it this time. I tried to talk my way out of my predicament, but because of the dangerous signals I had emitted the night before, I was being pressed against my will to the shit-kicker level of the insane.

The second evening I was in the pit, a fortyish-looking woman with tousled short blond hair entered the Tank. She wore a large blue cape over several layers of designer clothing and carried a typewriter. A youthful, nervous energy set her to pacing back and forth. Adding a touch of class to the ragamuffin's disorientation were two stylish East Side White women wearing a wealthy glow. At one point the overly clothed woman dropped her typewriter, and the case popped open releasing a flutter of pages. She dove to the floor, scrambling to pick them up while wailing over her predicament. This irascible little dust mop was in bad shape.

I was thirsting for anyone to come into this musty pit who wasn't scarily insane, so I approached the classy helpers with my best sane impression. My playwright-spiced rap won them over, and they revealed the name of the woman now squatted atop her fallen pages in catatonic stillness as Tinkerbelle. I was seduced by the perfumed scent emanating from the little nut job's finely coiffed empathizers. These two jewels in a shit pit elicited my promise to look after their disturbed waif. Upon agreement, they issued a hasty goodbye to the inanimate creature, before getting into the wind.

That night Tinkerbelle was out of her mind, stoned buried, with periodic droplets of emergence from her catatonia producing a stream of delirious fast-lane babble that sounded like an old 78 rpm recording. Her nonsensical blather over flipping out doing opium with Yves St. Laurent highlighted her madness. The following morning, after Tinker's drugs rested, she transitioned into an engaging, wit-filled personality, peppering me with stories of her days as part of Andy Warhol's crew. "I was one of the bright lights that shone from the Factory to Studio 54," she exhorted, as her jet set eyes sparkled, turning on her pale face. Under the dim light, the fragile decomposition of her fortyish beauty was fascinating. She was Blanche DuBois bottoming out—dark, crazed, and demure.

I kept Tank watch on Tinker for two nights as we did penance in the bowels of the nut franchise, where patients were routinely drugged and tied to tall-backed wooden wheelchairs until the elusive bed materialized. We talked about the sixties. I told her that many of my dreams had been born during that decade, and how every opportunity I'd received had come from the concept of American integration. She stroked my cheek as though I were a naive pup and said, "The sixties were great, but Whites didn't include you. They stole from you." Tinker's powerful dart caught my balloon square. I sought to defend my philosophy, and all she could do was laugh. "People are cruel. As they grow older and more frightened, they share love less and less."

"I'm too Black to feel that way," I said. "If I want to be an American outside of the Black walls, I have to keep taking my leaps of faith."

She gave me a hug that was soaked in pity, turning the tables, assuming the role of caregiver. "You still have miracles you believe in, huh?" she teased.

"For me, it's miracles or bust."

Tinker's rich connected friends came to her rescue, getting the hospital to release her for the NYU nut joint, a much nicer facility. Before Tinker was whisked away, her warm parting embrace signaled that our hellish nights had made us comrades.

I was happy for Tinker, but I was facing more observation upstairs on the ward where crazies went to celebrate their insanity—19 North. When I entered, music by David Gates floated through the air, softly pleading: "I want to make it with you." Prescription drugs ruled the house. Psychotherapy for smudged brains scored a distant second when it came to controlling the errant mental beast. There was a long line of patients standing in single file against the wall waiting for one of their thrice-daily drug hits. A nurse sat behind a Plexiglas window dispensing the drugs. Each dope fiend received two paper cups, one containing the dope and the other fruit juice to wash it down. As I stood transfixed, a short, pickled-faced Black man with glasses ingested his dose and approached me. We were practically nose-to-nose, when he gave me a goofy look and belched in my face.

This was my official introduction into the world of the legally insane. A short time later I was in an empty cafeteria, seated by myself, staring off into space, consumed with incredulity, when a thirtyish White woman with wild red hair, wearing very thick glasses, came upon me. She was carrying a magazine, and on its cover was a picture of Woody Allen. The magazine was her prized possession, and she cradled it with loving care. She asked me for a cigarette and I gave her one. After a few puffs the Woody lover placed her magazine on the chair beside me and left to hit the chow toss.

A Black woman, a visual mess, approached asking for a cigarette and I accommodated. She sat down and asked for a light. With her pungent body odor fouling my largesse, I played through until the lit match was blown from my fingers by a scream. It was the redhead who'd discovered that the Black woman was seated on her Woody. She came rushing over, and the two women got into a knock-down, drag-out, hair-pulling fight as pages of the redhead's heartthrob flew everywhere. Such was the atmosphere of 19 North: If you didn't drug the cracked nuts, they'd flip out on you.

During my evaluation the shrink wasn't sure if I was sane or not. It was all an exercise in mental masturbation. I left just enough doubt to keep the room-and-board coming. The bin offered refuge from my flop of a life. One of the few people I talked to, or who was willing to talk to me, was my creative brother Mitchell Weiss. Mitch had produced one of the best productions of *Bullpen*, bringing the likes of Denzel Washington and Giancarlo Esposito to the most fruitful period in People's Neighborhood Theatre's run. Their firepower added to our guerrilla band of hopefuls, detonating an impressive bang.

Mitch and I became welded matter. Proximity revealed his background nurtured in the last roundup of Manhattan's great theatrical culture. A gofer job for Kermit Bloomgarden and his production of *Equus*, Peter Shaffer's play starring Richard Burton, was where Mitch's administrative theatrical gums had been broken. Soon his standout usefulness found its way into Joseph Papp's confidence. Papp, the last meaningful king of New York theatrical wonder, had spotted Mitch's ebullient imagination and had afforded him the opportunity to be one of the final group of talented pups to come under his auspices. Mitch's haughty rise propelled the logic that he knew everything, and I knew much less. We rode that equation into an early minor theatrical disaster, before quickly balancing the equity on our respect sheets. In our second attempt we produced the best kind of Off-Broadway theatrical excitement in the pile.

"What the hell are you doing in there?" Mitchell asked.

"Half-hiding, half-confused, half-afraid," I whined.

"That's three halfs, one more than your share," he fired good-naturedly, probing for the perversity in my funny bone.

"Mitch, you are the only fucking person in my life who I can tell that I'm fucking scared to death and no longer have a fucking clue," I sputtered. "All I know is that after all the people you and I have made clap, I'm fucking broke."

"This is just a bump in the road for guys like you," he contested. "You've got real writing ability. Extract the drama out of your life and direct it onto the fucking page. You're one of the lucky ones who have that option."

"Fuck you," I uttered grudgingly, realizing there was little sympathy for the pity-slurping section in my portfolio.

"Look, I'm willing to donate pads, pens, and pencils. The key is for you to write about it, before you come back to your senses." He laughed before settling into a reflective mood. "Remember, the best thing you have going is that you're crazy, so this isn't that big of a stretch."

"Thanks, Mitch. You screwed up my sulk with that superior brand of friendship crap you have going." I hung up pissed, with the uneasy feeling resulting from having had my best interests being fired at me.

The ward reminded me of my early days of incarceration at Spoffard. The attendants ran a tight ship. The majority of us slept two to a room, and those who were able were required to keep their beds made and allotted space clean. The twenty-four-hour lite-FM music that was piped in acted as an additional drug that kept everyone moving at a languid pace. I had managed to convince my shrink that I didn't need mind-altering substances. With the exception of two sleeping pills every evening, I was left to my own mental devices. I filled my time by writing and interacting with the inmates.

I stayed in a small room with a large window that overlooked the FDR Drive and befriended my roommate, John, a plump, affable White man in his fifties. He had once been the owner of a small car service. His life's work went belly-up and his sanity followed suit. John was a neat freak who passed the time folding and unfolding his laundry incessantly, while airing out a delusion that he was a talented singer. It was enough to drive one crazy listening to him sing John Denver's "Rocky Mountain High." After days in that dental chair I yelled, "Will you give me a break?"

"Pipe down," he responded. "You Black guys are so angry." I laughed and he continued. "This is your first time here. Relax, I'll give you a good lesson about the nuthouse—never believe a fucking thing anyone says. Once you step across that line, reality turns into a lie."

Several days into my stay I was electrified by a surprise visit from Tinkerbelle. She was dressed and made up beautifully and quickly seized the room's oxygen with her magnetic energy. Tinker was carrying a large plant that she plopped in front of me. I moved it aside to take a good look at her. This was the first up I'd felt since landing on the North. Tinker was excited over a book she was writing entitled *Sometimes a Somebody*. It was an autobiographical portrait of her life as an almost star. She performed a passage from the book, turning the dreary, clanging cafeteria into a small theater. Tinker acted out an embarrassing snub she'd experienced at an A-list club. She captured the indigestible sorrow that torments the has-been who's fallen from the right lists. Tinker's physical soliloquy was funny, sad, clever, and naughty, and I was maximally enthralled.

Tinkerbelle pitched the idea of our working together, and I quickly agreed. I asked about NYU, and she told me that she'd decided to take a week to get her game in order and was to enter the facility the following day. Tinker assured me that her hospital stay was nothing more than a pit stop to oil her gears for the next push. I was sold and ready to run through a wall for her, but that was only half my reaction. There was a sad thread of tin in Tinker's golden performance. She had plunged to the level of doing her act on 19 North. Her hyper need to draw me into her pain stank with the profundity of her loneliness. Tinker's great spirit was at odds with the age lines that were gutting her relevance.

The plant was a gift for me, although I didn't have the slightest idea what to do with it. She also gave me a carton of cigarettes, which immediately drew the eyes of all of the grub-prone loonies in the room. Tinker thanked me with a warm kiss for caring during her desperate nights, before exiting the room with a storm's giddyup.

After ten days of fending off the real world, it was time to face the music. They decided to kick my legally sane ass out. The most important thing I learned in Bellevue was how crazy I wasn't. Most of the patients had little responsibility for their own actions; I was not fractured enough to meet that threshold. I dreaded my reentry into the lives of the family and friends I'd taken a powder on. The assignation of crazy Black husband was not an easy tag to surmount. I had let Anne down by bailing on her. Would she give up and declare our situation unworkable? Was that her best move? I certainly couldn't blame her. She had visited me most days, bringing a roast beef sandwich along with her frustration and confusion. No immediate changes were in the works, just more of the same—a lousy job and useless dreams, a bad way to instill confidence in someone you love. I clung to Tinker's offer, which was akin to being on a life raft made of paper towels. But it was the going dream.

After a few days of ingesting humble pie, I slunk back into my dimmed fate and was anxious to visit Tinker, in search of a helpful blast. When I arrived on the ward, I discovered that NYU was the Waldorf compared to 19 North's rumbling atmosphere. I sighted Tinker in long shot as she approached down a long corridor, and she didn't look good. As she drew closer my suspicions swelled to the point of shock, as I was confronted by a withered canary minus fifteen important pounds of feathers that a week and a half's time had plucked from her drug-petite frame. Tinker was dressed in pajamas and bathrobe and seemed paranoid. It was clear that my savior wouldn't be saving anyone soon. Tinker took me by the hand and led me to the atrium where there was a piano. She sat down and began to play a Joni Mitchell–tinted ballad she'd written called "Who's Child Am I." The haunting nature of each chord spelled trouble.

"What happened?" I asked.

She stopped playing. "I can't eat and I can't sleep."

"Why?"

She prefaced her answer with a thought. "I decided that the reason that I like you is because you're a dreamer who needs to believe that the past mattered. But the sixties were a hallucination, and those of us that are hanging on do so out of our fear of inconsequentiality."

"Come on, you're just down. You need to find a way to get some food and rest."

Tinker became irritated by my simplicity and fired, "Get out of the sixties, Dennis, it was all an illusion. A time when you could believe anything you wanted to believe, but keep a pipe filled with something or facts will fuck you. I'm going to be fifty fucking years old. Even Paris can't change that."

She began to play again, and I asked, "What about us and the work we were going to do?"

Tinker smiled, leaned over, and nuzzled her face in my beard, then said, "I love you, Dennis, but it's not going to happen."

She resumed playing, becoming so absorbed in the music that it blotted out my presence. I split, having to contend with the loss of my most recent inspiration.

Several weeks later I got a call from one of her friends, who told me that Tinker had jumped from a roof in Manhattan, ending it all upon impact. It was a great loss, though not a big shock. I was used to tasting the death of others, but this one lingered as though a lightbulb had gone out, with things feeling somewhat dimmer.

A memorial service was held in a classy hall on Central Park West. The joint was filled with crystal White veterans of the Studio 54 sect. It was a surprise when one of the women who had brought Tinker into the Tank asked that I speak at her memorial. I accepted, affirming my belief that our brief meaningful connection had mattered. Steven Gaines, the writer who would subsequently chronicle the event and Tinker's life in *Vanity Fair* magazine, captured the high-level outpouring of love and respect that Tinker's peers felt. Sylvia Miles, the actress, cut through the love with a stern reminder that many of the people in Tinker's life had helped shove her off that rooftop by ignoring her obvious instability. I addressed the crowd and thanked Tinker for having had a profound impact on me. Her death had taught me that longevity was a dose of hemlock for the dated soul.

After Tinker's death I took the next year off. The harsh Reaganite atmosphere provided a cold outdoor shower every morning. My biracial family was operating under enormous strain. The excitement of the "us against the world" high was flattening. The world was winning.

TWENTY-EIGHT

Show business mopped much of its pigment up after the blaxploitation film period of the seventies. These often-maligned films afforded a multitude of African American actors and storylines a back alley of expression. When the eighties rolled around, Black artists were in the midst of a great drought. Opportunities were scarce. Bruce and John were the only *Bullpen* stable members with a legitimate shot at a higher rung. In Bruce's case, fame and fortune grabbed him by the scruff of his neck, jerking him into the stratosphere. We had been dreamers together, and it was tough when the industry's handicap separated our paths to opportunity.

I took my ass-whipping poorly, acting as though I had landed on an iceberg, increasing the call of inebriation's denial of my frostbitten psychological extremities. A theater rat in exile casts a dark, gooey shadow. I was in need of something to direct, important scenes to break down. There were no more actors to provide the vital improvisational lines that fired up a scene's utilities. Like any middle-timer, I was on the fuck-off wheel, a place where those who had leaped the first hurdle on the road to success went to die. Marriage, children, and money problems called for maturity, but I couldn't give up my pursuit of rejection. I wallowed in this new White deal I'd learned called guilt, and agonized over my stone's descent. With only a few fingers still visible, I latched on to a new lifesaver, Alcoholics Anonymous, but I was playacting. My desire to bury my senses beneath substances remained as strong as ever, empowering my weaknesses' arrogant stab at romancing the most lethal White lady the streets ever pimped—crack. Initially, the drug leveled my booze head, skimming off its obnoxious excesses, but that floorboard caved quickly, and the hidden dominatrix that was crack brought me to my knees, extorting pathetic whimpering sounds for mercy.

The best opportunity to slash my throat arrived in an unusual way. Bruce had once been involved with Geraldo Rivera's former wife. Somehow this led to his recommending me to Geraldo's people for a consultancy gig on Rivera's syndicated special on the proliferation of drugs in America. I was a great admirer of Geraldo's. I first became aware of him because of legal work he practiced for a Puerto Rican gang called The Young Lords. They hung out on familiar East Harlem turf at 111th Street, between Lexington and Park Avenue. The Young Lords were happening around the same time as the Slum Lords, and on the streets the smell of Geraldo's commitment wafted well. Years later, when ABC News affirmatively acted on Geraldo's behalf, giving him a camera and much of his head, he brought the first gutsy pair of Latin balls to television reporting. He was also a big Lennon admirer, which added to my respect quotient.

Geraldo's producer brother, Craig, told me that he wanted to film a crack house. I wasn't up on crack houses, but I wanted the gig, so I contacted Ray, a close friend who had a sharp instinct for trouble. He was living in a crack-infested neighborhood in the heart of the venal South Bronx, and after a bit of coaxing he agreed to turn his crib into a den for a day. Ray had one stipulation: the TV people had to put up some money for the drugs. I was able to bed that detail with Craig, and the gig was a go.

On the night of the shoot I was met by a van carrying a small crew of Geraldo-ites: a cameraman, his assistant, and Craig. Our trip to Ray's joint was enshrouded in good cheer. To the at-large public, crack was in its infancy, and the cutting-edge quality of the assignment moistened their journalistic undergarments. Ray's place was a battered one-bedroom tenement apartment, the prototypical crack house. He had lined up a number of addicts, promising them a few free hits if they allowed themselves to be filmed. Before long, the junkies were puffing and the camera was rolling. The clouds of smoke filling the bowls of crack pipes engorged my addiction with blood. We filmed a young teenaged girl. Predictably, she had become a prostitute whose money supported her chemical agony. It was a tragic story. Technical difficulties called for her to repeat her tale several times, and in between takes she indulged her obsession with the pipe.

It was this visual that snapped my twig, compelling me to leap forward. Under the guise of a crusader against reportorial abuse, I decided to defend the young girl's virtue by volunteering to go on camera alongside her. At this moment the cameraman approached and asked to speak with me in an adjoining room. Vic volunteered his history of alcoholism and recovery in Alcoholics Anonymous before pleading with me not to go on camera. But the cloud had spun a web of denial that had closed the door on reason. I bullshitted about the importance of America's need to see my informed take on the drug's reality. Vic continued to plead with me to no avail. I went back into the main room and convinced Craig to shoot me in the act, and, in short order, I was puffing for America.

Vic's grim face sat behind the camera's eye as I puffed and pontificated, loving every toke. It was junkie paradise: free drugs along with a self-righteous reason to suck glass. Everyone in the room but me knew that I was a very sick man. We ended the shoot, packed up, and headed back to Manhattan. After a few blocks I stopped the driver and insisted that I had to go back. I came up with a bullshit reason that everyone saw through. Before I hopped out of the van, Vic tendered one more shot, but my mind was fixed on Ray's joint. It would be two days before I slithered out from under that rock.

My action dissolved the final straw, ramming my marriage's degree-of-difficulty needle into the red zone. My tissue-thin judgment forced Anne's hand, driving her and Keelan away. It was an act of self- and child-preservation. Her timing was good; they would be spared the ugliest part of my slide. When I finally found my way home, I was met by a damning note dangling before my nose. The note made it clear that Anne was done. They'd fled to Long Island, where Jack and Ellen stepped forward and dealt domestic aces for my young family in distress.

It was 1986, the year of the Strawberry Mets, a great team that raised hell on every rung of its climb to a World Championship. The shock of Anne's leaving forced me to abandon my poisons. I went to AA, and my old buddy, Mitchell Weiss, hired me to work for him on his new gig as general manager of the Big Apple Circus. I called Anne repeatedly, trying to lure her back with my makeover. I had begun writing a musical with a young songwriter, Paul Scott Goodman. All sterling brownie points, but nothing budged her resolve.

Irony ruled and it seemed appropriate that I would join the circus. My life had become a tapestry of disparate acts hectically performed under a big tent. I was confused and frightened over the loss of my loved ones. I bullshitted myself into thinking I could win them back with the razzmatazz that the circus fronted, but it was my dormant junkie's self-absorption that was feeding my delusions. I never missed the opportunity to watch the trapeze artists rehearse, always wishing that I could somehow absorb the coordination and confidence they exhibited, until one of the flyboys told me, "The circus is a place for spangle-covered losers."

I was on the ring crew that raised the big tent. The European workers were tough and regarded the American workers as lazy, pampered obstructionists. Their superior expertise enabled them to break balls with a vengeance. A few days before opening, I was relegated to the crew that shoveled the elephant shit. I was dung!

On my thirty-fourth birthday, I was consumed with self-pity, so I threw away my shovel and picked up the pipe, initiating a rapid descent through the cracks, ultimately landing in my old neighborhood. I'd fallen to the point where I was sharing pain with the lowest form of eighties nigger: a gutter-curb-level crack addict. Within a month I went from 214 pounds to 170. I was a powerless genie trapped in the belly of a glass bowl. The term 24/7 was birthed to describe one's need to please the crack dominatrix's lure, twenty-four hours a day, seven days a week.

During the height of my addiction, I employed every scheme imaginable to feed my mistress. As the phone book filled with one-shot opportunities thinned, my desperation led me to a special woman named Nicole whom I'd befriended on 19 North. Aside from Tinkerbelle, she had been my favorite certified lunatic. Her ward name had been Piss Pot. During her more inspired declarations of self-loathing, Nicole would urinate on herself. This stamped her persona non grata, narrowing her companion pool to the flies that danced to the tune of her wretched fumes. I was intrigued and began probing beneath her exterior. I learned that she was a former schoolteacher from a good family that abandoned her after she'd exhausted their multiple attempts to help. Nicole wound up at the bottom of the mental health barrel, shuffling from dirt-shit institution to dirtier shit institution. She revealed tidbits of information as we slowly developed a modicum of mutual trust. Beneath Nicole's insanity was a wise, learned being whose sophistication could baffle the observers' contrasting visual, yet her sudden episodes of piss-soaked rage were explosive enough to induce famed Mafia don John Gotti into running for cover.

I had assumed the role of de facto guardian, and it was a fascinating assignment. After Bellevue, I continued to visit Nicole in an attempt to aid her fight to peak above her fog. Her slow but steady improvement was one of the most improbable occurrences since the '69 World Champion Mets. Finally, when she won her release from Bellevue, it was a great day for winners. Nicole allowed her hair to grow longer and began to take pride in her appearance. Over sixty and covered in psychological scar tissue, she was a portrait of courage. One of my most memorable celebrations occurred when we filled her first Lithium prescription in the outside world. Our relationship slowed when Nicole's continual improvement flew in the face of my cracksville occupancy. I cut off contact because I couldn't deal with Nicole's reaction to her knight in shining armor riding his stallion off a cliff.

As my addiction worsened, my self-esteem tapped out and I contacted Nicole, alarming her with a bullshit emergency. She loved me and immediately offered her help. When I arrived at her apartment, I was a funky mess with a spasmodic crack twitch. Nicole immediately saw through my bullshit. She gave me a hundred dollars before calling me on my addiction. Like any junkie, I lied until the bullshit stung enough to make her cry. Nicole feared that if I stayed this course, I would soon be dead, but I was numb to her angst because in my state crack trumped love in a heartbeat. It was a drug that transformed logic into evil, making it easy to defraud one of the greatest examples of human courage I'd ever known. Upon grabbing the cash from her hands, I dashed, leaving Nicole in tears. Her painful worry would be our parting number. The residual effects of the hard knocks she'd endured would join forces to punch her clock before I could make amends.

Things had gotten so bad that I was tiptoeing up against a precept I had sworn by: Thou shall not mug anyone for drugs. But my habit was lobbying for a little late-night waitress hunting. I begged my close friend, Ernie Wilkins, to lock me in his apartment in order to protect me from myself. I was up against the writing on the wall that read: try or die. I chose to try, and after a twitchy, sweaty two-day trip to hell, I was able to secure a bed in a detox facility. Project Return was the name of my latest lifeline, and I writhed through four days of psychological torture, my longest period without the drug in months. Upon my release, my well-wishers loaded me down with a stack of Alcoholics Anonymous and Narcotics Anonymous adverts. As their smiling faces and hearty handshakes faded, I was back in the devil's ballroom.

There was a scent on the streets named lure. With so much rock being smoked in Harlem of 1987, the atmosphere had become one large bowl. Black and Puerto Rican junkies had turned the majority of the neighborhood denizens into hostages, who were beaten, robbed, and often killed for their meager earnings, as inadequate locks and bolts failed to shield them from crack's terrorism. How could America have allowed these jungles filled with death, pain, and suffering to exist on its soil? The human carnage that the eighties crack epidemic served up was the most debilitating whack that disenfranchised pigment-dipped victims had taken since slavery. Welfare, teenage pregnancy, addiction, and Black male incarceration created a human cesspool that leaked its government-approved bile all over the Gipper's Rockne-desecrating decision not to signal for a fair catch when standing under the nation's Colored football. The consequence of allowing the pigmented pigskin to hit the ground detonated an aimless, retrogressive bounce, settling inches from its own goal line.

I walked the streets on my first day of sobriety, and my stomach became queasy as the scent challenged my resolve. When not eluding bill collectors or the landlord, I cowered in darkness, having lost electricity. With the heat shut off, I wrapped myself in an overcoat and blanket, fighting off an unforgiving winter's ass-whupping, clinging to the belief that each day sober made me a day stronger. With the exception of AA meetings, I tried to remain as still as a post, staring at the blank walls of my empty apartment, fearing that moving an inch would lead to a slip that would translate into another horrible run. With a thimbleful of faith covering my nonexistent prospects for the future, I was bound to survive.

I would have starved without the little plastic bags filled with rice, Spam, lemon concentrate, and sugar taped to my door each morning by Ernie Wilkens, whose brotherly help kept hope alive that I could somehow grow another pair of oars. The average disadvantaged crack junkie knew nothing about hopes and dreams. Their suicide wish was an environmental issue; mine had been self-inflicted. Having gassed out on ghetto pain, my White side took over. I inhaled AA pamphlets before contacting Vic, the cameraman who had tried to head me off during the Geraldo taping. I told him I was ready to make a real go of sobriety, and in typical AA fashion, he vowed to help me help myself.

Sobriety was hard business, and Vic was an effective taskmaster. I was penniless, so he committed to feeding me a few times a week, which was one of the worst punishments of the entire ordeal. Vic's cooking was so awful that he could have been brought up on assault charges, but his leadership was strong during his sponsorship of my resurrection. The worst thing about the life of a recovering substance abuser is that he is left to face the tall wave of debris accumulation that descends like a ton of bricks, burying him in his junkie madness. Gagging on this bitter medicine was a gut-searing endeavor.

One day the doorbell rang, and as was my norm I let whoever was leaning on the button exhaust himself, but these callers wore me out and I responded. There was a diverse coalition of Black, White, and Puerto Rican—a salt-and-pepper male set, illuminated by a gold-skinned Latina woman. They identified themselves as Jehovah's Witnesses. An attractive middle-skinned Black man, who was as calm as I was irritable, offered a smile brighter than a movie's premier. Armed with *Awake!* magazine, he began to communicate his religion's thrust. After a few blasts he stopped cold and scrutinized my sunken body language, which seemed to amp his silence. After a naked forty seconds or so, he moved closer and looked me in the eyes. Mine plummeted.

"You need help, don't you?" he crooned. His words hung until coming down on me like a net. My humbled non-answer lobbied for the affirmative. We moved into the living room and its two remaining chairs. I plopped into one, while the others remained standing. The calm brother broke the silence. "What's troubling you?"

The physical authenticity empowering his compassion cracked the dam, unleashing my sob story into six absorptive ears that cradled a two-hour, twelve-hankie testimony. After affording me the opportunity to wring myself dry, the calm brother stepped forward and committed his church's help to my latest phoenix makeover fund. In turn, he solicited my promise to give his faith an honest listen. Over the next several weeks, one or a combination of the others pumped my doorbell at 7:30 A.M., the mission being to jerk me out of my 3:00 P.M. to 5:00 A.M. cycle of depressive isolation.

Upon opening my eyes, the devil in me would fire up a cheap cassette player with the Doors' classic album *Soft Parade*. I strangled the volume dial, testing the depth of my above-and-beyond Samaritan's commitment. Their objectives commenced with goading me into the shower. They soon augmented my meager dietary allotment with bulky, grainy, healthy staples of rice and vegetables. With little alternative and less seasoning, I gratefully approached the mush as though it were an important medicinal component. After a week of basic deprogramming, they implemented a massive one-man cleanup, directing me toward the grimiest corners of the apartment, pumping self-pride as the emotional thrust behind the positive spirit that comes with one's own enhancement. As I moved about my tasks, they painted silk-screened images of their religiosity drawn from the Bible and the *Watchtower*. I'd fallen into an unlikely source of absolute serenity that put my recovery into fast-forward. Between AA meetings, Vic, and a makeshift Kingdom Hall, my shit-level losing streak had been highjacked by this confluence of positive pressure.

I went to Kingdom Hall to worship beside my concrete angels. I wanted to honor their home turf when telling them of my decision to move on. I leveled with the calm brother about both my unforgettable appreciation for their help, as well as my heart's bottom belief that I could respect and learn from anyone's choice of religious expression, but I could never be a conscientious soldier on any single path. Calm brother turned up his high-beam smile and offered his embrace before assuring me that the quantum leap in my welfare was reward enough. It was a lovingly fond farewell. Only AA rivaled the Jehovah's Witnesses in selflessness.

Now showering and answering my doorbell without fear, I responded quickly to the buzzer one afternoon, and was knocked back into a pleasurable part of my past upon the sight of Gail Sheehy. Her smile had Cavalry written all over it. After a warm, lusty embrace, she took a spin around the set of my ashened saga in all of its drab, barren cleanliness before suggesting, "Let's get out of here and get something to eat."

An expensive restaurant later, we played with hours of conversation. Gail's reason for drawing me out of my shadow was to solicit my counsel during her first attempt at writing for the theater. A workshop she was attending required the crafting of a one-act play. Her respect for my old theater chops ripened the timing for a sounding-board reunion. After a number of poignant, well-received suggestions, Gail's newsdar leapt on my stories about the new toxic waters edging up on White America's consciousness—crack. In typical fashion, the poison's genesis bubbled for years in the ghetto destroying everything it touched, except mainstream denial. The force of the epidemic was now ready to extract payment for our majority's negligence as the scent of deadly rock began tickling the noses of MTV's founding White suburban teenagers.

Gail suggested I write down several of my anecdotes, thinking that the woman who published her magazine pieces might be interested. When she laid a moniker on the editor in chief, my first thought was that the name Tina Brown felt like a Black one. My stomach's impatience with White folks shuffling me off to the chitlin' circuit was thinner than a rat's hair, and when confronted with strains of the newly affirmed niggerized cap, I'd get in the wind. Gail broadsided my paranoia-inflated pessimism, revealing that Tina Brown held a mother-country-level Caucasian pedigree and was in the throes of commandeering *Vanity Fair* magazine, a monthly that was riding the arc of a hyper hot thing.

Despite the proposition's swelling legitimacy, writing had become anathema to me. My contract with sobriety had forced me to abandon the thought of being a meaningful writer, because my darkest trip cues were embedded in my creative pursuit. The still-fresh lessons from my recent hell reminded me of the last time I had sought to benefit from my writing stripes, when I offered a bemused crack dealer private writing lessons in exchange for credit. He had laughed through his retort, "If you down to teaching me, you ain't worth shit." I'd come to full agreement with my former tormentor, and chose to douse Gail's inspiration with lukewarm comport.

Crossing my first important Alcoholics Anonymous threshold of stitching together ninety successive clean days of sobriety elicited a Mardi Gras energy level of support from my AA family. Pumped beyond my ego's means, I took a stab at showcasing the new model for Anne's inspection. After responding to a few heart-racing snapshots that bore a strong resemblance to the man she'd bargained for, Anne passed, choosing to honor the sturdily constructed preservatory wall she'd commissioned.

My ninety-day pink orgasm gave way to a reality heist that sent me sprawling. People were no longer willing to credit me for sobriety alone, so my life's worth came under sharper scrutiny. The simplicity of fighting back from death's door offered few of the complexities that pulling one's own weight demanded. The initial head slap was the final eviction order from my landlord whose essence spelled: "Nigger, if you ain't out in thirty, the police insure that you'll be gone in thirty-one." Homelessness is no joke, and thirty-two days later I tasted a mouthful of that misery, doing a short trick in one of the decade's controversial human refuse bins. My homeless-shelter pastime consisted of remaining awake to guard off the crazies or watching disposable toddlers bounce off cots too close for a child's dreams.

I begged, borrowed, and slurped together enough money for a flight to Tampa, Florida, parachuting out of the previous ten years with little more than my jeans could carry, landing on the empathetic futon of Gerri's largesse. It would be the last time that she and I would reside together under the same roof, and although it wasn't a sexual rapprochement, an instinctive gut connection wrung the last vestiges of our past love in an attempt to fill each other's empty halves.

Shortly after parking double digits into his calendar box, Avery stepped into the Black adolescent, man-of-the-house maelstrom booby trap, a traumatic, disorienting hurdle Boomer dads placed before offspring who finished second to the generation's altered tastebuds that made abandonment's bitter porridge palatable. Despite my tenuous value, Avery reached through his anger, embracing his scuffed, fallen gene donor, exhibiting an imposed maturity that chafed at an absent father's guilt center. I tried to maintain a consistent relationship with him, but during a child's formative years, if you've left, you're gone. Five-foot-eleven with rich Black coordination beyond his ten years, Avery was able to vent his frustration on the basketball court using his reasonable shot at kicking the shit out of his drug-weakened, enigmatic, vanish specialist. His occasional upper hand scraping my nose into the hot Tampa asphalt was good medicine for Avery's no-fault ailments.

My month-long stay in retro familia generated a bonded look at our painful never-to-be's. Denial dilution ate away at our momentary uplift, and a dark, melancholic cloud gathered. During our marriage I had fancied myself a combination of Gil Scott-Heron's soulful intelligence, John Sebastian's cool goofiness, with Waylon Jennings's middle finger empowering Marvin Gaye's brash opposition to what was going on. My deity's phone number had been planted on Lennon's speed-dial as cocaine flourished under its advert of harmlessness, circa 1979. It all added up to an out-of-control, overmedicated brother who had driven his first bride batty. Little did I know that the loss of the naiveté and security of one's first impactful love was the only hit allowed off of that pipe.

Memories of our oil-versus-water angst produced footage in my mind of the painful past when I drunkenly mistook Gerri's beloved potted-plant arrangement for a urinal. This gross act of miscalculation dissolved the blinders shielding our compatibilities' inherent dysfunction, leaving us with a paid-up lifelong purchase of unused love that slowly soured in storage. The most painful puzzle I would never solve was the clash between Gerri's love and my hedonistic, artistically inclined curiosity. Her terrestrial teenaged presence enriched my youth beyond any scenario imaginable, but one of the major snakebites on high-school-sweetheart mythology is the belief that youthful inexperience and arrogance make "forever together" a perceptible certainty. In a time of instant erections, with pert, ripening breasts playing smartly, the "love is enough" cotton candy spins fluffily on its cone. Under the weight of time and scrutiny, that cotton can contract into a less-than-enticing, shriveled red sickle of bad sugar.

Of the slight mist of confusing what-ifs that permeate life's backlog, the scent that stands out most prominently is that of the first woman a man touches all four bases with, an indelible benchmark. What an oddity that one of time's sweetest fragrances would fertilize soil, producing rows of unsightly ache-ids. I sensed that we were closing out the final statement of our teenagers-to-parents union, and I was hell-bent on anesthetizing the pain as the final curtain fell.

With our limitations bench-pressing four times our options' weight, I took a stab at calling my old friend John Ballard. It was a desperate roll of "what the hell" dice up against the back alley's wall in hope of a lucky readout. Upon contact and an all-points update, Ballard tossed me a Southern Californian life raft, offering the opportunity to work and live with him. There was one splashy caveat: I had to provide my own transport.

Gerri and my ideas bowled spares attempting to score the funds to fuel a California strike. Our dearth of prospects sent me on a feeble-minded rummage through clumps of papers in my back pocket that had been sat on since New York. Buried in the crumpled matter was an abused page from an old phone book with Bruce Willis's number. I dialed the number, and, after going through two or three paid filters, the phone found Bruce. He offered an unchanged friend's welcome. At this point our worlds resided on opposite sides of the spittoon, but he was still full Bruno. He was in the throes of negotiating with the unreality that comes with a runaway winner's accuracy in LA's high-hang district. Bruce's television show was still popular as he readied his pole for the difficult vault into feature films. He had just completed his first shot, *Blind Date*, with Kim Basinger.

My bizarre appearance in Geraldo's theater found its way back to Bruce, so he wasn't surprised that I'd been bitten by street rock. But he was happy and relieved that I was on the AA train and immediately offered to pay for my flight out. He was hip to the fact that the recovery initiative in California was sweeping the entertainment community and thought it was a good idea for me to continue my recovery in that vibe. His filters took care of my ticket, on top of wiring a thousand beans of esteem. I slapped two-thirds of the coin on Gerri. The money wallpapered the airport sadness with delusional thoughts of tomorrows that would dissipate by the time my LA-bound plane reached Phoenix.

Nineteen eighty-seven began to smell like a good year, or such was the feeling as John Ballard whisked me from LAX. By nightfall, I'd encountered three ladies who escorted me to a party in Beverly Hills. My flip from hell to Hills in one leap was one of life's magical hors d'oeuvres.

The next day I went to an AA meeting, seeking to lather the edge off of my grandiosity. This simple positive action led me to one of the most fascinating person's imaginable, Rift Fournier. Rift was a prominent producer in the industry who helped pioneer television's celebrity-talk-show addiction. He had a syndicated show on the air and had recently filmed up-close video profiles on the likes of Ray Charles and several other deep-grooved show-business luminaries. Rift was an exceptional athlete and star hockey player, who would have had his pick of athletic scholarships had he not been two-by-foured by the disease of polio. He would spend his entire adult life in a wheelchair, but you'd never know it, given the power and character emmanating from his presence.

He was chairing the meeting when I caught his eye. At the close he surprised me by asking that I lead the Serenity Prayer. I drew a startled blank, and Rift chimed in with the first couple of words, pulling me back. After the meeting he rolled over and laid his rap of introduction down. I discovered that Rift had earned his enticingly post-fifty, weathered charisma firing from behind the soul of a Black jazz musician who kept his own time to the rhythms he played. Similar to Rift's successful hack at disability, he'd managed to transcend his Caucasian birth stamp on his all-encompassing journey on the road to sobriety cool.

"Come with me," Rift commanded. He led me to his specially built automobile, equipped to accommodate his "crippled thing." He got into the car, effortlessly swinging his dead legs under the wheel, shattering my impulse to patronize his condition. Rift had every conventional reason to shout epithets at the hand he'd drawn, and yet he became indignant at the suggestion that his disability was anything more than an annoying allergy. We cruised back and forth on Sunset Boulevard for hours, with Rift encouraging me to spill my fears, loves, hates, and mistakes. He was part Chuck Griffin, part Jimmy Cagney—a genuine tough guy who didn't take shit from a little bit. I'm the easiest lay in the world for mentors of his stripe, and I pounced on Rift's offer to be my West Coast AA sponsor.

Gail Sheehy called to nudge me closer to writing my crack anecdotes. It seemed like years had melted in the few short months since Gail had applied salve to my crack-parched spirits. I was now ready to take her suggestion seriously and began sketching a number of street-rock war stories. Sobriety freshened my perspective as I applied the varnish to American pigments' urban holocaust. The bizarre jazz chord in the mix was the amazing fact that I was stitching my sludge together seated on the outdoor patio of a beach restaurant, sipping club soda, with McGuinn and the Bryds pumping "Mr. Spaceman" live through my headphones. The song's zany energy collaborated nicely with the sound of the waves rolling in.

My timing as a recovering addict in late eighties LA was fruitful. It seemed like everyone who was anyone was in the program. Rift took me to a number of high-profile AA meetings that were filled with actors, directors, and producers of considerable bump. My sober run through Rift's star-studded pens of chemical befuddlement restored my appetite for a good game of spangled White ball. My integrationist convictions played in my favor in this makeshift community's search for answers more powerful than their own. Respect for Rift was so high that his tailwind afforded those he sponsored first-class treatment. The recovery seekers were painted in a demure shade of selfless white that boinked my crossover jones. Commiserating with rich, successful recovering junkies in a new BMW on the freeway amplified the distance between the privileged Caucasian Twelve-Step brigade and their darker-skinned brethren whose enlightenment was often found in death or jail. Had I not sought to believe in a colorblind America, I would have been Black-whacked along with the other bottom feeders at the tail end of this insidious disease.

On an electrifying night to be an LA have, a friend borrowed the use of an office that was located on Venice Beach. The lively freak shows that powered the boardwalk's daytime left with the sun, and the night shift's haunting stillness lured the thick-walleted romantic callers to its shore's edge. Our purpose was to lay down the final anecdote in my crack collection for Gail. My lovely patron's enthusiastic commitment to the work spiked the creative impulse upward, and the words began to play like musical notes. With my friend on the keyboard, I narrated the story of Iris, a beautiful, young Puerto Rican woman, whose crack addiction eventually took her apart in layers. I'd witnessed her first pull on hot glass, and by evening's end, after dragging her extraordinary beauty through a gutter of slimy, two-bit dealers, the sun would find her awash in empty crack vials. A startlingly swift character makeover pained those like myself who knew her, and in the time it took for one to spell the words *crack whore*, Iris would be on the wrong side of a sheet that was being drawn over her face. A homicidal blowjob for crack swap found her knees in a tight squeeze, when a maniacally psychotic trick forced Iris to swallow a coke bottle for his perverted pleasure.

As the anecdote drew to a close my guts were churning over the untapped beauty and sensitivity that my tempestuous street victim had left on the table. Suddenly, it was as though gratitude inhaled a popper, lifting humility so high that I was inspired to bow to the grace of a power greater than myself that had spared me from Iris's fate. I went to the window, searching for something to thank, and was greeted by a klieg blast of a full moon. Its voltage was so strong that it brightened the foam at the end of each wave until it sparkled. I felt like one fortunate Black American.

Capping Iris's memory portended the end of my LA recovery. I'd gotten into fantastic physical shape, made a few dollars, and, with Rift's dutiful head slaps reminding me that sobriety was what refeathered the phoenix, I was ready to fly east with the intention of reengaging with my biracial family.

TWENTY-NINE

My lurid anecdotes preceded my arrival in New York. Guarded skepticism was an attitudinal uptick indicating my increased respect for the game of hope. I found a job as a bicycle messenger and tore ass around the city, inhaling car and bus exhaust for a living. My sobriety was to encounter its sternest test when I found my way back to Leola's lair. With no place else to live, Rift convinced me to gulp the arsenic that came with a bed under my mother's roof. Leola was at her drill-sergeant best, making the living conditions difficult. She attributed my problems to the lack of God in my life and marrying "that White gal." Every night without fail my mother would crack open a new keg of fire-and-brimstone at her religious tavern. As bartender she served one drink, the Lord's word, and the bottle was stamped 100 PROOF. Two shot glasses and I was whacked out of my head. It was hell, but I accepted Rift's notion that penance built character.

I clung tightly to a rigorous AA-influenced workout schedule, enabling me to retain the stiffness my upper lip required when forced to surf through the flaming echo of clicking cigarette lighters igniting stems filled with bad intentions. Hopscotching through my deadliest weakness required the help of a strong support system: California Rift, New York Vic, and a new addition to the team, John O'Donohue, who ponied up his experiences gained in a twelve-step sobriety résumé in its fifth year. These guys stabilized my walls of containment, hunting down and destroying red flags before they surfaced.

"You need God, boy! You need God!" were the words fueling my fourth most dominant influence's 3:00 A.M. proclamation, anointing my misfortune of being on her late-shift God-patrol beat. Leola's wake-up blast rattled me out of a dead sleep with a vengeful hammerhead's force. My mother's smash-mouth enlightenment was lovingly intended, but her love stung. In an act of exasperation I called Barbara Kopple, and she invited me to live in the loft that housed her company, Cabin Creek Films. I acted as a helpful anything guy to support my weight on the premises. Barbara was mindful to keep the cupboards filled with staples, and her Cabin Creek vittles kept me going.

My LA crack anecdotes' fortunes were swelling like Jiffy Pop, when an enthusiastic conversation with Gail alerted me to a meeting scheduled with *Vanity Fair*'s Tina Brown. My crud bits were timed well, coinciding with the mainstream's whitening-hot focus on crack, and suddenly I was a legitimate flavor of interest. Several days later I was moving my head about like a confused yard dog as an elevator lifted me to the clouds section of the Condé Nast Building, where I was to meet *Vanity Fair*'s head person. I'd heard bits and pieces about Tina Brown before the meeting, and the portrait drawn was that of an erudite UK wordsmith. My ignorance prepared me for a tea-sipping Thatcher-esque figure, so when a born-blond, hot, fashion-pampered, late-Boomer power babe extended her hand, all my preconceptions flew out the window. I was impressed by the sensual thrust behind Tina's sharp journalistic instincts when she jabbed her vision into a writer's consciousness. She would brandish her viewpoint on the author's mind's torso leaving nary a bruise. Tina was a late-1980s set companion in the rising female executive's chest of stilettos encased in velvet.

Also attending the meeting was Wayne Lawson, the magazine's executive literary editor. His task would be to shepherd me through my virgin print run. As Tina Englished on about the direction of the piece, I was having a difficult time holding on to a straight face. I couldn't believe that the recent psychological rat shit I'd ingested in tenement basements would lead me to the highest paying writing job I'd ever scored. When Wayne and I began working on "Between the Cracks" in late 1987, he didn't know that I was a writer who had gone through a crack experience. His read-up was that he'd be working with a former crack addict with a single-shot tale to tell. My determination to impress Wayne produced the best writing of my career. His attention to the melodious tones between the written words inspired a revival of forgotten lessons from my failed musicians' stab. This observation changed my approach to writing. I discovered that many of my almost-good-enough musical impulses that had disappointed me now invigorated my prose with a score to boogie to. Drafts became musical charts, and my instinct to compose buzzed my craft. Wayne's delight was fueled by the open depth I brought to our good chemistry that sautéed the vignette of the gifted editor and grateful student who generate a simpatico that rarely ebbed.

After the meeting I was high on a cloud as I headed down to Cabin Creek cradling my new bundle of opportunities. I had been clean for about eight months, and the world had pulled back its blinds. The road back to Anne was moving forward, but there were obstacles. I had to address the damage I'd laid on her family. I would rather have ingested monkey-shit tablets than face Jack. I'd fired some horrible blanks at a man who was a straight-shooter.

I had only seen him once since my return from the West Coast. I had come to visit Keelan and waited for him outside on the lawn, avoiding contact. As Anne readied Keelan, I was left to play the inconspicuous big Black guy on a Bellmore, Long Island, sidewalk. The moments felt like bricks as I shuffled with the agony of dragging the McCormack family through the cans, bottles, and crack vials that lined the curbs of West Harlem's ghetto streets. I'd fulfilled the worst White fear scenario of the stereotypical nigger moving into the neighborhood, exhibiting bone-nosed-crude behavior, subsequently dragging the community's property value down. It was clear that I had a date with the back of Jack's hand.

After five minutes that lasted an hour, Keelan came running out of the house. He made a dash for me, offering a much-needed hug. Jack emerged and walked into the yard. I hailed from a distance as he attended to a minor yard detail. He turned and said, "Hello, how ya doing?"

"Fine," I said.

He turned and went back into the house, but his demeanor had offered a glimmer of hope.

Anne's and my choice to give our marriage another go was hastened by Jack and Ellen's decision to buy a house in Avon, Connecticut. This put Anne on the choose seat, with her next move depending upon our move. The dilemma forced the music out into the open: Should she stay or should I go?

I reached out to John O'Donohue, who at the time was engulfed in his own marital separation. This allowed for us to become brothers-in-exile. We were fighting different addictions: mine, substances, and his, a bad romance that had his heart by the throat. I gave wise counsel when it came to relationships other than my own, and John had mastered the rudiments of sobriety. The shoe wore well.

One Saturday afternoon, John came to Cabin Creek to visit and we got to talking about Jack and the family. I asked if there was any way he might help me break Jack's ice. John was a McCormack favorite, an Irish Catholic cop who had ascended to the rank of lieutenant in the NYPD. Jack had been out of the cop game for ten years, but he still had a number of friends on the force. They often turned notes into chatter on occasions like Keelan's christening, where grandfather and godfather made deposits on an easy friendship. John didn't leap into my plea. He equated the chore of cracking an Irishman's skepticism to pouring warm water on a block of granite expecting its dissolution, particularly with my intention being to approach Jack without warning. But I laid it on heavy, and the scuff marks on the knees of my rap won him over. He agreed to act as a friendly broker at a Long Island sit-down.

The following day John pulled up in a total piece of shit for a car. The sight of the embattled vehicle fired up my nerves, and I had to suppress the urge to construct a bad omen. I hoped that Jack wouldn't be on the front lawn when we gasped up. We honked, belched, and stalled on the Long Island Expressway, knotting my stomach into a spaldeen, before arriving at Jack's crib. The family was preparing for its move to Connecticut, and much of the furniture and other belongings had been shipped out. Anne, Keelan, and Ellen were at the beach, and Jack was occupied supervising moving activity. The emptiness in the house was numbing, bearing little resemblance to the place where so many good times had played. Jack walked through our surprise appearance with blinders, choosing to focus on his work, while John and I wrung our hands sitting in the area that a kitchen had once warmed.

When Jack joined us, the gesture read like a distracted courtesy nod. John rolled up his sleeves and attempted to cut through the density of an uncomfortable silence. He tossed his line into their mutual well of blue fraternity, and they slowly fished out topics for conversation. I sat there planted in silence as the two of them rapped. Surprisingly, when John sought to lure me into the conversation, after a moment of silence, Jack nodded me in. It was becoming apparent that Jack had done a bit more carpentry on his olive branch than I had dared to imagine. I talked about the *Vanity Fair* deal, careful not to oversell my new beginning. With the humility of a chastened bullshit artist, I made my footprints light. Jack was reasonably responsive to my interlude, but it was also clear that my new show-business hopes and dreams were thinnish air.

Anne, Keelan, and Ellen returned home to the surprise of the three of us, still sitting together. John greeted everyone warmly, inspiring Ellen to roll the dice by inviting him and me to join them for dinner at her sister's house. Anne's Aunt Mary and Uncle Don were favorites of mine. Don was a retired New York City fireman, and I had a hero thing for firemen. I used to tell him, "You guys are the toughest because you can't bullshit fire." He was a textbook example of a guy I expected to gag on Nigraphobia, but we kicked it together from the outset. I was a smoker, and Don's calendar had pushed him into the age of having to sneak his butts around family and medical trip wires. When we would burn one in the basement, it gave us the opportunity to discover crossover New York roots that ran through Satchmo's music to the all-engaging sports pages. He was a memorable stripe in a flag I was darning in protest of the bum sticker of inflexibility glued to white-haired civil servants' character.

It was a pleasant evening, sprinkled with flecks of healing. I understood why the family would have a hard time reinvesting in me, but it was harder on Anne who had to make the sale. She had to convince them that I would not pull my Black-junkie burnout act again. The dearth of data on cocaine recidivism, whose high percentage would subsequently stun the recovery trade, was not available when Anne went to bat for the authenticity of my shiny new focus. Her determination to restart our hearts together left her out on the shaky plank of indemnifying my sobriety. As the night wore on, the ice between Jack and me began to drip. Jack's fondness for me, along with the upward graph my sobriety was riding, would induce the old codger to take a tentative gamble on burying the hatchet slowly. In turn, I would offer mounds of verifiable evidence to support his risky wager.

Despite the difficult work that lay ahead, I took time to swoon over the uniqueness of my American experience. The Black guy's beloved Irish friend clears a path for the Black guy's reconnection with his Irish roots—an odd, diverse compilation found only beneath the American umbrella.

When I told my mother that I was going back to Anne, she and I were drawn into a ram-butt confrontation. "Irish root!" she proclaimed, suggesting that Anne was practicing in the Celtic version of the old-world Black word *rooted*. My mother's version of this treachery described the manner in which a woman turns the object of affection into a helpless sycophant by mixing her menstrual fluids into her cooking. "I don't know how the Irish do it, but everybody got their ways. You gonna go back to the girl that turned her back on you?" she questioned. "You dumb, boy; you the smartest of the dumb." Her steadfast plutonium blew up my intentions, and the debris flew with impunity.

My mother's hi-fi noise was drowned out by the stereophonic hit I would take from a significantly more influential resource. "Are you Black or White, motherfucker, because the room between the two has been boarded up?" Chuck exhorted.

He thought that my marriage-resuscitation effort was misguided Tom-ism. Chuck's slap left a reality print indicating I was on the wrong end of an unintended yank of my dark roots from its soil. The separation would drain half of the color from my vision. I'd turned once too often toward my penchant for selling rock 'n' roll to its forepersons, but in this heated racial climate I was munching on Molotov collard greens, subsequently blowing my face off its pigment identification card. My refusal to accept Chuck's non-negotiable "enough White is enough" ultimatum provoked his dropping my ass on a suburban curve and driving off for a decade before glimpsing in the rearview mirror. By the end of the eighties the split would be so wide and the isolation so profound that I would emerge as the only Black person in my dreams.

Shortly before Anne's parents left for Connecticut, she told them of her intention to stay on Long Island. Her reentry into the pigment zone was met by a racist welcome mat from housing agents bent on potholing her search for an apartment. A perversely enlightening process would begin upon Anne's finding suitable living quarters. Her affirmative reaction would act as a starter pistol, setting the landlord's heart racing over the prospect of adding an affable, pretty, single White woman to the roster. The rent snatcher's wet dream would climax with an oral agreement. Subsequently, Anne would bring her mother, along with our three-year-old toddler, whose large brown eyes peered affectionately from behind a face tinted in gold, to map out decorative possibilities. In each case the landlord would break out in a rash of Jim Crow–tosis upon sighting Keelan's biracial brew. With the force of the degradation that accompanied an egg-pelted ambush, Anne and Ellen would be stung by the apartment's instant unavailability.

Their multiple experiences with blatant institutionalized racism provided a rare look at what White people of goodwill find difficult to believe exists. My beloved pigment novices were forced to view a racist esteem jack from the front row. Anne's son was darkening the face she saw in the mirror, activating the Black shark smarts of a deceptive survivalist. The choice of riding her White-ness back into demand ached because it meant hiding her son's identity. But gritted teeth lost out to the painful reality of having to do business with an insidiously corrupt clan of obstruction mongers. In short order, under the "White is right" resolution, Anne scored an apartment in Freeport, Long Island. This experience hammered into place her final sociological enlightenment plank. Repeated arbitrary prejudicial sightings burned off the last layer of her reflexive White denial. The completion of Anne's reality infusion boded well for the enormous undertaking of mothering an African American male.

I arrived back in Anne's life with an ebullient sobriety, highlighted by a *Vanity Fair* job. Within a month of our reunion, we found ourselves on Jones Beach being photographed by a professional photographer. The completed article had boarded the vanity portion of the Tina Brown express that was idling in the station.

The LA anecdotes delivered the *Vanity Fair* piece a stark portrait of the urban crack cocaine experience. Tina's instinct to leapfrog her demographic competitors by slipping my lurid tale into the '87 Christmas issue, bordered by profiles of Bette Midler and the incandescent Fred Astaire, added an eye-widening edge to her Yuletide greeting. Her deft timing and unusual sense of humor resulted in a career-solidifying success.

When the article hit the stands, the unvarnished peril that came with crack addiction, housed in Tina's perfumed, literary bordello, struck a resounding chord. As with most topical matter, gutty, societal pulse reading wins the match. The popularity of the article was so pervasive that HBO optioned the work before its newsstand value expired. I was hired to write the screenplay, which created an opportunity to join the Writer's Guild, bestowing a degree of perceived professionalism upon me. The wide buzz was reminiscent of the days when Noel and I were frequent flyers in crystal White society. I was again speaking at countless upscale gatherings of influential White folks who were answering a call to arms in the war on drugs. My balanced fortune prompted an interest in young Republicans. I became intrigued with the possibility of reconciling my differences with their party. Reagan's watch had so soured me on the promise of his America that I again committed the sin of painting all White conservatives with the same ignorant race-dipped brush.

One of my old Hotchkiss buddies, a Republican good guy, invited me to speak at the Young Republican's Club about ghetto turmoil. I was seated by an attractive young woman whose effervescence produced its own electrical currency. Her name was Ann Liguori. Ann was a radio sports jockey swimming against the tide of male resistance in a profoundly sexist industry. She would break ground, break balls, and break hearts as part of the first group of pioneer women to settle the wild terrain of the male locker room. We both had the type of personality that lent itself to instant friendship. My sportsology bent was floored by her determination to fight the good fight against the specter of White male exclusion in the world of play.

I delivered my rap to the young conservative pups with nonjudgmental zeal. The invigorating high wattage emanating from this pool of bright Republican energy was reminiscent of a good Hotchkiss night out. I told of my recent excursion into the bowels of their city's most fearsome eyesores before steering their focus toward the statistical fact that a relatively small percentage of the Black population comprised the news-friendly violence and tomfoolery that defined Black citizenship. The pigment majority was comprised of a pool of evolving Americans ripe for a solid pitch to join a new team. The needle on their response swung into the pep-rally zone on the enthusiasm meter. After a slew of thoughtful, insightful questions increased my perception's stamina, the house was vibrating with possibility. My megalomaniacal teaser was a surefire shelf life casualty. Sadly, my deaf-eared Repups would sign on to the Horton-ization of the 1988 electoral joust. The short-term wins that Black political footballs produced were too great to pass up.

Several months after the crack article's windstorm settled, I was contacted by Barney Collier, writer and editor for *American Way* magazine. His reading of "Between the Cracks" led him to offer me an assignment, but I was apprehensive. The unique elements that led to the success and excitement of the crack piece was a once-in-a-lifetime experience, and I was content to close that book while ahead. But Barney Collier wouldn't give up. He continued to pitch his considerable woo my way, prodding periodically and increasing the attractiveness of his offer. As the *V-Fair* glow surrounding my finances began to dissipate, his persuasiveness grew. Finally, I made one of my better decisions when I accepted the assignment to write "Pilgrim Among the Privileged," a retrospective view of my Hotchkiss days.

I was still relatively ignorant as to the print game, and was fortunate to land in Barney Collier's basket of literary obsessions, a productive journalistic finishing school if ever there was one. I enjoyed a sense-memory implosion quarterbacking my return to Hotchkiss under Barney's tutelage. Much of Barney's career was spent as a foreign correspondent who fished and snagged dangerous gets like Latin American revolutionary, Che Guevara. Whereas Wayne Lawson's touch had been that of a symphonic conductor, Barney's chops were more likely to have been tendered in the midst of jungle crossfire. His world-honed sensibilities marinated in the frightful realities of Third World atrocities had somehow produced a nimble, risk-taking optimist who believed that there was no bottom to a story and the writer with the deepest well of inquiry honors the craft's intent most. Topic matter and stewardship fused into a cathartic labor of love, allowing me to reconnect with my upper-middle-class-to-sky-box-level White roots. My return was highlighted by the discovery that many from my past offered glowing retrospective accounts of my contribution to the Hotchkiss community. After this invaluable affirmation, the coin I was drawing for the assignment became house money.

In the midst of a frenzy of activity, I received a call from Wayne informing me of Tina's decision to offer me another assignment. Topping this mind boom off, the gig was a cover story on Bruce Willis. Bruce had become TV's hottest heat-seeking missile since the Travolta launch in the mid-seventies. With a hit show and two feature films to his credit, the breadth of Bruce's opportunities had secured him a place in one of our generation's culturally infused snowballs that the success god let roll from atop a snowy mountain. Its rapid descent increased the bauble's circumference, allowing it to achieve boulder status in the celebrity flatlands. He was receiving a grade-A education working with the likes of James Garner, Malcolm McDowell, Cybill Shepherd, and Eva Marie Saint, high-altitude stuff for a guy who, three skinny years earlier, was washing his chops' laundry on ghetto stages.

The most fascinating element of Bruce's success was that his early days had suggested he would freak out under such intense pressure, but I'll be damned if he wasn't practically driving his own bus through the hills of Hollywood success. He hadn't shed all of his New York–barroom bluster, bringing on the occasional swath of bad publicity, but as was predicted back in our old pre-rehearsal bullshit sessions, American White guys fell in love with him. His fans were drawn to his biracial concoction—the Elvis thing. Bruce was strapped in to all the requirements the legendary Sam Phillips of Sun Records had cited for popular success: burning desire, legitimate talent, and credibility that only a few early blue-collar scuff marks could garner. Add the all-important dose of Black do-it fluid, and the explosive concoction comes rocking out the petri dish with enough rhythm to bring sober teenage girls to orgasm.

Bruce found himself in unchartered waters when receiving a then-whopping five million dollars for an action movie called *Die Hard*. The industry went a little bat shit over Bruce's unprecedented coin snatch. His first two pictures had made money but didn't bust any blocks, and the industry feared impending gate collapses by the force of heavyweight moneymakers like Stallone and Schwartzenegger. It was a dicey gamble by Fox because Bruce was TV, and the public was unpredictable about which size screen they wanted their heroes' images on.

As our pot boiled over, with the first draft of the HBO project's deadline looming and four other suddenly viable commitments, Anne's editorial responsibilities were put under extraordinary pressure. Her decade of plow work as a wordsmith duckling answered the difficult call with a swan's maturity. In a fifteen-month period she would coax four drafts from four different projects out of a harried writer, racing to ingest the overflow that ran down the sides of his suddenly crammed plate.

A few days after accepting the assignment, I spoke to Bruce and we established from the outset that we would play it straight up, letting the most interesting chips fall on the pages. Within days I was on an aerodynamic javelin headed for California, hiding beneath my Walkman, listening to Marvin Gaye's last studio album, *Midnight Love*. I clung tightly to Marvin's music. His voice kept things

Black enough to strike a balance between reality and the insanity I was enjoying. My quick return to LA as an important media guy had my old rehabilitation friends bursting with pride. When attending AA meetings and sharing my good fortune, I was embraced as a symbol of the miraculous powers of sobriety. In one year I had gone from helpless and hopeless to hanging out and happening.

The roach in the potato salad was contending with the fact that this wasn't the America I'd fancied; this one was almost totally White. When you arrived at the airport in Los Angeles and your business was with the communications machinery, Black people ceased to exist. Rift Fournier took me to dinner at a fancy, industry-hip oceanside restaurant. Before the club soda arrived I bitched, "Where's the niggers?"

"Pallie," he laughed, "White people are too busy fighting for their own freedom to care much about yours. This brain malfunction you have about people coming together is fool's gold. Times have changed, and that bell don't chime no more."

Rift took his hard-earned right to shoot straight seriously. The intensity boost in his eyes would rise to the level of a blitzing linebacker's when he turned up the volume.

"In the sixties, the objective was how much we could do to help Blacks. Now the issue is what can the Blacks do for me? With the exception of the exceptional, White people don't think much about your citizenship. People made a lot of money under Reagan, and it changed the game. Wise up, better men have crumbled under that much piety. That shit could drive you back to the pipe. This little *Vanity Fair* swish you got going is as meaningless to me as that cheap boiled-down shit you used to smoke. Remember that? I'm not in your life to keep up with your fluffy fantasies. My concern is your sobriety, so here's the raw: Make the most of your special nigger status for as long as it holds up and go to a lot of meetings. The key to your life is staying sober, and the best way for you to get the most out of that half bucket of talent you have is not falling into the trap of thinking that you're as great as you have to believe you are in order to make it. Read me, Pallie?"

The intensity in Rift's eyes subsided, until his demeanor's flaccidity left him quietly picking at his fish. I juggled mixed emotions: respect for the honesty in Rift's sponsorship against my inability to accept his stark skinny on America.

After that sobering hit from Riftsville, I commenced work on Bruce's trip. Our first meeting was in his trailer on the Fox lot, where he was shooting his *Moonlighting* series. In between setups he would dash over to the editing rooms and work on his *Die Hard* picture, which was also financed by Fox. The time between our work and his success was so short that internal changes were hardly visible. The obligatory PR star shield that protected him from the public was now firmly in place, but in dimmer light Bruno was the same guy—pinball active to the max, with more expensive toys.

He was living in a house on the beach in Malibu, and it was here with his star garb closeted that Bruce could ooze with the wowie of his existence, exhibiting some of the "why me" twitches of a big Lotto winner. Before a budding superstar processes his or her altered state, a whole lot of faking is going on. But his amazement favored humility over arrogance, so the extra half-hop in his step was inspiring. His recent Emmy award for his characterization of David Addison in *Moonlighting* meant a lot to him. Bruce was vulnerable to critical shots at his acting ability. He picked up the award and held it proudly. Unfortunately, it was only temporary salve for a wound that would never completely heal.

In the midst of Bruce's wattage, his stunning wife, Demi Moore, who was in her third trimester of pregnancy, entered the room. Her sharp Liz Taylor–esque beauty snapped Bruce to attention, and his shit-eating smile validated the fact that it was her world, and we were mere servile inhabitants. This brought out the bowing and scraping that typified the stereotypical oafish American man's way of dealing with pregnancy, as Bruce focused on her slightest whim. His attention span was fraying as his long day sought to settle in with his woman. I took the cue and made my departure.

The following day I met the photographer who would be working the piece. I didn't know very much about photography, so when Annie Leibowitz was introduced to me, her sharp, engaging, pertinent sense of humor was taken at face value. I wasn't aware that she was a high-powered figure trucking a platinum résumé. My ignorance served me well, affording the chance to work in an awe-stripped atmosphere with a great artist. It was fun. Annie and her staff did their bit shooting Bruce, while I spent much of the day with Demi watching a young woman in her twenties grapple with the onrushing changes she'd undertaken. Pregnant and married to one of the hottest stars in Hollywood was quite a meal. An actress of note, Demi pushed the pause button on her career, choosing to focus on the baby's blossoming during her maiden pregnancy. Her knight in studio armor was at her beck and call, and for the moment Demi's star glowed brightest in Bruce's far-flung galaxy.

Bruce was taking a number of pictures on the beach in a white linen suit, with the ocean backing him up. From a distance, through the patio's large glass doors, I watched the best image-capturers in the business buff the Jersey boy's ass like it was Gary Cooper's. A rush of vicarious thrill swept over me watching Bruce pose. I relished the optimism at the core of absurdity's sway on all things human.

On our last day together, we huddled over an editing machine on the studio lot, watching forty rough minutes of the film *Die Hard*. It was unnervingly good, as each scene played larger than the one before. A year later it would become apparent that after Schwarzenegger's and Stallone's success with their aloof superhero characters, Bruce offered a welcome change of pace as the action hero that a guy would feel comfortable doing shots with in a bar. Bruce's foible-tinged White-Black sense of humor was perfect for his characterization of John McClane, the superhero next door. The film's unusual sprinkling of plot-connected roles for Black actors was outstanding, and if Bruce wasn't directly responsible for this, I sure as hell know he wasn't uncomfortable.

The phenomenal success of *Die Hard* would bury the paltry five million dollars the industry was screeching about, by growing into a multisequel franchise that rained money into the swimming pools that matter for a decade, while boosting Bruce into a grassroots superstar, much like the other Jersey Bruce. At the end of Bruce's workday, we sat in the trailer trading barbs and insights, with a little bit of old Harlem retro jive. Before hopping a metal pony that was waiting to take me to the airport, I experienced the only sighting of confusion in the gig's space, when Bruce closed himself off in a tiny trailer compartment jammed with uniformed Hollywood percentage-seekers. I felt a subliminal hint of concern that Bruce's outstretched stardom could take him to some strange once in an only places.

My flight home was filled with thoughts of the unique wild-card quality underlying our Americanism. Those daring to dream can enter the national Easter-egg hunt, and the rare few who find the egg are transformed eons above their forceps humble forecast. Watching Bruce Willis's arc up close had generated some pretty satisfying thoughts about the American dream.

The article was a success, and apparently the piece helped assuage fears that Bruce's wild-man image would hurt the film. Demi said she thought it was the best piece written about her husband to that point. Wayne Lawson did a great job leading the assemblage of all the puzzle pieces I had brought home with me. A key was his tasteful respect for people's privacy as he encouraged me to dig deeper for compelling elements without rummaging through the target's bedroom drawers for bits of saleable depravity. The dignity salvaged in this exercise in Peeping Tomism made celebrity-stalking tolerable. With Tina Brown, the class of journalism's new, red-light district supporting our effort, a spectacular cover story of the subsequent blockbuster movie emerged, cementing Bruce's place in the big-dollar lava flow.

THIRTY

The Bruce story made me a hot Black freelancer for a splash of time. There were so few African Americans who did this gig that every time I showed up on the scene writing for A-list publications, like the *New York Times*, jaws would drop. It was an interesting front-seat to the show except for one dangling Bowie knife: the scene was unapologetically White. Disillusion was seeping in.

Meanwhile, on the other side of the divide, the Black folks' verdict was in: Fuck White folks! It wasn't as though they were harboring continuous anger; they had simply submitted to the neon fact that attempting to interact would bring disappointment. The NIGGERS NEED NOT APPLY sign had hung on too many doors for too long. Young Black and Latino leaders were breathing life into the corpses that littered the mean streets of the Bronx and Manhattan. The likes of Al Sharpton and Freddie Ferrer were emerging as grassroots difference-makers and knew that the passivity in Dr. King's integration message clanged off of this generation's ghetto-scorched ears. Activism that snorted when mistreated played into Reagan's polar-ization strategy, forcing Black leadership into White faces like never before. The historical result of sep-arate agitation produced a transcendent step for-ward with the presidential candidacy of Jesse Jackson initiating one of Dr. King's strongest dreams: pigmented legislative identity.

I was strung out on integration, so it was hard to return to the old neighborhood with my tottering philosophy. My vibe and delivery were drugs better suited for the disingenuous half-attempts made by liberal White toe-dippers. I'd become a lounge act with limited reach, a nowhere man's zone of duty.

Sour fumes began to emanate from my magazine run when *New York* magazine hired me to do a story about the growing chasm between Blacks and Whites. The premise asked the question: What happened to integration and all of its lofty goals during the sixties? This topic scared the shit out of me. I don't think I wanted the answers, but as always, money had the last word.

I interviewed a number of choice Blacks and Whites, from the ghetto to the White suites of power, and the consensus was that integration was an illusionary blip on the country's historical racial screen. The negativity and ambivalence that soaked the assignment was disappointing. The hostility that Blacks showed, along with the indifference of the Whites was depressing. My old friend from Hotchkiss, John Terenzio, summed up the prevailing sentiments in his interview when he opined, "It's over, Denny, the commitment isn't there." John's simple words were like weasels gnawing at my flesh. Once my closest White confidant, John had ingested the full Black-stereotype-busting experience, and yet, even he wrestled with the tentacles of exclusion.

My special nigger status was falling from its White branches as I threw my research against the wall, killing the story. Several months of disheartening face jobs with virtually every source I interviewed had ratified Rift Fournier's boiler-plate analysis as the basic law of the land. I was not happy, and with no one left to bluff, my privileges and opportunities began to disgust me. I lapsed into the worst of my bad demeanors, the big brood, where my penchant for optimism turned inward, kicking the shit out of my self-esteem. I shut down print opportunities, except for one.

I had written a piece for the *New York Times* that previewed an upcoming Broadway play, *Checkmate*. The production starred the first lady of Black dramatic theater, Ruby Dee, along with Paul Winfield and an old acquaintance, Denzel Washington. This article, which was accompanied by a Hirschfeld cartoon, brought me an interesting opportunity from the *Times* Sunday magazine. They wanted me to go to Miami to do a piece on the rush to prominence that the talented actress Melanie Griffith was making as a result of her star turn in Mike Nichols's brilliant comedy *Working Girl*. I didn't want to do it, but the well-cooked edict that one didn't turn down the *New York Times* seduced me into accepting a trip to Miami that would turn out to be a dangerously unwise blessing.

Within a few weeks I was seated at a Kennedy Airport bar in an ugly mood. The fact that Art Garfunkel's vocals on the *Bookends* album were feeding my Walkman didn't help. I was experiencing marginalized-Black attitudinal combustion.

The prisons were filling up with Black male flesh. It was difficult to think of anyone I knew from my past who had not been ensnared by the system. When old Lyndon Johnson freed the slaves in 1964, this couldn't have been what he envisioned. Too many of us stumbled through our second reconstruction period like drunken sailors on leave in a foreign country. We'd gone from victimization to incarceration. Hundreds of thousands of Black men's lives were terminated prematurely inside chambers of incarcerated horror. The judicial system was weighted so heavily against Black male skin that their guilt was virtually assured, and any additional haggling would be over time meted out. The Reagan administration's unremitting lashes kept the warehoused pigment stock at bay as 1988's White hunters made no distinction between the good Willie Hortons and the bad ones. We all felt at risk.

I was feeling hungry, angry, lonely, and tired when I boarded the plane. The stewardess blocked the entrance to first class, assuming I had made a false Black step. After showing her my ticket, I was compelled to help her through her embarrassment. I don't bash innocent race ignorance. We searched for ways to laugh about it as she committed to my comfort.

With my negatives on fire, I white-knuckled it with the engine's roar. My mind climbed back atop its soapbox, aching to hear beyond the absent sounds from the Black middle class. With the exception of our courageous clergy, the backbone of pigmented advancement was missing in plain view, unable or unwilling to fight the street-shitster image that desecrated their phenomenal amount of catch-up work in post-King America. Stevie Wonder's *Innervisions* came up through my Walkman, dousing the flames.

"I'm on my way to Miami to interview a movie star," I coached. "I should feel good about that. Here I am, sitting in first-class, eating shrimp cocktail; that should constitute a victory. Gratitude, damn it, gratitude. Change the music, pump some early Dylan." The drink that the stewardess was serving to the guy next to me looked three times its normal size. I shouted at myself, "Think about what that drink will do to you. Remember your last worst day. You don't want to go back to that insanity, do you? Hell no . . . I think? Gratitude. Think of what you have to lose. Two years ago you were street soot. You've come back from the dead. Brothers don't do that. How many times are you going to dance with the reaper before he takes your Black ass home with him?"

Joni Mitchell's "Judgement of the Moon and Stars (Ludwig's Tune)" provided a Band-Aid that seemed to stem the bleeding. As we descended upon Miami, I was thankful that I had dodged the big bullet. Walking though the terminal, I searched through my fancy leather carry-on bag for the address to my luxury hotel. While waiting for a cab, the insidious blade of addiction began to jab at me again. John Lennon screamed into my headphones about being crippled inside. As I entered the cab with my weaknesses in command, I instructed the driver, "Take me to the Black section."

My demons were kicking my ass as the cab driver searched for a cheap motel in the Black-hole section of Miami. We came upon a small hooker shack, and the cab driver wanted to know if I'd lost my mind. I told him some bullshit about researching a project, but he didn't buy in. I was already backing into the culture of deception with my dark hunger showing. It was a hot night, and the hooker shack was teaming with vermin. The entire establishment smelled like a butane-fired bowl of crack.

I approached a group of street niggers who had that drug feel to them and began to speak in our native tongue.

"Anyone out here straight?" which meant "Who has the drugs?"

One guy looked at my bag, and the sight of its well-kept leather sparked his interest. He asked, "You the po-lice?"

"If I am, that's your ass. If I'm not, you can get high all night. You a gambler?"

He examined me closely and his verdict, "What you want? I can get you anything."

By midnight I was seated with a burnt-out group of thirsty demons leering at me as my hands shook holding a bowl of rock. I was scared to death; I could feel myself transforming into that monster. Enshrouded in the smoke was all my good sense, leaving me naked with my old nemesis. The junkies paraded in and out of the room as I continued to pay and smoke. I had picked up my own private dealer who was supplying me on the spot. I was a sweating pool of mess, cramming C-notes into the glass menace. Suddenly, there was a loud bang at the door, a fear slap that knocked me out of my stupor. The junkies in the room sat quietly. I scrambled to find a weapon. With only an ashtray at my disposal, I ran to the door and bluffed, "What's up!"

"Open up," the voice on the other side yelled. "There's some people coming here and they gonna rob you."

It smelled like a setup. I threatened, "Tell them motherfuckers, if they want some . . . then bring some."

The voice spoke, "Why don't you let me in, man? I'm just trying to help."

"Bullshit, the Red Cross don't send niggers sound like you."

"Fuck you," shouted the voice. "It's yo' ass!"

I didn't answer; I held on to my ashtray as though it were a legitimate weapon. The voice on the other side remained silent. I backed away from the door, and, after minutes of tension, I told my dealer, "Sell me some more shit."

An hour later the threat was a distant memory. The dope fiends in the room looked like reptiles—taut, scaly, ashened predators—all Black, practicing death with no purpose. Did I want to die for nothing? I envisioned the headline: ANTI-DRUG FRAUD DIES OF OVERDOSE. I jumped to my feet and started screaming. It was an attack of mass hypocrisy. I had allowed for my indignation over the Black plight to bury me at the bottom of the plight's pole. I continued to scream obscenities at the top of my lungs, and the junkies scrambled like roaches when the lights are turned on. I started throwing motherfuckers out. After their departure, I attempted to break my drug paraphernalia, but with each thrust the pipe stuck to my hand. With product still on the premises, I couldn't bring myself to do it.

At 3:00 A.M. I was searching for my bottom. At this point I was smoking death every five minutes, hours before I was to interview a movie star. The drug had turned me into a sprinkler; I was sweating like a pig. I called Anne in a panic, confessing that I had slipped and fallen hard. She called my manager and friend, Josh Silver, and he quickly called me. Josh went into career-saving mode, and he concocted a bullshit story to buy time. The cockamamie pudding he whipped up was that I had been robbed and was the victim of horrible circumstances. Josh was one of the best friends I'd ever had, and his love for his clients rivaled that of Broadway Danny Rose's, but it was clear this wouldn't fly. I agreed because it was either that or all-out panic. He convinced me to flush the remaining drugs down the toilet. We fought over that one, but I complied. Josh quickly hung up in order to lay the false tracks with Melanie's people.

As I lay prostrate on a drug-soiled bed, ten paces beyond wired, sleep was an impossibility. Even chain-smoking had lost its appeal. I got up and ran to the bathroom to examine the toilet bowl once more to see if any of the crack had resurfaced. I cursed my attitude: using Black anger as an excuse for self-destruction. What kind of cockeyed bullshit was that? I had crawled up under the toenails of pure niggerdom—unreliable, incompetent, and full of shit. I wanted to run, but there was no place to hide. Sanity's sliver preached, "You're going to get up, shower, and fall on your sword."

The hot, humid Miami morning had the drugs pouring through my sweat ducts. On the way to the interview I stopped to pick up a role of paper towels and wiped my brow and chest continuously, but the droplets were in free fall. I had trouble walking in the lobby of the hotel because of a jarred depth perception. I found a phone and called Anne, who adamantly opposed the big lie Josh had cooked. She wanted me to level with Melanie. I disagreed, because I thought the truth would end my career. The phone booth was filling with irony. It was crack that made me, and now it was going to snuff it all. Personal responsibility weighed heavily over my head, when I entered the elevator with sweat-a-poppin'. The ascent to my downfall was a quick one.

I was greeted by an assistant at the elevator who led me to the production offices. Melanie Griffith and Don Johnson had two floors to themselves to do their business. This was the final year of Johnson's *Miami Vice*, the volcanically successful television cop show. The assistant inquired about my health, as I dabbed my forehead and neck with the paper towel. I told her I was trying to adjust to the Florida heat. She seemed to buy that, but it was not her job to wonder why.

I sat in the waiting room with my now squishy paper towel, when, suddenly, one of the most beautiful women I've ever seen up close entered the room. She was fashionably lean, dressed in tight black jeans. This was the closest I'd ever been to someone with Marilyn Monroe–like charisma. Her deep-dish foxiness was so consuming that for an instant I forgot how terrible I felt. Melanie's reaction was the unkindest cut of all: her selflessness was painfully sympathetic over my fake mugging. I shuttered beneath the lie, increasing my guilt, which increased my sweat. She wanted to call the police and stir up a ruckus on my behalf. I've never met anyone so willing to stroke a gargoyle. Such a sweetheart, and I'd let her down by not bringing my best.

Having already made a fool out of myself, I wasn't going to do the same to her. I asked if there was somewhere we could talk in private. We entered a side room, and I was literally squinting from the starlight that framed her face. I managed to croak out the words, "I fucked up." Her smile drew lines of confusion, and I reiterated sternly, "I fucked up." This got her attention. I drew a deep breath into my sore lungs, released it, and said, "After two years of sobriety, I had a terrible slip last night, a complete meltdown. I've been up all night slamming it hard. I'm unprepared to do this interview, and at the moment I'm scared as hell."

Melanie paused for what felt like a month. I tensed up, waiting for the temperamental shrapnel to fly. Finally, she said, "I'm nine months sober, and I understand what you're going through."

A deal-making point for the existence of a god was evidenced by the incredible result of my honesty. Before long the movie star and I were sharing war stories about our weakness for drugs. I was dazed, caught between too good to be true and more than I deserved. I confessed my fear of being exposed, with the *New York Times* steamrolling my career's little shack. She offered me full protection, but first I had to do something for her.

"Anything," I answered. *Angel of mercy*, I thought.

She insisted that I go to an AA meeting with her immediately.

"Is that it?" I whimpered.

Melanie rubbed my shoulders and said, "That's it."

In short order I was flying up the highway with Melanie in Don Johnson's foreign sports convertible. Though her comportment was angelic, she drove like an addict pursuing a score. Melanie continued to talk about the importance of getting back on the horse in order to prevent my slip from turning into a slide. I asked her why she was going out of her way to be so helpful. Melanie told me she could remember times when she needed strong nonjudgmental help and was afraid to reach out to people. Her AA experiences had taught her humility, so helping people mattered. I pled gratitude for her stringing a silver lining through my nightmare, but she wasn't interested in any of my post-crash conversions, so I clammed up and watched her, savoring the closeup.

The sweating stopped, and my clothing felt gamey. Lack of sleep was becoming an issue. We pulled into a parking lot of a small community center. Inside was a crowd of White hard-hat types having coffee and mulling about as they waited for the meeting to begin. The faces of recovering alcoholics were so comforting that it inspired tiny flecks of relaxation, despite the room's NASCAR feel. The meeting started and the speaker, an old White guy, a machinist with twenty years of sobriety, told his story. I hung on every word. After his testimony, he opened up the floor, and several people shared their experiences. At the end of the meeting, I was invited to introduce myself. After two years I once again was copping to day one on the road to sobriety. I apologized to Melanie for fucking up her *New York Times* opportunity, before sharing my American Black guy anxiety and how racial demons were kicking my ass. After lending a respectful ear, these grizzled, navy-blue-collar White survivalists grabbed ahold of my head and screwed it on. Several made the point that what we shared as addicts and alcoholics transcended race. One participant stated, "I used to hate Black people, because I hated myself. Once I put the bottle down and found sobriety, I discovered that I didn't really want to hate anyone."

Melanie sat beside me as I witnessed the common goal of sobriety level the playing field. She wasn't the pampered movie star, or I the spoiled writer. So many of the things I was obsessing over were asphyxiated in this atmosphere of gratitude and hope. After the meeting, the people embraced me as only AA folks can. These guys' necks were as red as Georgia clay, and yet they were filled with nothing but genuine concern for my well-being.

I was silent, as Melanie sped to the airport. Sleepless anxiety, guilt, and repentance had broken me down. My stomach had given out, and I was getting sick. Melanie pulled to the road's shoulder and fished out an antacid pill that settled me down. Throughout my petrified state, Melanie continued to assure me that we would find a way to get the interview done over the phone. She cajoled, "The most important thing you have to do is stay sober for the next twenty-four hours." We arrived at the airport, and my movie star got out of her car and walked with me to the terminal. After saying goodbye, she waved until disappearing from sight. Melanie saved my job, my sanity, and my faith in people.

As the plane soared up the East Coast, I counted my ironies. This episode was launched on the back of my growing dissatisfaction with White America, and it ended with me pouring out my heart to a group of genuinely concerned

Reagan Democrats. I later discovered that on the day Melanie held my hand, the motion picture industry had announced an Oscar nomination for her role in *Working Girl*. You would think that on her big day she would be in seclusion, praying to the Oscar gods, and yet she chose to nurse a fallen fellow junkie. The *Times* spiked the article for reasons that had nothing to do with my behavior. I was immediately given another assignment on Denzel Washington. Melanie took the spiking in stride. At that time she was poised to have a monster career. She honored her commitment to me. Aided by her PR person, Elliot Mintz, Melanie went to generous lengths to cover my ass. Their effort was above and beyond normal expenditure.

Melanie steamrolled a way out for me and split. Much like Dorothy in *The Wizard of Oz*, I would never see or hear from the good fairy again. Her gentle largesse helped tip the scales in my final victory over white-powder dependency. Never again would I belly-up to that gamble, exposing myself to the lady in any of her tempestuous outfits. I dove into serious self-inventory. My using was tied to my self-esteem, and my self-esteem, in large part, was tied to the state of my relationship with mainstream America. If I allowed racial anger to get the best of me, I was a dead man, plain and simple. As a committed integrationist, I would have to come up with a plausible way to deal with the heartbreak of our near extinction.

The trauma that blows through African American citizenship is difficult to contend with, because too often sight restrictions trump individuality. A quiet paralysis gripped my optimism as I stared in the eye of my truncated citizenship. The Miami experience liposuctioned the poisonous self-pity out of my attitude, restoring sobriety, but the dilemma was jabbing me crazy as I grappled with my American value. My infected perspective's salvation would finally find me on a trip to the European continent.

Europeans have their ethnic prejudices, but Black American males who work on movies ain't one of them. This shock opened the door to unimagined comfort in a Caucasian majority. The weight of being Black among White American mainstreamers was heavier than I'd realized. A simple replacement of mutual fear with mutual curiosity provided an unexpected blast of liberation. This shocking esteem rebate lifted a safe from my shoulders I didn't know I was carrying. Unfathomable optimism fed wet disorientation, arousing my senses. This unexpected delivery of pure helium blew my overstuffed mental graveyard to smithereens, grinding tombstones and the cynical corpses beneath them into nourishment for the new lot's chance at restoring a bit of its lost innocence.

This new freedom would serve me well when I scored the opportunity to write a screenplay for Markus Gruber, a writer and director from Cologne, Germany. Markus and I met in Berlin, when he invited me to see his superb documentary about Maceo Parker, famed saxophonist and leader of the backup band that injected the wiggle into James Brown's hips. After the movie we had a meal, and he asked if I was willing to write a screenplay based on the autobiography of Black American writer Chester Himes. We quickly agreed on a deal, and I was on my way to Cologne.

The Germans in my creative circle impressed me with their profound appreciation for African American artistry. I stayed in the loft of a duplex apartment with a local radio personality, Petra Mueler. Petra was an avid Black music fan and had every important piece of African American popular music. Her lengthier European attention span enabled an appreciation for the great honor it was to interview former masterful somebodies, from Smokey Robinson on the high end to long-buried R&B live wire Bobby Womack. It was like stepping back in time to the Blue Note, my old neighborhood's portal of sounds.

Ensconced in my little loft above Petra's archival vault of spades, with artists like the Four Tops rising from my host's trove, I'd come to the end of the first draft of Chester Himes's extraordinary life. Despite an abundance of talent and character his journey had been marred by his bitterness toward America. This project unleashed a jackhammer to my sensibilities. I was staring into a cracked mirror.

Himes was a brilliant writer who had had a flash hit, *If He Hollers Let Him Go*, in 1947. In his youth he had done a stretch in the penitentiary, where he discovered that his gift for words was worth pursuing. Shortly after his release, Himes wrote his great novel, one of the best American portraits of the isolation and struggle of the urban African American male ever written. Unexpected success for this promising debut inflated future expectations, until he came nose-to-nose with the fact that Black American novelists had short shelf lives, and with astonishing quickness, Himes found himself a frustrated janitor. He would soon join the exodus of great literary talent that was making its way to Paris. Authors Richard Wright, James Baldwin, Ralph Ellison, and other creative Black wordsmiths found more respectful freedom in the wider-minded city of lights.

> American Negroes are unique individuals, funny but not clowns, solemn but not serious, hurt but not suffering. We are absurd.
>
> —CHESTER HIMES*

---

*From *My Life of Absurdity: The Latter Years*, vol. 2 of *The Autobiography of Chester Himes* (New York: Thunder's Mouth Press, 1976).

Chester's pain reduced the tenets of the early postwar Colored man's plight to the base of its insanity, creating a degree of separation from the baffling contradictions that had poisoned his former nation's credo. He split the States when his anger bubbled over into a dangerous red zone that was driving him to the brink of violence.

> I had always believed that to defend my life or my honor I would kill a White man without a second thought. But when I discovered that this applied to White women, too, I was profoundly shaken. Because by then, White women were all I had left.
>
> —CHESTER HIMES**

Chester's fear was that America's apartheid madness would force him to spend his life in a cell for carrying the burden of having slain his only panacea, so he saddled up the wind and galloped to Paris, where a pleasant transitional period provided enough psychological testicular inflation to continue his craft. But Himes's brilliant work couldn't escape his diseased racial attitudes, a malady prevalent among proud, scarred Jim Crow survivors.

Himes and I were both angry, confused Black men in our early forties when we arrived in Europe. But Chester Himes's anger over America's apartheid injustice scalded his psyche, separating him from his love of country, a love I still retained. I could understand his pain, but given the difference in our generations, I had more faith to hang on my American hook. Chester's superbly articulated disgruntlement sanctified his ex-patriotism, but I couldn't bring myself to give up the national inheritance our ancestors staked me to. Ground-floor ownership in America's miracle is one of the most valuable possessions a contemporary human can possess.

Cologne's odd movie of solid Caucasian neutrality was the perfect atmosphere for me to come to an epiphanic dawning. Chester's America was not bound to accept his citizenship, offering soured recourse loaded with gut-wrenching indignities. His pain was one of the rungs that supported my climb to relative relevance. For me to assert the value of my half-filled pouch of citizenry couched behind the scar tissue of Chester and his generation's empty pouch struck me as a cowardly rebuke of all they'd suffered. I doubt Chester would have hopped sovereignties so quickly had he been in an America that was clearly turning the corner on its pigmented future.

**From *The Quality of Hurt: The Early Years*, vol. 1 of *The Autobiography of Chester Himes* (New York: Thunder's Mouth Press, 1971, 1972), p. 4.

Despite my occasional periods of marginalized-Black attitudinal combustion, an honest crunching of future numbers made it a decent bet that the long-range value of our union's most diverse hours were ahead of us. It was incumbent upon myself and fellow Black Boomers, who were the first to ingest the quantitative, legislative scrambled eggs at the post–Civil Rights table, to move the yard markers. Initial sightings of equality's goal line had pierced the last vestiges of our ancestor's once-black fog. I spent a few moments endorsing the plaque I was holding with the word *asshole* written across it, awarded to me for the lamest inflated-victimization howl.

Dusk on the horizon dampened the loft's light. I pulled myself away from Himes's inadvertent shove in the right direction and went to the window. In that moment the sight of an old bare cobblestone alley produced an odd effect. A setting sun glamorized the antique passageway, offering the view of a determinative fork. The right direction was illuminated by the sun's pinpoint reflection upon a better path to play. This revelation was a bolt of B12, nailing my left ass cheek square. The rush painted an unwipeable shit-eating smile across my face.

On my way back to the States I made a business stop in Davos, Switzerland. After settling in to a quaint little hotel room, I took a stroll on the promenade, with my Walkman feeding me sounds only Aretha Franklin can make. My enjoyable cloud was parted by two girls around seven years old with shaggy blond hair who were following me. I stopped, they stopped. I continued, and they followed suit. I turned and inquired, "Hi, how can I help you?" but my English didn't penetrate, so I blew them a kiss. They turned and dashed off. I continued my walk, until discovering that my shaggy blond stalkers had returned with several of their friends. I asked two women who were seated at an outdoor café if they spoke English. When one of them answered in the affirmative, I pointed to the children and asked, "What's going on?" She spoke to the children in their language and then said, "They have never seen a Black man before. They think you're the biggest chocolate bar ever."

This information induced the warmest smile my face could chart. One of the two original blondes handed me some flowers. I was so taken by the kindness embedded in her innocent expression that I feared the old chocolate bar might melt. I wanted to give them something in return, but all I had was two baseball cards I'd bought for Keelan. One was Kirby Puckett, the all-star outfielder for the Minnesota Twins, and the other was Don Mattingly, the indefatigably professional first baseman for the Yankees. I handed the cards to the children, and they stared at them oddly, not knowing the game, but favoring Puckett, whose round brown physique was an Almond Joy. I took a sweeping bow before them, blew another kiss, and continued onward, clutching my flowers as they waved goodbye.

As I came to the edge of town, that special human buzz that rewarded positive existence was cooking. I was moved to contemplate if I'd rather be a chocolate bar or a victim, choice food for thought as I geared up for another plunge into a new decade of racial absurdities practiced on American soil.

RECONCILIATION

Got the will to Love.

—**Neil Young,**
"Will to Love"

THIRTY-ONE

Harlem, Summer 2000

I'm seated in the Apollo Theater working on a film. New York Times Television has given me the opportunity to write and design a documentary on Jimi Hendrix and Sly and the Family Stone for the Showtime cable network. The Apollo is one of the great Black music dives of all times, where both Sly and Jimi did work on their musical GEDs. Throughout the summer, we've filmed and interviewed classic rockers from the sixties in the great houses their music once inflamed. LA's Whiskey A Go Go, San Francisco's Cow Palace, and New York's Bottom Line and Electric Circus hosted classic rock when its legend was fresh.

I have not been on 125th Street since my crack down days, when Harlem's greatest street was a ghost after 6:00 P.M. The Clinton-inspired Black renaissance is now in full swing. The number of storekeepers and shoppers that crowd the area is reminiscent of the sixties during the days of James Brown, when his appearances at our caramel Carnegie Hall generated more human rhythmic energy than anywhere it has ever existed. It's been a long time since I've seen Black folks this pumped. The joy and optimism that surrounds the Apollo is an indication of how the lot of the terminally depressed has improved. Those left for dead in the eighties are sporting new badges of inclusion, and the buzz on the streets reeks of elevated esteem. Clintonism's expanded sense of the concept of inclusion loosened the grip of the conservative vice that compressed the previous decade. The national notes that flowed from the big guy's saxophone were that of a complicated bluesman that still vibrated below the belt. Like most great bluesmen, life was too colorful to place pigment before substance. Harlem's vibe has gotten the message.

My old friend and former AA sponsor, Vic, is the cameraman. We've just finished filming the *New York Times* music critic, John Perales. After the interview Vic, director Nina Rosenblum, and I sit in the empty theater and discuss the film's focus: the rare and complicated Boomer musical gem Sylvester Stewart, wild child of integration and front genius for the group Sly and the Family Stone.

Sly had been young musical prodigy whose deep church roots inspired a vision of an all-inclusive strain of gospel rock. Black Christians are a loving lot who will extend a hand to anyone, Black or White, who respects the Holy Ghost. Equality under the Lord blew away the notion of a weaker anything. Sly's baptism in church democracy taught that inviting a Black female trumpet player to play alongside a White male saxophonist created a larger talent pool for his young King-LBJ idealistic vision. A vital injection of inflamed passionate guidance by one of the music industry's most rebelliously talented heavyweights, Columbia Records' David Kapralik, was Sly's topping "it" factor. David had deftly taken all the behind-the-scenes bullets, shielding his new young artist from his most vulnerable disability, executive bullshit. This combination of King-influenced visionaries had cleared a path for the young genius's brilliant musical compositions to electrify the public air waves. A transcendental experience resulted in a new crossover audience that chipped at Motown's expiring patent on that distinction.

We break for lunch, and I hustle to my new favorite spot, the stone benches that frame the entrance to the State Building on 125th Street and Lenox Avenue. I didn't believe that these streets would ever soften to the point where one could sit outside in the heart of Harlem without anxiety, but I'm peacefully chowing down while preparing my notes for the afternoon's work. The sounds of Anita Baker's best jams feed my headphones when a familiar face interrupts my groove. A number of squints later, recognition seeps through. It's an old friend from way back in my Black life, but the reunion quickly fills with sorrow when he informs me that he's on his way to a funeral home to pay his respects to the memory of George House. His news would have been less jarring if he'd fired a gun.

The last time I saw Mr. George was in Tampa, Florida, where he and his family had moved. I was in the final throes of kicking my crack addiction and was embarrassed to be in his presence. He greeted me warmly, and I played upfront about my recent drug problems, and, without a hint of judgment, Mr.

George encouraged me to stay on the rail of recovery because there were still opportunities out there to run down.

My friend asks if I would like to accompany him to the funeral parlor a block away. "No," I say, "I have to get my shit together. I'll be over there." The old friend pats me on the back and continues on. I'm in a shocked state of memory search. I was so fortunate to come under Mr. George's wing, when he espoused the tenets of Black pride and power long before the concept's official horns blared. Anita's sounds turn into mourning music as 125th Street strikes again with its penchant for pathos.

When I arrive at the funeral parlor, I am directed to the room where the open casket is on display. The parlor is empty except for a grieving female peering into the coffin. Upon closer inspection I see it's Mr. George's daughter, Michelle once a baby sister, now a relative stranger. I stand beside her over the body and begin crying uncontrollably, completely losing it. Michelle takes my liquidated emotions to heart, embracing me, and the comfort feels right against breasts that didn't exist in our last days of hay. Michelle understands how much I loved her father, and all of the nurturing her woman's compassion can offer strokes me through the knees-steadying process.

I leave the funeral home and start walking, and before I know it I'm on 135th Street and Amsterdam Avenue. My mind is scouting for memorable pangs of Mr. George past, when he pushed me on the White stage during the early sixties. Fortunately, meaningful interaction was playing its best hand, but neither of us could have known how far Black people would come from those early days, when shining shoes was an acceptable career choice, to Colin Powell's appointment as chairman of the Joint Chiefs of Staff—lifetimes of progress, now only lifetimes away from equitable citizenship. Back in the days of our car-waxing expeditions, during a train ride, Mr. George beat my ear with another of his potent brain washings. "You got to be for integration, boy," he blasted, "cause real freedom is freedom from prejudice. No matter how hard things get, you can't get your piece, unless you make your peace with White folks."

Freeport, Long Island, 1990

The highlight of year was the birth of my beloved Arielle, the first and only daughter I would ever have. She was distinctively planned, and her arrival staked an additional claim for my marriage to Anne. This event completed our rehabilitated commitment. Jack's soft spot for his grandchildren offered the opportunity for me to reestablish my mettle, and I had pretty much earned my way back into the McCormack family mainstream.

On May 5 in the early A.M., Arielle Justine Watlington was born. When she emerged from the womb, she looked exactly like her brother, Keelan. "It's the same recipe," the attending nurse stated in response to my astonishment. Anne looked angelic in her post-delivery exhaustion. An early cell phone was available, and, moments after the delivery, I called Ellen and she was able to speak with her daughter. At 4:00 A.M. I left my wife to sleep off her triumph.

When I arrived home, I was drained. I had an appointment that morning to shoot a television pilot, so I chose to forego sleep. I settled into a blissful limbo, savoring the instant eternal love I felt for my little girl. I turned to the chairman of the board for his take. Sinatra had a new video called "A Man and His Music." I slipped my copy into the VCR and watched the last glimpse of his winter's magic. When the greatest dago of them all shook hands with Michael Jackson during the Quincy Jones–led Sinatra recording session, it made Sammy's recent passing a bit easier to take. Proud thoughts of Frank's and Sammy's indirect influence on my beautiful biracial daughter's birth were a cherishable American dividend.

The day after my daughter's birth, Jack and Ellen arrived at the hospital. Arielle was their seventh grandchild, so they were seasoned pros in the grandparenting game and played accordingly. Jack and I left the room to take a peek at the new family member, and while walking down the hall the old guy extended himself, expressing his happiness over my attempt to turn my life around. Peering through Plexiglas, we watched our blood mix squint in her tiny crib. The connection was comfortingly there.

We moved down the corridor, and Jack remembered that there were several items he'd left in the trunk of his car. When we got downstairs to the hospital's exit, he looked at me with eyes that froze one's soul and tossed me the keys, suggesting, "Why don't you go and get the things, and I'll wait here for you." The hurt in his expression indicated that he did not have the physical wherewithal to make the jaunt. I immediately made light of the visible vulnerability, covering any shred of embarrassment he'd conveyed, before dashing for the articles. As I headed back toward Jack, I could see in my long-shot view that his body language was shrouded in sadness. It was the first clear hint to me that he was not well.

The new baby's presence rendered our tiny apartment untenable, so we searched for a bigger place to live. Jack and Ellen were living in the town of Avon, Connecticut. Initially, that wasn't on our prospective list, but extenuating circumstances brought out its shanks. Jack had fallen victim to colon cancer. We wanted to be close to the family, so we settled in Simsbury, twenty minutes from the Avon home. Simsbury was a small, suburban town outside of Hartford, a well-kept community with a good school system that was overwhelming White. This personal peeve was overshadowed by the sum of the other parts. Jack's cancer was a problem that wasn't going away. It was a particularly difficult time for me because, of all of the mentors I'd accumulated, he was the most solid. The honesty in his rock-ribbed cop's values had become a template for something real to me. When we were thrust upon each other, I trusted him least while fearing him most. When Jack proved he wasn't racist under my tiny margin for error, it revealed mettle that stood out from the rest.

I'd been making a suitable living from my writing career, so Anne and I had the flexibility to shape our movements. Many mornings after seeing Keelan off to school, I would hop in the car and go over to Jack and Ellen's. We would sit at the kitchen bar, have coffee, and shoot the breeze. As his illness ate away at his physical capacity, I was compelled to spend as much time with him as possible.

Anne's sister, Kathy, her husband, Flip, and their children, Brian and Tara, also lived in Avon. Jack attended as many of his grandchildren's high school activities as he could. The prideful boost both of his athletically talented grandchildren provided was tonic for diversion. Brian was a football and wrestling stud, while Tara excelled at field hockey on a state level. I attended several of their meets with Jack, and on our drives to and fro we talked incessantly. Often the topic was race. One of my issues that ragged Jack's ass was the contention that the baseball from his youth, before Jackie Robinson, was really minor league and should be credited as such.

"That's bullshit! There were great players in the thirties and forties, just like there is today."

"If baseball hadn't been so racist," I argued, "at least a third of the game would have been Black and Latino, and a third of the White players who made it to the Majors would have never risen to that level. Thus, an inferior brand of ball."

I was inching up close to the line that might set off his Irish geyser. When pissed, he became silent. His face would redden, and you could tell that the flush of blood was urging him to tell me to fuck off.

"You know, Jack, how they have a section in the Hall of Fame for the old Negro League? Well, all baseball before Jackie Robinson should be cordoned off and called the old Caucasian League." His skin tone had crossed the crimson line to my topper, "See how racism screws things up."

After a few beet-faced miles, his contentiousness subsided, suggesting he had no sound arguments to refute my hypothesis. I think that Jack's late Black education influenced the edges of his White conservatism, nudging him in the direction of calling the whole spade a spade. On occasion it irritated him that I was rarely at a loss for words. His retort was a good one when he said, "Damn it, you could talk the ear off of a brass monkey," and we both laughed. He had a hearty sense of humor once he got going.

Jack grew up during the Depression, when the noveau White roamed the urban streets. There were many similarities between growing up during the Depression on the streets of New York and growing up poor and Black on the same streets during the sixties. The oddity of our union was that in many ways I had more in common with him than with many of the White kids my age. He didn't always agree with me, but he respected the hard knocks I'd encountered. Our interaction was the biggest dividend that accompanied my admission to the family. As Jack was going through his period of physical decomposition, the strength and character that he displayed were lessons that I hoped to remember when my maker started to reel me in.

Since Anne and I had reunited, my mother and I had engaged in a blissful, uneasy truce. I'd recently taken Keelan to meet her for the first time. I hadn't seen her since my days under her thumb in my post-crack gulag. She had slowed considerably. Leola was delighted to see her grandson. Keelan epitomized everything she valued in a Watlington child. He was bright and inordinately articulate, and she gave him her unqualified approval, deeming him a worthy recipient of her vaunted genes.

She had a doctor's appointment at the local storefront clinic. As we walked through the neighborhood, Keelan dashed ahead, drawn to the playground where the monkey bars his dad swung from awaited. As he climbed the joy pipes, my mother stopped and rested on a bench. There was a softness about her that only the needles of aging could invoke.

"So how you doing, Ma?" I asked as I sat beside her.

"I'm fine. There ain't nothing wrong with me that God ain't planned," she exhorted. "How you doin'? You still out there writing that mess?" she inquired.

"Yeah, as a matter of fact, and I'm doing okay," I whimpered.

"I don't know why you spendin' your life on that stuff. You should let the Jewish boys do the writing. What we need is more preachers. You missed what God put you here for," she uttered wistfully.

"I'm okay, Ma. Besides, the Black world is full with good preachers. We need more writers. There is a much bigger shortage of Jewish gospel preachers," I kidded, drawing a laugh from her. One of the better kept secrets was that my mother had a beautiful smile.

We summoned Keelan before resuming our journey and slowly ate up project turf on the way to the doctor. Her out-of-control blood pressure was wreaking havoc on her organs, but her dignity was as healthy as ever. At the clinic she accepted the doctor's unpleasant information with distain. He was a mere human. Leola took her marching orders from the Lord. I protested because I felt she was giving short shrift to science. She gave my protestation the back of her hand and set off on a litany of my well-chronicled faults, which was oddly comforting. It assured me that her verbal six-shooters were still well lubricated.

After the appointment, Leola gave Keelan some candy and a big hug. All in all, a very satisfying visit, and as she walked off Keelan and I watched the lumbering figure until she was the size of a fly. I gave young Keelan a tour of my old neighborhood and told him the G-rated version of some of the adventures I'd experienced. As Keelan and I headed home, we listened to Buffalo Springfield's "Expecting to Fly." It was a favorite of his and seemed to score the ghetto-street images well.

My mother and I had both managed to move beyond her objection to my marriage to Anne. On Thanksgiving Day I called my mother, and she was in good spirits. After the niceties, she surprised me when she asked to speak to Anne. I was reluctant to hand Anne the phone, fearing the unpredictable, but my mother graciously congratulated her on Arielle's birth. Leola's pleasantries represented a major thawing in the racial cold war. I was really proud of the old girl.

Spring 1992.

Anne and I were seated on the couch watching a parade of Democratic presidential hopefuls descend upon the New Hampshire primary. We were curious about a relatively obscure politician from Hope, Arkansas, who had managed to score a good deal of negative publicity over his alleged womanizing. His human shenanigans sparked my initial attraction. After the many years of old White guys, like Reagan and Bush, I was a bit turned on to an Oval Office contender with an active pointer. His wife, an accomplished lawyer in her own right, stood by her man on the nation's video polygraph apparatus, *60 Minutes*. It was an admirable attempt to control the damage, reducing some of the sting that his peccadilloes had wrought. This overweight, country nova was someone who looked like me.

My interest grew as I watched this cat fight onward, and his ability to salvage a second-place finish in the New Hampshire primary sent my eyebrows northward. In short order, he would win his first primary in the state of Georgia. When he stepped forward to make his thank-you speech, he praised all of his supporters who'd nudged him to victory. It was then that he sold me on the quality of his fortitude. He would later flaunt funk that only a grassroots gut could conjure, when jamming on his 'ophone with the house band on *The Arsenio Hall Show*. In the months to come, his momentum grew, and he would find himself leaning over the threshold of victory, peering into a new decade of faintly perceptible challenges. By November, when victory struck, the boy from Hope had shown the ability to hatch hope in others. His victory freed Republican-whipped liberals who'd become accustomed to soaking their bruised asses after witnessing innumerable Democratic concession speeches.

Hope, Arkansas's contribution to the nation's capitol came armed with an instinct for unity that exceeded the simplistic pigment-versus-Caucasian argument. Gender and sexual orientation were inspired to burst through liberal lip service checkpoints to a land of distinctive identification, sharing and benefiting from the young president's genuine hankering for a mood of respectful coexistence. His blue-collar touch was punctuated with impressive, brained-up pieces of paper with Yale and Oxford stamped on them. These were important documents helping to ward off the shit-kicker sticker that hovered above the first president to have received his Elvis shots. The Presley vaccination dissolved the southern White-only blockages to his heart, releasing the swivel that paid homage to his sensibilities' pigment pride. Conversely, a generation of middle-class pigment hopefuls could breathe a little easier.

The new commander in chief's childhood home had broken, and his bluish class background offered odds slightly better than mine of ever setting up in the Oval Office. The country's first Boomer prez's rural, southern background provided unusual exposure to salt-of-the earth, hardworking American Gibralter chips, whose wares were often soiled after a day's work. History's calendar had provided him with a ground folks' seat from which he had participated, learned, and jammed during the civil rights movement. Hope's boy's heart's wallet held a membership card in King's ring of offspring. He'd walked through the clearance engendered by Dr. King's successful breakage of the final pane of denial plaguing the races' ability to engage in civil discourse. His inhalation of this revolutionary American quarter step would eventually impact upon his presidential playbook, allowing this unusually bred country boy to embark upon the unprecedented presidential objective of nailing down the illusive Oval Office legacy as the president of inclusion.

Right out of the box as President-elect, he fired a shot across the political bow with his Nigraphobia-free appointment of Vernon Jordan to head up his transition team. Jordan was a solid chunk of iconic civil rights matter who'd launched his career as a powerful Beltway insider from his leadership position in the Urban League, a centrist civil rights organization that rose to prominence during King's splash. He was an accomplished lawyer who had influenced the organization with a pro-integration, pro-business wand. The oil dark, assiduously dressed Jordan was the picture of Black power like it ought to be. His selection as presidential point man sent a message to Black wannabes that the stage was set for pigment's hidden potency to emerge from the Republicans' darkened shadow.

One of the prospective beneficiaries of the president's anti-Nigraphobia vibe was my brother Calvin. He was four years younger than I, and the age difference effected a generational split. My mother had learned a lot from her travails with

her drug-plagued older sons, so when Calvin entered his teen years she'd concocted a number of effective clamp-down measures. Leola herded Calvin
through the Boys Club system, and, unlike her first experience, when we made
it up as we went along, she pounced on Calvin's early signs of unusually bright,
outspoken charisma. She barred the windows, locking a majority of that budding
talent under her watchful eye. Leola's best parental work insured Calvin's consistent flirtation above excellence's threshold. Her stamina goaded the development of Calvin's study habits, until he realized that he was a pretty smart guy.
By the time my mother loosened her vise-like grip, it was apparent that the parts
had glued together nicely. Calvin competed successfully among the best candi-
dates in the Boys Club program. His outstanding personality and good grades
made him a star in the same system I had helped to pioneer.

Calvin's hard work afforded him an opportunity to join the Hotchkiss family.
One of my proudest moments was standing in the admissions office with Calvin
and Admissions Office Peter Adams when it was decided that he would come to
the 'Kiss. My vicarious impulses partied hardy over my tangential share of
Calvin's feat of besting my smoke-and-mirror-aided admission with bonafide
qualifications. After eight years of scholarship, upon obtaining his bachelor's degree, Calvin enlisted in the army and did a lengthy stretch in Germany. When
he decided to join the army, it seemed like the craziest thing in the world, particularly while toting a degree, but he sensed opportunity in the armed forces
and took advantage of his stint, sandwiching an honorable discharge between
two master's degrees. Like many of his progressive Black brethren, he was willing to pay the price that came with opportunity's unyielding demands.

Calvin scored a job in George Shultz's State Department, before settling
down with his wife, Denise, and their three children in a Virginia suburb near
D.C. During his time in Washington, he juggled two jobs and law school until
obtaining his degree and passing the bar on his initial stab. He had executed the
plan that had been drawn up in the early sixties on how to reverse the fortunes
of the disenfranchised with little chance of sipping the American dream. Calvin
had joined the ranks of affirmatively delivered people of color and substance
who were again gnawing on the cement ceiling. In his late teens, he did a stint
in the center where he'd garnered a huge whiff of one of many of Chuck Griffin's instructional mantras: "You can compete with the White boy for the American dream and hold on to your Black shit. There's already enough White boys on
they side, make your skin count for something." Beneath Calvin's layers of
mainstream achievement was a proud Black heart that pumped street blood.
When the inevitable threats and taunts from the unenlightened street-sufferers
who inflated their cubes by castrating the educationally motivated tested
Calvin's manhood, the urban terrorists discovered that he'd been breastfed in

the land of kill or die and could whup somebody's ass, so the street-hardened grudgingly gave him his props.

Unfortunately, Calvin was an exception to the rule. The vaunted urban Black hoodlum of the nineties rarely missed a chance to denigrate pigment's symbolic, bespectacled suit-and-tie group that worked so hard living up to the responsibilities of our progress. Every time I see someone like Black conservative talk-show pundit Armstrong Williams playing his eloquent vocal harmonica for a Republican way of life that managed to elect but one drop of pigment to its congressional majority, it makes me want to throw a brick at my TV screen. It's embarrassing that our street-shit image has chased off so much talent. Williams, a coffee-bean-dark brother of ideas and passion, pumps a pro-responsibility agenda, penicillin for what ails our undisciplined Black underclass. But his powerful southern Black ideas are inaudible to the Black rank-and-file, whose ears freeze over to sounds shouted through a Republican megaphone. Williams is too valuable a contributor to toil on supremacist butt-boy duty, but it seems to beat relating to our race's hostile image that shreds his generations-old value chart. This unfortunate disconnect drives many of our finest to preach to a choir that still tolerates the Confederate flag.

A covenant between the streets and our middle class is essential to the growth of the African American's presence in the new global game. This in-race divide contributes to our perpetual position on the bottom of America's barrel. Brilliant young rap veterans like Chuck D of Public Enemy, Russell Simmons, P. Diddy, and, my particular choice for future president, KRS's Chris Parker, should offer a race line to talented brothers like Williams, Delroy Murdock, Robert George, Larry Elder, and others, so that together they might design areas of compromise fostering a narrowing of our race's divide.

Despite the positive thrust of our enriched Black middle, the public face of the Black urban male took its lumps throughout the decade. In April of 1992, I was in Nashville, Tennessee, doing research on a television-movie gig. The relatives of my subject lived in the vicinity and agreed to avail themselves for interviews. After the hotel's front desk rung up the news that my driver had arrived, I was soon greeted by an enormously fat, red-cheeked good old boy. He'd been alerted that I was a network writer, and his first words were "Are you Spike Leeeee?" I waited for his thick drawl to disperse before answering, "Yes." His jowls stiffened, and a scowl contorted his pasty features. I rethought my smart-ass reply when it dawned on me that Spike was probably high up on the country boy's uppity-nigger chart, so I took back my lie and replaced it with a better one: copping to the disguise of being a good southern boy from South

Carolina. A smile rewrote his frown, and we were on our way to Nashville's Black community.

It was a lengthy drive, and to pass the time my driver and I chewed the fat. When I drop my stereotypically unfair view of the chaw-and-spit boys, I'm often rewarded. My driver revealed himself to be a jovial presence with an engagingly sharp sense of humor. We talked about his beloved football team, the Tennessee Volunteers. "The best thing that ever happened to the Vols was when they let you Colored boys carry the ball. You guys are the best." I got a kick out of his heartfelt redneck compliment, and my up response encouraged him to paste more bonding strips on our odd coupling. He talked about his large family and his love of hunting, and I spoke about my grandmother and her indomitable, humble southern pride. We struck party-level agreement over our mutual love for grits. "You can bet your ass I'm wearing a lot of grits under this belt," he bellowed before laughingly patting his proud mid-body compound. It was a fun up, with my companion's fat jiggling rhythmically with each belly laugh.

My subject's family greeted me with open arms, pouring buoyant insights into my tape recorder. At one point, before reloading, I became distracted by the smell of greens, corn bread, and pig's feet. I stopped the interview and confessed to my wife's Irish roots and their immersion in corn beef and cabbage, pushing the scent of corn bread out of my nostril's range. My host proceeded to engorge me with enough soul food to resuscitate the sense's memory. When my jolly driver showed up he was invited in, and before long the peach cobbler would be making its way toward his second chin as he dove into the house's happy banter about soul food. On our departure the friendly sound of Jed Clampett's "Y'all come back now," was ringing in my head. As we pulled out of the driveway, dusk was drawing its curtain, soon to leave a starless, black-hearted theater in its wake. Me and the fat man were grooving. I was moved by his invitation to come and meet his family before splitting town. I agreed to alter my schedule in order to make his scene.

At the height of our groove, a sociological earthquake erupted. The country music on the radio that covered the dirt road darkness with honey was joltingly slashed by a newsflash from southern California: the policemen in the Rodney King trial had been acquitted. A massive "uh-oh" covered my thoughts. Reports of black rage exploded from the speakers, and just as quickly, a severe case of Nigraphobia blanketed our vehicle. My fat friend's demeanor plunged southward in an instant.

Rodney King was a Black man who unwisely engaged the police in a dangerous car chase. When they caught him, the cops decided they would convict and sentence him on the spot. Their snap guilty verdict was followed by a savage beating recorded on videotape by an amateur. The images shocked civil society.

The policemen were tried for the over-the-top ass-whupping by an all-White jury that fed them an acquittal. The infamous Simi Valley third finger lit the fuse to a factory of human explosives up north in LA's Black and Latino communities. White insensitivity and Black anger, sans leadership buffers filtering the invective, drove our better angels on strike. It all spelled *kaboom!* with emboldened, ugly idiocy filling the vacuum.

My fat friend's facial reflection in the rearview mirror was now a taut mask of separation. The ride turned scary, with my irrational suspicions outlining scenarios of a sudden swamp nap. Fortunately, that wasn't on his agenda, but he never said another word as the radio station chronicled the outbreak of riotous activity that exacerbated the wedge between us. When we arrived back at the hotel, I gathered my stuff and said, "Thanks," to which he replied tersely, "Yeah!"

I got back to my room and watched Black rioters play a mean game of havoc on my TV screen. The pigment-thick rioters were break-dancing on their own graves as the entire world looked on. With much of an embarrassed nation's compassion evaporating with each VCR hoisted, it was a frightening visual document of America's have-nots having their say.

THIRTY-TWO

After a decade of separation, Leif Thorne-Thomsen and I reentered each other's lives. Time had served him well, and the ten-year gap in our ages had narrowed. Leif led a healthy cyclist's life devoid of tobacco or alcohol, thus preserving his youthful fundamentals. A victory against the calendar and a second marriage producing three lovely daughters led to a comfortable life on an old farm in Massachusetts's Berkshire County. A surprise separation from his wife grew into a divorce, emptying the farmhouse. Leif needed the love of a family and invited Anne and me to move in. It took little contemplation before the major chords of our relationship resurfaced, and the music floated the fact that Leif was one of the most important loves of my life, so we were honored to share in his reconstruction. We had been looking for a larger residence, so our choice made for a good fit. In August of 1992, Anne, the kids, and I came to Massachusetts.

The house had been built in the early nineteenth century on fifty acres of land. It's rap sheet included stints as a ski lodge as well as a camp for the United Nations. The house was showing signs of wear, but the six bedrooms and four bathrooms meant plenty of room for everyone. We woke up in the morning to a view of cornfields and mountains and our three sheep grazing in their pasture behind the house.

After the new basic family structure

was in place, Leif's daughters, Gudren, Ella, and Ruby entered the mix—three beautiful Norwegian-German little girls who had inherited their father's wall-to-wall curiosity. In short order, the family added another member when my and Gerri's son, Avery, showed up. He was now a six-foot-four teenaged mass of achievement, whose excellence in the classroom and ball court was lighting up his Tampa high school. Avery had showed great resolve and character in overcoming the disability of a broken home. Gerri's God wand had blessed the kid's development with his kindergarten-to-graduation Christian school education. The Christian values component had supported a structure that helped Avery dodge the reaper that took out so many of his Tampa street peers. Anne was a committed stepmom whose honest engagement chemo-ed the debilitating "fuck Whitey" tumor, enabling him to sidestep much of the fear and ignorance that infests the teen pigment pool.

As I grew older I was forced to confront the negative ramifications that came with the family I'd busted. The shortness of breath that accompanies the thought of having left Avery on a fatherless raft never goes away. Phone updates and summer visits were a lousy way of parenting, often producing a difficult "love you/fuck you" tug-of-war that produced more victims than victors. He and I fought like hell to a long-distance draw. When Avery showed up on the summer of our new family's liftoff, he was a good-vibe surprise, having ditched much of the old anger and choosing to cultivate his place in the clan by adding a strong young voice from the contemporary Black South.

Avery and the girls pushed the diversity dial into the power zone, firing up my American high beams. The family dinners were happening, with Leif, at one end of a long table, and me, at the other, co-orchestrating these improbable affairs. A wide variety of influences broke bread at our spread. The invitees and drop-ins ranged from wealthy Ivy League–bred capitalists to rugged ghetto individualists. We were mining the gold nuggets that lay just beneath the establishment's rule book. Our diverse ages and backgrounds cooked into a recipe for interactive stew. Its brew empowered an inadvertent hoisting of the finger at the race, gender, and sexual-orientation stop signs, tearing them down before the eyes of our children.

The nineties saw the proliferation of a once-rare commodity, the African American millionaire. The entertainment community had always provided one of the best opportunities for Black people to obtain big coin. As America's obsession with professional sports grew, Black dominance on the athletic fields delivered unfathomable wealth and celebrity.

Michael Jordan, an oil-black North Carolinian phenomenon, who two centuries earlier would have been any auction block's number-one draft choice, did to the game of basketball what Ali had done to boxing: own it. But Jordan worked the clean side of the American street, transcending race with his brilliantly crafted public image and extraterrestrial athleticism. Athletes like Jackie Robinson, Hank Aaron, Connie Hawkins, Kareem Abdul-Jabbar, and Julius Erving had formed the plaster cast for the Jordan model. These icons past had provided the rungs that facilitated his ascent to the top of mainstream acceptance. By the time the nineties struck, the country's White power stream was ready to embrace the ultimate Black superstar on one condition: he or she must subscribe to the Simpsonian template of never making Whites uncomfortable. Jordan got the joke and wrote his own ticket.

The decade would also provide a handful of Black athletic titans who failed to live up to the mainstream's Simpsonian axiom: If we worship your Black ass, you better stay on the straight and narrow. Those who failed to make the grade generated scandalous sparks, igniting racial firestorms across the nation. Two of these athletes would shake my past sensibilities from its White trees.

I had the opportunity to work with Barbara Kopple, Kevin Keating, and Leon Gast on a film project in the summer of 1992. Barbara was directing an NBC documentary for prime time on the most compelling figure in boxing since Muhammad Ali, Mike Tyson. The film's mission was to connect the dots of Tyson's life leading up to his conviction for raping a young woman named Desiree Washington. We spent a week in Indianapolis doping out the steps that led to their collision.

A year earlier Black Expo, an annual convention that acts as a national network for the sharing of Black ideas, had drawn the nation's glare. This relatively obscure function had been an unlikely venue for a hotshot of ugly national publicity to detonate. Someone had the brilliant idea to invite Mike Tyson to the rehearsal of one of the highlight events, the Miss Black America Pageant. It was there that he met the young lady he would subsequently lure to his hotel suite. Desiree cried rape, and a muddle of "he said, she said" ensued. In surprisingly short order, Tyson was convicted and sentenced to ten years in real prison. I was reminded of something I had heard on the streets. "Clarence Thomas beat it, the Kennedy boy beat it, so Mike don't have a chance." Three years earlier, Tyson had been the single most valuable asset in the kingdom of professional sports. Whether the verdict was justice or ream job had lost relevance, because our team was now visiting an Indiana prison, where Tyson was on the other side of some seriously hard walls.

Tyson was a stone cold blade from the streets who thugged upon his destiny as the best pugilist on the planet. Former heavyweight champions Sonny Liston and, to a lesser degree, George Foreman had also come from the no-chance club of criminal survival, but in those better days thuggish behavior was frowned upon by the Black community. Its leadership's protection of the collective's dignity acted as a speed bump slowing down the gifted's impulse to indulge in public, street, niggeristic displays of the race's darkest laundry. Performers with stars above their heads had to publicly separate themselves from the culture's grimy fringe. Tyson's fame coincided with the outbreak of the hip-hop culture, which had hoisted its wind-whipped gangsta flag stamped with a dominant Black middle finger. His brethren's salutation to its fuck-'em symbol empowered Tyson to do his thing without shucking those concrete-bad street affectations. Unfortunately, there was no one powerful enough to impress upon Tyson that gangsta mythology was earmarked for the destructive path he had dodged, and a trillion dollars in prize money couldn't buy off that scent.

A few weeks later, back in New York, we went to Tyson's hometown hellhole in the Brownsville section of Brooklyn. This was a triple-X-rated ghetto, a collection of burnt-out tenement buildings in which people didn't live, they survived. On a day when the temperature read one hundred degrees, the atmosphere was steaming. Our seasoned documentary veterans were taken aback by the hellish conditions and refused to leave the van. As I peered out at unfamiliar broken concrete, jelly found my knees, but I knew that you had to meet hard ghetto with blind ghetto.

Barbara's burglar-bold cubes hung tough as the two of us entered the neighborhood together. We were flashing NBC logos, and fortunately the power of network attention enabled me to do some fast street-face work with the most important looking cats on Tyson's crowded stoop. After conversing in our native tongue, I elicited the support of several key figures who'd grown up with Mike. They led us to the roof, where a thirteen-year-old Tyson had once owned a pigeon coop. As we walked up the six flights of stairs in a scary tenement building, whose light sockets were waving white flags, it was a net-less tightrope walk, but the hard-core brothers were helpfully cool. After sizing up what we were going to shoot, Barb and I summoned our light-in-the-tripod teammates with the okay sign, and they pulled into the steam.

The children on the street were sweaty bolts of energy running wild. Suddenly, a white stretch limousine pulled into the block. The kids gathered around the majestic sight, and out of the car stepped the inimitable LeRoy Neiman, commercial pop-artist extraordinaire. Neiman had taken an interest in the project because the world of sports was on his art beat. Dressed in a white suit and hat, with his trademark waxed-handlebar mustache, he was a bigger-than-life necessity. He took several pieces of drawing paper and laid them out on the hood of his limo, then gave out a pile of crayons to the children. Neiman began drawing quick cartoon figures to stimulate the kids' involvement, and before long he had a funky art class going. His presence transformed the hot, tense atmosphere into a carnival of goodwill.

We filmed many of Tyson's home boys on the roof, using the old pigeon coop as a backdrop. Our impromptu love-in was punctuated by the echo of consistent gunfire throughout the neighborhood. My nerves began to play games with my stomach, and I went to the edge of the roof and looked down in the streets at the children dancing around the white limo, drawing equilibrium from Neiman's easy humanity. NWA's Dr. Dre on acid couldn't have composed a more bizarre street scenario, but things went off without a hitch. The neighborhood's pride in Mike Tyson's celebrity served up enough vicarious vittles to nourish a few hours of civil diversion.

Next on the Tyson trail was a trip to Spofford, the teenage detention facility in the Bronx where Mike and I had done undergraduate work. This was the first time I'd been back to the joint since my incarceration. Children's rights issues had grown into a cottage industry, so the protections against naked abuse of young inmates that had been commonplace during my stint had subsided. A very attractive Black woman now headed the facility. She was thrilled to have an alumnus who had beat the recidivism odds. I spoke to a group of inmates, and the futureless teenagers broke my heart. They flaunted their clueless tragedies before me in an atmosphere free of the slightest hint that their birth nation's ingenuity and wealth offered a citizen's menu of wondrous options.

I was photographed in my old cell staring through the barred windows, picking up on my old friends—moving vehicles. The bars in the windows solidified my kinship with Tyson. We were two hunks of ghetto shrapnel lodged in the distant zone of American opportunity, dodging the bullet-ridden fate awaiting most Spofford grads. Unfortunately, money and fame aren't enough to remove keyloid ghetto scars. Healed or not, they are always visible. It's a permanent condition.

On the morning of the Spofford shoot, I was weighted down with some heavy news: my beloved little brother and comrade Checko had joined Noel in the bygone file. Like Tyson, he was a victim of the gravity that draws a nigger to a street-shit death. It had all been so promising in the early community center days, before my brothers bought tickets in the street's drug lotto, in which the seductive prize money obscured the game's insurmountable odds. A temporary euphoria preceding the big draw offers the players a sliver's worth of bogus grandiosity, until its Vegas-weighted odds puncture the illusion. Torn, discarded tickets line the road to their coffins' or cells' auction block. The painful vial we couldn't duck was labeled TAUGHT BETTER. The fig leaf of ignorance that the uninitiated could claim offered little coverage for those of us who were exposed to life beyond the gate.

The last time I saw Checko, his youthful energy and magic had dissipated under the pressure of a pathetic crack addiction. He was in his late twenties but looked fifteen years older. Checko's hustles had soured, and he was living a drug-to-mouth, petty-scheme-to-petty-scheme existence. The news was hard on Anne, but she wasn't surprised. We had known from the word on the street that the deathly lurk was zeroing in.

Barbara suggested that we go to pay our respects after the shoot. We entered the small funeral home, and seated in the parlor was a lone figure enshrouded in grief. It was Noel's wife, Linda, whom I hadn't seen since the day of his funeral. Our painstaking coffin-to-coffin relationship produced a numbness that accompanied avoidable death. My heart broke for Linda, who had been very close to Checko and his deceased young wife, Vanessa, who several years earlier had fallen victim to cancer.

I stood over the body, and Checko stories began racing through my mind. I could see his eleven-year-old face beaming with pride, when he held watch as we shot heroin in tenement hallways. We praised him for his quick-minded maturity; he had been cool beyond his years. My capacity for grief was at its low ebb, so I chose to think of how turned on Checko was to his senses the first time he heard James Taylor's "Fire and Rain." His joy in that moment was a nice memory to focus upon, sealing off my sorrow. I turned to Linda, and we fought to connect, but so much time had passed, the words weren't there. We hugged, exchanging pain-filled eyes.

When Barbara and I left the parlor, I thought, "Boy, did we fuck up." Noel, Checko, Bobo, Barker, Little Stevie, Wild Cheeko, Chuck and Anna's youngest son, Eric, and countless others, once important soldiers for the center's dream, had never seen a thirty-fifth birthday. The dream became a burial ground for outstanding young men. It was as though we'd never dreamed at all.

The other athlete who, given his image, was the least likely Black celebrity to become vilified by White America, emerged on the nation's radar screen, and his appearance cut deep. It was the summer of 1994, and I was returning to New York from a speaking engagement in Washington, D.C. The engagement was successful, with applause and other gestures of appreciation still warming my insides. I was in a good mood upon my arrival at Penn Station, and with Bono lobbying my headphones for "Pride (In the Name of Love)," I hopped a yellow horse. When the cab took off, all seemed right in the world as an all-news radio station spurted positive Wall Street numbers at me. The greed blast was interrupted by the news that O. J. Simpson was now a fugitive from justice. O.J.?

I asked the driver to take me to Nina Rosenblum's office in the Tribeca Film Center. When I arrived, Nina was transfixed by the sight of a white SUV moving slowly down a highway in Los Angeles. O.J. and his main man, A. C. Cowlings, were being pursued by the LAPD. Simpson's wife, Nicole, had been killed in an unimaginable act of savagery, and initial indicators of guilt pointed at the Juice. It was one of the most unlikely scenarios I could have imagined. The drama on the television screen was thick with the possibility of O.J. committing suicide, and that was just the tip of the sadness, for it was clear that, if apprehended alive, one of the most beloved Black American crossover heroes would be ashes.

Juice had been a beacon of moderation during the turbulent times of transition from Negro to Black. He was one of the first finished models of Dr. King's work to come off the integration assembly line. Handsome, talented, and humble, Black folks admired him for his excellence and White folks loved him for his accessibility. His knack for making Whites of lesser endowment feel comfortable in his presence was his gold coin. He brushed off the stifling criticism from the extreme Black left, choosing to pounce upon loosened White attitudes to seize his full citizenship.

O.J.'s arrival on the nation's television screens had coincided with the youthful Summer of Love in 1967. I had watched through a heroin-induced haze as the Juice ate up college turf with a glutton's ferocity. The following year Muhammad Ali was iced after refusing to enter the military, but his first foal produced a new Black yearling whose intent was to buck the Joe Louis handbook of amiable comportment. At the 1968 Olympics, two African American sprinters, John Carlos and Tommie Smith raised defiant black-gloved fists on the winner's podium, directing the world's attention to American pigment's new posture of defiant resistence. In the midst of this turbulent national drumbeat, O.J. struck a compromise between White fear and Black anger, and he cleaned up. My father would say, "I never thought I'd see the day when America would let a nigger share the national stage with Arnold Palmer," referring to the popular ad campaign that O.J. and the golf icon collaborated on for the Hertz Corporation.

In 1973, while playing for the Buffalo Bills, the Juice laminated his crossover iconic sticker at Shea Stadium. With the press bearing down on him, and the Jets' Hall of Fame coach, Weeb Ewbank, working his last game, the high-grade New York electricity lit the nation. Juice captured the hearts of American sportsmen by breaking every one of Jim Brown's stone-written 1,863 drops of dominance embedded in his hallowed season's rushing record. After forcing the greatest athlete to ever play the game into the unfamiliar position of second place in the record books, O.J. crashed the oncoming millennium when crossing the 2,000-yard barrier. Millions of onlookers stamped a nearly indelible *S* on the crossover prince's torso. His post-game press conference was a thing of beauty, when O.J. insisted that his hard-working offensive line share in his accomplishment on camera. He introduced each member with short, sincere terms of endearment. The group was a biracial collection of behemoths that was a portrait of America at its most comfortably integrated best. After his multiple-barrier-shattering day, O.J. held the deed to the nation and was inspired to sell its shares to all comers interested in good-time color-blind crosspollination.

When I was working on the film *Champions* with John Ballard, one of the actors on our wish list for the lead role was O.J. Simpson. Juice had done well in the world of feature films. He wasn't much of an actor, but the sheer force of his celebrity tinted his shortcomings with the same kind of lighting that exaggerated a late-night pickup's appeal. A meeting was set up at the Sherry-Netherland Hotel. Normally I was not one to go gaga over celebrities, but the Juice was extraterrestrial. He was in town to host *Saturday Night Live*, which in itself was quite a statement on his unique stature. This was before athletics garnered assignments of such girth.

When we arrived at his suite, he greeted us in a bathrobe, and my first impression of him startled me. As anyone who has ever met the Juice will tell you, he has the largest head in the history of craniums. I was someone who was well versed in head jokes, having been subjected to more than my share, but like his running ability, Juice was in a class by himself. He greeted us graciously, and his affable manner played through immediately. We were getting along well, when the groove was interrupted by the doorbell. It was a delivery person from Bergdorf Goodman, a ritzy upscale department store in Manhattan. Juice signed for the package and took it down the hall to the bedroom. On Juice's return we picked up where we left off, when suddenly the air was pierced with the melodious voice of a young woman.

"Oh, Juuuice!"

A goofy grin came across his face, directing my attention down the hall, where standing in the bedroom doorway was the most beautiful silhouette of a young woman's body imaginable. Her transparent nightgown revealed the cut of a luscious female frame, and her blond hair shimmered. O.J.'s composure hit a bump, and a hand-caught-in-the-cookie-jar expression crawled across his face. At the time he was still married to his Black wife, and the publicity that had accompanied his happily married status was a large part of his image. O.J. was worried that I would try his behavior under a racially traitorous statute. He braced himself for my indignation, but I put him at ease by telling him of my recent homogenization. His relief thickened the fabricated thread between us, because he didn't want anything to screw up the blond down the hall's control of his blood pressure. When our business was over, and we were at the door about to leave, I pulled Juice to the side and asked, "What's her name?"

He leaned over and whispered pridefully, "Nicole."

The following day I was scheduled to meet O.J. down at NBC's studios, where we would discuss the more intricate elements of the screenplay. As Juice walked down the hall, a number of agents, managers, executives, and hangers-on buzzed around him like flies. Various Not-Ready-for-Prime-Time Players were bouncing off of the walls, caught up in the high-energy stakes that came with live TV, but Juice was as cool as the unused side of a pillow. I was Joe Nobody times two, and yet he couldn't have treated me more graciously. He was solid: John Wayne without the swagger, Jim Brown without the attitude. I was blown away by his ability to handle all of this activity so smartly.

As I watched the slow-moving chase that was bearing down on the white SUV, my heart hit the floor. My hero was about to become one of the most polarizing racial figures of the twentieth century. After a long trial, Juice was acquitted by the judicial system, firing up an incredulity-gripped Black population that had rarely witnessed victory. A wealthy Black man, with a lawyer who looked like our rank and file, had chipped the bared teeth of jurisprudence. With indignance providing the foreplay, the White population exploded upon the climactic verdict. They were outraged over their ultimate brown-skinned hero's betrayal of their trust, thus rendering their own sentence: life without parole in lepersville. The lion's share of the Black celebrants had but a wisp of who and what O.J. represented, and there was certainly no allegiance to his posh Brentwood address, but the underclass will grab psychological victories wherever they can.

I liked both Mike Tyson and O.J. Simpson. Mike represented what I once was and O.J. represented what I wanted to be. Disorientation fed my sorrow as I witnessed my two borders collide in disgrace.

Christmas of 1992 was special. I called my mother to tell her that I wanted to visit on the twenty-sixth, and in true Leola form, she began to rag my ass.

"Well, if you comin' you better be here by seven-thirty because I got church."

"But Ma, that means I'll have to leave at four-thirty in the morning," I protested.

"Well, that's how it's gonna have to be," she iron-fisted.

My mother didn't negotiate, so I took the deal. "Okay, Ma, I'll be there," I conceded.

On the morning of the twenty-sixth, as I pulled out of the yard in the early A.M. darkness, I was comforted by the fact that the only human oak tree in my life was still standing. When I arrived, my mother was putting the final touches on her Sunday go-to-meeting outfit. The moment I entered, she sprayed her ritual of slapping me from pillar to post.

"You, boy, have wasted your life. I heard about that thing that you wrote in the magazine about drugs. Ain't you got no shame? And that play you did with the toilet and everything."

She was on a roll when she referred to the open toilet on the set of *Bullpen*. It didn't seem to matter that my offenses had a decade's wear on them.

"Ma, I'm doin' good. You're too old and too lame to like anything James Cleveland ain't singing," I challenged.

She offered me breakfast and I refused, citing my aversion to her Black cholesterol specials: grease soaked eggs, sausage, and heavily buttered toast. "That stuff could stop a bull's heart," I teased.

"Ahh, boy, come in the house. You been eatin' it all your life. Remember when you was gonna be a Muslim, until you found out they was against the pig. That whole thing lasted until dinnertime." Her guns were blazing. "How's your family?" she inquired.

"Fine, everybody had a good Christmas."

"Good, you know I talked to yo' gal, and she's a nice gal. But if you was gonna go that way, you should have gotten a Jewish gal. They a little closer to your skin, and they'll make your money go farther, but that gal you got ain't bad. She took you back when you weren't worth the air you was breathing," she conceded. I was left to ponder her verbal gymnastics when she said, "Let's go, I don't want to be late."

When I started the car, a tape of Stephen Stills music blasted. "Changing Partners" was the tune, and I immediately turned it off, for the car could barely contain the frown on my mother's face. We arrived at her church on 116th Street between Fifth and Lenox Avenues. I helped her out of the compact vehicle, and as she started up the stairs I felt weary of being cuffed around and more than ready to wave goodbye. She stopped, turned, and fired, "Come on, boy, I want you to meet my pastor." I was reluctant because I envisioned my morning's hazing in stereo. "Come on. Besides, I have a gift for you," she commanded. I trudged up the stairs slowly. "Come on, boy!" she shouted, and I picked up my pace.

When we entered I was greeted by all of her church brothers and sisters. They hailed me as though I was princely matter. "This is my son I told you about who writes plays and things," she stately proudly. The pastor and his disciples showered me with praise as my mother beamed. I hadn't seen such pride in me from Leola since I played Delancey Street in my Elvis days.

One of the women asked, "Is he the one married to the White gal?"

"I'm the one," I stated through a surprised grin.

The minister said, "We'se all God's children, and the White ones are just as important as the Black ones."

"A-fucking-men," I whispered to myself.

Apparently, my mother had exposed her true feelings in the house of the Lord. She was really proud of what I had done with my life. Leola would never admit that outside the confines of God's crib, but the truth shined in the sacred light. The minister told me how much everyone loved "Mother Watlington" for her great service to the church and her kind and gentle nature. What? I was now convinced I wasn't in a church, I had entered the Land of Oz. I don't think I ever felt more like a worthy son during my entire life as Leola's roaming enigma. I wanted to split while the feeling was good, and as I was about to do my good-byes my mother placed her heavy paw on my arm and pulled me to the side.

"Here your gift, boy," her whisper roared. She handed me a bottle of Goya olive oil. "This was blessed by the minister. You put a dab on your forehead every day and the Lord will do the rest."

I looked at my mom and was so moved that liquid found my cheeks. It was the first tears I could remember my mother evoking without the aid of corporal punishment. I hugged her, and the grip on her return hug was the tightest it had ever been. I bounded down the steps. As I landed on the crack-ravaged pavement, I was totally disarmed. Any resentment I might have harbored had been washed away by her show of blessed love.

February 1993

I was in Los Angeles working for two Emmy Award–winning television producers, Marian Rees and Anne Hopkins. I had been hired as a writer on a television project about a historical medical figure named Vivien Thomas. I stayed with my agent and former big brother from the Peddie School, Jim Sarnoff, who was living with his family in Pasadena. Jim and his wife, Vizma, were great hosts, and I got on well with their two young sons. On the morning that Vizma awakened me at 4:30 A.M. with an emergency call, I rushed to the phone. Anne delicately informed me that my mother was dead. I stood in shocked silence as Vizma draped her warm, sympathetic love around my shoulders. I couldn't grasp the fact that this clamorous voice in my life had been taken.

On the day of the funeral, everyone gathered at our old apartment before heading to the church. Ironically, Anne was a star of the pre-funeral gathering.

Her gracious demeanor elicited genuine warmth. My mother's congregation turned out, packing the church. Leola had done a great job with her life after my father's death. Although I was often at odds with what I considered her religious fanaticism, when her life was hammered by losing the only man she had ever loved, she had put her faith where her mouth was by allowing the Lord to nourish her in this wonderful congregation of true believers.

At the time, Barbara Kopple was in the midst of an exhausting promotional tour for the Mike Tyson project. I didn't think she would be able to make it and was moved when she and Kevin Keating were there to pay their respects. Many other White friends made their way out into the winter night. The salt-and-pepper audience was invigorated as the gospel chorus sang their hearts out in honor of my mother's soul. The greatest thing about Black funerals is the music. It infuses the proceedings with a dimension of emotional rescue that outfitted each participant with temporary wings. My son, Keelan, held my hand, and I could feel the excitement that rushed through his body as he experienced his first uncut Black spirituals. The minister, who a few short months earlier had blessed my Goya oil, was intoxicating as he preached the virtue of my mother's existence. He reminded us that Leola was not really leaving, that she remained alive in anyone who had ever had the opportunity to know her. The Reverend captured the spirit of her tenacious will and unflappable faith in her Lord Jesus Christ.

As I soaked in this magnificent departure, I scanned the crowd for posterity. Its makeup was a far cry from the America that had birthed Leola. She'd died in a significantly better country. It was a moment of pure transcendence that an ardent integrationist could appreciate.

The following morning the burial procession endured a brutal hailstorm. At my mother's gravesite the conditions were so terrible that the minister shortened his prayers, and everyone dashed for cover. The hailstones began gathering on the back of my neck, numbing my senses, but it was difficult to leave her side. I remained standing under a barely adequate tent, watching the stones form a blanket of glistening pearls on her coffin. The Lord's bejeweled sendoff was further indication that her indomitable faith had been appreciated. I defied my frozen extremities, holding on to the moment, unwilling to accept the fact that the king was dead.

THIRTY-THREE

On a cold February day, shortly after my mother passed, I was home alone enjoying a soothing shower when the phone rang. Faced with the dilemma of interrupting my bliss or letting the phone exhaust itself, I chose the former and slipped and slid until reaching the receiver.

"Hello, yeah, man, what's up?"

It was my agent, Leo Bookman, from the William Morris Agency.

"Do you know anything about Black cowboys?"

"Sure," I replied.

"I might have a job for you. TBS is doing a piece on Black cowboys, and they're looking for a Black writer."

"Well, that's my specialty."

After I hung up I took a deep breath. I barely knew that Black cowboys ever existed. Fortunately, my agent didn't probe beneath my snap response, because with the exception of a few roles played by Sammy Davis, Jr., it was my understanding that cowboys were White.

Esteemed documentarians, Bill Miles and Nina Rosenblum, were producing the film, along with Pat Mitchell, our TBS executive, who provided an unusually constructive hand from the hire-and-fire wing of the operation. Nina was largely responsible for my getting the job, but the opportunity to work with Bill

Miles was the real lure. He was to be my first Black boss in the industry. Bill's relatively unsung career as a filmmaker was obsessed with preserving the legacies of the likes of Paul Robeson and the Black patriots who served in World War I. I was pumped for this job and dove head first into the research, only to run into a psychological meat grinder.

The subject's matter was sunk deep in the bowels of slavery. I was shocked to discover that one-third of cowboys in the Old West were Black. Many were runaways from the colonies on the East Coast, which acted as a veritable Triple-A farm team for Black cowboys. Troubled slaves were welcomed to join the struggle to tame our Western regions.

If you're the unlucky Black man stuck with the job of researching the period of American slavery, life sucked. My ancestors were regarded as sophisticated livestock, so there was little respect for the slave who had endured hard work, under horrible conditions, without compensation. A handful of months of this was enough to make one's Black ass burn, because the only conclusion leaping from this pile of painfully stained American laundry was that White people were fucked up. After a couple of days of hate-Whitey convulsions, I regained perspective, focusing on my children and how their options had grown. My urge to broad-brush White folks by placing past tormentors up against the wall and administering character death by firing squad subsided. Despite the hanging curveball's girth, the humanity etched in my wife's Caucasian face cemented the bat to my shoulder. She had invested in one America.

I vaulted over the Black pain and focused on how vital slaves were to the development of the American miracle. Black cowboys were some bad cats who helped stretch our national boundaries from coast to coast. Their unacknowledged patriotism sprang from the colonies' first womb. Their courage and heroism was responsible for everything my children and grandchildren might ever achieve. I wanted the film to reflect my buttressed pride in my slave roots. Beneath the layers of searing injustice are a slew of colorfully impactful American pioneers. If their legacies were to draw national attention, it might help nudge the topic of slavery beyond the reflexive gridlock of indignation and guilt.

The joyful enlightenment I had stumbled upon was dampened by the fact that my father-in-law had entered the final stages of his battle with cancer. Jack bounced between poles of hopeful chemotherapeutic floor shows that ended each performance with the revelation that progress was illusory. While filming I was often sobered by the discouraging words crawling through the phone lines. In November of 1993, *The Black West* project was in the editing process, when I received word in New York that Jack had passed. I was paralyzed by the thought that the old guy was gone. He and my mother falling off the count in the same year was a poignant reminder of how much instability life offered. It seemed as though these two pillars had been around forever, and despite the obvious cracks, their departure was incomprehensible.

I stayed in New York continuing to work, and several days later I hopped an iron horse to Merrick, Long Island, where I was to meet the family at the wake. I was still in denial over Jack's death; in my heart he would remain alive until I saw him laid out. As the train roared I flashed upon on a decade-old incident. I had been laid up in the hospital with an appendix in revolt. This was during one of my persona non grata periods, shortly before I was to spin off to Bellevue. I was a cash-empty, dispirited bloke, and, had I not fallen sick on a midtown bus and taken to a decent hospital, I would have wound up in a cheap ghetto chop shop.

I'd crapped out to the point, where death had fallen out of my list of top-ten worst things that can happen. The nurses doped my anxiety into a fitful sleep. When I awoke I thought I was hallucinating, when standing before me was a smiling Irish senior whose thick white hair defied the aging process. It was Jack McCormack on family duty, and despite my wide-screened propensity for screwing up, he'd come to bolster my spirits. Jack's patriarchal touch was most effective when one of his flock was in dire need. With typical Gaelic reserve, he shrugged off his dead-of-winter drive from Bellmore as no big thing, but to me his gesture topped all the drugs in the nurse's cabinet. The old man's cameo left me with a kernel of hope that things would work out.

My recollection vaporized as the train pulled into the Baldwin station. After a soused group of teenagers authored a loud, raucous departure, we pulled out of the station and my thoughts returned to the old guy with the Depression-era sanity. Jack was a straight-shooter with little desire to impress at the expense of his laminated principles. While my personality often darted all over the map, he rarely failed to deliver the meat and potatoes cooking in his pot of basic truths. I was so Black, and he was so White, yet we made it work. By the end of his life we'd driven the divisive color issue into irrelevance's benign chamber.

When I got off the train at Merrick, I waded through the dark night, searching for the funeral parlor. When I found the joint, the entire family was there engaged in reflective musings as they celebrated the old man's existence. I made my way to the coffin, and there he was, as handsome as an old White dead guy gets. The proof was before me, and I had to accept the painful truth that his steady hand had left the oxygenated merry-go-round.

The following morning when I arrived at the funeral home, I dashed downstairs to take a leak. When I hit the lower level, there were approximately a dozen cops packed in blue, many of them holding rifles. In honor of Jack's big cop status, they were preparing for a multi-gun salute. My presence provoked a instinctive collective gasp. "Who the hell is that?" was the question that ran the table of surprised faces. Flashbacks of my criminal past besieged me. I held my hands above my head and cracked, "I've never been in a room with this many cops without handcuffs on." My quip acted as an icebreaker, and we engaged in a mutual laugh. "As unusual as this may seem, I'm family," I declared, and the blue boys rolled with the oddity. The old guy's sense of humor would have chimed over this one.

After the funeral my new friends put on a show, blasting away in unison to honor Jack's service. On the way to the cemetery, they shut down Northern State Parkway. Several motorcycle police leapfrogged each other, closing off the entrances to the public as the procession made its way to Jack's final resting place. He owned the road, free of the traffic that had so often irritated the hell out of him.

Keelan and I drove in our car, listening to a Neil Young recording of "Star of Bethlehem." As the procession snaked down the highway, I clung to images from the previous year, when Jack's only son, John, had married his fiancée, Colleen. During the week that led up to the event, Jack talked about his desire to attend the wedding in good stead. The old guy fought the good fight, and fortunately his medication cooperated. His reward was a sufficient surge of energy on the day of the union. When he and Ellen danced at the wedding, I was moved by their ebullience, seemingly oblivious to the diminishing amount of sand left in the old guy's hourglass. This was Jack's last public triumph.

When it comes to Francis John McCormack, I plead guilty to hero worship. I couldn't find the clay in Jack's feet if the words Play-Doh were stamped on them. I was knocked out by the amount of character he exhibited when I sky-dived into his life. I had put his cop-scrubbed middle-class values to a sharp test, and he had rarely failed to exceed expectations. After Jack was planted, it became official: The Lord had added another M.V.P. to his roster of eternal voices.

Months later my angle on slavery proved that you could attract more Americans with honey than vinegar. On a hot summer day, at the end of a round of the family's yearly hay-bailing initiative, I climbed the stairs to my bedroom. Fatigue had broken me down like a three-legged card table, and I collapsed on the bed. Rigor mortis was invading when the fax machine chimed in. Duty got the best of me, and I trudged over to the machine. To my great surprise it was a message informing me that I had been nominated for an Emmy for writing *The Black West*. Adrenaline seized the moment, firing up my exhausted limbs, and I ran out to the fields where Anne was still working the tractor. Several of our work mates mulling around the backyard were puzzled at the sight in the distance of Anne and me jumping up and down on a swath of hay like newly minted maniacs.

On the morning of the awards ceremony, I fulfilled a commitment to a former employer and friend, Patricia Duff, to visit a youth group sponsored by her foundation in South Central, LA. Patricia was a longtime political and social activist who had just married New York billionaire Ron Perlman. She was at the height of her influence and spent significant amounts of energy and capital on up-kick programs like this one. The goal was to help Black and Brown kids who were trying to dig themselves out of the gangsta dead-end future that had been exacerbated by the ravages of the Rodney King gang bang. Patricia's charitable eyedropper laid a taste of tangible hope on this group of tottering teenagers at risk. The hundred or so faces reminded me of my days with the center, and I delivered a rousing spiel in our native tongue on a street kid's right to dream, using the nomination as my credibility chip. Implacable ghetto pessimism dies hard, and I could feel my rap shrink under the collective assumption that my chance of winning was negligible.

That evening I attended my first big-time show-biz back pat, and I discovered that these events were so long one could knit a sweater for an elephant. Finally, my category arrived and everything sped up. As the presenter did his rap, they showed a clip for each nominee. After the *Black West* clip, I prepared for my coach to turn back into a pumpkin. Then my name was called. My table of TBS executives erupted, banging out stunned applause. Befuddled, I was left with the task of making my way to the stage. The light found me on the way, and flashes of déjà-vus broke out. I was reminded of the last time a spotlight had followed me so closely: It had been during my attempted escape from the Spofford correctional facility. The irony empowered a huge smile as I entered the blur of acceptance and thank-yous that played without mishap. I left the stage with six inches of air beneath my feet.

Early the next morning I was swimming laps in an empty pool at the Miramar Hotel in Santa Monica. I stopped when the closeup of a pair of ankles at the pool's edge distracted me. I looked up and squinted into the sunlight, trying to make out the facial features of a man who, from my low angle, looked ten feet tall. It was Anthony Quinn, the Rushmorian-weighted, award-winning actor, holding the hand of a cute blond toddler. This was the stuff of dreams. I climbed out of the pool and shook his hand before introducing myself and telling of my award. He smiled and his face wore the wisdom of an old lion, before he imparted his recollection of the thrill he had experienced when winning the Oscar for his work in the film *Zorba the Greek*.

Quinn rubbed some prideful liberal salve over my accomplishment, indicating his delight with the social progress embedded in my pigment's distinction.

But time grows old fast in the presence of an eighty-plus-year-old screen legend, and my few minutes wrapped in a blink. He reached for the hand of his toddler, turning in the direction of his intended destination, walking a few steps before stopping.

"Just remember," he advised. "The first one is usually the only one, so enjoy it."

His parting smile was soon the back of his head as he escorted the young child into the hotel.

Later that morning, I went back to the kids in South Central and elongated my high by delivering a direct hit of Black success. Ten minutes before I was to speak, a White biker, a Hell's Angels type wearing a leather jacket, helmet, and shades turned heads when he roared up. It was a blast to discover that beneath all of those red-assed symbols was John O'Donohue. My old *Bullpen* sibling had moved to Los Angeles to feed a successful career as a television character actor, ultimately, hitting on a recurring role in the popular dramatic series *NYPD Blue*. Anne had gotten the message to him that I was on the West Coast. We hugged in a typical, big-hearted O'Donohue way, when he said, "I heard you were doing this, and I wanted to help." John always had my back. I put my arm around him, and we walked into the community center with some of the kids studying John closely, emitting strains of recognition.

When I fronted the audience holding the trophy, the faces were lit as though the golden lady bore special powers. Now that I had them, I used the Emmy to rap my message in some hard native tongue. "I'm a street nigger who couldn't, and did anyway. Can't sing, can't dunk, can't rap, and I still won." The crowd roared as I held the trophy above my head. Their high-beamed attention was a mixture of disbelief that I had won and astonishment that I'd come back to share my good fortune. I used my moment to goose the importance of King's twin six-shooters: education and integration, wrapping the two precepts in a package and stamping it with the helpful Clintonian respect his administration consistently pumped into the Blackstream. I could feel my words connecting with a willing trove of ghetto listeners. It was as though I had won the award a second time.

The old Thorne-Thomsen farm in the Berkshires was lit up over the news of Leif's impending nuptials. While reconstructing his life, he had fallen in love with Aimee Rivera, a Hotchkiss alumnas. Although she was in her twenties, Aimee's maturity and poise played well beyond her birth certificate. Aimee's background was seeded in Hispanic Manhattan, primarily on the Upper West Side. Her curly black hair and golden skin tone were identical to Noel's. She was also in possession of his indomitable Latino will. When she landed on the Berkshire scene, Leif was doing low-level depression, sorting through a confused future. Aimee's sophisticated street sanity pulled a nicked-up, cynical idealist out of his doldrums.

Preparations were set for them to tie the knot. It was fitting that they chose the United Nations Chapel for the ceremony. Leif and I stood at the altar. We'd reversed our positions from the ones we held decades earlier at the wedding Gerri and I had shared. This time I was the best man and he was in the proverbial hot spot. The event's gathering of friends and family did justice to its U.N. backdrop. Many different hues coated the faces of those who came together, from Sadie Rivera, Aimee's madre and my home girl, who carried a Ph.D. in street savvy, to Mary Thorne-Thomsen, Leif's eloquent mother, a near century's worth of progressive teaching acumen that had influenced generations of upper educational aspirants.

When the ceremony began, Leif's three daughters, son Eli, and longtime Hotchkiss friend, Rick Mayer, joined us at the altar. Eli, the surprise star of my first wedding, was now a strapping six-foot presence in his twenties. Keelan sang "Amazing Grace," setting the stage for Aimee's arrival. Three bridesmaids preceded Aimee's entrance on the arm of her proud father, Salvador.

Aimee was as beautiful as hope and promise could suggest. I focused on Leif as he watched her approach the altar. Overcome by emotion, he punctuated his joy with an unusual show of tears. This Dr. King dividend was comprised of four Puerto Ricans, six Whites, and an African American, who together formed an enclave of supportive love when the clergyman pronounced Leif and Aimee husband and wife. Flecks of our Hotchkiss past seasoned the air. Headmaster Olsen's genuine stab at diversity had initiated the process that subsequently provided his beloved protégé with a loving Puerto Rican wife and a proud Black brother.

After the ceremony, we split the United Nations, hopping into a horde of vehicles that made their way to the South Bronx for the reception. It was held in Castle Harbor, a neighborhood bar with an after-hours joint's bent to it. In the rear was a large banquet room where the festivities played out. The neighborhood was planted in South Bronx's proud soil, a gritty reminder of Tom Wolfe's choice of location for *Bonfire of the Vanities*, where White folks held their breath and floored the gas pedal. Checked emotions got busy to the blare of Latino rhythms. Great food and fine toasts provided the fuel that sent our interactive Barrio-chic boiling pot soaring into a rich, Oprah-esque ghetto night.

Sadly, the marriage initiated the end of our makeshift family. Leif's move into his new life flattened the coalition's dynamic, and like so many good things in life, we were forced to contend with the aftermath of dispersal. Another of my America bubbles had burst. Illusions were at low tide.

Summer 2000

After twelve years of estrangement, the result of bad racial residue, Chuck and I buried the hatchet. I had been itching to reconnect, but there was little opportunity to break the ice. Chuck was noted for his steadfast, never-look-back philosophy, and I didn't want to go through the disappointing aggravation that came with one of his cold dismissals.

Chuck's many decades of overdrive were taking their toll, as heart ailments, diabetes, and a fried prostate rode his broad back as he crept across the line of his seventy-third spin. I tried to invite Chuck to watch Keelan play in his opening football game. Keelan was in his first year at Hotchkiss, and I thought the big man and I would break our impasse while watching Keelan perform on the same field that had hosted our street-prep classic three decades earlier. But I discovered that the phone number I had for him had gone cold. I went back to the old neighborhood to look for information. After standing on the corner of 115th Street and Lexington and scouting familiar faces, I drifted toward Noel's old building. Curiosity led me to the entrance, but I couldn't get in. Security measures were much tighter, and you had to be buzzed into the building. Finally some kids let me in, and I went to Noel's apartment on the first floor and knocked. My intention was to ask the residents if I could take a glimpse of my history.

I was surprised when Noel's mother answered the door. She recognized me, despite the three chunks of ten that had passed since our last glance at Noel's funeral. I was at a loss for words when she invited me in, because I fully expected that the Velasquezes would have moved on. Mrs. Velasquez had always been kind and gracious to me, and thirty years of life's toll had not changed her demeanor. We talked about Noel and his daughter, who was experiencing a successful career in the U.S. military, before looking at a number of faded photographs of Noel's image. It felt like we both welcomed this refresher course in his memory, but at our commemoration's climax, a sad silence ensued. We were struck by the sorrow that Noel's incomplete life exacerbated; his tape had run out too quickly. When we parted I held on to her frail hand, and we shared a mutual warmth. I wanted to tell her that I loved her son, but the words didn't come. I regret their not having found me.

I don't think that I ever quite got over Noel's nonsensical departure. There are a handful of people in your life whose death kills a part of your soul. As I walked back to the corner, I tossed morbid memories past focusing on the weight of loss. I was reminded of something I heard the great football coach John Madden once say, "Losing is worse than dying, because you have to live with losing."

On the corner I got lucky and ran into a former blood who gave me Chuck's new phone number. After my experience with Mrs. Velasquez, I was pumped for contact. Then the Sly-Hendrix project happened, affording me the opportunity to seek Chuck out bearing gifts. From a pay phone a block away from the center, I called and we connected. Quick joy indicated that the grudge's coat had been shorn, and we both were thinking that our next encounter would break the lock. I offered him a job doing voice-over work on the film. After ten seconds of thought, his raspier, slower vocal cadence fed my ear a warm, compliant: "Are you crazy, nigger? What time and where I got to be." I was thrilled

We sent a town car to pick up Chuck. I was so excited that I was firing off hyped-up teenaged sparks, and the old gray king did not disappoint. He and I picked up our rhythm from good times past. Nina Rosenblum was aware of our history together, and gave Chuck the royal treatment. After parking his body you could see the performance lights turning on, and before long, he was spinning tales of his bulging yesteryears in an atmosphere of respectful adoration. For a few moments Chuck repossessed thirty years of calendar pages, offering a glimmer of his prime. He told of the time I quarterbacked a championship game on a broken leg and won. That was a clear signal that I was on his good memories list, because he knew that story was pure helium to me. It was great to see my de facto dad speak pridefully of our trip together. Ironically, we were again the only Black people on the scene, but we both seemed to have made peace with that boulder. It was vintage Chuck Griffin, and the imbibers got a great buzz.

In a quiet moment between setups, I asked about his various ailments, and he spit in their eye. "I ain't gonna worry about the shit. Life was meant to kill you."

I brought Chuck up to speed on the project before we laid down his audio tracks. It was clear that the ham embedded inside the old actor was as fresh as ever, and his vocal blasts served the film's archival images perfectly. After the work was done, I walked Chuck downstairs to the car and told him, "I love you and miss you and I'm really grateful for what you have done for me." I waited nervously for his reaction to my sentiments. He gave me his widest smile to chew on before stating, "You'se my son." I kissed him on the forehead, helped him into the car, and watched it speed off.

In the fall of 2001, Chuck called and asked if he could come to hunt on our land. I jumped at the chance because it provided an opportunity to spend a week together. Anne and he had put to rest the gross misunderstanding that had occurred between them during the *Bullpen* fiasco. Chuck was the first person from my inner circle to meet Anne at a time when her White face was a blackhead on the tarp of convention. I had wandered way off the reservation, bringing the devil's child into the tent. This stunt had the word *ostracize* written all over it, but one meeting with Anne and her colorblind sincerity initiated a suspension of convention. They dressed each other in accommodating garments and wore them unflinchingly. It was a relief to watch them resume the positive practices of their unique past.

Chuck pulled up in his SUV, slowly maneuvered his large frame out of the front seat, and yelled, "Annie Mac!" his favorite name for my wife. We could tell from the joyful tone that this would be a retro encounter. I was concerned over Arielle's first lengthy dose of Black bombast, but she and Chuck took to each other thoroughly, and by the end of his stay they had adopted each other as grandpa and granddaughter.

As far as Chuck's hunting prowess was concerned, there was not much left of the old warrior but the heart and the gear. Age's robbery of his energy limited him to short bits of activity. More often than not, he would take a quick look around the property, come back in the house, and crash on the couch, where I would find him sound asleep in camouflage fatigues. On one excursion we hopped into his vehicle and drove off into the fields. We sought to scale a hill where Chuck felt he could gain the best vantage point for scoping out prey. As he jacked his four-wheel drive to the summit, the wheels found the muck that tall grass obscures. After several attempts to free ourselves, the verdict was hopelessly stuck. Our only solution was to walk back to the house and call Leif to crane us free.

I offered Chuck the option of staying with the vehicle while I did the leg-work, but he insisted on making the trek. After the first fifty yards, his body re-belled, bending him over, and, with his hands clutching his knees, he gasped for oxygen. Profuse streams of sweat drenched his bearded face. I feared for his life as I helped him to the ground.

"How ya doin' man?" I asked. "You think you going out on me? Shake this shit off." He smiled between gasps. "Come on, man. You got to pull this shit out. I can see the headline now: Greatest nigger in Harlem history dies on a nonde-script piece of Berkshire turf."

"I ain't goin' nowhere yet, nigger!" were the words that replaced the heavy breathing as his faculties coalesced. "What's this thing about you and death, boy. I keep tellin' you—a lot worse things can happen to a nigger than dying. You need to reevaluate that shit."

That last note let me know that the old man was all right.

"See, man, I figure we still got some hell to raise," I said. "Besides, I'm not worrying about me dying. I'm worried about your ass dying."

As our laughter helped him to his feet, the difficult task of moving on still lay ahead. We thought about taking him back to the vehicle, but the incline was too dicey. We decided to continue onward, when Chuck said, "Stand in front of me, son, and hold still." I did so, facing him. "No, turn around," he commanded. I complied. He placed his hands on my shoulders and ordered, "Go slow." I became his human walker, and we moved at a snail's pace the half mile back to the house. When I was a kid I had leaned heavily on Chuck's shoulders as he led the way to my survival, and now as the exhaust from his heavy breathing moistened my neck, I was determined to usher him to safety.

Hours later, Leif and a couple of friends showed up with a four-wheel drive vehicle with a crane and dug the car out. The rare opportunity for Leif, Chuck, and myself to be together invited a dip into the time machine. Despite a variety of degrees of separation, we found our groove from the late sixties that connected the three of us so often in that time of all times. With Chuck's breathing apparatus restored, we began to polish our antique memories. I was again the kid, Leif, the mentor, and Chuck funding it all with his iconic street capital.

Chuck was a bit embarrassed by his loosened grip on sufficiency, but his dreams remained undaunted. By the time the children came home from school, he had wiped away the incident and, with Arielle seated beside him, began to tell of his future plans. It didn't matter that his plans had little chance of realizing themselves. Chuck's gift was to lay out big dreams and invite younger people's imaginations to surpass them.

THIRTY-FOUR

2004

It is 4:00 A.M., and I'm on my way to New York on a writer's trip. I grab my legal pad and a handful of unlabeled music cassettes before heading out into a dark country morning. I fire up the ride, slam a random tape into the deck, and move out. I'm delighted to discover that my choice is Dylan's "Mr. Tambourine Man."

I love writing on the move. Much of my work has been written in cars, city restaurants, rural diners, and foreign countries. Some of my best work was written in Nicaragua and Honduras. Our embassies in those countries invited me to show a few of my films in honor of Black History Month. The ability to be Black in February has put a lot of food on my table.

I once asked Ray, my close friend, what he thought about Black History Month, and he snorted, "What about the rest of the months?"

"Damn, man, it takes progress to reach perfection, and this is progress," I replied.

"You been living in the woods too long, sniffing that clean air, so you believe in Santa Claus," he laughed.

"You still in and out of tenement buildings too much," I tossed, "so to you the world smells like an old shoe."

Ray paused for a moment, then let loose a burst of infectious laughter and said, "Maybe you're right, but you notice they slipped us the shortest month." We both fell down laughing.

I have been driving in a dark fog for an hour. Route 22's dividing line is barely visible on my low-beam crawl. As the sun begins to wink through the clouds, I pull over to *On The Run*, a gas-and-coffee joint. After feeding my car, I cop my caffeine and motor off into a newly lit reality. I'm still toying with Ray's February rant and am reminded of a question my daughter, Arielle, once asked.

"Why is the penny brown and the other coins silver?"

Talk about a loaded question. "Lincoln's picture is on the penny," I told my little girl, "so they made it brown because he freed the slaves who were also brown."

"Was Lincoln poor?" she asked.

"What?" I replied.

She asserted, "The penny is the poorest coin."

"The penny isn't poor, it's first," I floated. "No matter how much money you have, it always starts with the penny. It's an honor."

Arielle seemed pleased with my jive and skipped off to other inquiries. I was left wishing that my bullshit was more truthful. I asked Ray what he thought about Arielle's question and he said, "Simple, pennies is the niggers in the coin pile."

I'm in Manhattan cruising down a newly awakened Central Park West. First stop is my monthly visit to the John Lennon memorial, a small patch of sacred turf in New York's Central Park named after one of his better acid songs, "Strawberry Fields." As I look down on the memorial's centerpiece with the word IMAGINE emblazoned across it, I'm thinking about our country's invasion of Iraq. Peace through bloodshed has become the national strategy. What would you have thought about preemptive war, John, and the early national gag order that asphyxiated dissent?

A gray wind blows through the memorial, darkening the atmosphere. I'm chilled by the thought of the American kids my children's age blowing up in Baghdad. The axe-wielders are chopping the olive branch to bits. Where do we go from here, and who will bring nonviolent peace initiatives to the international conference tables? My curiosity draws me closer to the memorial, until I'm close enough to listen for the sound of the Walrus weeping.

After writing several pages in Central Park, I enter the city's motorized morning nightmare, inching northward to a place most motorists try to avoid, the ghetto. I pull up on First Avenue and 113th Street beside Jefferson Park and take out my legal pad, looking to siphon off some inspiration from my former stomping ground. I get out of the car and, after paying the parking meter for my car's right to exist, I hit the old playpen. It's a cold day, and the park's sporadic patches of trees and shrubs are naked. It still feels great to walk the dirt fields that I played my best football on, but in harsh daylight there is no hiding the pathetic neglect that has fallen upon a once thriving hotbed of Italians, Puerto Ricans, and Blacks.

As memory inflates past athletic exploits, my Walkman is pumping Crosby Stills and Nash's song. "Pre-Road Downs." The lyrics surge as I come upon the spot where Alfred Mealy gave me my first joint. The still, lifeless soil where Alfred and I once stood activates a chronic sense of guilt. When my destructive drug past wedges itself onto the radar screen, the cold reality of my history emits poisonous residue, setting off an alarming hiss. How many people died from the dirty needle that almost took me out? I'd shared that needle with dozens of people. Maybe some of them didn't make it.

When the peace-and-love boys came along in the sixties with a bong, a hope, and a chemically infused prayer, they inadvertently piloted an out-of-control aircraft through the looking glass. To be fair, they were in their twenties, and any of us who've made it across the fifty-year stripe have discerned that in those years one doesn't know one's ass from a hole in the ground. In large part, these young cultural icons were just pissing in the wind. Tragically, the bong would morph into a free-base pipe, heaping shame on their wooden ships.

I'm now standing atop my old footprints, where Alfred punched my ticket to the Gomorrah-decorated hedonistic drug-sprayed ball. I stayed on the dance floor catching thrills and dodging disaster for decades. The high crime of addiction was my willingness to turn loved ones into hostages, traumatizing them senselessly.

I'm staring at my old bedroom window, sitting in my father's favorite bench spot beneath it. The memories coalesce, invoking scenes of my early childhood, when I would peer four flights down into a cloud of Kool cigarette smoke, with the sounds of Mel Allen's baseball play-by-play poetry cutting the air. Inevitably, the latter stages of the game would turn dad's coarsened grumbles into audible epithets, earmarked for Yankee manager Ralph Houk's Bronx hit boys after they'd jabbed another victorious pin-striped dart into my dad's ass. My recollection pricks open a soft scab of regret: I never found a way to convince my father that I loved him and appreciated his yeoman's effort of corking the leaks that consistently sprung in our family's impoverished vessel.

Seated in the old man's spot, I'm sketching notes from a half a century of expired calendar pages. Many of my best American thoughts often materialize when I measure my life beside my father's. Robert Sr.'s life as a Jim Crow survivor was entrapped in a block of perpetual futility, while I've had the privilege to think as freely as the price of my actions would bare—a quantum leap beyond the old man's birth stamp.

I've been so immersed in thought that I didn't realize that a woman with a cartful of groceries is a few feet away, staring at me. Upon quick inspection I realize she's a bonafide former neighborhood beauty, Joanne. In our youth Joanne was vivacious, intelligent, and completely out of my reach. We were friends because it was the best I could do from the back of a long line of heat-seekers. She looks worn, almost as though life has been beating her with sticks.

"I haven't seen you in so long that it's hard to imagine you still above ground," she says. Joanne gives me a warm hug, disappearing in my arms. My embrace falls to her waist, and I can feel the imprint of her ribs. Joanne's skeletal figure suggests too many losing eyeball-to-eyeball confrontations with the dreaded pipes and needles. Upon our release, she says, "Let me see, last thing I heard about you is that you married a White girl."

"Now how is it that no matter who I meet from back in the day, if they know nothing else, they know I married a White girl?"

Joanne pinches my cheek and says, "Because that's news. The only Black men I know who have White women is pimps."

"Well, I ain't pimping. It's straight-up love, marriage, children, and brown rice. I'll tell you something else, my wife's father was five-oh, high up in the narcotics unit."

Joanne laughs, "He know about all the drugs you shot?" She again howls with laughter. "You look good, like you doing okay. That White girl must be keeping you healthy."

"Yeah," I say. "I've been lucky."

"What you doing around here?" she asks.

"Sniffing old memories. You see . . . I'm a writer, and I'm working on a few things"

"A writer? I thought that pad you was writing on meant you worked for the welfare or something." We both laugh, before entering a pre-departure awkwardness. "I'm proud of you," she says. "You left this hell and wound up with a great White job and a good White woman."

Before parting, I surprise her with a kiss on the lips and say, "I've been waiting thirty-five years to do that."

Sheepishly, she whispers, "Disappointed?"

"No. It was every bit as sweet as I thought it would be."

I glide through the projects on my way to the basketball court, where Chuck once coached my brother, Robert, on how to take no prisoners. My younger brother, Calvin, also spent a stint polishing his manhood on this hallowed turf. My baby sister, Harriet, who was probably the best round ball talent of us all, dominated the paint among her peers. I cop a seat on a bench, and my view is that of a tall Black kid bundled up from head to toe shooting jump shots. I count for a while, and at one point the kid has a nine-for-ten stretch. How he's able to shoot that well wearing an overcoat is a wonder, but as the cold air turns his breath into exhaust, he keeps firing away. His pigment-rich face is that of a serious warrior who is intent on shooting his way out of the ghetto. Unfortunately, as in my time, basketball has remained a Black kid's front-row dream, despite the unrequited ambition filling the cracks in the worn pavement beneath him.

You'd think after all of these years, my jump-shot warrior would have more options instead of fewer role models. Despite far more egregious treatment during my stage of Jim Crow's apartheid, oddly, it was easier for Black kids to reach across racial lines for their heroic influences. In today's world, where there is a wider platform for exchange, far less of it seems to occur. This ironic happenstance has been one of the most perplexing developments to waft its way through my five decades. I'm fortunate that the brainwashing I received from American television in the fifties and sixties flooded my mind with so many positive White images that when the riotous racial acid defaced the nation's poise in the late sixties, I was incapable of hating Whitey indiscriminately. Hell, Green Bay quarterback Bart Starr taught me some valuable lessons about courage as the field general under my adopted godfather, the great Lombardi.

Starr played quarterback for the University of Alabama when apartheid was as prevalent as a stiff bang of good bourbon. Fortunately, no one sought to tell me that Starr played for a machine that viewed me as less than human, and thankfully, I was able to skim his greatness from the bitter details. Starr's no-quit leadership during the do-or-die last-ditch effort of the 1967 NFL championship game, when he scored the gutsiest game-winning touchdown of the decade, was a colorblind seminal uplift that I was free to absorb.

If I were a teenager today out there shooting those jump shots, I would not have had the indiscriminate, youthful worship rights for heroes with choices that ran from the multitalented performer Mickey Rooney to Nobel Prize–winning diplomat Ralph Bunche, with all kinds of variations in between. White people may not have rhythm, but they sure as hell are colorful. The overall positive qualities that make White Americans special must be factored into the Black assessment apparatus. These days that's a tough haul, because Black kids have little interest in White heroes who aren't willing to embarrass themselves mirroring Black street culture.

Who will fill the leadership vacuum? The arrow seems to point at an unforeseen candidate. "Ain't no way them record-scratching porch monkeys gonna fly," was a friend's comment in the early eighties, supporting a consensus that sooner or later the big White slap would catch up with rap. To the mainstream's cultural astonishment, these feisty street exhibitionists waded through empty crack vials, laying new cement with fresh Adidas prints. They barked gut-level poetry through percussive rhythm, a foolproof, megaphonic Black meal ticket. The explosive naiveté, virulently untainted by Horatio Alger's mythological piety, drove the chutzpah arrow off its dial. The monkeys didn't just fly, they soared, with their creative courage coalescing into a uniquely independent African American voice. They would formulate an unprecedented battering ram, smashing Black, conventional, liberal fears of Caucasian retribution. An important assist from their White punk peers' emancipatory energy that percolated a few miles south on the Lower East Side of Manhattan cleared its generation's sinuses for an on-coming wave of unabashed young Black "burn down the missionism."

Now what? The hop-beat founders who brought creative farts and slaps to mainstream prominence produced a list of extraordinary men and women too numerous to mention. Many of them were middle-class, educated visionaries who took the baton from the boys on the stoop and asserted their non-conformism in terms that could only have put smiles on the faces of their be-bop predecessors. The unexpected predominance of the rap pioneers' art finds itself in the role of defining the new ideal for heroic Black leadership. These Malcolm-laced, King-dipped, founding Black gems started a revolution that holds a significant slice of my myopic young jump-shooter's American esteem in the belly of their product. The Dres, Latifas, Cubes, Smiths, Simmonses and Doggs are peering into their sons' and daughters' generation with more options and clarity than street-bred sensibilities have peeped since the ships docked.

In what innovative way will they contribute to Brother Jump-Shot's move beyond his psyche's obsession with a few pounds of entrapped air? Will their contribution enlighten his task when he faces the nation's racial potholes in the forefront of his consciousness?

The jump-shooter's perceived tiny margin for inclusion in society's main well lures him down a path of his own exclusion. He is unaware of a rarely artic-ulated mammoth truth trapped in the discordant racial background noise. My decades reveal that our country has made amazing progress on that young man's behalf. Our public leadership should call for a pause, turning the volume way down in order to lay a pat on our nation's back, with a major shout out of appre-ciation for the astonishing societal progress that has occurred.

On my life's watch I've witnessed and have been part of positive changes that are almost beyond comprehension. During my childhood in the South in the fifties, I was taught to stare at my shoes when talking to a White man. If my favorite new jump-shooter were led into a public facility where water fountains and bathrooms were labeled White and Colored, he would think that he had landed on another planet. I was one of the millions of Black Boomers who ran the obstacle course through Colored, Negro, and Black, subsequently landing on the board in a space that read African American. My life's timing has allowed me to see the empty glass I was born in fill to the halfway mark.

The African American is a special breed of human, and I am grateful to have been born one. My reverence for my slave ancestry punctuates this conclusion. My jump-shooter must know that he is a secret shareholder in his country's prodigious wealth. The buckets of sweat that poured from his forebears' brow into the soil helped water the seeds that would sprout into the greatest national miracle in the history of peoplekind. The courageous slave legacy embodies perseverance, ingenuity, and foresight that commands its own stripe on our flag. My hip-hop–energized bundled-up warrior should know that he can wrap himself in this uniquely distinctive symbol that the likes of Public Enemy's Chuck D has infused with new relevance. If he can hurdle that revelation, the value of his citizenship would brighten the width of his horizon, allowing him to stand among his national relatives with rights no one could deny.

After having dumped the weight of our race's future reckoning on the younger bang-and-scratch brigade, what would I do to communicate this theorem to my young pavement-leaper? I would start by asking the president of the United States to sign an executive order bestowing belated citizenship on all recorded slaves, paying symbolic homage to the patriots who were among the first respondents the embryonic nation ever called upon. In addition, there should be an education fund to help heal the clubfoot of illiteracy that saddled the race. This point often provokes White folks into ordering their feet to do their stuff, hightailing it from the slightest wisp of renumeration, but we were the only people walking our soil who had to surmount criminal charges in order to read. Sadly, the impact of those restrictions still linger.

I walk on the court, say hello, and ask my star for a shot. He accommodates my wish, and I brick it badly. The shot caroms off the side of the rim, with the ball skirting well off the court. Embarrassed, I run it down, and when I return the ball he gives me his best "get off the court old man" look. I acquiesce and bow out awkwardly, respecting his court ownership. Bizarre solace brightens my mind as I walk away hoping that the young man will someday step off a basketball court in his middle age with the options that bared the freedoms I've been fortunate to exercise. Optimism surrounds me, blasting away at the reflexive pessimism I was born to. Despite the large but decreasing hill of race ignorance left to vanquish, I feel confident that both my nation and my jump-shooter will merge over the next fifty years. Five decades from tomorrow it's a good bet that vital, pervasive pigment relevance will serve our nation's global participation well.

The following morning at 5:40 A.M., I am combing my notes by car light in a North Canaan, Connecticut, Stop and Shop supermarket parking lot waiting for dawn's break. I'm geared up to answer the process-server who subpoenaed me on behalf of my clothing's lawsuit against my runaway mid-section. In times like this my only salve can be found on the Hotchkiss track. For ten years the school's tartar-trimmed football field has been the battleground where I fight to skim the fat from my excesses in my Boomer male battle to fit comfortably into compact cars. As the night's curtain slowly parts, I reach into my magic bag of unlabeled cassettes and draw an ace with my favorite Springsteen album, *Nebraska*. The intimacy of Captain America's dawn-lifting soul music gets me to scratching on my pad as daylight slowly puts car light out of business.

I'm focused upon a recent experience with my good buddies Timmy Hitchcock and Blade Brokaw. We recently got together in Blade's Norfolk, Connecticut, backwoods crib. Thirty winters have melted, and yet our sturdy friendship has stood tall. Despite extra pounds and obligations, our three-way hell-raising spark ignites something special that puts the clock on defense, driving it back several decades before political correctness ruined people's fun. Timmy and I have adopted conventional marriage and parenthood, but like always, Blade painted his own path. After a marriage and multiple relationships, he pulled into the new century with a successful contracting business and two bright, studly young-adult sons.

After Timmy's days as a rebel without a pause, he gravitated toward his family's trucking business, and, with his brother Marty, came to eventually man the ship's helm. Timmy is my U.S. White oak, always there to remind me that solid, rural, conservative American values aren't dirty words. Our home-boy-level interaction is a balancing measure when my urge to crap on his prototype's political behavior flares without distinction. Over the years Timmy's and my ghetto-to-Berkshire connection has fueled our game of brothers, providing an irreplaceable spice in my stew. Yes, Virginia, street pigment and rural Caucasia can draw from the heart, and Hitchy and I have been doing it since computers were the size of Buicks.

After enough liquid had been consumed, the room was painless as Willy Nelson's music seized control of the cabin's groove. I was seated across from Blade, who was wearing a comfortable chair with drink in hand and a twinkle in his WASPish eyes. The age thieves had gone light on his fifty years, and he still retains much of the form I'd witnessed thirty-plus years earlier. Our first encounter had been at the bash in Greenwich, Connecticut, where Noel and I met his father. Blade and his younger brothers were in pajamas, awaiting their dad's 8:00 P.M. sign-off.

Our kinship was staked in our different takes on his dad, mixing a nice balance of Blade's reality and my hero worship. I'd gone a few rounds with Bill Brokaw in his prime, earning my quarter-sibling stripe. This enabled Blade and me to sip from the old guy's memory reservoir, sharing varied interpretations on its taste, but we both loved the multi-tentacled, enigmatic ball-buster. It was that old ball-buster who stitched together the opportunity for three unlikely musketeers to enjoy one hell of a run.

Daylight begins to invite customers into the parking lot, cuing my split. I'm soon careening on Route 44 heading into my flukishly attained cradle of privileges. As I approach the Hotchkiss campus, I'm still holding on to the memory of the man who plucked the biggest string on the ukelele that's been my life. A tape of an experience in Germany is on my mind's screen, showing a scene of me standing at the top of the stairs of the battered Riechstag with Leon Russell's "Bluebird" blasting my earlobes. I was joyously overcome by the improbable odds of being in Berlin and gave Brokaw a primal shout out of gratitude for hatching the whole scheme.

As I break for a stop sign at Hotchkiss's four corners, a rush of teenaged metabolic blood-thinner speeds everything up, and I harken back to the last time I visited Mr. Brokaw shortly before he was planted. "You were one of the best gambles I've ever taken," he said. "You made me a winner, and I'm proud of you." Those four words are my dust-proof gold medals that will never lose their bling. Bill Brokaw believed that racism was a coward's tool and selflessly plowed new ground in the early wilds of Nigraphobia so that a ghetto-ite could glimpse the rudiments that belied a level American playing field. In his final years, bad behavior soaked in booze tainted his legacy, so it's incumbent upon me to beat the drum for the selfless part of the old gang-banger's soul.

I'm seated in my car beside the Hotchkiss football field in the process of wrapping my knees, preparing the oldest, fattest, slowest version of Dennis Watlington yet to take on the hallowed track. I haven't yet found the America I've been chasing all these years, but its growing freedom has established its existence. The unfinished business encourages me to get on the track and bust my ass with forward motion, keeping the emerging America I crave in my sights.

ABOUT THE AUTHOR

Dennis Watlington is an Emmy Award–winning documentary filmmaker, a television writer, and a playwright. He lives in the Berkshires of Western Massachusetts with his wife and two children. *Chasing America* is his first book.